Germans

and

African Americans

Germans and African Americans

TWO CENTURIES OF EXCHANGE

Edited by Larry A. Greene and Anke Ortlepp

UNIVERSITY PRESS OF MISSISSIPPI
JACKSON

www.upress.state.ms.us

The University Press of Mississippi is a member of the Association of American University Presses.

First printing 2011
∞
Library of Congress Cataloging-in-Publication Data

Germans and African Americans : two centuries of exchange / edited by Larry A. Greene and Anke Ortlepp.
    p. cm.
  Includes bibliographical references and index.
  ISBN 978-1-60473-784-4 (cloth : alk. paper) — ISBN 978-1-60473-785-1 (ebook : alk. paper) 1. African Americans—Relations with Germans—History. 2. African Americans—Germany—History. 3. Germans—United States—History. 4. Germany—Race relations—History. 5. United States—Race relations—History. I. Greene, Larry A. II. Ortlepp, Anke.
  E185.61.G37 2011
  305.800973—dc22   2010016182

British Library Cataloging-in-Publication Data available

Contents

Introduction

LARRY A. GREENE AND ANKE ORTLEPP

Germany and African Americans, in the minds of most citizens of the United States, have very little connection. Many were astounded at the more than 200,000 Germans who turned out to hear President Barack Obama in 2008, then Democratic Party candidate, speak in his Berlin visit. For many of those surprised Americans, the only connection they could determine was a vague remembrance of black soldiers stationed with the U.S. military in Germany at the end of World War II through the Cold War era in the Federal Republic of Germany (West Germany). Although nearly 3,000,000 black soldiers were stationed on German soil in the more than half century since the end of the Second World War, this impressive figure was largely unknown as were the many issues it raised for both governments, soldiers, and German citizens. It was one of those statistical anomalies that did not alter the reality of African Americans and Germany as a nonevent or nonrelationship in the minds of most. We hope that this volume will clarify the long, but not well-known connection, and contribute to a greater understanding of that relationship to the thousands of Berliners and the multitude of Americans viewing and listening to Obama. Our focus will be upon the African American and German connection in the nineteenth and twentieth centuries and how that connection shaped the African American freedom quest and both their attempts at ethnic self-definition.

The American incomprehensibility of German fascination with Obama is the result of not only a lack of historical knowledge of the German and African American connection, but also only the vaguest awareness of the degree to which Europe and Germany have changed demographically since World War II. Europe in the early twenty-first century is no longer the racially homogeneous monolith that it was in the opening of the twentieth century. The guest worker program in Germany, France, and other European countries in the 1950s and 1960s brought tens of thousands of immigrants from former colonies in the Mid-East, Africa, Asia, and the Caribbean to European soil. Many more seeking economic relief or religious and political freedom immigrated to the continent since. The evidence of change on the racial and cultural demography of Europe is evident in the popularity of African American, Afro-Caribbean, and African music from jazz to rhythm and blues to hip-hop to reggae to ska among not only European youth of color, but also white European young people.[1]

European youth were not the only ones affected by the visible changes in the racial composition of European cities like Frankfurt, Hamburg, Berlin, Paris, and Amsterdam. European scholars of American culture motivated by these home-grown changes and the emergence of the American civil rights movement took a fresh look at the influence of race on American literature, history, and art. The formation of the Collegium on African American Research (CAAR) in 1992 and most recently Blacks in European Studies (BEST) in 2005 reflect the growing European interest in African American and African diasporic studies. This inter-est has progressed beyond the examination of these diasporic cultures as sepa-rate research entities, but rather seeks to investigate their interconnectedness and their relationship to Europe. With the increasing globalization of culture, we witness the evolution toward the globalization of scholarship. To that end this volume has brought together scholars from Europe and America, to share their research on the African American and German connection.

The focus of the African American–German interaction in this volume is upon the nineteenth and twentieth centuries, but with the recognition that a German relationship with Africa antedates those centuries. While Germany was only a minor participant in the trans-Atlantic slave trade compared to the na-tions of Western Europe, it gained knowledge and had contact with Africans even with its limited black population and colonial involvement. Sander Gilman's pioneering work *On Blackness Without Blacks: Essays on the Image of the Black in Germany* (1982) explored representations of African peoples in German philo-sophical, literary, and scientific traditions from Blumenbach to Kant and Hegel. This rudimentary contact with Africa stimulated German academic interest in African languages and peoples. Abba Gregory from Ethiopia taught the German scholar Ludolf the Amharic language while he learned Latin in 1652. Anton Wil-helm Amo (ca. 1700–1753) from Ghana was an African philosopher, fluent in German and Latin with an understanding of French, Greek, and Dutch. Amo was a respected teacher in Wittenberg and Jena.[2] German intellectuals, for the most part, like their European counterparts of the 1600s and 1700s, considered Africa to be an exotic and even barbaric place inhabited by primitive peoples.

Despite the negativity of German and European perceptions of black people in Africa and the New World, there developed an interesting interplay between German support for black freedom and opposition to it conditioned by time and space. Eighteenth-century German Moravian missionaries converted Africans to Christianity in colonial Pennsylvania and on St. Thomas and other Caribbean islands with the support of Count Nikolaus Ludwig von Zinzendorf.[3] The Mora-vians offered blacks spiritual equality which blacks in the process of their conver-sion to Christianity adapted to their need of complete freedom. In another ex-ample of black conversion of the secular European Enlightenment human rights ideology to their needs, black soldiers fought with the British and their battlefield opposition, the Continental Army and militias, during the American Revolution in their quest for freedom promised by both sides. This freedom quest led blacks to fight along with the Hessian mercenaries hired by the British crown to shore up their numbers in the conflict. As the defeated British troops and their Hessian allies departed after the American Revolution, their black troops were evacuated with them to Nova Scotia, England, and Germany in the 1780s.[4] Germany in the nineteenth and twentieth centuries as noted earlier served as a source of both support and opposition to that historic quest of African Americans for freedom and independence in the modern age.

The Essays

In the prologue to this volume, Victor Grossman, a white American GI who received political asylum in the early 1950s, reflects in his personal memoir on the freedom quest of black GIs who sought refuge or asylum in the German Democratic Republic (GDR).[5] America in the two decades following the end of the Second World War was a racially divided society with the southern states having instituted as racially a segregated apartheid-like society as South Africa and similarly disfranchised its black population. To some it may seem strange, that many African American GIs found German people more hospitable and racially tolerant in the immediate post–Third Reich years than the white American occupying army in Germany. The U.S. Army contained many white southerners and others who thought that the military should reinforce America's racial status quo and caste system abroad.[6] Victor Grossman in his essay notes that some of the black GIs he knew were romantically involved with German women and had incurred or would soon incur the wrath of the American military bureaucracy. African American writer and expatriate, William Gardner Smith, in his novel, *Last of the Conquerors* (1948), published only four years after the Second World War, commented ironically through his black GI protagonist on finding more racial tolerance and democracy in postwar Germany than in the United States. Grossman's collective autobiographical approach describes the motivation for defection of black political refugees, their struggle to maintain their identity while adapting to a new land, and their perceptions of America from a far-off land. How East Germans viewed and treated their new visitors also shaped African American identity formation and the perceptions of America by those black exiles.

The struggle for freedom and equality in American society is constantly accessed by black Americans whether in American-occupied Germany in the mid-twentieth-century or nineteenth-century America. The essays by Mischa Honeck and Jeffery Strickland dissect the relationship between black and German communities in nineteenth-century Cincinnati and Charleston. Germans were an immigrant minority in Cincinnati and Charleston searching for their place in America as were the African American inhabitants of both cities. Immigrants to nineteenth-century American cities were often the recipient of nativist fears of inundation by foreign "others" and suspicion of disloyalty and subversion. They were seen by some as a necessary economic evil and by others as a threat to the labor interests of native-born whites. Sometimes these fears erupted into nativist riots, like the infamous anti-Irish Catholic Philadelphia riot of 1844 or the 1855 attack on the German community in Cincinnati. German-American communities, like other immigrant groups, were concerned with assimilating into American life while maintaining their culture. African Americans in northern cities were often denied such basic citizenship rights as voting; they faced widespread employment discrimination and were subjected also to mob violence like New York City's murderous draft riot in the summer of 1863.[7]

Honeck and Strickland explore the relationship between African Americans and Germans with particular sensitivity to the ways in which concepts of class and ideology brought from Germany created diverse racial views within German communities. These racial perceptions were also shaped by the varied ways regional patterns of race relations shape German and black interactions, especially in the North and South. For a portion of European ethnic groups, assimilation meant emphasizing the "whiteness" held in common with the native-born white majority and a view of blacks as outsiders. The impact of the growing scholarly field of "Whiteness Studies" influences the scholarship of Honeck and Strickland.[8] Honeck's perceptive essay on Cincinnati addresses the relationship between Peter Humphries Clark, the black principal of the Western Colored District School, and August Willich, the German immigrant editor of the *Cincinnati Republikaner.* Willich's support of abolition and opposition to racism were derived from his radical socialist beliefs from the failed 1848 revolution in the German states. His support of black causes and lobbying of German working-class organizations to support abolition and equal rights for blacks earned him the hostility of the conservative German-American elite and German Catholics who were generally quite hostile to abolition and black equality. Both men respected each other, and Clark embraced the causes of the "oppressed Hungarians and German socialists in their efforts to throw off the yoke of despotism."[9]

Charleston, unlike Cincinnati, was in a slave state, but similarly its German population was viewed with some suspicion by the city's white southern population. Blacks were the primary patrons of German merchants whom the city's non-German white population ignored. These social and economic contacts confirmed the status of German immigrants as outsiders. Strickland describes a city in which the Civil War and the onset of Reconstruction placed a native-born white population seeking to retain their antebellum status and an assertive freed black population seeking equality and participation in the city's governance on a collision course. Strickland's essay explores the transition of Charleston's German population as neutral nonbelligerents between the city's conflicting black and white populations in the antebellum era, to a supporter of the Democratic Party, and their goal of white supremacy in the post–Civil War era. He quite cogently analyzes the connection between German immigrant goals of assimilation and acceptance by native-born whites with the deterioration in the relationship with African Americans in the postwar South. The incompatibility of German immigrant goals and the Freedmen's goals of assimilation, civil rights, and political rights are highlighted in this essay's exploration of the way in which the Civil War and Reconstruction remade Germans as southerners and continued the casting of African Americans as the perpetual "racial outsiders."

On the other side of the Atlantic, throughout the late nineteenth century and early twentieth century, a relatively small number of African Americans traveled to Germany to study in the excellent universities, among them W. E. B. Du Bois, who became a major historian and civil rights leader.[10] In 1901, four African American agronomists from Tuskegee Institute arrived in the Germany colony of Togo in West Africa to aid German efforts at cotton production.[11] Entertainers and black college choirs found bookings in the theaters and concert halls of Germany. In the post–World War I era, Paris became the European capital for the black musical entertainment boom and those thirsting for jazz brought to Europe by African American musicians. German cities, in the Weimar period of the 1920s, became an important secondary venue for these touring African American entertainers. They often enjoyed higher wages and incurred less racism in Europe than in America. Leroy Hopkins in "Louis Douglas and the Weimar Reception of Harlemania" observes the fascination for black musical entertainment in German society. Louis Douglas, the principal focus of Hopkins's essay, came to Paris in 1925 with his dancing partner, Josephine Baker, in the wildly popular *La Revue Nègre* in 1925. He went on to a musical career and film career in Germany, returning to the United States in 1937. Douglas had roles in such German films as *Einbrecher* (1930) and *Der brave Sünder* (1931), but it was in *Niemandsland* (1931) that he received his greatest critical acclaim. This liberal antiwar film angered German nationalists and was released in the United States in 1934 as *Hell on Earth*.

The essay by Leroy Hopkins is a sophisticated analysis of the reception of black artists and themes in the popular entertainment culture of Weimar. The complexity and ambiguity of the German critical and popular response to Louis Douglas, Josephine Baker, and other black entertainers and musical revues crisscrossing Germany is skillfully assessed. German nationalists and conservatives, like their French counterparts, were highly critical of black entertainers and music which they saw as denigrating European culture. German and French liberals extolled the virtues of this "primitive" and "spontaneous" art compared to the European loss of naturalness which they asserted were killed by war, materialism, industrialization, and modern society. In many instances, the criticism is more illuminating about European culture and the response to African American art than it is about black art itself. The essay artfully negotiates the difficult intellectual terrain between Weimar praise and acceptance of cross-cultural diversity and simultaneously subscribing to nineteenth-century minstrel-like racial stereotypes.[12]

The rise of Hitler's Third Reich and the Great Depression reduced the African American cultural presence in Germany. The turn toward fascism and anti-Semitism transformed the positive image that many African Americans held of Germany toward a decidedly negative one. The widely publicized, but inaccurate story of Hitler's refusal to shake the hand of Jesse Owens at the 1936 Berlin Olympics contributed to the politization of sports as did the Joe Louis–Max Schmeling boxing matches into Aryan/fascism versus American/democracy. The image of Germany as a racist totalitarian state was solidified in the consciousness of many African Americans. Analogies between the racist Nuremberg Laws of the Third Reich and the Jim Crow laws of the southern United States began to prolif-erate throughout the African American press in the 1930s. Larry A. Greene's es-say examines the manner in which the African American press incorporated this analogy into a sustained campaign for civil rights in the mid-1930s and acceler-ated with the beginning of World War II into the postwar period. Greene asserts that the "Double V" campaign initiated by the *Pittsburgh Courier* in February 1942 and joined by African American newspapers all across the country was the beginning of the modern civil rights movement. Central to that campaign was the analogy between America's segregation system and the anti-Semitism of Nazi Germany, which illustrated the hypocrisy and contradictions between American professions of democracy, criticism of Hitler, and the toleration of similar injus-tice on American soil.[13]

The irony of the Nazi–Jim Crow analogy and the Double V campaign inaugu-rated by the African American press is personified in the lives of fifty-one indi-viduals who fled Nazi-controlled Germany and Austria and taught in nineteen historically black colleges located mainly in the South. All but two of the exiles were Jewish who sought political asylum from the Nazi horrors of the genocidal Third Reich and found an academic career in the racially authoritarian states of the Jim Crow South.[14] Berndt Ostendorf's biographical essay relates the unique career of a non-Jewish political refugee, Julius Lips. Ostendorf examines the ca-reer of Lips with emphasis on his brief two-year academic career at Howard Uni-versity and the novel he wrote after his return to the communist East Germany, *Forschungsreise in die Dämmerung* (Field Trip into the Twilight), where he was appointed rector of Leipzig University in the early 1950s.[15] Ostendorf's essay deft-ly explores the ideological contradictions in the life of a man who in the preface to his novel blames white racist capitalism for the plight of African Americans, but in the main narrative blames African Americans for much of their situa-tion. Lips reacts negatively to the bourgeois nature of Howard University, thinly disguised as Hilltop University in the novel, and the mulatto composition of a portion of its faculty. Only in part is the Lips critique a legitimate condemnation of intraracial color prejudice and bourgeois materialism among African Ameri-cans; it also represents his despair at the disappearance of the so-called primi-tive essence of African culture among African Americans. While Lips does not reflect the dominant views of most German refugee professors at historically black colleges, his ambivalence is reflective of some liberal German intellectuals, who, while claiming as positives an alleged preindustrial simplicity, nobility, and spontaneity of black peoples unspoiled by modernization, often cross the line to a valuation of stereotypic primitivism.

Germans in the immediate post–WW II era did not have to rely on old Wei-mar images of black entertainers, prewar or wartime Nazi propaganda, or the travel memoirs of returning exiled scholars like Julius Lips to gain a sense of African American culture. The occupation period ushered in a period of extend-ed contact with African American GIs who were a significant part of the huge American military presence over the more than half century since the end of the Second World War. Maria Höhn's essay examines with penetrating insight the German and American debates on interracial relationships. Neither country had been receptive to interracial relationships and the U.S. military discouraged black servicemen from marrying German women.[16] As the 1960s civil rights movement in America intensified, its impact was manifest on black soldiers in Germany who were less willing to tolerate interference in their relationships or adhere to the de facto segregation of bars and restaurants to GIs sanctioned by the American military and adhered to by German owners. African American GIs were defining civil rights not simply in terms of political and economic equality, but also in terms of social equality. Höhn explores the irony of an American government that as part of denazification immediately following the end of World War II forced the abolition of the Nuremberg Laws and their ban on marriages between Aryans and non-Aryans, but tolerated the many state laws banning interracial marriage until 1967 when the U.S. Supreme Court declared such laws unconstitutional. She also examines the attitudes of black soldiers who felt less racism in Germany than in the United States and perceived their greatest problem in Germany was the racism of the American military, even though German attitudes toward interracial relationships were not especially positive.

Sabine Broeck's provocative essay looks at the reaction of the "progressive" segment of the German community, rather than the federal or local government attitudes toward African Americans in Germany and in the United States, at a time when the civil rights movement was at its most intense in the 1950s and 1960s. She finds African American and German interaction was characterized by white romantization and adoration of black endurance, moral power, suffering, and immersion in the style of black rhetoric. Broeck analyzes the work of writers, like Max Frisch, whose 1954 essay "Begegnungen mit Negern" ("Encounters with Negroes") circulated this view of African American culture and history throughout the German high school curricula. Contained within this "paradigmatic intellectual text" is a "pro–civil rights sentiment" coupled with a kind of nineteenth-century abolitionist paternalistic exoticized and eroticized stereotypic depictions of black social and religious gatherings. Broeck calls for rejection of this kind of "pornotroping" and the establishment of a new paradigm beyond racist stereotypes and benevolent paternalizers that would allow progressive Germans to construct a more positive view not only of the historic American civil rights movement but contribute to the discourse on the racial diversification of Europe and the contemporary antiracist discourse in Germany and Europe.

Hans Jürgen Massaquoi's personal commentary on the racial history of Germany and the United States in the twentieth century provides unique empirical insights into the racial discourse on diversity, the creation of national and personal identities, and the perception of minorities in those countries. Massaquoi's triple identity as a mixed-race person of African and German heritage born in Hamburg to a German mother and African father in the Weimar era and later naturalized as an American citizen gives him a kind of Du Boisian "second sight" into both Germany and America.[17] Frank Mehring analyzes the autobiographical writings of Hans Massaquoi in an essay comparing American and German attitudes toward blacks, mixed-race people, and racial assimilation. Massaquoi survived the terrors of the Third Reich, the deflating discovery that the American occupation army contained antiblack and anti-Semitic elements, and upon immigrating to America another shocking discovery that the realities of American de jure and de facto segregation hardly made the United States a racial paradise. Mehring explores this journey of personal transformation followed by Hans Massaquoi as he becomes an American citizen and an eyewitness to the national transformation of America brought about by the civil rights movement. Mehring's essay demonstrates how inextricably intertwined are the narratives of personal and national transformations.

West Germany's relationship to the black quest for freedom and equality is complex and at various times ambivalent. For some African American troops stationed there it was a liberal oasis compared to the blatant racism they experienced in the United States, especially in the South. For Afro-Germans, like Massaquoi, their lack of acceptance and respect in Germany was psychologically painful and sometimes economically damaging.[18] The essays by Astrid Haas and Aribert Schroeder focus on different aspects of a complex and ambivalent portrait of depictions of race in America by the East German theater community and internal racial policies of the East German state (German Democratic Republic). Haas critically reviews the presentation of two classic African American dramas from the civil rights era, *A Raisin in the Sun* and *Blues for Mr. Charlie*, while Schroeder assesses the life of Ollie Harrington in East Germany, one of the most prominent African American cartoonists and journalists, who sought political asylum in East Berlin in November 1961 following the death in Paris of his good friend and fellow writer, Richard Wright.[19]

Astrid Haas observes that in the official propaganda of the German Democratic Republic the United States was the epicenter of political reaction, racism, and imperialist aggression, but the intellectual and popular images were more complex and diversified, acknowledging the existence of an anticapitalist, antibourgeois, proletarian culture. African American literature and drama protesting racial injustice in America was considered such an oppositional culture to the dominant capitalist hegemony. Haas examines the East German critiques of these plays which acknowledge the plays' oppositional stance to America's dominant racial hegemonic doctrine, but clearly notes East German critics observed that the plays had not progressed to a Marxist-Leninist analysis. Haas deftly negotiates the ideological terrain of GDR critics who praise, but also clearly state the limitations of reformist civil rights ideology from a socialist perspective.

Aribert Schroeder's essay on Ollie Harrington is based on extensive research in the Stasi (GDR secret service) files now open on Harrington and his associates in East Germany. Schroeder reveals the contact between African American Communist Party members visiting the GDR and Ollie Harrington. While Harrington was a committed communist, he was an independent thinker and at times critical of GDR cultural and political policies from a socialist perspective. The Stasi spied on him and used informants to report on his activities and thoughts. Their suspicions were based on his criticism of GDR cultural policies restricting expression and travels by artists and intellectuals whom he thought required freedom of expression to improve life and discourse in a socialist state. Harrington is important because he provides insight into the perspective of the African American left and the GDR's views on race, the African American civil rights movement, and the African national liberation struggle. The essays by Schroeder and Haas meticulously examine the interaction between the GDR cultural ideology and security apparatuses, African American drama, and African American exiles like Harrington to give a detailed picture of the limitations on intellectual and artistic discourse in the GDR.

It is abundantly clear that authoritarian states like the communist GDR or fascist states like Germany and Italy under Hitler and Mussolini have always sought to limit political, intellectual, and artistic expression to support government doctrine and policies. However, even states with democratic structures like the United States and West Germany (Federal Republic of Germany) have at times tolerated limitations placed on the freedom of their citizens. For instance, the U.S. Government tolerated for decades the political disfranchisement of black voters in the southern states and bans on interracial marriages by those states.[20] Maria Höhn, in her book *GIs and Fräuleins* and in the essay in this volume, describes the symbiotic relationship between American military authorities and conservative German authorities who sought to discourage African American GIs from socializing with, dating, or marrying German women. The limitations placed on the freedom of choice of both black soldiers and German women is especially ironic considering America's claim to have fought the Second World War in order to preserve democracy and to combat Germany's virulent Aryan supremacy doctrines. The irony is further expanded by the reality that these interracial relationships developed in a nation whose previous racist regime was committed to ethnic cleansing and genocide as a means of preserving racial purity and acquiring *Lebensraum* (living space) out of the territories of other nations.

Damani Partridge in a thought-provoking essay examines the psychological and sociopolitical aspects of interracial relationships in postwar Germany. Popular interpretations of these relationships have tended to simplistically portray German women as naively romantic and ignorant of the difficulties of interracial relationships or exceedingly practical and functional economic predators seeking food and material comforts that black GIs could provide. While there is some truth in these interpretations, the reality is often more complex according to Partridge.[21] The "black body" serves not only as an object of desire but a conduit to Americanization through the absorption of various vestiges of American culture from music, dance, gender relations, to consumption patterns. The rejection of traditional taboos against socializing with men of color or any racialized others, like Jews, is not only a personal statement, but also the rejection of male patriarchal authority to police the sexuality of women and to define heterosexual relationships in a more democratic way. Partridge would agree with Annette Brauerhoch that a segment of those women involved in interracial relationships can be viewed as "'protofeminist rebels.'"[22] The freedom to explore interracial relationships ultimately involves a rejection of traditional European aesthetic standards of physical beauty, white male patriarchy and definitions of German identity, and limitations placed on women's roles and right to choices.

Eva Boesenberg in "Reconstructing 'America'" traces the development of African American Studies in the Federal Republic of Germany as an outgrowth of the emergence of American Studies in West Germany after World War II. American scholars like Charles H. Nicholas, who taught at Hampton Institute, became the director of the JFK Institute at the Free University of Berlin for ten years, the pioneer revisionist historian Kenneth Stampp taught in Munich in 1957, and Edward Clark taught the first black course at the University Kiel in 1958. In the 1960s, black artists like James Baldwin and the Alvin Ailey Dancers toured Germany, and the international media coverage of the civil rights movement brought the issue of race in America to the center stage. An accompanying development was the establishment of courses in African American Studies on college campuses across America, which had an impact on the American Studies curricula at German universities. These growing influences culminated in the establishment of two organizations: the Collegium for African American Research and the Black European Studies. German scholars are on the cutting edge of research in the field of African American Studies and have pioneered the research and publication on the trans-Atlantic connection between African American and Germany.

Conclusion

Why has German interest in American race relations and African American Studies been so pronounced and consistent over the years and equal to or even greater than in many other European countries with larger black populations and much longer colonial traditions in Africa? Any explanation has to consider the German university system, which has integrated African American literature and history so thoroughly into the American literary and historical cannon. Yet this structural answer is only a partial explanation and reflects a deeper interest and connection to New World race relations.

African Americans and Germans have played reciprocal roles in each other's quest for freedom, national identity, and redefinitions of identity. African Americans have longed used foreign nations as positive or negative reference groups in the struggle for equality. Germany has had its place in this freedom quest of African Americans, as blacks have played a part in the discussions of German identity formation.

Blacks, whether in Africa or as part of the American nation, have in a number of ways been part of the discourse, albeit a secondary theme, on nationhood for Germany. Soon after Chancellor Otto von Bismarck's successful efforts at German unification in 1871, Germany organized the Berlin Conference of 1884 and brought order to the great scramble for colonies in Africa. Germany as a preeminent nation in Europe naturally sought its own colonial empire and rationalized its reign over African peoples in terms of economic benefit, geopolitical considerations, and racial supremacy like all other European nations.[23] Nazi elements in their quest to topple the government in the Weimar era included the bogus charges of rape by French African troops as part of the "Black Horror on the Rhine" campaign to associate racial defilement with the legacy of the Versailles Treaty. Upon the assumption of power, Nazi propaganda portrayed the United States as a racially mongrelized nation whose African American and Jewish minorities retarded America's development and threatened European civilization like the so-called communist barbarians to the east in the Soviet Union. In the post–World War II era, the German press and German student leftist groups by the 1960s were favorable to the African American civil rights movement. German students sent a petition in support of the movement to President John F. Kennedy in 1963 and four years later the German SDS (Sozialistischer Deutscher Studentenbund) student organization declared its solidarity with the "black power" movement in the United States. The German Rote Armee Fraktion (Red Army Faction) and the Bewegung 2. Juni (June 2nd Movement) radical groups adopted similar clothing to the African American radical Black Panther Party and supported such leaders as Kathleen Cleaver and Angela Davis.[24]

The identification of German moderates and liberals with the civil rights movement and German radicals with various factions in the black power movement, while sincerely supportive of the struggle of these groups, it also served their own ideological needs. By opposing racial oppression in the United States, their support highlighted American hypocrisy and contributed to the changing image of Germany from the racist past of Aryan supremacy in the Third Reich years. For German radicals, through their identification with certain American countercultural and black power groups, they found allies in the global movement against colonialism and imperialism.

Similarly, African American connections to and use of Germany was to satisfy their own needs within the American context. Blacks pointed out the inconsistency in the American Revolution against Great Britain while denying them the very freedoms they sought.[25] Frederick Douglass, Peter Humphries Clark, and other black abolitionists praised the German-American, German, Irish, and Hungarian supporters of black freedom. After the Civil War, the freedmen protested the return of lands promised them by their former owners who proceeded to deprive them of their civil and voting rights, noting that they had opposed the secessionist southern whites who formed a separate foreign nation which raised an army and took American lives on the battlefield.[26] During World War I, African American newspapers taking the lead from white newspapers, which portrayed Germans as descendents of the "Hun" barbarians committing atrocities in Belgium, linked the barbarism allegedly committed by Germans to the barbarity of American racial violence and lynching in their designation of the equivalent "American Hun."[27] During the First World War and postwar era, the black press emphasized the absence of racism in France and the acceptance of African Americans as equal human beings in contrast to the United States. To a lesser extent these articles typified the depictions of Germany and the rest of Europe in the 1920s.[28] Germany appears as a negative reference group in the Nazi–Jim Crow analogy in the 1930s and was the main component in the civil rights

"Double V" campaign inaugurated by the African American press during World War II. In that same time period, the left-oriented black intellectuals and journalists in the African American press extolled the virtues of the Soviet Union as a classless society free of racism.

After the Second World War with the beginning of the Cold War, the Soviet Union was transformed into a negative reference group threatening the American position with Third World countries of color that can only be combated by eliminating Soviet propaganda advantage of racial inequality in America.[29] The Nazi–Jim Crow analogy dissipated in the African American press, but did not disappear. Germany was now treated as a positive reference group; with writers like William Gardner Smith in *Last of the Conquerors* (1948) through his protagonist comments on American soldiers stationed in Germany finally tasting equality and democracy in Germany of all places. A view echoed nearly thirty years later by former general and later secretary of state, Colin Powell, in his autobiography, *My American Journey* (1995), reflects also on the irony and meaning of freedom of movement, association, and activities during his tour of Germany for African American servicemen in the 1960s and 1970s. Mutual connections and perceptions of Germans and African Americans have continually evolved over time and space depending upon mutual needs and will continue to do so in the future.

Notes

1. See Maria I. Diedrich, Theron D. Cook, and Flip Lindo, eds., *Crossing Boundaries: African American Inner City and European Migrant Youth* (Münster, Germany: Lit Verlag, 2004); Cathy Covell Waegner, "Rap, Rebounds, and Rocawear: The 'Darkening' of German Youth Culture"; Irina Novikova, "Black Music, White Freedom: Times and Spaces of Jazz Countercultures in the USSR"; and Heike Raphael-Hernandez, "'Niggas' and 'Skins': Nihilism among African American Youth in Low-Income Urban Communities and East German Youth in Satellite cities, Small Towns, and Rural Areas," in *Blackening Europe: The African American Presence*, ed. Heike Raphael-Hernandez (New York: Routledge, 2004).

2. Sander L. Gilman, *On Blackness Without Blacks: Essays on the Image of the Black in Germany* (New York: G. K. Hall, 1982); Hans Werner Debrunner, "Africa, Europe, and America: The Modern Roots from a European Perspective," in *Crosscurrents: African Americans, Africa, and Germany in the Modern World*, ed. David McBride, Leroy Hopkins, and C. Aisha Blackshire-Belay (Columbia, SC: Camden House, 1998), 5–7; Peter Martin, *Schwarze Teufel, edle Mohren: Afikaner in Bewusstein und Geschichte der Deutschen* (Hamburg: Junius, 1993), 308–27.

3. Katherine Faull Eze, "Self-Encounters: Two Eighteenth-Century African Memoirs from Moravian Bethlehem," in McBride, Hopkins, and Blackshire-Belay, eds., *Crosscurrents;* Daniel B. Thorpe, "Chattel with a Soul: the Autobiography of a Moravian Slave," *Pennsylvania Magazine of History and Biography* 112 (1988).

4. Benjamin Quarles, *The Negro in the American Revolution* (Chapel Hill: University of North Carolina Press, 1961); Philip S. Foner, *Blacks in the American Revolution* (Westport, CT: Greenwood Press, 1975).

5. See Victor Grossman's fascinating memoir explaining why he and other GIs, black and white, defected and the life they found in East Germany: *Crossing the River: A Memoir of the American Left, the Cold War, and Life in East Germany* (Amherst: University of Massachusetts Press, 2003).

6. Maria Höhn, *GIs and Fräuleins: The German-American Encounter in 1950s West Germany* (Chapel Hill: University of North Carolina Press, 2002).

7. Ray Allen Billington, *The Protestant Crusade, 1800–1860: A Study of the Origins of American Nativism* (New York: Macmillan Company, 1938); Iver Bernstein, *The New York City Draft Riots* (New York: Oxford University Press, 1990).

8. Noel Ignatiev, *How the Irish Became White* (New York: Routledge, 2008); David R. Roediger, *The Wages of Whiteness: Race and the Making of the American Working Class*, 2nd ed. (New York: Verso, 2007); David R. Roediger, *Working Toward Whiteness: How America's Immigrants Became White* (New York: Basic Books, 2005); Matthew Frye Jacobson, *Whiteness of a Different Color: European Immigrants and the Alchemy of Race* (Cambridge, MA: Harvard University Press, 1998); Jennifer Guglielmo and Salvatore Salerno, eds., *Are Italians White: How Race Is Made in America* (New York: Routledge, 2003); Karen Brodkin, *How Jews Became White Folks and What That Says about Race in America* (New Brunswick, NJ: Rutgers University Press, 1999).

9. Bruce Levine quite impressively explores the divisions within Cincinnati's German community over the issues of slavery, abolition, and African Americans in "'Against All Slavery, Whether White or Black': German-Americans and the Irrepressible Conflict," in McBride, Hopkins, Blackshire-Belay, eds., *Crosscurrents.*

10. David Levering Lewis, *W. E. B. Du Bois: A Biography of Race, 1868–1919* (New York: Henry Holt and Co., 1993), 127–46.

11. Andrew Zimmerman, "Booker T. Washington, Tuskegee Institute, and the German Empire: Race and Cotton in the Black Atlantic," *Bulletin of the German Historical Institute* 43 (Fall 2008): 9–11.

12. For the debate over foreign and modernist influence on French culture, see Herman Lebovics, *True France: The Wars over Cultural Identity, 1900–1945* (Ithaca, NY: Cornell University Press, 1992).

13. Patrick Washburn, *A Question of Sedition: The Federal Government's Investigation of the Black Press during World War II* (New York: Oxford University Press, 1986), 11–40; Patrick Washburn, *The African American Newspaper: Voice of Freedom* (Evanston, IL: Northwestern University Press, 2006); Barbara Diane Savage, *Broadcasting Freedom: Radio, War, and the Politics of Race* (Chapel Hill: University of North Carolina Press, 1999).

14. Gabrielle Simon Edgcomb, *From Swastika to Jim Crow: Refugee Scholars at Black Colleges* (Malabar, FL: Krieger Publishing Company, 1993), xiii; See also Robert Boyers, ed., *The Legacy of the German Refugee Intellectuals* (New York: Schocken Books, 1972); Martin Jay, *Permanent Exiles—Essays on the Intellectual Migration from Germany to America* (New York: Columbia University Press, 1985).

15. Julius Lips, *Forschungsreise in die Dämmerung. Aus den Aufzeichnungen und Dokumenten des Professors Smith über sein Leben an einer Negeruniversität* (Weimar, Germany: Kiepenheuer, 1950).

16. For an in-depth look at American and German racial policies, especially interracial relationships, see Höhn, *GIs and Fräuleins;* Heide Fehrenbach, *Race after Hitler: Black Occupation Children in Postwar Germany and America* (Princeton, NJ: Princeton University Press, 2005). Fehrenbach provides a thorough analysis of the difference in German government policies and popular attitudes toward black and white occupation children.

17. W. E. B. DuBois, *The Souls of Black Folks* (Chicago: A. C. McClurg, 1903). In this classic volume, Du Bois, a historian who studied at the doctoral level in Berlin, suggested that African

Americans were gifted with a "second sight" or inner vision into the depths of American culture by their very exclusion from it.

18. Ika Huegel-Marshall, *Invisible Woman: Growing up Black in Germany* (New York: Continuum, 2001), is the autobiography of a mixed-race woman growing up in postwar Germany; May Opitz, Katharina Oguntoye, and Dagmar Schultz, eds., *Showing Our Colors: Afro-German Women Speak Out* (Amherst: University of Massachusetts Press, 1986), is a collection of essays and interviews that is historical, autobiographical, and contemporary explorations of race in Germany from the point of view of Afro-German women; Katharina Oguntoye, *Eine Afro-Deutsche Geschichte: Zur Lebenssituation von Afrikanern und Afro-Deutschen in Deutschland von 1884 bis 1950* (Berlin: Hoho Verlag Christine Hoffmann, 1997) is a history of Afro-Germans from the late nineteenth century through the first half of the twentieth century.

19. Oliver Harrington, *Why I Left America and Other Essays* (Jackson: University Press of Mississippi, 1993). Harrington's explanation for living in the GDR given in this book is not consistent with the facts unearthed by Aribert Schroeder in his essay.

20. Höhn, *GIs and Fräuleins*, 126–54, 177–97; For southern attitudes toward miscegenation and interracial marriage in the nineteenth and early twentieth centuries, see Charles F. Robinson II, *Dangerous Liaisons: Sex and Love in the Segregated South* (Fayetteville: University of Arkansas Press, 2003). For an exploration of interracial marriage in more recent times, see Renee C. Romano, *Race Mixing: Black-White Marriage in Postwar America* (Cambridge, MA: Harvard University Press, 2003). See an examination of miscegenation in American literature in Werner Sollors, *Neither Black Nor White, Yet Both: Thematic Explorations of Interracial Literature* (Cambridge, MA: Harvard University Press, 1997).

21. For a sophisticated analysis of the relationship between American soldiers and German women, see Tamara Domentat, *"Hallo Fräulein": Deutsche Frauen und amerikanische Soldaten* (Berlin: Aufbau-Verlag, 1998). For an excellent study of an interracial relationship in the nineteenth century between a German woman and an African American man, see Maria Diedrich, *Love Across Color Lines: Ottlie Assing and Frederick Douglass* (New York: Hill and Wang, 1999).

22. Annette Brauerhoch, "Foreign Affairs"—"Fräuleins as Agents," Panel VI. Germanness and Gender. http://www.Unc. Edu/depts/europe/conferences/Germany celeb9900/abstracts/brauerhoch Annette.hmtl (April 4, 2003) cited in Partridge's essay in this volume. For an important discussion of the impact of race on the perceptions of national identity, see Fatima El-Tayeb, *Schwarze Deutsche: der Diskurs um "Rasse" und nationale Identität, 1890–1933* (Frankfurt: Campus, 2001). See an excellent examination of the issue of interracial marriage, race purity, and the 1912 Reichstag debate in the paper of Tina Campt, "The Body and Identity: Essential/Experimental/Constructed" at Goldsmith College (London, UK: 1999). For a discussion of these issues in Nazi era, see Clarence Lusane, *Hitler's Black Victims* (New York: Routledge, 2003).

23. For the varied impact of Africa on German intellectual, cultural, and literary thought, see Sara Friedrichsmeyer, Sara Lennox, and Susanne Zantop, eds., *The Imperialist Imagination: German Colonialism and Its Legacy* (Ann Arbor: University of Michigan Press, 1998); Lusane, *Hitler's Black Victims*, 43–56.

24. Martin Klimke, "The African American Civil Rights Struggle and Germany, 1945–1989," *Bulletin of the German Historical Institute* 43 (Fall 2008): 98–103; see Martin Klimke's comprehensive study, *The Other Alliance: Global Protest and Student Unrest in West Germany and the U.S., 1962–1972* (Princeton, NJ: Princeton University Press); Timothy Schroer, *Recasting Race after World War II: Germans and African Americans in American-Occupied Germany* (Boulder: University of Colorado Press, 2007).

25. Arthur Zilversmit, *The First Emancipation: The Abolition of Slavery in the North* (Chicago, IL: University of Chicago Press), 85–138.

26. Eric Foner, *Nothing but Freedom: Emancipation and Its Legacy* (Baton Rouge: Louisiana State University Press, 1983), 39–73.

27. William G. Jordan, *Black Newspapers and America's War for Democracy, 1914–1920* (Chapel Hill: University of North Carolina Press, 2001), 155–62.

28. Tyler Stovall, *Paris Noir: African Americans in the City of Light* (New York: Houghton Mifflin, 1996); Petrine Archer- Straw, *Negrophilia: Avant-Garde Paris and Black Culture in the 1920s* (New York: Thames & Hudson, 2000); Arthur E. Barbeau and Florette Henri, *The Unknown Soldiers: Black American Troops in World War I* (Philadelphia, PA: Temple University Press, 1974).

29. Mary L. Dudziak, *Cold War Civil Rights: Race and the Image of American Democracy* (Princeton, NJ: Princeton University Press, 2000).

Germans

and

African Americans

Prologue

African Americans in the German Democratic Republic

VICTOR GROSSMAN

When the Soviet authorities hunted for a location for deserters from western armies, why did they choose the city of Bautzen for what was to become a small but unusual experiment in internationalism affecting, among others (including myself), a handful of African Americans? Certainly not because it was so ancient. Bautzen, first recorded as a city in 1002, had been hit again and again by city conflagrations, battles and sieges by Hussites, Saxons, Swedes and, last of all, when the Nazis decided to make it a fortress city, by the Red Army. A few ruins or empty lots resulting from the final battle in April 1945 were still visible when we lived in Bautzen, though its bridges and the autobahn had been repaired by 1950. Nearly all of its medieval buildings had been destroyed in one or the other century, except for the big Gothic cathedral, one of the only churches in Germany used by both Roman Catholics and Protestants, divided neatly in half by a small fence through the middle. Many handsome Renaissance and Baroque buildings had survived, though they were often in need of repair. It was hardly the church or the architecture that determined the Soviet choice of Bautzen.

I also doubt that its role as center of the Sorbs had much to do with it. The Sorbs, a small minority struggling to preserve their culture and their West Slavic language, dominant here a thousand years earlier, had been reduced by German repression to fewer than 100,000 people living in the bayou landscape of Lower Lusatia to the north or the gentle landscapes of Upper Lusatia around Bautzen, at the foot of the low Erzgebirge mountains separating the larger Saxony from Czechoslovakia. When we foreigners arrived we found triple street signs: in German, in faded Russian from the first occupation years, and in Sorb. Official buildings and state-owned shops had bilingual signs, and Sorb women wearing numerous wide skirts and black bonnets with long ribbons were fairly numerous. Because the Sorbs had been oppressed and their language forbidden by the Nazis the Soviets viewed them as allies, which led to a few special privileges in the first postwar years. When the German Democratic Republic was founded in 1949 it passed laws decreeing equality and the encouragement of the Sorb language and culture. But I doubt that this had much to do with choosing this area.

Bautzen is best known in the rest of Germany, above all, for its penitentiary, and the jailing of political prisoners here by the Soviets and then by the GDR (including some Nazi war criminals) has cast a shadow on the city since German unification in 1990. Few seem to recall that the institution, known originally as the Royal Saxon Prison, was built not in 1945 but in 1900. All I learned about it when I arrived was that the head of the Communist Party of Germany, Ernst Thälmann, had been imprisoned there by the Nazis until 1944, when he was transferred to Buchenwald concentration camp and murdered. I think the presence of the prison, the main section of which was known as "Das gelbe Elend" (The Yellow Misery) because of the color of its brick walls, was hardly of any importance in connection with us. There were two more likely reasons for deciding on Bautzen. First of all, it was of medium size, with somewhat more than 40,000 inhabitants, and was an industrial center with widely varied industries, from the big LOWA railroad-car factory, biggest of its kind in the Soviet bloc, to plants weaving cloth and producing printing machinery, leather goods, and even church organs. This created a wide variety of job opportunities. However, it was not a major urban center like Dresden, Leipzig, or Halle, where oversight was difficult and people could easily "get lost in the crowd." In Bautzen it was possible to keep an eye on possibly undesirable activities, criminal, alcoholic, or conceivably political. (And indeed, more recent revelations show, not surprisingly, that the State Security apparatus of the GDR was always keeping an eye on this strange group of wanderers from the other side of the Iron Curtain.) But the main reason for choosing Bautzen, I feel certain, was its distance from any western borderline, including the border to West Berlin, without sitting directly and uncomfortably on the Czech or Polish borders (like the larger nearby cities of Zittau or Görlitz).

All these questions were of some importance for me, for I was to spend nearly two years in Bautzen. A few months too young to get drafted during World War Two, I attained my bachelor's degree at Harvard College in 1949 and then, convinced by my left-wing views that the labor union movement was a crucial factor in history, I worked at unskilled factory jobs in Buffalo, New York. When the war in Korea began, the draft was revived and I became an unwilling recruit in January 1951. In those years—and over a decade before this requirement was ruled unconstitutional by the Supreme Court—this meant signing, or possibly refusing to sign, a statement saying, "I am not and have never been a member of any of the above organizations." Of the more than a hundred listed, many defunct and nearly all left-wing, I had been in about a dozen, and I planned to refuse to sign. But, suddenly confronted with this fateful document, pure, sharp fear of admitting my very leftist past in the icy climate of Cold War USA, where I had already become a sworn-in soldier, caused me to sign in ashen silence and the hope that, if I remained inconspicuous, no one would check up on me for the next two years. But a check was made, perhaps because a fellow student had denounced me, and in August 1952 I was ordered to appear before a military judge in nearby Nuremberg. Knowing that the stated penalty for concealing one's past could be up to $10,000 and five years in prison, I panicked and deserted, swimming across the Danube, then part of the demarcation line between the American and the Soviet Zones of Austria. After two weeks in a cell in Austria and two months in a pleasant but isolated room in Potsdam near Berlin, Soviet officers sent me to Bautzen in November 1952, together with three Welsh soldiers whose main interest soon turned out to be less politics than beer.

Until private rooms could be found for us, we were put up in a hotel with free room and board. Until jobs could be found, we were given pocket money. After rooms were found for each of us, we were also given a monthly ration of food and tobacco equivalent to that which Soviet officers received. This ceased, however, when the USSR turned over administration of our group to the GDR authorities late in 1953. From the start we were quite free, faced with one restriction only: we were not permitted to leave the county of Bautzen without special permission. I soon found other army deserters in the town; there were thirty or forty in all as it later turned out. They were there for a variety of reasons, but it soon became apparent that quite a few shared the same alcoholic interests with the Welshmen.

Charles Lucas was a definite exception. Charlie, an African American, lived in a well-furnished apartment near the "Square of the Red Army." I never heard him speak about his past, and asking any such questions violated the tactful etiquette of the Bautzen "Ausländer." Therefore I must rely largely on the rumors of other ex-soldiers, who said that Charlie, a soldier in West Germany, had been ordered to break his ties with a German woman; in the 1950s the U.S. Army sternly discouraged such relationships with black GIs. When Charlie proved stubborn, he was warned that he might be sent to fight in Korea. So, instead, he joined her in the then easy crossover from West to East Berlin. The woman soon returned but Charlie remained and, like me a year later, was sent to Bautzen where he worked in a big state-owned bakery. I was told that he was a "brigadier" there, a foreman. During World War II he had been on a U.S. Navy ship, in the stewards' department like all black sailors, in his case as a baker.

In Bautzen Charlie was something of an institution; he was greeted heartily everywhere. His special appeal for children made one think of a friendly Pied Piper of Hamlin. One reason for his popularity was his boxing. Bautzen was not blessed with many distinguished athletes, so those few known beyond the city limits became heroes. I watched him only once in a bout in hometown Bautzen—where the fans cheered enthusiastically. A club evaluation from May 1952 said:

> Lucas has been in the Boxing Section since October 9, 1951. He is popular with sport friends . . . and known as a decent fellow. He leads a steady life and avoids alcohol and nicotine. Unfortunately he is hard to understand since he knows only a few words of German. He trains irregularly, but when he does, hard and intensively. But it is doubtful whether he can improve greatly since he is 36 (born on December 10, 1916).

The fight I saw may have been his last one.

Actually he spoke more than a few German words but tended to mix them with English. Whoever knew both languages understood him perfectly. Letters between boxing clubs in the area suggest that in Upper Lusatia (Oberlausitz) he was viewed rather as an exotic; no surprise, for I believe that in that out-of-the-way region he was the first person of African descent most people had ever seen.

Foreigners of any kind were quite rare in those years in Bautzen, so all of us, even those with white skins, were fairly conspicuous. At any one time there were on average about fifteen U.S. Americans, ten Britons, five or six Frenchmen, plus one Algerian and five or six Moroccans who had deserted the French army rather than fight in Vietnam. A few were Dutch; one was from Mexico, and another from Spain. Not many of the deserters were leftists or even politically minded; most had gotten into difficulties with their military authorities because of financial difficulties, AWOL problems, some mostly minor transgressions; if they wandered over from West to East Berlin the Soviet authorities may have tried influencing them to stay to avoid punishment in their units. A few like Charlie were involved with women the army disapproved of, sometimes because they came from East Berlin. Charlie was the only black for a long time—until a young Nigerian arrived, to be followed later by the men mentioned below.

There was always a turnover. I believe that a large proportion of the American defectors had had unhappy childhoods, came from broken family relationships, and had no real trade or profession other than the army. Men who had found female partners in Germany, in some cases marrying and raising children, almost always settled down and stayed. Others, usually with only rudimentary German, no learned trade, and frequently with alcohol problems, were often lonely and homesick and sooner or later made their illegal way to Berlin and then back to the West, no great problem in that city before the Wall, when subway and elevated systems crossed the border every few minutes. Once back, however, they faced prison sentences which varied greatly, from one to ten years. Even this did not deter them.

But every few months in the GDR press we would see another facsimile photo of a handwritten and signed statement by a defector, usually explaining his move eastward with a rejection of U.S. imperialist policy in Korea or elsewhere in words which sounded anything but normal for GIs or other soldiers. Such published statements were probably aimed at displaying resistance to U.S. policy even among American troops, at exerting a sort of blackmail effect to discourage the signer from going "back west"—or perhaps for both purposes. I suppose that I also wrote and signed some statement of this kind but I cannot recall any, and none by me was ever published. Soon after we read such statements a few Soviet officers would drive in with two or three new men, for whom rooms and jobs were soon found, the latter usually in one of the local factories.

I, too, had received a room, subletting it from a clearly reliable family, and I hiked a mile or so each day to the big LOWA railroad-car factory where I helped carry lumber. In April 1953, the usual two Soviet officers arrived in Bautzen, as always in civilian clothes, and asked if I wanted a different job. After lugging heavy lumber for five months, often in cold weather, I was all ears. It seems the authorities in charge, worried about the foreigners' heavy drinking, their frequent absenteeism at work, and the troubles some got into, had decided to turn the local Soviet officers' club into a clubhouse for us Ausländer. This "Klubhaus der Internationalen Solidarität," as it was now titled, was the Weygand Villa, a mansion built about 1900 by a Bautzen millionaire as a wedding present for his son. Each room had been designed in a different, Oriental or otherwise exotically unusual style. Its use as a Nazi military hospital until 1945 and then as a Soviet club meant that much of its glory was covered over or run down, but it remained an imposing building, which has since been completely renovated for use by people of wealth for marriages and other ceremonies.

The clubhouse was staffed with Germans and with two foreigners, Douglas Sharp, an Englishman, and myself. We were both fluent in German, nonalcoholic, and considered politically reliable. Douglas had some administrative experience and I could get along to a degree in French. My new job was to organize cultural activities in a pre-television era. We had a library with English and French books, a weekly film which I tried to translate simultaneously into English and sometimes into French as well. We had chess, table tennis, and billiards tournaments, occasional dance evenings, and English classes that I developed for some of the wives. After a slightly controversial debate with the German club director about gambling I also organized hitherto totally unknown bingo evenings with self-made cards, a fifty-pfennig limit, and all receipts immediately paid to the winners. We went on excursions, with free bus fare and a paid day off if needed. Once we went to a skiing resort for a weekend and one day we helped out at various jobs in one of the new collective farms.

I witnessed no racist incidents involving Charlie but was told by others of one probable case. It seems he took a woman friend on one of our bus excursions. When a young Englishman used loud, foul language, Charlie told him he was with a lady, and he asked the man to "clean it up." The reply was angry, and a dispute followed. There may well have been an unspoken racist undertone. At a bus stop the dispute became physical. Perhaps the challenger did not know Charlie's boxing background, but after Charlie knocked him down two or three times he decided to call it quits. That is the only time I know of Charlie getting angry: otherwise, he was a solid, friendly rock among the often-difficult relationships in and around the clubhouse. When we constructed our own volleyball court there, for example, Charlie was one of the first to join in the work. Once several of us were invited to nearby Löbau, where the Free German Youth group was celebrating the organization's anniversary with a party and fireworks. When Charlie demonstrated how to jitterbug—and despite official disapproval of such decadent influences from the West—he became the hero of the evening.

Our clubhouse had opened in May 1953, exclusively for us foreign deserters and our personal guests. It was a good idea in general, I think, but by August my own position there had become untenable. I was caught between the complaints and demands of the foreigners and attempts by the German staff to keep them satisfied and out of trouble, especially those who preferred regular drinking to regular work. Some found that if they asked clubhouse director Heinz Schattel for handouts they almost always got them, especially if they hinted that a rejection of the requested 200 or 300 marks would lead them to consider "taking off for the West." That could result in criticism of the director and his staff from the Soviets or, after the USSR relinquished control in 1953, from the GDR Interior Ministry authorities in Dresden or Berlin. Since I could speak German, English, and some French and worked in the clubhouse, and Schattel spoke only German, I often had to interpret such tricky negotiations, trying to show impartiality or, actually, sympathy for both sides. The frequent conflict of interests proved too much for me and ended in a mild nervous breakdown. Charlie Lucas, I should add, never came begging. But then he worked regularly and didn't drink!

Just when my two weeks of convalescence ended, the GDR authorities started a school for us. It had obviously been realized that the jobs held by many of the largely unskilled Ausländer were often harder and less well paid than the average and also lacked any real incentive. We needed to learn proper trades—like the majority of Germans. The decision came at just the right moment for me, so I happily quit as "Kulturleiter" and became a pupil and apprentice instead.

The official aim of this schooling (which now included the possibility of providing temporary living quarters for up to six new arrivals until private rooms could be found) was officially phrased as follows:

> This home serves as temporary location for persons of foreign nationality who have applied to live in the German Democratic Republic in order to participate actively in the preservation of peace and the construction of socialism. The main task of the Special School of International Solidarity, therefore, will be the reeducation and job training of these persons with a right to asylum who will one day return to their homelands as patriots in order to support their own working class in the fight to preserve peace and improve their living conditions.[1]

This latter question of returning to our homelands, I might add, was never raised or discussed except perhaps privately. Indeed, every effort was made to keep the Bautzen foreigners from returning westward.

The schooling lasted a year and was attended by all the foreigners, who received an average factory wage of 300 marks a month, with an additional 340 marks for wives and 25 marks for each child. Each new arrival was given a one-time sum of 750 marks to purchase clothing and an interest-free credit for furniture if moving into an unfurnished apartment. Although I was in Leipzig by then, I was later lent 2,000 marks for furniture purchases when I got married. For the first three months we had classes every day in the clubhouse: spoken and written German, simple mathematics, "Fachkunde" (industrial vocabulary and methods as part of our apprenticeship) and Staatsbürgerkunde or civics, in which an elderly anti-Nazi (and communist) struggled to teach us about the structure of the GDR as well as rudimentary Marxist ideas about historical dialectics and the like.

In 1964 the *Washington Post* columnist Jack Anderson warned very belatedly about this menacing school for deserters: "There is no telling how many have been sent to the espionage, propaganda and sabotage school in Bautzen."[2] To paraphrase Mark Twain once again, this report was "highly exaggerated." For a few of the older "rummies," already in their forties, almost any teaching seemed rather utopian; the nervous little teacher of German looked fearful each time he faced some of those tough old soldiers. A younger teacher who spoke fluent French got along much better in his classes for the more sober Frenchmen and, separately by necessity, for the North Africans, who were all illiterate and spoke more or less limited French and German. The one Algerian, by no means unintelligent, still believed the earth was flat!

In the second four-month period, we had classes in the clubhouse two days a week and went for the other days to a workshop in the LOWA railroad-car factory to learn, like so many other apprentices, how to file metal properly and carry out similar basic activities. Classes in the final months, which were all held in a special room set aside for us in the factory, were devoted to specialized training in one of four trades. I chose lathe operator; Charlie chose metalworker. Others could choose to become painters or carpenters, if I recall correctly.

Over the Whitsuntide weekend in June 1954 the Free German Youth organized a huge gathering, a "Deutschlandtreffen" (the GDR was still demanding unification in those years, in contrast to Adenauer in the Federal Republic). A few hundred thousand young people from all parts of the GDR and a much smaller number from West Germany congregated in East Berlin. A fair number of East Germans also used the opportunity to cross over and visit West Berlin, some as agitators, others as sightseers—or shoppers.

The school staff chose several of our "better students" to go along: in the main those who could be counted on not to get too drunk, cause trouble, or flee to the West. Aside from two members of the amazingly large German clubhouse and school staff (over thirty in all), our group included Charlie, myself and one other American, an Englishman, a Frenchman, and two Moroccans. Like most GDR participants we traveled in freight cars with temporary benches, singing much of the way. Upon arrival everyone got a lunch bag and the address of a place to sleep, often in schools. But we Bautzen foreigners were welcomed by a special group from the Ministry of Interior. Perhaps that meant State Security; we neither knew nor cared, I think, for they were friendly young men and women, were not nosy, and helped us find our way around East Berlin to the main events, like the giant opening ceremony in Walter Ulbricht Stadion (later renamed "Stadion der Weltjugend"; Stadium of World Youth) but torn down after 1990 and currently destined to become the site of the Bundesnachrichtendienst (like the CIA).

Each night we were driven to the vacation home of the ministry on a pretty lakeside near Berlin. Otherwise, we were free to go where we wished. Charlie met a pretty English teacher who lived in the newly built Stalin Allee and invited us all to visit and look out from the roof over the giant construction site and an adjacent area, still a wide field of ruins, which was built up some years later—and where I have been living since 1961.

Back in Bautzen, Charlie, though usually smiling, clearly had problems. We met the good-looking neighbor woman who came to clean up, perhaps to cook, and perhaps for other reasons. Her husband did not seem to mind; rumors had it that their apartment upstairs was gaining new appliances and furniture faster than usual—thanks to Charlie. But the rule among us foreigners was: Don't ask too many questions. He later moved to another street but could not seem to find a steady companion. Perhaps language and other difficulties were factors. So we were all happy to hear that he was planning on marriage. I vaguely recall the woman: not too young, no beauty, but pleasant and intelligent; it was said she had a desk job with the railroad company, or Reichsbahn. On the wedding day, or so I was told, a crowd of friends and fans went to the Standesamt. Just about everyone was there—except the bride! Her absence was a mystery. Only recently, researching for this paper, I heard it suggested that perhaps, as a member of the dominant GDR party, the SED, she was not supposed to marry a "stateless" westerner, our category at that time. Other possibilities present themselves. Whatever the reason, it was a terrible blow!

My more recent research uncovered a surprise. Charlie did finally find someone, it would seem. He was married on March 31, 1956, to a textile worker from Bautzen. Why did they marry in Leipzig? We must guess at the most likely reason. Marriages with people of color were in those days virtually unknown and undoubtedly not universally approved. It cannot have been a happy marriage. Were the pressures caused by differing nationality but even more by their differing skin color too strong? I cannot answer. Manfred Noack, the director of the clubhouse from 1955 to 1959, recently told me the following. Only six weeks after the marriage, on June 12, 1956, the LOWA factory called to say that Charlie had not come to work, something unheard of with him. Was he ill? Manfred immediately went to his apartment—and smelled gas in the hallway. The door was unlocked; he ran in, opened a window—and found Charlie slumped at a table. An ambulance took him to the hospital, but it was too late. On the table next to him lay a letter to a woman, probably his new wife, and two books, one by Karl Marx, the other the Bible.

Lucas was not the only African American to pass through Bautzen. Arthur Boyd, whose family had raised cotton in South Carolina before moving north to Long Island, was stationed in Berlin when he fell in love with an East Berlin woman then visiting West Berlin. In 1953 a daughter was born and Boyd, who had never had alcoholic or other difficulties with the army, decided to defect to the East. On April 30, 1953, they were sent to Bautzen, a day before the clubhouse was opened. Ingeborg Boyd was not very enthusiastic about life in Bautzen or the connection with the clubhouse. Years later, in any case, she complained about having to march in the May Day parade although it was hot and she was again pregnant. But when the trade school began the following September Arthur completed the course and became a journeyman metalworker, evidently a very good one. He told me with a laugh that he had twice been honored as an "Activist," an award for those who achieved greater productivity. This did not always earn him friends, especially when his foremen held him up as a good example, saying: "Just look over here, Herr Boyd has again produced nearly twice as much as the others." This might lead to more efficiency with higher, more realistic production standards and pay rates, but this did not necessarily bring more popularity. Boyd always had difficulty with the German language, evidently, and this also made it more difficult to find many friends. He also sang and was a good hobby instrumentalist on drums, but in styles as yet largely unknown in the GDR in those early years.

As soon as possible the family moved to East Berlin, where Ingeborg Boyd became manager of a co-op grocery. All in all they had six children. When they were together, I recall Ingeborg talking almost ceaselessly while Arthur remained largely silent. According to his son Leroy, who went to school in East Berlin and later became a construction manager, his father was proud of the awards but always homesick for the United States. He argued with his son, who, raised in an East Berlin school, was very skeptical about the good things in the USA—such as all the many cars—which his father talked about. His homesickness was partly due to his language problem, Leroy believed.

About 1967 Arthur and Ingeborg visited us with their oldest daughter Karin, who was then fourteen. When my wife asked her about her hopes for her future she said she wanted to become an actress. Knowing that many girls at that age dream of such a career, and mindful of possible difficulties because of her brown skin color, I recall having some private doubts. She did indeed achieve her goal, however, and after completing her studies at the State Dramatic College in Rostock and also singing lessons she was engaged for ten years at the prestigious Maxim Gorky Theater in Berlin. But sadly and stupidly, her color did indeed prove a definite handicap with directors who believed at the time (as they had for so many years in the United States) that they could not give her any substantial "white" roles. Quite probably for that reason she left the GDR legally with her young son in 1983. She has since had many theater and television roles and was particularly admired for her supporting role in István Szabó's very successful film "Mephisto" about Gustav Gründgens. She is now a stage and television actress and director in Munich, with guest performances in Berlin, Stuttgart and elsewhere.

Arthur and Ingeborg were divorced in 1975. After the unification of Germany, Arthur went to the U.S. consulate in West Berlin to apply for a passport or visa to return to the USA, possibly to see his parent or parents. From reports I heard he was immediately put into uniform and sent back to the United States without any notification of his waiting family in Berlin. The U.S. Army officials who met me at John F. Kennedy Airport in 1994 spoke of another ex-soldier whom they had apprehended and who no longer spoke much English when he arrived at Kennedy. From the description I believe this must have been Arthur Boyd. Evidently he, like me, was then discharged from the army without serving any sentence. Like me, he returned to Germany and now lives in Land Brandenburg.

His son Leroy, although he had argued against his father about the merits of the USA, was not blindly devoted to his memories of the GDR. He spoke in his interview with West German Radio about learning that the family was under observation by the Stasi, as were probably all residents from the United States or other unfriendly countries. Ingeborg also reported an unsuccessful attempt to win her over to work for the "Stasi." However, when Leroy Boyd also visited the USA after this had become easily possible, he found that he did not feel at home there, only partly because of his not-so-perfect knowledge of English, and he, too, returned to Germany.[3]

James William Pulley, born in Pennsylvania in 1936, was another African American soldier who deserted the U.S. Army. He was stationed in Augsburg in July 1955 when, according to what he told the West German radio team, he simply went with a girlfriend to her hometown in Halberstadt in Saxony-Anhalt, crossing the border in uniform and on foot and then checking in at the police station. "Frankly, I didn't have a clue about East or West and suddenly I was in the East . . . I wanted the girl-friend and didn't bother worrying about other matters."[4] His wife (not the same person) says, "It was love!" (It should be noted that in 1955, before the Berlin Wall was built, the East-West borderlines were porous and permeable.)

When Pulley arrived in Bautzen the clubhouse was still there, directed by Manfred Noack, and improved over past years by the addition of one of the earliest television sets in the GDR, a present from the responsible government organization, the Interior Ministry. The trade school had continued, though with fewer apprentices, and Pulley was taught metalwork, like most of the others, and was already working as a boilermaker in the LOWA railroad-car factory in Görlitz, a sister factory of the LOWA plant in Bautzen. But evidently he had not yet completed his apprenticeship. This is how Manfred Noack tells the story:

> We actually wanted him to finish learning a trade. But he went his own way and disappeared one day, we didn't know where. And then we and our foreign friends went on vacation for two weeks in Bad Schandau and when we arrived we saw on the billboards: "The Negro singer James Pulley will perform in Bad Schandau with the Black and White Dance Orchestra" . . . At first we said, "That can't be true!" But then it turned out to be just that; I have some of the pictures here. He had his way; he did not want to be a metalworker but a singer. And he got his way and became a singer.[5]

This is the way Pulley tells the story about how he and his wife went to a dance one evening in 1957:

> A band was playing and we were sitting next to the stage and I was beating out the music with my hands the way I'm doing now, and the pianist kept looking down at me. In the break he said,
> "Come on up here. Say, do you love music?"
> I said: "Naturally!"
> "Can you sing?"
> I said, "Naturally I can sing."
> "Really?"
> I said, "Yes."
> "Well, after the break you come up here and . . ."

So I said, "What should I sing?"

And they already had a singer who sang soft pop stuff so I sang sort of Rock'n'Roll. And he hired me on the spot.[6]

Pulley took singing courses and became known as an industrious fellow with a good sense of humor. He became a very popular singer, partly because of being an exotic African American from the United States, but also because he displayed plenty of energy singing and easily captured his audiences. He evidently tried some of the pelvis gyrations that reminded people of Elvis and were officially greatly disapproved of in those days, and on one occasion he provoked a tumult which ended in throwing chairs. But aside from such occasional run-ins with the staid, conservative etiquette still ruling the music scene but always assailed by new fashions and new customs leaking in from the West via radio, television, and personal visits, Pulley, often wearing a white suit presented to him by the central concert agency, sang around the GDR with many of the best-known singers and sometimes went on tour with them as far as Tashkent. He sang American songs for the most part, but also new GDR hit songs. One report, presumably from a Stasi informer, said: "this concert was in order since he represented the genuine America. At earlier concerts with the Bodo Weise Orchestra there were some complaints since the Negro singer included some pelvis gyrations in his program."[7] But in general, Pulley made a good impression with everyone.

His wife, Ursula, was also impressed: "You will have noticed that my husband is not a great orator. He went onto the stage and he sang. He achieves an extremely sympathetic effect with the audience and has a fine, warm voice. And they also liked the songs, of course. James was always a modest fellow, a quiet pole. But really quite hot all the same, if you know what I mean."[8] He and his wife were able to settle in a pleasant house in Berlin and own a dacha outside Berlin—like half of all the East Berliners, but also own—like very few East Berliners—an expensive Volvo with a trailer. Pulley told the *Berliner Zeitung*, "I was treated exactly the same as everybody else, neither discriminated against nor particularly favored."[9]

When the GDR disappeared in 1990, so did many concert possibilities and especially television performances, since GDR television was replaced almost 100 percent by West German channels, owners, and managers. But Pulley was able to make out after a while, singing at nostalgic East German get-togethers or, more regularly, in programs on passenger cruise liners. "We've been almost everywhere . . . ," he told the West German radio team. "We were in Mombasa twice, and we were in England, in Scotland, in Jordan, Israel, Egypt, Monaco."[10] He had no interest in returning to the USA, where he knew no one. And, as he summed up in an interview with the magazine *Der Spiegel*, "My homeland is the old GDR."[11] Or, as he told the radio team, when he was asked what he considers himself: "I thought it over and came out with—'I'm an African American GDR citizen of the Federal Republic.'"[12]

Raymond H. Hutto, an African American from Georgia who crossed into the GDR in 1954, also learned a trade in Bautzen and earned his master's papers at the giant *Schwarze Pumpe* coal and gas complex in Upper Lusatia (not too far from Dresden). *Der Spiegel* quotes him as saying that when the Wall fell: "I was a little fearful . . . I told my wife that we would never have it so good again."[13] And, indeed, after unification he lost his job.

Der Spiegel prints a similar quotation from the widow of Willie Avent, an African American and former sergeant, also a deserter, who died in 1994. After mentioning that her husband had been awarded the "Silver Pin of the National Front" and was a member in excellent standing of the "Association for German-Soviet Friendship" (actually an organization in which nearly all German workers formally joined up), Erika Avent is quoted as saying: "He was more a GDR citizen than an American." He once said, when the Wall fell, "Now the quiet life is a thing of the past."[14]

In September 1954 I left the school and clubhouse in Bautzen, a journeyman lathe operator, in order to attend the Karl Marx University in Leipzig. After the large initial group which I had been part of, there was only a trickle of new participants. By 1956 only three foreigners were learning a trade there and the Interior Ministry was questioning the political and financial effectiveness of the project. The Berlin Wall and related measures along the entire German border in 1961 virtually ended the arrival of new deserters and finally, in 1963, the Home of International Solidarity was closed for good, though some assistance was given its alumni when required.

Aside from the tragic end of Charles Lucas, the handful of African American deserters who went to the GDR and Bautzen managed by and large to adapt quite well and integrate successfully into society, as I did. This does not mean that there were no racist undercurrents in the GDR. Dating and perhaps marrying a person of color was quite acceptable to some young women and may even have been additionally desirable because of the vicarious acquaintance with the "outside world," especially the western world, which it involved. To them, skin color differences represented no drawback to a genuine love affair or marriage. But others, especially those belonging to older generations, most certainly looked askance at such connections. This may well explain Charles Lucas's difficulties in finding a wife, the reason for getting married in Leipzig and perhaps even the tragic end of the marriage. This is speculation, of course, but antiblack prejudices were hardly eliminated completely despite the stress on internationalism in education, from kindergarten on up, as well as in some very popular books, plays, and films opposing race prejudice. There were also widespread and often effective campaigns on behalf of discriminated or threatened African Americans like Paul Robeson, the Wilmington Ten, and Angela Davis, who paid greatly publicized and well-received visits to the GDR as soon as they were able to.

Some political officials on all levels may have encouraged antiracist sentiments in part because they involved a critique of the "imperialist USA" and thus fit into the general political direction of the GDR, at least in its first decades. There were always many people in responsible jobs who sang the officially approved melodies because of their careers. But there were always many others who were very convinced internationalists.

In the last two decades of the GDR the problems became more complex when not only our handful of deserters and a small number of African students came to the GDR, but also several thousand young people who arrived on a governmental contract basis to learn a trade and especially to work, while sending money home or saving money or equipment to set themselves up economically once they returned home. The first to come were Algerians, then Cubans, Mozambiquans, Angolans, and especially many Vietnamese followed. With this larger influx, some problems were almost inevitable, sometimes due to what GDR citizens perceived as special advantages granted the foreigners—desirable homes in the new, relatively modern high-rise building blocks, special paid time in working hours to learn German, and at times lenience in occasional but luckily quite rare clashes. Since all groups except for the Vietnamese consisted largely or entirely of young men, there were also problems involving competition for women partners, especially at discos. The GDR authorities, inexperienced in such matters, sometimes committed well-meaning or stupid blunders.

More important, in my opinion, however, were the infectious antiforeigner feelings increasingly seeping over from West Germany via radio, television, personal contacts and, in one case, at least, by what might be called literature. In the earlier GDR years, whenever one saw someone reading a thick paperback book wrapped in brown paper to conceal its title one could be quite certain that he— or usually she—was reading a dog-eared copy of *Gone with the Wind*, which had been removed from GDR libraries. (Only in the last year or so of the GDR did one publisher see fit—and get an OK—to print it, despite its Ku Klux Klan bias.) Perhaps this one book was not so important, but the nasty racial epithets which increasingly circulated during the final GDR years originated, I am quite positive, in the Federal Republic. They were directed especially at the larger groups of foreigners—Turks, Arabs, Vietnamese, but also at blacks.

The GDR was a complicated mixture of many currents, changing views and pressures, both internal and external, and far from the monolithic, almost totally negative structure which has been pictured so universally, both before and since its demise. This also applied to the problems of xenophobia and racism. As far as the clubhouse and school were concerned, at first, and especially under its early Soviet administration, there were doubtless hopes of winning a few propaganda points in the East-West conflict. But it soon became apparent that aside from the transparently dictated and hardly convincing declarations made by the deserters when they first arrived, there were no points to be won. Nevertheless, the experiment was continued, at great expense, and I know that the two directors, Heinz Schattel and his successor Manfred Noack, as well as others who worked in the clubhouse, were motivated completely by their deeply felt belief in an internationalism which fitted in with their commitment to their communist beliefs and principles.

Although I know of only five African Americans who attended this school, it is interesting to note that all got along very well and had a list of accomplishments to their credit, except only in the tragic case of Charles Lucas.

Postscript

1. Much of the material for the radio feature quoted above was taken from documents of the GDR Interior Ministry now being kept in the Bundesarchiv in Berlin-Lichtenfelde, which state that in all about 150 U.S. Americans lived in the GDR. Of these, of course, only army deserters were sent to Bautzen.

2. In the article referred to above, *Der Spiegel* quotes U.S. sources investigating for the Department of Defense as saying somewhat ambiguously about the U.S. deserters: "About 40 of these destinies have since been cleared up however: the Americans had been hiding in the former GDR, 10 are still living in the new Federal provinces."

Notes

1. Arna Vogel and Christian Blees, "Der Cowboy im Sozialismus, US-Amerikaner in der DDR," *Westdeutscher Rundfunk*, Cologne, October 5, 2004, 6.

2. Jack Anderson, "US Misfits Train as Red Spies," and "The Washington Merry-Go-Round," *Washington Post*, June 13, 1964, 39.

3. Vogel and Blees, "Der Cowboy im Sozialismus, US-Amerikaner in der DDR," 10.

4. Ibid., 11

5. Ibid., 12.

6. Ibid.

7. Ibid., 13.

8. Ibid., 14.

9. *Berliner Zeitung*, April 25, 1995, 3.

10. Vogel and Blees, "Der Cowboy im Sozialismus, US-Amerikaner in der DDR," 22.

11. *Der Spiegel*, April 10, 1995, 97.

12. Vogel and Blees, "Der Cowboy im Sozialismus, US-Amerikaner in der DDR," 22.

13. *Der Spiegel*, April 10, 1995, 97.

14. Ibid.

An Unexpected Alliance

August Willich, Peter H. Clark, and the Abolitionist
Movement in Cincinnati

MISCHA HONECK

"A German has only to be a German to be utterly opposed to slavery. In feeling, as well as in conviction and principle, they are anti-slavery," penned Frederick Douglass, the famous black abolitionist and newspaperman, in August 1859. Douglass later modified his statement, welcoming above all "the many noble and high-minded men, most of whom, swept over by the tide of the revolution in 1849, have become our active allies in the struggle against oppression and prejudice."[1] Douglass's assessment of the immigrant revolutionaries from German lands, although overblown, is understandable. In fact, the liberal and radical "Forty-Eighters" were anything but a solid bloc—they encompassed a spectrum of different ideological outlooks, regional backgrounds, and occupational orientations. Their ranks included university professors, lawyers, army officers, journalists, craftworkers, and ordinary laborers. Yet, and this is what piqued Douglass's curiosity most, almost all shared a profound aversion to the American institution of slavery. In public speeches and writings, they attacked this system of bound labor, which, they judged, grossly belied the founding ideals and democratic promises of their host country. In concert with native-born antislavery fighters, the Forty-Eighters swelled the ranks of a protest movement the transnational and multiethnic dimensions of which are still vastly underexplored.

This essay offers a fresh appraisal of the German-speaking refugees of 1848 during the run-up to the Civil War by probing their relationship to another group of beleaguered agitators: America's abolitionists. Specifically, it focuses on the companionship of two radicals, the German-born socialist August Willich and the black educator Peter H. Clark, in the immigrant stronghold of antebellum Cincinnati. It sketches how both individuals and their adherents joined forces in the long, often-dangerous battle to eliminate slavery and argues that cooperation helped them mitigate their differences in a society steeped in racist and nativist thought. Even as these activists pressed for emancipation in different, sometimes conflicting ways, their alliance led them to raise questions about America's developing mores that are startling in their intensity and farsightedness. Returning to these figures, however, does not only elucidate their interrelated lives and ideas.

More important, it also sensitizes us to alternative expressions of community at a time that witnessed a growing convergence of race and citizenship, when democracy became increasingly wedded to the nation.

Tributes to a Hero

In December 1859, America's abolitionists bade farewell to their fiercest warrior. John Brown, the antislavery revolutionary, had been hung for his ill-fated attempt to launch an insurrection among the slaves of Virginia. In the days following the execution, friends and sympathizers across the North commemorated Brown in various public gatherings (Oates 1984, 354–55). This was also the purpose of a meeting that took place in Cincinnati's Over-the-Rhine district. Over-the-Rhine, home to Cincinnati's German-Americans, was a bustling community: small shop owners, artisans, crafters, apprentices, and ordinary laborers constituted the backbone of a culture that was predominantly working-class. Many of these German-born workers were organized in the local *Freimänner-* and *Arbeitervereine*, the freethinking and workingmen's societies that gave public life in this plebeian milieu its distinctively radical features. August Willich, editor of the *Cincinnati Republikaner*, a publication of the Social Workingmen's Club, had announced the previous day that the *Arbeiterverein* was to hold a memorial meeting for John Brown.[2]

Around two o'clock in the afternoon, a formidable crowd started marching into the hall of the German Institute. However, not all who attended the meeting were of German descent. As one observer put it, there was "a motley crowd of both sexes, diversified by every hue common to the human species," including the "bronzed Frenchman, the pale-faced American, and the rubicund Teuton." To the rear of the podium, the American flag was dressed in mourning as were the portraits of Washington and Jefferson to its left. In front of and a little to the right of the podium, the black-red-golden flag of German republicanism stood unfolded. Shortly after the meeting had begun, a delegation of African Americans entered the hall, exhibiting a flag of their own and fastening it to the ground alongside the others. Cheers and salutes followed and did not ebb until the African American standard bearers took their seats.

The first to take the floor and address the interracial crowd was August Willich. He electrified the audience by denouncing the ignorance of the Irish, depicting the evils of slavery, and by telling his hearers "to whet their sabers and nerve their arms for the day of retribution" when the institution and its supporters "would be crushed into a common grave." The crowd responded with thundering applause, indicating a unity later described by Willich as "the inner bond of humanity, [which] brought forth a harmonious melody sung by races and nationalities separated by nothing but outward appearance." Among those who followed the German-American labor leader was Peter Humphries Clark, the black principal of the Western Colored District School. Clark proclaimed to those present that they were "in the midst of a revolution that had to be fought to the death," and that the events now transpiring "were more holy, more momentous to the well-being of man [. . .] than those of '76." Clark also thanked the German-Americans in the audience for doing justice to his race. By attending, they not only demonstrated their love of freedom but also their willingness to make common cause with people of a different color. Willich returned the compliment in the next edition of the *Republikaner*, praising Clark's speech as "the most stirring elaboration on the idea of freedom" that was delivered on that day.[3]

The gathering of people as diverse as Willich and Clark was extraordinary and in many ways unexpected. This is echoed in the extensive coverage of the Over-the-Rhine meeting in the local press. Not that many articles, however, were friendly. The *Cincinnati Daily Enquirer* issued the report of an eyewitness who could not fathom how German- and Anglo-Americans could sit on the same bench with "the copper-colored African and the greasy-skinned and odorous Ethiopian." The *Enquirer* went on to marvel how a foreign people who had failed politically at home were "to teach the descendants of the men of '76 their first lessons in Government" while all they had in mind was "to favor 'negro equality.'" The *Cincinnati Volksfreund*, a conservative German-American newspaper, was equally indignant. It held that the only thing the Brown sympathizers had accomplished was to "stigmatize the great men of the Revolution," most of whom had owned slaves themselves.[4]

Willich and Clark were not only attacked for their political beliefs but also because their collaboration defied one of the principal social ideologies of the time. From a conservative vantage point, promoting radical ideas was one thing, but it was quite another to cooperate "with the vilest of the African race."[5] What was it that made a German revolutionary of 1848 and a black abolitionist defy the assumptions of antebellum racism and join forces, apart from the fact that they both hated slavery? Was their alliance genuine, based on an appreciation of one another as equals, or was it merely driven by political interests? To which extent did the different cultural and ideological backgrounds play a role and how were they received by the other? To answer these questions, Willich and Clark need to be examined within the social topography of a city notorious for ethnic conflict at that time.

The political careers of Willich and Clark began literally oceans apart. The descendant of an old Prussian Junker family, Willich first emulated his ancestors: he served in the army. But the hierarchical structures of the Prussian military soon collided with his Enlightenment beliefs. These had sprung from conversations with Friedrich Schleiermacher, the famous Berlin theologian and philosopher, who had mentored August and his brother after the death of their father. Willich eventually resigned after embracing republicanism in an open letter to the king. The revolutions of 1848–1849 gave him the chance to put his political ideas into practice. By then, he had become part of the Cologne circle around Marx and Engels and adopted a socialist outlook focusing on workers' rights and social improvement through *Bildung*. At the side of Hecker, Sigel, and Struve, Willich fought against the reactionary forces in the Palatinate and Baden. His military training and eloquence made him one of the most dashing and skillful commanders of the democratic militia. Willich, beloved by his soldiers, allegedly took no privileges and shared their hardships to the very end.

After the revolution was put down, Willich emigrated to London where he became a member of the Communist League. But political differences with Karl Marx soon generated personal friction. The factions split and in 1853 Willich left London for good. He joined the Forty-Eighter exodus to the United States, moved to Brooklyn, and from there on to Washington, D.C. Working as a cartographer for the government, Willich made the acquaintance of the émigré politician and lawyer Johann Stallo, one of Cincinnati's most respected German-American citizens. Stallo was impressed with Willich and persuaded him to relocate to Cincinnati. Willich arrived in 1858, ready to start his editorship in a city reeling under the impact of race, class, and pre–Civil War party politics.[6]

Peter H. Clark was born and raised in Cincinnati as the son of a black barber and the grandson of a Kentucky slave woman and her white master. He was given the best education available to an African American at that time—courses included Latin, history, and philosophy—but that did not shield him against discrimination. Prejudice, Clark recollected in 1873, "has hindered every step I have taken in life."[7] During his apprenticeship in printing he was fired by a new master who refused to train blacks. After taking over his father's barbershop, he got into a controversy with a white customer who was offended by Clark's policy to provide equal service to blacks and whites. The field, however, in which Clark invested most of his energy, was teaching. But his plans to elevate African Americans by educating them faced huge difficulties. While the Ohio legislature allowed blacks to organize their own public schools, it left them direly underfunded. Clark's disputes with the Cincinnati School Board led to his dismissal in 1853; the official reason was heresy. The charges raised against Clark were that he engaged in free-thought discussion circles and had his students question essential Protestant doctrines. It was not until 1857 that he was reinstated.

In the meantime Clark started acting on a wider political stage: along with his uncle, the black civil rights pioneer John I. Gaines, he participated in the Ohio Conventions of Colored Men; he edited and published his own abolitionist weekly, the *Herald of Freedom*, which he had to discontinue after only four months due to financial difficulties; and in 1856 he temporarily moved to Rochester to serve on the editorial staff of the *Frederick Douglass' Paper*. Presumably through Douglass's patronage, Clark was invited to a national meeting of radical abolitionists in Syracuse where he gave a brief but memorable speech. "If you wish to abolish slavery," he told the delegates, "you must combat it wherever it is found, whether in political parties, in churches, or in your own homes."[8]

A Divided City

Antiblack sentiments were especially strong in Cincinnati, a city where ethnic rivalry became a growing concern in the first half of the nineteenth century. Strategically located on the Ohio River, the "Queen City of the West," as Cincinnati was affectionately called by nineteenth-century Americans, soon developed into a major trading center attracting an increasing number of merchants and settlers. The growth rate was breathtaking: in 1825 the United States census estimated 15,000 inhabitants; at midcentury this number had skyrocketed to 115,435 and kept rising (Bertaux 1993, 130). But Cincinnati was not only among the fastest-growing places in the country. It also had one of the nation's most diverse populations, a fact that did not escape contemporary observers. As the Swedish traveler Fredrika Bremer thought, Cincinnati was a "pre-eminently cosmopolitan" city, while the German-born novelist Emil Klauprecht marveled over the "prevalent confusion of tongues" in the river town (Benson 1924, 247; Klauprecht 1854, 2).

A large portion of Cincinnati's inhabitants consisted of European immigrants, the majority coming from Ireland and Germany. In the 1840s and 1850s nearly two million poor and starving peasants left Ireland; many of them were bound for the New World. While most Irish settled on the Eastern seaboard, particularly in larger cities such as New York and Boston, some decided to go farther west. By 1851, the Irish constituted nearly 12 percent of Cincinnati's overall population (Taylor 2005, 24). However, their chances to thrive in this city as a group were limited. Coming from an overwhelmingly rural, traditionalist, and provincial background, the Irish were largely unprepared to meet the requirements of an emerging industrial market society (Miller 1988). Another disadvantage was their religion. Almost all the immigrants from Ireland were Catholics who arrived in America in the midst of a fervent resurgence of Protestantism; many native-born Americans were suspicious of the folkways of the Irish and treated their religious customs with disdain.

The Germans left an even greater mark on Cincinnati's urban landscape. According to an 1859 estimate, they comprised about two-thirds of the city's foreign-born population (Cist 1859, 165). Lacking a national center, the German immigrants had grown up with separate regional identities, and the cultural idiosyncrasies they held dear continued to blossom in the New World (Miller 1989, 2). From the very beginning, German-speaking immigrants had a stake in Cincinnati's development. David Ziegler, a veteran of the Revolutionary War and a native of Heidelberg, became the city's first mayor in 1802. Among the earlier arrivals was also Martin Baum, a successful banker and entrepreneur who prospered in the nascent transportation industry. Jacob Kornblüth and Sebastian Meyer, both merchants of German descent, made a fortune in Cincinnati's booming textile factories (Levine 1992, 183–84).

A community as multifaceted as the Queen City Germans was not free of internal strife. Spending the winter of 1846–47 in southern Ohio, the historian Franz von Löher deplored that his emigrated countrymen had "split into strong factions, religious and political, and in serried ranks continually menace and attack each other."[9] The immigrant generation that came to Cincinnati after the events of 1848 only widened this gap. As in previous years, the bulk of these newcomers were laborers, adding to the already impressive number of foreign-born workers that had been crucial for Cincinnati's economic development. That much becomes clear in the following remark of city chronicler Charles Cist:

"[T]o the industry of foreigners, Cincinnati is indebted in a great degree [. . .] . Their presence here has accelerated the execution of our public improvements, and given an impulse to our immense manufacturing operations" (Cist 1851, 48).

There had always been a striking presence of German-born laborers in the city, but the newcomers raised their share of Cincinnati's entire male workforce to over 43 percent by 1850. Another important aspect was that they figured comparatively high in the skilled professions, undoubtedly a consequence of their training in the European apprentice system. As the English traveler Isabella Bird underlined during her stay in the Queen City, the "Germans almost monopolise the handicraft trades, where they find a fruitful field for their genius and industry."[10]

The new arrivals, however, had more to offer than strong hands and sturdy backs. Unlike other immigrant groups, many of them were not only hard working but also well organized and politically educated. They had been at the heart of Germany's failed democratic revolution and had imported its tenets—universal human rights, abolition of privilege, national unity—to the New World. Led by their intellectual spokespersons, they reshaped Cincinnati's German-American community with new civic organizations, thereby hoping to sustain their home-grown social and political ideals in an unfamiliar environment. This was certainly the case when fourteen friends responded to the call of revolutionary legend Friedrich Hecker and established the *Cincinnati Turnverein* in 1848, the first of its kind on American soil. Other associations quickly followed: radical workers founded the *Arbeiterverein* to combat unfair wages and working hours; freethinkers, sticking to their Enlightenment heritage, met in *Freimännervereine*, where they debated all kinds of literary, moral, and scientific issues (Levine 1992; Wittke 1962). Although a minority, these revolutionaries and agnostics were shrill enough to unnerve their conservative kinsmen as well as many churchgoing Anglo-Americans. This oppositional group of Germans, Isabella Bird noted, "are a thinking, sceptical, theorising people: in politics, Socialists—in religion, Atheists. [. . .] Skilled, educated, and intellectual," she concluded, they "constitute an influence of which the Americans themselves are afraid."[11]

The profound distrust of these newcomers among older immigrants betrayed a more immediate concern as well. By the mid-1850s, Know-Nothingism had become a major force in the region, and tensions between Cincinnati's German-American population and local nativist bands were doubtlessly amplified by the sociopolitical activities of the Forty-Eighter democrats. The most ferocious nativist onslaught in this decade was the election riot of 1855. After their candidate for mayor had been defeated, Know-Nothings went on a rampage against the Queen City's foreign-born residents. The German-Americans, in order to defend themselves, barricaded the bridges leading into Over-the-Rhine and summoned their militia units. So severe was the fighting that civil order could not be restored for three days (Baughn 1963).[12]

When attacking the foreign-born, nativists cared little about intraethnic distinctions. During Archbishop Bedini's visit in late 1853, nativists and radicals had still united against Catholic immigrants; three years later, German-American radicals themselves became victims of nativist aggression. Marching back from a picnic near Covington, members of the *Cincinnati Turnverein* were assaulted by a mob of Ohioans and Kentuckians. Rocks were thrown and pistol shots were exchanged, drawing blood on both sides.[13]

Anti-immigrant unrest was a sad reality, yet it barely exuded the intense racial contempt which native- and foreign-born whites heaped upon America's oppressed black population. Bordering on slaveholding Kentucky, the Queen City was seen by numerous African Americans as a gateway to a better life. Virtually from Cincinnati's incorporation as a town, however, municipal authorities treated people of a darker hue as a caste inferior to all others. "I thought upon coming to a free state like Ohio that I would find every door thrown open to receive me," the fugitive slave John Malvin reportedly said. "But from the treatment I received by the people generally, I found it little better than in Virginia."[14] Even though the 1802 State Constitution of Ohio disallowed slavery, it remained silent on the issue of civil rights for blacks. This provided sufficient leeway for the enactment of the Ohio Black Laws of 1804 and 1807, which excluded African Americans living in the state from much of its public activity. The rationale behind these laws was to discourage further settlement of blacks, particularly of fugitive slaves, in the region; but since they were never fully enforced, Ohio's black population rose slowly but continually. In 1820, a little more than 400 African Americans resided in Cincinnati; thirty years later, the city had one of the North's largest free black communities: an estimated 3,237 people—roughly 2.8 percent of the city's overall population (Taylor 1993, 99; Taylor 2005, 28–37).

Most blacks in Cincinnati came to dwell in the highly polluted quarters near the docks commonly referred to as "Bucktown" or "Little Africa." It was a struggling neighborhood: signs of privation and decay were everywhere. To the nineteenth-century journalist Lafcadio Hearn, Bucktown conveyed the image of an early urban slum, a "congregation of dingy and dilapidated frames, hideous huts, and shapeless dwellings."[15] Residential segregation by race, however, was not a familiar concept yet. Some African Americans, if they could afford higher rents, also moved into adjacent white working-class districts. According to one statistic, the Irish were most likely to have black neighbors, but there were also blacks who could be found living next door to German-speaking families. In 1850, for instance, 235 blacks were counted among the residents of Over-the-Rhine, Cincinnati's "Little Germany" (Taylor 1986, 26–30).

Another major contact zone between blacks and whites was the workplace, a sphere that became a major breeding ground of racial antagonism. A vast number of Cincinnati's blacks were manumitted or fugitive slaves who had acquired marketable skills during their time in bondage. But despite their ambitions and their willingness to work, blacks were largely restricted to unskilled or semi-skilled labor by their white employers. More than 80 percent of the city's black labor force earned their daily bread as barbers, cooks, steamboat workers, or domestic servants (Taylor 1986, 26). Poor, illiterate, and disenfranchised, Cincinnati's African Americans rarely went up the social ladder. "In this very state they are free, but they are not recognized as citizens," commented William Unterthiner, the Austrian-born pastor of St. John Baptist Church, in 1845. "In short, they are regarded as things."[16]

Further factors that denied blacks equal treatment on the labor market were laws which made it illegal to hire African Americans who did not possess a certificate of freedom and, more relevant still, the widespread refusal of white workers to work alongside a person of color (Horton and Flaherty 1993, 87). White resentment of black wage labor often exploded in violence as in the bloody riot of 1841 when Irish dockworkers attacked their black colleagues, leaving many dead and wounded (Taylor 2005, 118–26). Recent scholarship, however, has stressed that it was not only economic rivalry or the fear of competition that relegated African Americans to the bottom rung of society. As David Roediger underscores, for low-class Anglo-Americans and for poor Irish and German immigrants, distancing oneself from those who occupied the lowest rank in the country's social hierarchy was also about emphasizing one's whiteness, about asserting citizenship in a predominantly white republic (Roediger 1999). To be accepted as white meant not to be black, to be exempt from the burdens and inferiorities commonly associated with the black race.

In spite of these social and political barriers, Cincinnati's black population, as has been pointed out, rose slowly but steadily. Its proximity to the South made the city relatively easy to reach for runaway slaves seeking a safe haven from bondage. Because of this, Cincinnati was also on the front lines of the Underground Railroad and the movement to abolish slavery. From the very beginning, free blacks had managed to build an intricate network that provided food, shelter, clothing, and other services to help fugitive slaves in need. Community leaders like Henry Boyd, John Gaines, William Henry Harrison, and Peter H. Clark coordinated these movements, occasionally calling upon the support of white abolitionists with whom they conspired (Horton and Flaherty 1993, 72–75).

The history of white abolitionism in Cincinnati began in the early 1830s and reached a first critical moment in 1836 with the publication of James Birney's *The Philanthropist*, the main organ of the recently established Ohio Anti-Slavery Society. Uncompromising in tone and content, the *Philanthropist* rapidly antagonized the city's conservative white majority. Although Cincinnati was geographically northern, it looked southward politically and economically. Its mercantile elite had strong business relations with the South and could not afford to lose traders and planters from this region against whom much of the abolitionist propaganda was directed. When Birney refused to moderate his antislavery criticism, outraged citizens took matters into their own hands. On July 12 and again two weeks later on July 30, 1836, a proslavery mob stormed the office of the *Philanthropist* and wrecked havoc on the printing press. On the second occasion, the rioters, infuriated over abolitionist ideas of racial equality, also set on fire several buildings in which black and white people were known to mingle. Birney survived the assaults and resumed his editorial activities in the fall, but not without a heightened sense of caution.[17]

Even though Birney remained in the city with his newspaper until 1847, his ordeal exemplifies that protesting against the racial status quo in the negrophobic climate of antebellum Cincinnati came at a high price. Abolitionists, whether black or white, had to endure personal danger and public isolation. This situation had not changed substantially in the 1850s when slavery was attacked by another group of Cincinnatians who had fled from the political turmoil of the Old World.

Abolitionists from the Other Shore

"Our Teutonic brethren are found guilty of the crime of loving liberty too well. Truly—a heinous crime in this age and country!" the *Cincinnati Daily Commercial* remarked with some irony at the peak of the slavery controversy.[18] Republican papers like the *Commercial* were obviously pleased that numerous German-Americans had placed themselves in the forward ranks of the Anti-Nebraska movement, and were now among the city's most fervent opponents of the "peculiar institution." This was especially the case with a generation of radical workers and their intellectual spokesmen who had settled in Cincinnati after the events of 1848. Unlike other immigrant groups, these people were not only highly skilled but also well organized and politically educated. They had gone through the storm and stress of Germany's failed democratic revolution and had imported its core tenets—universal human rights, social equality, national unity—to the United States. To sustain and spread these tenets, they founded organizations such as the *Arbeiter-* or *Turnverein* and newspapers like the *Cincinnati Republikaner,* the very paper Willich took over after his arrival (Levine 1992).

For the liberal and radical Forty-Eighters, slavery was a moral anachronism, a flagrant contradiction of the founding ideals and democratic promises of the country they had emigrated to. In 1854, a convention of German exiles drafted the Louisville Platform, a manifesto of principles that became a cornerstone of German-American radicalism prior to the Civil War. The platform declared slavery "a political and moral cancer, that will by and by undermine all republicanism." In addition its authors called for the repeal of the 1850 Fugitive Slave Act and for banning the extension of slavery into the new territories. This same sentiment also prevailed at the 1855 meeting of the national *Turnerbund,* then the leading Forty-Eighter association in the United States. Again the delegates took an open stand against slavery, denouncing the institution as "unworthy of a republic and directly opposed to the principles of freedom."[19]

Meanwhile, there were also large parts of the German-American populace who did not agree with this kind of disagreement with slavery. The older and more conservative German immigrants had little sympathy for the missionary zeal of the newcomers; they repeatedly branded them as hotheads and dreamers who were totally ignorant of the social and political realities in their adopted homeland. All they did, one pre-1848 immigrant grumbled, was "flood our cities, beg, lament, criticize, and gloat in a revolting way."[20] This viewpoint was particularly widespread among German Catholics who moreover voted principally in line with proslavery interests—not because they regarded chattel slavery as a positive good, but because they had come to identify opposition to it with the extreme Protestantism of the evangelical abolitionists (Hochgeschwender 2006). That some of these religiously inspired activists, in order to achieve their goals, would even sacrifice national unity, a central tenet of Catholic political theology, only fueled the hostility of German Catholics toward abolitionism. Papers like the Catholic *Wahrheitsfreund* branded such approaches as "irrational" and vilified its spokesmen as anarchists "who boldly labor for the destruction the Union, hilariously awaiting the day of their so-called victory."[21]

But instead of deterring the revolutionary veterans, this conservative backlash only made them more conscious of their political identity. By the middle of the decade, Cincinnati's Forty-Eighters had succeeded in constructing a vibrant counterpublic: newspapers like Friedrich Hassaurek's radical *Hochwächter* or the liberal *Volksblatt* emerged as important outlets for German-American programs of social reform and were relentless in their attacks on the South's "peculiar institution." However, resistance to slavery and the laws associated with it was not confined to the editor's pen. In the tumultuous weeks following the Kansas-Nebraska Act, German-born radicals were among the first to publicly express their indignation over this contentious law. One of their platforms called the Nebraska bill "a disgrace to America and this age," while another went even further in its condemnation by turning against interpretations of the free-soil doctrine favoring whites only. Free land in the West, the drafters insisted, should be handed out to all qualified applicants, "irrespective of color."[22]

To native-born abolitionist groups, such resolutions signaled that strong antislavery convictions also blossomed in ranks other than their own. Interestingly enough, however, the first English speakers in the region to salute the immigrant radicals were not white abolitionists, but African Americans. As early as 1852, Ohio's blacks, among them Peter Clark, saw parallels between the recent European struggles and their own struggle for liberty and publicly expressed solidarity with "the oppressed Hungarians and German socialists in their efforts to throw off the yoke of despotism." They even encouraged teaching German in their schools, believing that this would "prove a great auxiliary to our cause."[23] A few months earlier, the state's free black community had already shown their appreciation for the Old World radicals in a more substantial manner: on his fundraising tour through the United States, the German revolutionary Gottfried Kinkel received donations from numerous people, including a group of Cleveland blacks. But their decision to support Kinkel's cause angered many in the conservative Anglo- and German-American press, resulting in defamations of Kinkel as an abolitionist and "representative of unbelieving Germany."[24]

The Anglo-American reform community in Ohio also took note of the antislavery democrats from overseas, but it was not until 1858 that they openly welcomed them as allies in a common struggle. In this same year, Cincinnati's antislavery German-Americans staged a major demonstration in support of William Connelly, a writer for the *Daily Commercial* who had been tried and incarcerated for hiding a couple of fugitive slaves. Further difficulties arose from the fact that the attempt to recapture the blacks had ended in a deadly fight, in which at least two persons were severely injured. One was a slave catcher from Kentucky, the other was the fugitive Irvine Broadhus, who later died from the gunshot wound he received defending his freedom (Coffin 1876, 582–88; Conway 1904, 253).

The Connelly trial lasted several days and was covered by every major newspaper in the city as well as by the nationwide abolitionist press.[25] In a crowded courtroom, prosecutor Stanley Matthews had to contend against a defense team put together by Levi Coffin; it included ex-governor Thomas Corwin and Johann Stallo, who had broken with the Democrats over the question of slavery's extension. By the time Connelly went to jail, he was an antislavery hero. Unitarian and Methodist delegations flocked to his cell, hailing his efforts for the hapless fugitives.

On June 11, the day the prisoner was released, Cincinnati's German-American opponents of slavery also paid tribute: Connelly's lawyer Stallo headed a large procession of Turners that honored the liberated prisoner with a torchlight parade. The rain poured down in torrents but, as the *Ohio State Journal* reported, this did not "dampen the enthusiasm of the multitude, which [. . .] must have numbered fully 3000."[26] In the ensuing ceremony at Turners' Hall, Connelly, who was sharing the speakers' platform with Stallo and the radical newspapermen August Becker and Friedrich Hassaurek, received loud ovations for stating that he would not have rejected the blacks even "if I had been sure that the gallows would be my recompense."[27] This display of interethnic fraternity made a huge impression on some of the older abolitionist organizations. Delighted by the performance of the Turners, the Ohio *Anti-Slavery Bugle* commented: "Let us be of good cheer; the principles of freedom are not only extending themselves but are gathering strength in their development in new and unexpected sources."[28]

"A Republic of Labor and Intelligence"

His record as a revolutionary leader catapulted Willich to the forefront of Cincinnati's German-American labor and free-thought movements. What set him apart from most other local radicals was his communist background. "The Reddest of the Red," as he came to be nicknamed, resumed his crusade for the rights of labor in America. The *Republikaner*, the paper Willich took over after his arrival, was the propaganda tool of the city's German-American Social Workingmen's Club (*Sozialer Arbeiterverein*). Its mission was to educate the German-speaking working population and sensitize them to the social and economic grievances in a rapidly expanding capitalist society. In his inaugural statement as chief editor, Willich made clear that he had no intention to stray from the path of his predecessors. "As the organ of the workingmen, it will try to promote the material as well as literary interests of the working classes against capitalism," he assured his readers. Willich further pledged to bring the socialist creed to life with a program combining political action and intellectual training: "Based on this platform, we intend to support all those reforms that are supposed to make this republic a truth for everyone, to turn it into a community of free men which only acknowledges the authority of two interrelated powers: for a *Republic of Labor and Intelligence.*"[29]

Cincinnati's "Little Germany" proved a fertile ground for the kind of intellectual socialism Willich and his radical Forty-Eighter comrades wanted to disseminate. They organized plays, lectures, concerts, and staged public celebrations to honor such fighters for mankind as Thomas Jefferson, Friedrich Schiller, and Alexander Humboldt (Conzen 1985, 148–59; 1989, 44–76). They also engaged in political demonstrations dedicated to fellow revolutionaries such as the Italians Orsini and Garibaldi who carried on the battle against aristocracy in Europe.[30] All this reflected a deep concern for *Bildung*. Without knowledge, the laborer, Willich argued, could not identify and tackle the everyday social iniquities he was exposed to.[31]

Anglo-Americans strolling through Over-the-Rhine tended to look with amazement at these unfamiliar spectacles; what roused their ire, however, was that these foreign-born radicals united once every year with native-born skeptics to pay homage to Thomas Paine, the English-born pamphleteer whose image at that time was that of a notorious infidel. Public worship of Thomas Paine had a well-known history in Cincinnati, dating back to the early 1850s. Two ceremonies, the 1859 and 1860 anniversaries of Paine's birthday, marked the zenith of this cult (Kistler 1962). On January 29, 1859, more than two hundred German-American freethinkers and workers formed a procession and marched to Melodeon Hall where they joined a gathering of Anglo-American Paine admirers. Speeches were held in both languages and resolutions adopted, all with the intent of rescuing the Enlightenment radical from oblivion.[32] Next year's celebration attracted an even larger crowd, an estimated one thousand people. The hall was packed as August Willich and Robert Treat delivered orations "of the most ultra-heretic character," in which they hailed Paine as an apostle of religious freedom. After that, emotions were further set ablaze with a catalogue of resolutions; the second one proclaimed the movement's intellectual manifesto, a rationalist version of the Declaration of Independence. It began: "That we hold these rights to be the inherent and inestimable birthright of all mankind, the right to think for themselves, the right to differ from any or all others, without which the right to think is worth nothing."[33]

Peter Clark was surely elated over the rising devotion among Cincinnati's German-American revolutionaries for Thomas Paine, a man of great symbolic importance to him as well. Part of what had led to Clark's removal as a teacher in 1853 was his interest in the works of the English-born radical. "His views of God," a local newspaper reported, "were not those given by the revelations of the Scriptures, but from the book of nature." In this the article was not mistaken. Clark had been an enthusiastic participant in the meetings of an association named "The Liberals," and it was obviously there that his fascination for Painean ideas was bred.[34]

All his life, Clark experimented with new moral-philosophical systems since the one furnished by traditional religion had in his view come to bear the imprints of proslavery thought (Frederickson and Herz 2002). Although he never broke with the chief denomination among his black peers, the African Method-ist Episcopal Church, he concurrently set out to explore a host of theological alternatives. Clark, a humanitarian who had grown "tenderhearted toward all who suffer," had a propensity for teachings providing a rationalist outlook and encouraging a social gospel devoid of racial hierarchies. This is what attracted him to Masonry, an order in which he served most of his life. For the same rea-son, he also established ties to the city's liberal Unitarians (Gerber 1988, 179–81). Thomas Paine was one of the main guides on this spiritual journey, a quest that drew the black educator increasingly close to Cincinnati's evolving community of Anglo- and German-American radicals.

For Clark, fighting to end slavery in the South and campaigning for the rights of blacks in the North were two sides of the same coin. Though officially a free state, Ohio both legally and socially hampered the ability of its African American population to reap the harvests of freedom. This systemic inequality felt more than repugnant to a man of talent such as Clark; his experiences taught him that the ones who had placed all the obstacles in the path of his people were the least likely to remove them. Rather than relying on white support, he wanted to teach blacks how to help themselves. "Give us the opportunity of elevating ourselves," Clark demanded in an address to the Ohio legislature, and "remove the disabili-ties that cramp our energies, destroy that feeling of self-respect, so essential to form the character of a good citizen."[35]

Like so many black activists at the time, Clark was convinced that educa-tion was the key to African American self-improvement. He followed his uncle Gaines in the assertion that blacks would never earn the respect of the white majority without proper schooling: "We must be their equals in human knowl-edge, improvements, and inventions, and until we are, all schemes for equalizing the races upon the soil are nothing but cob webs."[36] Therefore, when offered a teaching post in Cincinnati's first black public school, Clark happily rose to the occasion. Except for a few interruptions, he would be employed in this field over the next four decades—first as teacher, then as principal. Education became the institutional framework for his intellectual aspirations, shaping his reputation as an ethnic leader and public speaker.

Lessons of Race and Class

Toward the end of the 1850s, slavery seemed more firmly entrenched and power-ful than ever. Public opinion in the North had also grown more hostile to slavery, but this was less the result of abolitionist propaganda than the perceived victo-ries of the Slave Power—the Fugitive Slave Act, Kansas-Nebraska, the Dred Scott case. Tensions within the movement heightened. And when John Brown invaded Harper's Ferry, moral suasion and nonviolent protest, the two mainstays of Gar-risonian abolitionism, seemed to have become all but a thing of the past.

Clark was of this opinion. With similar impatience, he awaited the dawn of a desegregated America in which the "distinction of Irishmen, German, and

African may be lost in the general appellation of American citizens."[37] Unlike the Garrisonians, however, Clark felt that slavery could not be eradicated without bloodshed. The black educator, though a man of letters, acknowledged that from the vantage point of the oppressed violence could not be ruled out as a last resort. Was this not the legacy enshrined in the Declaration of Independence, a document hallowed by black and white intellectuals? Natural rights, after all, meant the right to resist—if necessary with force. While this line of reasoning gave the Garrisonians serious headaches, it was a crystal-clear affair to Clark. To his satisfaction, he found this same clarity of thought among Willich and his plebeian revolutionaries.

A dedicated socialist, Willich presented the news of the day as evidence of an unfolding class struggle. According to his understanding, the great social conflict was between labor and capital, between the producing and property-holding classes. Slavery, he believed, represented this conflict in the most glaring manner. It had to be opposed not primarily because it was a crime against the black race but because it stood for a system of capitalist exploitation that could be found both on the plantation and in the factory. Willich told his readers that the situation of the white laborer was unlikely to improve unless he also confronted those who kept the black laborer in chains, unless he realized that "black and white slavery derive from the same principle." As long as the white worker allowed slavery to persist, he "will not even have set foot on the battlefield for the advancement of human rights."[38]

Since the communist editor viewed American slavery primarily through the lenses of class conflict, there is little wonder that he defined resistance to it on the basis of this very notion. This is reflected by the many commentaries on John Brown's raid printed in the *Republikaner*.[39] In Willich's opinion, Brown swung the axe not merely at black slavery; he laid it deeper, striking at the root of the ancient division of mankind into masters and servants. Brown might have started out as a religious fanatic, but his death on a Virginian scaffold situated him alongside recent European martyrs of freedom such as Robert Blum or Felice Orsini. As part of this universal revolutionary continuum, he came to epitomize moral principles that reached across nations and historical epochs. "Old Brown's deed [. . .] forces us to take sides—The way we judge Old Brown is the way we choose," Willich insisted in a Manichean fashion. "On one side, the rights of man, equal to all—the principle of good. On the other, the laws that uphold power and bondage—the principle of evil."[40]

The fact that Willich and Clark both expressed their abolitionism in the contexts of free-thought rationalism and liberal education arguably strengthened their alliance, which was tested only two weeks after the John Brown meeting in Over-the-Rhine. On December 18, a group of black men—Clark was allegedly one of them—attended a fair organized by the *Turnverein* but were sent away as their presence annoyed several white visitors. Although it later turned out that Clark was not among the expelled, the incident sparked a heated debate in the local German-language press, and Willich wielded his pen fervently in defense of the black educator. Portraying Clark as a man "who, thanks to his superior social and academic skills, would hold an eminent position in any civilized society,"[41] Willich rebuked all those who judged people on the basis of skin color instead of merit. He also published a declaration issued by the expelled blacks, who stated that they had left the *Turner* fair "with regret, especially since we had nourished great ideas of your friendship for our race."[42]

Willich belonged to the few radicals among the German-American opponents of slavery who went farther than merely protesting its expansion or fighting slavery in the abstract. His egalitarianism did not include a color line which privileged certain races over others. Pushed to the lowest ranks of antebellum society, African Americans, according to Willich, were just as oppressed as the white proletariat in the slums of London and New York and were therefore entitled to solidarity. They, too, had been suffering the affliction of not receiving their due, which made them potential revolutionary agents. They, too, had a capacity for intellectual development and needed the leadership of people like Clark who were able to incite it. Willich had been more than thrilled by Clark's performance at the John Brown ceremony. He thought that his speech "should have been witnessed by all defenders of the trade in human flesh. [. . .] How embarrassed, how mean would they have felt, had they listened to the stirring words of the black speaker whom they despise so much."[43]

Such interpretations of the slavery conflict left many of Willich's white readers dumbfounded: Even though they might have disliked slavery, they had no intention to tear down the social wall that separated them from the blacks. Willich thought otherwise, thereby inviting the scorn of the conservative press: the anti-abolitionist *Volksfreund*, for instance, branded him a "German nigger worshipper" and accused him of promoting racial amalgamation.[44]

Far from being discouraged by this kind of slander, Willich continued to ponder over the racist incident at the Turner fair. Particularly annoying to Willich was that the expulsion had occurred in his own social milieu, and that some perpetrators were German-born Turner. In his view, they had not only violated the tenets of Enlightenment humanism but also undermined the notion that the Germans, especially those with a revolutionary background, were the true agents of social progress. As Willich warned his peers, "the sympathy, the trust of the oppressed nationalities and races, we must not abuse it, we must not run from it like cowards if we do not want to betray our own people, our own race."[45]

It is interesting to see how Willich tried to garner support for the African Americans not only by evoking political ideals but also by appealing to ethnic honor. As spearheads of the liberation movement in Germany, he argued, the revolutionaries had taken up the struggle for freedom and justice back in Europe; as such, they were now continuing the struggle in the United States under new circumstances, and their enemies were numerous: Irish Catholics, protestant nativists, and, above all, southern slaveholders, who stirred bitter memories of the European aristocracy. Willich suggested that it was imperative for the revolutionaries to maintain a strong group consciousness in the face of this opposition. The trauma of 1849 was still fresh; and if the radicals wanted to learn from history and refurbish their tarnished self-image as a revolutionary elite, they had to avoid schisms and steer clear of anything that discredited the movement as a whole—such as incidents of racial discrimination.[46]

The Civil War tore apart entire communities—in that respect, the alliance between Willich and Clark was no exception. Willich assumed command of a German-American regiment and led his men into battle at Shiloh, Chickamauga, and Chattanooga; meanwhile, Clark continued sounding the abolitionist trumpet behind the lines. But while the war separated the two men geographically, it did not eradicate the concerns that had brought them together. Willich and Clark, that much is clear, knew and respected each other, thus openly defying the mainstream norms of antebellum Cincinnati. Their relationship illustrates that African- and German-American collaboration in pre–Civil War America was not always a matter of expediency. It shows that the ideological affinities between African- and German-American radicals could translate into a practical solidarity which taught those participating in it important lessons. On the one hand, Willich, who was used to seeing a world stratified by class, learned to make common cause with people who considered race to be the dividing line in American society. Clark's flirtation with socialism in the 1870s, on the other hand, can be read as a belated result of his encounter with Willich and the other German-born radicals that had invited him to speak at their John Brown ceremony (Gutman 1965). Brief as it was, their alliance put the idea of a colorblind democracy into practice, allowing strangers to become fellows.

Notes

1. "Adopted Citizens and Slavery," *Douglass' Monthly* (August 1859).

2. The following account is based on reports in the December 6, 1859, editions of the *Cincinnati Daily Enquirer* and the *Cincinnati Volksfreund*, and on the December 2, 3, 5, 1859, editions of the *Cincinnati Republikaner*. The *Weekly Anglo-African* covered the event in its December 17 edition for a larger African American readership. See also Bruce Levine, *The Spirit of 1848: German Immigrants, Labor Conflict, and the Coming of the Civil War* (Urbana: University of Illinois Press, 1992), 223.

3. Willich promised to publish Clark's speech in the December 6 edition of the *Republikaner*, which is unfortunately missing. Amid many threats, Willich also headed a torchlight parade in honor of John Brown through downtown Cincinnati; see Moncure Daniel Conway, *Autobiography, Memories and Experiences*, I (New York, 1904), 269.

4. *Cincinnati Daily Enquirer, Cincinnati Volksfreund*, December 6, 1859.

5. *Cincinnati Daily Enquirer*, December 6, 1859.

6. More detailed accounts of Willich's life can be found in Charles D. Stewart, "A Bachelor General," *Wisconsin Magazine of History* 17 (1933): 131–54, and Lloyd D. Easton, *Hegel's First American Followers: The Ohio Hegelians: John B. Stallo, Peter Kaufmann, Moncure Conway, and August Willich* (Athens: Ohio University Press, 1966), 159–203.

7. *Dayton Herald*, September 26, 1873.

8. *Radical Abolitionist*, I (July 1856), 98. For more on Clark's upbringing and early occupations, see Lawrence Grossman, "'In His Veins Coursed No Bootlicking Blood': The Career of Peter H. Clark," *Ohio History* 86 (1977): 79–95; David A. Gerber, "Peter Humphries Clark: The Dialogue of Hope and Despair," in *Black Leaders of the Nineteenth Century*, ed. Leon Litwack and August

Meier (Chicago: University of Illinois Press, 1988), 173–90; Mary E. Frederickson and Walter Herz, "A Matter of Respect: The Religious Journey of Peter H. Clark," *A.M.E. Church Review* 68 (2002): 25–36.

9. Franz von Löher, "The Landscape and People of Cincinnati, 1846–47, trans. Frederic Trautmann," in *Ethnic Diversity and Civic Identity: Patterns of Conflict and Cohesion in Cincinnati since 1820*, ed. Henry D. Shapiro and Jonathan D. Sarna (Urbana: University of Illinois Press, 1992), 42.

10. Bird, *Englishwoman in America*, 119. See the figures used in Levine, "Community Divided: German Immigrants, Social Class, and Political Conflict in Antebellum Cincinnati," in *Ethnic Diversity and Civic Identity*, 50.

11. Bird, *Englishwoman in America*, 120.

12. For a more detailed description, see William A. Baughn, "Bullets and Ballots: The Election Day Riots of 1855," *Bulletin of the Historical and Philosophical Society of Ohio* 21 (1963): 267–72. A general overview over the development of nativism in antebellum Cincinnati is provided in Baughn, "Nativism in Cincinnati before 1860" (M.A. thesis, University of Cincinnati, 1963).

13. The anti-Catholic coalition of nativists and immigrant radicals in 1853 is discussed in Michael Hochgeschwender, *Wahrheit, Einheit, Ordnung: Die Sklavenfrage und der amerikanische Katholizismus, 1835–1870* (Paderborn: Schöningh, 2006), 190–91. For reports on the clash between Cincinnati Turners and local nativists at Covington, see "Die Vorgänge in Covington und Newport," Turn-Zeitung, May 12, 1856, in *Jahrbücher der Deutsch-Amerik. Turnerei*, ed. Heinrich Metzner, Bd. II, Heft 3 (New York, 1894), 112–19. Additional attacks on German-American Turners and other German-American groups in Ohio are mentioned in Emil Klauprecht's *Deutsche Chronik in der Geschichte des Ohio-Thales und seiner Hauptstadt Cincinnati in's Besondere* (Cincinnati: G. Hof & M. A. Jacobi, 1864), 192–93.

14. Malvin is quoted in Richard C. Wade, "The Negro in Cincinnati, 1800–1830," *Journal of Negro History* 39 (1954): 43.

15. Lafcadio Hearn, *Children of the Levee*, ed. O. W. Frost (Lexington: University of Kentucky Press, 1957), 32.

16. Patrick McCloskey, "Cincinnati in 1844–45: According to Father William Unterthiner, O.S.F.," *Queen City Heritage* 41 (1983): 43.

17. For further descriptions of the proslavery riot of 1836, see Levi Coffin's autobiography, *Reminiscences of Levi Coffin* (Cincinnati: Western Tract Society, 1876), and chapter 4 of Charles Edward Stowe, *Life of Harriet Beecher Stowe* (Boston: Houghton, Mifflin & Co., 1891).

18. *Cincinnati Daily Commercial*, May 12, 1860.

19. *Louisville Daily Democrat*, March 4, 1854. *Verhandlungen der Turner-Tagsatzung zu Buffalo, vom 24. bis 27. September 1855*, Sozialistischer Turnerbund Papers, New York Public Library.

20. Quoted in Martin W. Öfele, *German-Speaking Officers in the U.S. Colored Troops, 1863–1867* (Gainesville: University Press of Florida, 2004), 4.

21. *Der Wahrheitsfreund*, June 7, 1838, and November 21, 1850, quoted in Hochgeschwender, *Wahrheit, Einheit, Ordnung*, 264, 361.

22. Reports of the 1854 state convention of Ohio's German-American radicals can be found in the *Daily Cincinnati Gazette*, March 24, 25, and the *Cincinnati Daily Enquirer*, March 25, 26, 1854

23. "Proceedings of the Convention of the Colored Freemen of Ohio, Cincinnati, January 14, 15, 16, 17, and 19, 1852," in *Proceedings of the Black State Conventions, 1840–1865*, ed. Philip S. Foner and George E. Walker (Philadelphia: Temple University Press, 1979), 277. In 1849, the Ohio legislature allowed blacks to run their own public schools. These schools had to be segregated, however. See also Taylor, *Frontiers of Freedom*, 161–74.

24. This is how Kinkel was labeled by the *Ohio State Journal*, according to Wittke, *Refugees of Revolution: The German Forty-Eighters in America* (Philadelphia: University of Pennsylvania Press, 1952), 89. Another critical article appeared in the *New York Staatszeitung*, February 21, 1852.

25. See, for instance, the May 1858 editions of the *Daily Cincinnati Gazette*, the *Cincinnati Daily Times*, the *Daily Enquirer*, and the *Daily Commercial*. German-language newspapers at the trial were the *Cincinnati Volksfreund* and *Tägliches Volksblatt*. The *National Anti-Slavery Standard* informed a larger abolitionist reading public about the Connelly case. See also Coffin, *Reminiscences*, 582–88.

26. *Ohio State Journal*, June 12, 1858.

27. *Cincinnati Daily Commercial*, June 12, 1858. The ceremony also made headlines in the *Cincinnati Volksfreund* and *Daily Enquirer*.

28. *Anti-Slavery Bugle*, June 19, 1858. The June 26 edition of the *National Anti-Slavery Standard* carries another abolitionist account of the Turner demonstration.

29. *Cincinnati Republikaner*, December 6, 1858.

30. Reports of a demonstration in solidarity with the Italian revolutionary Felice Orsini can be found in the May 18, 1858, issues of the *Cincinnati Daily Enquirer*, the *Cincinnati Daily Commercial*, and the *Cincinnati Tägliches Volksblatt*. On public sympathy with Garibaldi, see the July 7, 1860, issues of the *Cincinnati Daily Gazette* and the *Cincinnati Daily Enquirer*.

31. *Cincinnati Republikaner*, February 26, March 17, 1859.

32. *Cincinnati Daily Commercial*, January 31, 1859; *Cincinnati Daily Enquirer*, January 30, 1859; *Cincinnati Daily Times*, January 31, 1859; *Cincinnati Republikaner*, January 31, 1859. The German-American impact on the nineteenth-century cult of Thomas Paine is examined in Mark O. Kistler, "German-American Liberalism and Thomas Paine," *American Quarterly* 14 (1962): 81–91.

33. *Cincinnati Daily Enquirer*, February 1, 1860; *The Cincinnati Daily Times*, January 30, 1860. Other significant accounts of the meeting are printed in the *Cincinnati Daily Commercial*, January 30, 1860, and the *Cincinnati Republikaner*, January 30, 1860.

34. The quote is taken from Frederickson and Herz, "A Matter of Respect," 27. The Cincinnati School Board's investigation with regard to Clark's religious beliefs is documented in the August 6, 7, 8, and 9, 1853, editions of the *Cincinnati Daily Commercial* and the *Cincinnati Daily Times*.

35. "Address to the Senate and House of Representatives of Ohio, January 1856," in *Proceedings of the Black State Conventions*, 311.

36. Gaines made this statement in 1858. The black leader urged his peers to consider the value of education and send their children to school. Gaines, "What is the Duty of the Colored American Parent?" in *Ninth Annual Report of the Board of Trustees for the Colored Public Schools of Cincinnati* (Cincinnati, 1858), 8.

37. "Proceedings of the Convention of the Colored Freemen of Ohio, Cincinnati, 1852," 277.

38. *Cincinnati Republikaner*, October 3, 1859.

39. See, for instance, "John Brown. Entweder—Oder," *Cincinnati Republikaner*, October 22, 1859, or "Schiller and John Brown," *Cincinnati Republikaner*, December 9, 1859. The former article also found its way into William Lloyd Garrison's *Liberator*. It was translated and appeared on the title page of the December 9 edition.

40. *Cincinnati Republikaner*, December 3, 1855.

41. *Cincinnati Republikaner*, December 20, 1859. The debate was most intense among the *Republikaner*, the *Cincinnati Volksblatt*, and the *Cincinnati Volksfreund*.

42. *Cincinnati Republikaner*, December 26, 1859.

43. *Cincinnati Republikaner*, December 5, 1859.

44. *Cincinnati Volksfreund*, December 25, 29, 1859.

45. *Cincinnati Republikaner*, December 27, 1859.

46. Eventually, the Turnverein complied with Willich's demands. In a meeting on December 29, a majority of the Turners present adopted a resolution censuring all forms of discrimination on the basis of race or color as incompatible with the principle of human equality; *Versammlung vom 29. Dezember 1859*, Papers of the Cincinnati Turnverein, Cincinnati Historical Society.

Works Cited

Baughn, William A. "Bullets and Ballots: The Election Day Riots of 1855." *Bulletin of the Historical and Philosophical Society of Ohio* 21 (1963): 267–72.

Benson, Adolph B., ed. *America of the Fifties: Letters of Fredrika Bremer.* New York: The American-Scandinavian Foundation, 1924.

Bertaux, Nancy. "Structural Economic Change and Occupational Decline among Black Workers in Nineteenth Century Cincinnati." In *Race and the City: Community, Work, and Protest in Cincinnati, 1820–1970,* ed. Henry Louis Taylor Jr., 126–41. Urbana: University of Illinois Press, 1993.

Bird, Isabella Lucy. *The Englishwoman in America,* ed. Andrew H. Clark. Madison: University of Wisconsin Press, 1966.

Cist, Charles E. *Sketches and Statistics of Cincinnati in 1851.* Cincinnati: Wm. H. Moore & Co., 1851.

———. *Sketches and Statistics of Cincinnati in 1859.* Cincinnati: City Council, 1859.

Coffin, Levi. *Reminiscences of Levi Coffin.* Cincinnati: Robert Clark & Co., 1880.

Conway, Moncure Daniel. *Autobiography, Memories, and Experiences,* 2 vols. Boston: Houghton, 1904.

Conzen, Kathleen Neils. "German-Americans and the Invention of Ethnicity." In *America and the Germans: An Assessment of a Three-Hundred-Year History,* I, ed. Frank Trommler and Joseph McVeigh, 148–59. Philadelphia, 1985.

———. "Ethnicity and Festive Culture: German-Americans on Parade." In *The Invention of Ethnicity,* ed. Werner Sollors, 44–76. New York, 1989.

Easton, Lloyd D. *Hegel's First American Followers: The Ohio Hegelians: John B. Stallo, Peter Kaufmann, Moncure Conway, and August Willich.* Athens: Ohio University Press, 1966.

Foner, Philip S., and George E. Walker, eds. *Proceedings of the Black State Conventions, 1840–1865.* Philadelphia: Temple University Press, 1979.

Frederickson, Mary E., and Walter Herz. "A Matter of Respect: The Religious Journey of Peter H. Clark." *A.M.E. Church Review* 68 (2002): 25–36.

Gerber, David A. "Peter Humphries Clark: The Dialogue of Hope and Despair." In *Black Leaders of the Nineteenth Century,* ed. Leon Litwack and August Meier, 173–90. Chicago: University of Illinois Press, 1988.

Grossman, Lawrence. "'In His Veins Coursed No Bootlicking Blood': The Career of Peter H. Clark." *Ohio History* 86 (1977): 79–95.

Gutman, Herbert G. "Peter H. Clark: Pioneer Negro Socialist, 1877." *Journal of Negro Education* 34 (1965): 413–18.

Hearn, Lafcadio. *Children of the Levee,* ed. O. W. Frost. Lexington: University of Kentucky Press, 1957.

Hochgeschwender, Michael. *Wahrheit, Einheit, Ordnung: Die Sklavenfrage und der amerikanische Katholizismus.* Paderborn: Schöningh, 2006.

Horton, James Oliver, and Stacy Flaherty. "Black Leadership in Antebellum Cincinnati." In *Race and the City,* 70–88.

Kistler, Mark O. "German-American Liberalism and Thomas Paine." *American Quarterly* 14 (1962): 81–91.

Klauprecht, Emil. *Cincinnati, oder, Geheimnisse des Westens,* 2 vols. Cincinnati: C. F. Schmidt & Co., 1854.

Levine, Bruce. *The Spirit of 1848: German Immigrants, Labor Conflict, and the Coming of the Civil War.* Urbana: University of Illinois Press, 1992.

Miller, Kerby A. *Emigrants and Exiles: Ireland and the Irish Exodus to North America.* New York: Oxford University Press, 1988.

Miller, Randall, ed. *States of Progress: Germans and Blacks in America over 300 Years.* Philadelphia: German Society of Pennsylvania, 1989.

Oates, Stephen B. *To Purge This Land in Blood: A Biography of John Brown.* New York: Harper & Row, 1960.

Roediger, David R. *Wages of Whiteness: Race and the Making of the American Working Class.* London: Verso, 1999.

Stewart, Charles D. "A Bachelor General." *Wisconsin Magazine of History* 17 (1933): 131–54.

Taylor, Henry Louis Jr. "On Slavery's Fringe: City-Building and Black Community Development in Cincinnati, 1800–1850." *Ohio History* 95 (1986): 5–33.

Taylor, Nikki M. *Frontiers of Freedom: Cincinnati's Black Community, 1802–1868.* Athens: Ohio University Press, 2005.

von Löher, Franz. "The Landscape and People of Cincinnati, 1846–47, trans. Frederic Trautmann." In *Ethnic Diversity and Civic Identity: Patterns of Conflict and Cohesion in Cincinnati since 1820,* ed. Henry D. Shapiro and Jonathan D. Sarna. Urbana: University of Illinois Press, 1992.

Wittke, Carl. *Refugees of Revolution: The German Forty-Eighters in America.* Philadelphia: University of Pennsylvania Press, 1952.

Zucker, A. E., ed. *The Forty-Eighters: Political Refugees of the German Revolution of 1848.* New York: Columbia University Press, 1950.

German Immigrants and African Americans in Charleston, South Carolina, 1850–1880

JEFFERY STRICKLAND

Historiography

Most scholarship dealing with the South during the mid- to late nineteenth century supports a black/white paradigm and ignores the racial and ethnic diversity in the region (see Holt, DuBois, Foner; Powers 1994; Rabinowitz; Williamson). The recent investigations of German communities in the region have revealed complexities that reject the black/white paradigm (see Bauman; Greenberg; and Page). However, the scholarship on the Germans in Charleston has not challenged the longstanding assumption that the Germans had become white southerners prior to the Civil War (see Bell 9–28; Reinert 49). Moreover, scant scholarship focuses on the ways interaction between Germans and African Americans challenged white southern norms. Antebellum Charleston was the prototypical Deep South city, and it served as the financial, political, and intellectual center of South Carolina's slave society. White supremacy prevailed in a caste system that oppressed African Americans, and nearly all white southerners aspired to slaveholding. It appears that most Germans did not aspire to own slaves, and this affected their status in southern society (Bergquist 57, 59, 67; Higham 9). Although most elite white Charlestonians viewed the Germans as white, they did not accept Germans into the urban establishment during the antebellum period.

Germans, primarily from Hanover, Oldenburg, Holstein, Mecklenburg, and Bremen began to arrive in Charleston in the mid-1830s (Bernheim 529–33). In 1860, 1,894 Germans or 9 percent of the white population lived in Charleston. Second-generation German-Americans increased the population to 2,848 people or 12 percent of the population. In 1870, the German population in Charleston totaled more than 1,800 people or 8 percent of the white population. Second-generation German-Americans increased the population to 3,524 people or 15 percent of the white population. In 1880, 1,537 Germans still lived in Charleston and the second-generation German-American population reached a height of 3,868 people or 8 percent of the entire population. African American migration increased the portion of the black population from 17,146 or 42 percent in 1860 to over 27,000 or 54 percent in 1870 (See 1860, 1870, and 1880 Census). At the same time, African Americans and Germans dispersed throughout every ward in the city, virtually ensuring interaction on a daily basis. Germans created important social institutions to assist with their transition into southern society. John A. Wagener emerged as the leader of the German community. The fifty-six-year-old native of Prussia had settled in Charleston in 1833, and he helped organize various associations, including the German Fire Company, the German school, the German Lutheran Church, and *Der Teutone* German language daily (Silverman and Gorman 44). In the latter newspaper, Wagener distinguished himself as a prominent émigré and journalist (Faust 368–69). The numerous German secular organizations held various social activities throughout the year. The *Fusileers* rifle company held picnics at the *Schutzenfest* in suburban Charleston, and the festival entailed a target shooting competition, dinner, and dancing. The *Turnverein* held gymnastics exhibitions, and German dramatists and musicians performed regularly at German theaters. The Germans even held their own Fourth of July celebrations. Similar to German settlements throughout the United States, religion occupied an important role in the German Charlestonian community. The Germans primarily worshipped at St. Matthew's German Lutheran and St. Paul's German Catholic Churches. The majority of the Germans were Lutherans and a fewer amount Catholics (Bernheim 529–33).

Economic Relations

During the antebellum period, free and enslaved African Americans traded with Germans at a time when white southerners would rarely do so. Although trading with slaves was against the law, many German shopkeepers found this trade too lucrative to avoid. In turn, the Germans earned a steady clientele of African American consumers and increased their profits. In many instances, German grocers catered to working-class blacks, often selling merchandise in small quantities, and remaining open early in the morning and late at night. Germans sometimes extended credit to stimulate repeat business. These business transactions intensified after emancipation because African Americans had more wages to purchase foodstuffs and other items. At the same time, many black Charlestonians expressed their dismay with German business practices, mainly the Germans' refusal to extend credit, and accused the Germans of economic oppression. Importantly, the Germans had demonstrated relative disinterest in slaveholding, the economic lifeblood of Charleston's slave society.

The Germans' ambivalence about slaveholding defined their antebellum experience. In the 1860 federal manuscript census, there were only seventy-four German slave owners in the city (thirty-one came from Hanover), and they were underrepresented at every occupational level. Three Germans owned more than twenty slaves but most owned only a few. More important, many Germans had the economic means to own slaves but they chose not to enter the slaveholding class, and they were underrepresented among people of means who chose to own slaves. The historian Walter Kamphoefner investigated slaveholding among Westphalian immigrants in Missouri with a view toward their socialization patterns, and he determined that German immigrants were underrepresented as slaveholders in nearly every wealth category (115–17). The same was true in Charleston.

Many of the Germans had readily established themselves in the merchant trades of Charleston at a time when merchant trades were not widely respected by white southerners. Instead, white South Carolinians respected cotton and rice planting—and planting relied on slaveholding. Not only did most Germans appear disinterested in planting and slaveholding, they were overrepresented as shopkeepers and their business practices raised the suspicions of native-born Charlestonians. White southerners perceived that Germans, particularly shopkeepers who sold liquor to and traded with slaves, undermined the slave society in Charleston. The Court of General Sessions prosecuted hundreds of German shopkeepers for selling liquor to slaves and trading with them for property requisitioned from their masters during the 1850s (Lesesne 84–85). In addition, the police arrested countless Germans for loitering or allowing African Americans to loiter outside their stores—probably under the presumption that the Germans were conducting an illegal trade with them (see, for example, *Daily Courier*, November 21, 1853, April 7, 1854, July 12, 1855). As mayor of Charleston, William Porcher Miles reorganized the police force to better control these illicit dealings that he believed undermined the slavery system (*Daily Courier*, October 13, 1867). Judge David L. Wardlaw lectured a convicted shopkeeper about the evils of trading with slaves. He considered the "evil influences" of foreigners, who depended on trade with slaves against the interests of the citizens of South Carolina. Wardlaw concluded, "If the delivery and sale of liquor to slaves was to be carried on constantly, there was no telling how many fires and murders and thefts would be the consequence" (*Daily Courier*, May 7, 1860). Wardlaw's commentary is relevant for understanding the ways in which white citizens of the South perceived "foreigners," especially German shopkeepers, were undermining the slave society in which they lived. Jacob Schirmer, an influential German southerner, noted that the fines against shopkeepers for selling liquor to slaves were the highest allowed by the law (Schirmer, January 30, 1858). In 1860, there were only two German immigrants on a police force that was mostly comprised of white southerners. White Charlestonians continued to discriminate against German immigrants until the Civil War afforded some Germans the opportunity to prove their dedication to Charleston and the Confederacy.

White South Carolinians seceded from the United States and fought a Civil War to preserve slavery. The German Charlestonians' response to the Confederacy, however, was mixed, and most of the Germans who fought for the Confederate army were not committed to a slave society. Captain W. F. Bachman wrote about the German Volunteers that "there was not a man in the company who owed allegiance to the Confederate States every man being a foreigner and unnaturalized" (Lonn 119–20). There were countless reasons why an individual German immigrant might join in the fight—personal honor, a sense of adventure, occupational opportunity, and military prowess. During the Civil War, many German businessmen remained in the city to protect their property. Sally

DeSaussure, an elite white southerner, wrote her sister, "The unexpected shelling of the City has caused great excitement and indignation, and will perhaps help us, in bringing many foreigners in particular to think it's now time for them to defend their lives and property, the shelling has caused great alarm, and a general move to the upper part of the City" (DeSaussure). Following the Civil War, white southerners and German elites emphasized the Germans' meritorious service while African Americans rarely viewed the Germans as ex-Confederates (Bell 9–10, 17–18; Lonn 119–21; Ratzel 164). It deserves mention that when the Germans laid the cornerstone for the new German Lutheran Church after the Civil War, Confederate memorabilia were among the items included in the cornerstone's vault (*Daily Courier*, December 27, 1867). This was an indication that German elites sought to identify with that Confederate past in hopes of becoming southern.

As thousands of emancipated African Americans began earning cash wages, Germans increasingly conducted a cash-only business with black Charlestonians. They often refused to extend credit or charged high prices for foodstuffs and other items, creating resentment in the African American community, especially during economic downturns when cash was not readily attainable. Although most German shopkeepers had not been slaveholders, they had regressed into a different form of economic oppression.

Social Relations

Social relations between both groups peaked in the years immediately following the Civil War, a period in which race relations were in a constant state of flux. The postwar sociopolitical climate allowed for mixed households and even sexual relations that challenged the long-existing racial hierarchy in Charleston. In another example of sociocultural exchange, African Americans attended the annual *Schutzenfest* where they provided entertainment and participated in various games. These exceptional social relations declined throughout the 1870s and coincided with the failure of Reconstruction.

In 1860, there were very few examples of African American and German household interaction other than German households with slaves. German women domestic servants, living mainly in German households, sometimes worked alongside African American domestic servants. Slaves toiled in the households of some Germans. And in a few instances Germans boarded with African Americans. The Civil War and Reconstruction created new opportunities for racial and ethnic interaction, and many Germans exhibited a marked degree of racial tolerance. This was a brief moment in time when African Americans and Germans could live together without fear of persecution. In 1870, more German men and women boarded with African Americans than ever before. In rarer instances, German men lived with African American wives. Claus Hand, a baker from Hanover, lived in the first ward with his black wife, Emma, and their two children, Elizabeth and William, and both were identified as "Mulatto" in the census. Ten years later, the Hand family had moved to the third ward, probably because they needed larger accommodations for additional children. Importantly, Elizabeth and the Hand children were identified as white in the 1880 census, effectively demonstrating the malleability of race in the postwar South. At least two other Germans who lived with their African American wives in 1870 had left the city in 1880, possibly indicative of increasing tension over interracial relationships which accompanied the failure of Reconstruction. Some German women entered into sexual relations with African American men. In 1867, Augusta Finck left her German husband for William Overton, an African American Civil War veteran who had been boarding in the Finck household. The police arrested them in Wilmington, North Carolina, and returned them to Charleston where the incident was well documented in the local press. In the 1880 census, sixteen blacks and fifteen mulattos identified a German mother and seventeen blacks and twenty-nine mulattos identified a German father.

Germans and African Americans also interacted at community social events. Beginning in 1868, the Germans had held an annual *Schutzenfest* and an accompanying parade. The festival quickly became the "Mardi Gras of Charleston" and the city's most important annual leisure event. Following each parade, thousands of Charlestonians traveled to the *Schutzenplatz* in the suburbs. African Americans not only participated in the various games at the festival, but they also provided theatrical and musical entertainment. White southerners nearly always segregated their social events and did not allow African American participation.

Although the *Schutzenfest* began as a harmless ethnic festival, its accompanying parade quickly turned into an exhibition of white supremacy. White rifle clubs paraded in their uniforms with guns and Confederate memorabilia. These martial displays were political statements, and the Germans had invited the white rifle clubs to join them. Together they contributed to the resurgence of white supremacy in the city (Schirmer, April 1871). On May 1, 1871, Schirmer remarked with pleasure "a superb procession paraded the Streets . . . for the first time since the war, four uniform companies armed with rifles paraded" (Schirmer, May 1, 1871). The role these white rifle clubs played in the restoration of white supremacy has been well documented (see Kantrowitz; Williamson). The festival's popularity declined with the so-called Democratic Redemption of South Carolina government, possibly because the level of black participation challenged those same norms. The Germans had already begun to restrict African American access to the festival in the mid-1870s, requiring advance-purchase tickets and invitations.

In March 1871, five thousand people, including the entire German community and non-Germans in Charleston celebrated the Prussian victory in the Franco-Prussian War at the *Schutzenplatz* and *Freundschaftsbund Hall*. The Prussian victory had resulted in the unification of Germany and stimulated a wave of nationalism in Germany and among Germans living abroad (*Daily Courier*, March 8, 1871; *Daily Republican*, March 8, 1871, March 9, 1871). The speeches delivered that day demonstrate the heightened level of German ethnic pride. Alexander Melchers, president of the *Schutzen Gesellschaft*, delivered the welcome address: "Let us not forget that we came from this people, and whether in a strange land or not, let us be proud of our origin and name. May we never forget this day, and may it live long in our hearts." George Keim encouraged the Germans to "remain Germans in fidelity, in faith, and in unity." The Reverend L. Muller stated, "Though we have become citizens of another country, in heart we remain the children of our old Mother" (*Daily Courier*, March 9, 1871). The 1871 municipal election occurred at a critical point in the development of German identity in Charleston, and German ethnic nationalism played an important part in German immigrant voting behavior.

Political Relations

Following the Civil War, German political organizing on behalf of the Democratic Party undermined the efforts of black Republicans to maintain political power. It was clear that the Germans were divided, and some Germans, albeit a minority, quickly declared their allegiance to the Republican Party. Democrats and Republicans both courted German voters, and the Germans used their moderate position to form a German political machine that nominated one of their own for mayor in 1871 (Kleppner 153–54, 158). Not surprisingly, this led to political conflict between African Americans and German immigrants, culminating in a riot that hindered future relations.

During Reconstruction Germans across the United States tended to maintain their antebellum loyalty to the Democratic Party (Les Benedict 71). German Lutherans across the country continued to support Democrats (Kleppner 153–54, 158). In Charleston, the Germans were conflicted between their antebellum allegiance to the Democratic Party and loyalty to their German ethnicity. In the main, the Germans recognized they might earn political representation in the Republican Party, but they knew it would stimulate conflict with white southerners. German elites became politically active on a larger scale than they exhibited before the war (Keil 22; Levine 9–10). Though not every German was a Democrat, a small group of affluent German Democrats represented the community as a whole, while most Germans tended to their businesses until it was time to vote (Ratzel 163–64). These German elites promoted community loyalty to the Democratic or Citizens' Conservative Party (48–50). The historian Randall Miller has observed, "German ethnicity dissipated rapidly in the postwar South, especially in the cities where the influx of poor ex-slaves transformed the political and cultural calculus from ethnic into racial terms. Germans became white southerners first, Germans second" (14). Yet this process was more gradual in Charleston and it was not complete until 1876.

Germans were among the Democratic and Republican Party leadership in Charleston. In 1865, German Democratic politicians John A. Wagener and Franz Melchers were among the twenty representatives from Charleston to the state convention (*Daily Courier*, September 5, 1865, September 28, 1865). In 1866, two Germans—United States marshal J. P. M. Epping of Oldenburg and Benjamin Riels, a grocer from Prussia—served on the Committee of Thirteen, and they helped formulate the Republican Party platform (Baggett 53; Schirmer, February 1866). The platform included public schools supported by property taxes; public improvements with contracts awarded on an equal opportunity basis; revision of the entire law code and reorganization of the courts; support for the elderly, disabled, and poor people; equal protection for both the landlord and tenant; and the abolition of imprisonment for debt and corporeal punishment for convicted criminals. Perhaps the most radical portion of the platform pertained to land redistribution to poor African Americans and whites (Du Bois 381, 390–93). Epping demonstrated his commitment to the Republican Party when he recommended that African Americans consolidate their political power and not allow the "old oligarchy" to take away their civil rights. He likened the Republican Party platform to the "Magna Charta of South Carolina" and he hoped the platform could unite African Americans and whites (*Christian Recorder*, May 18, 1867; *Daily Courier*, March 22, 1867, March 27, 1867).

In 1868, Wagener, Melchers, and several Germans formed the German Democratic Club in an attempt to elect Germans to political office. The Germans admitted their former political apathy, but they believed it was their duty to support the Democratic Party to "revive law and order, progress and the general welfare." The German Democrats recognized their dual status as German-born and "citizens of Charleston." They considered Reconstruction an "impossible scheme" and a "fangled experiment," and they opposed the Republican Party and its "fanaticism" and "despotism." Ignoring white privilege in southern society, the Germans stated:

> That whilst we having come as strangers in the land, have by thrift and industry acquired property and wealth, have been content to undergo a long term of probation before having been permitted the rights of citizenship, the colored people of the South might be satisfied and would act wisely to acquire property and influence in the same manner. (Minutes, August 26, 1868, German Fourth Ward Democratic Club, South Caroliniana Library, Columbia)

The Germans had achieved rapid upward mobility at the expense of African Americans (Jacobson 9). The Democratic Party of Charleston nominated an all-white ticket, and included a German immigrant (*Daily Courier*, November 4, 1868). Republicans formed an interracial ticket, including a German immigrant, and it resembled the interracial political alliances that formed throughout the South during the late 1860s (Dailey 2, 4, 5). The Democrats' white supremacist strategy had failed in Charleston and throughout the South in 1868. Republicans dominated the first post–Civil War municipal election in Charleston (*Daily Courier*, November 12, 1868, November 13, 1868). In future elections, Democrats supported conservative Republicans whenever possible and attempted to divide the Republican Party.

In the subsequent municipal election of 1871, the Citizens' Conservatives (Democrats) defeated the Republicans in "ethnic politics" (Fraser 291). German elites initiated the movement to nominate John A. Wagener for mayor on the Citizens' Conservative Party ballot (*Daily Republican*, July 31, 1871). The Germans used the name "Citizens' Conservative" to emphasize their status as citizens, and because the Democratic Party had changed their name in most southern states to the Conservative Party. Their intentions were to attract moderate Democrats and Republicans, and to shy away from white supremacist political rhetoric (Perman 6, 10, 26). At the same time, many white southerners questioned the Germans' commitment to the Democratic Party. The German elites at the helm of the machinery had threatened to support the Republican Party if Wagener did not receive the Conservative nomination. This was indicative of the German community's overall moderate political position, and willingness to use the Republican Party to gain representation if necessary. Wagener's German supporters even met with the Republican Party to discuss the possibility of a fusion ballot representing the interests of both parties. Many white Charlestonians initially objected to Wagener's nomination, but they feared the Germans' defection threat and eventually supported the nomination (*News and Courier*, September 21, 1875).

Republican critics complained that Wagener's Citizens' Conservative Party resembled a Democratic political machine. James Brennan, an Irish political activist and manager of the *Southern Celt*, an Irish Nationalist newspaper, accused Wagener and the Germans of raising ten thousand dollars to buy Irish votes. Francis Warrington Dawson, an English immigrant and editor of the *Courier*, recognized that many people viewed Wagener "as the candidate of a German party," but Dawson viewed Wagener as a German "citizen of South Carolina, with whose interest and welfare he has been identified for many long years" (*Daily Courier*, July 24, 1871). The editor of the *Daily Republican* determined, "The Democracy of Charleston are making a desperate effort to secure the vote of the foreign element. The nomination of General Wagener was intended solely for the purpose of securing the German vote" (July 29, 1871). The Wagener party machinery attempted to capitalize on their German mayoral nomination, and they began a naturalization drive that inspired hundreds of German immigrants to become citizens in order to vote their candidate into office. Democrats in cities throughout the United States had adopted the strategy of naturalizing immigrants to assist in building their constituency. Voter fraud in Charleston closely resembled the corruption and naturalization mills of Boss William Tweed and Tammany Hall infamy in New York City (Callow 211). The deluge of naturalizations attracted the attention of the Republican Party and government officials in Charleston, and they disputed many naturalization certificates that had previously proved sufficient for local and state voting and other legal dealings. Election officials stationed a trial justice and constable at each precinct to arrest persons attempting to register to vote fraudulently. Officials arrested several people for attempting to register at more than one polling place or on naturalization papers belonging to others. Republicans felt obligated to patrol the polling places and challenge naturalizations, suggesting that Wagener's supporters may have been the greater offenders.

Conservative whites feared a coalition between poor whites and blacks (Carter 144). White southerners viciously opposed black suffrage rights and Republican rule, and white Charlestonians used violence and intimidation against white Republicans and African Americans in an attempt to regain political control (Jenkins 154; Rable xi). Jacob Schirmer, a leading German-American, objected to the presence of prominent whites, including Germans, at Republican political meetings. Schirmer consistently referred to white Republicans as "White Niggers" and "White Negroes" (March 22, 1867, March 27, 1867). Germans were well aware that public support for the Republican Party would hurt their social standing and whites would boycott their businesses.

Violence routinely occurred during Charleston's municipal elections as whites and African Americans attempted to gain or maintain political power (Barnes 2). White southerners used political violence against African Americans to maintain control. Daniel E. Huger Smith, a leading white Charlestonian, recalled that elections were "bitterly contested" and "pandemonium ruled!" (140–41). African Americans in Charleston were not easily intimidated and the black community had a reputation for aggressiveness that had its origins in slave insurrections and resistance (Jenkins 133). Black Charlestonians sometimes rioted to assert their claim to racial supremacy (Gilje 87, 97). The historian George C. Rable determined, "The incidence of black-initiated violence was higher in the South Carolina lowcountry than in any other part of the South . . . Whatever the extent of 'radical' violence, South Carolina Democrats were hardly innocent victims" (171).

An important election riot took place between German immigrants and a militant faction of African American Republicans during a torchlight parade just days before the municipal election in 1871. The riot exemplified the declining relations between both groups. During the procession, around five hundred African Americans carrying torches marched through Charleston's main streets, and they fired rockets and Roman candles into the air. The marchers expressed their discontent with the Germans when they sang "John Brown is marching on," proclaimed their disapproval of Wagener, and threatened to "burn down every dammed Dutchman's house." Indicative of racial and ethnic divisions, the various ward clubs carried banners with the slogans: "No Republican votes for sale," "Irishmen, stand by us, we have stood by you," and "Equality before the law for all men and all creeds." Men, women, and children participated in the procession. When several young white males threw rocks and bricks into the procession, a group of African American men retaliated and the riot ensued (*Daily Republican*, August 1, 1871). A group of militant African Americans targeted German shopkeepers and their stores, suggesting economic conflict between both groups (*Daily Courier*, August 1, 1871, August 2, 1871; *Daily News*, August 1, 1871). Schirmer noted, "A procession to night of Negro Men, Women, and boys marched thro' the streets in a most boisterous manner, demolishing more or less many stores belonging to Germans, throwing missiles into private houses and acting most shamefully" (Schirmer, July 31, 1871).

Following the riot, African American Republican politicians lashed out at the Germans and their political machine, making no apologies. The Reverend R. R.

Cain determined that the Germans had nominated African Americans who were "no doubt worthy citizens" but they were "not representative" of African American interests. Lieutenant Governor Ransier connected Wagener's Citizens' Party with the "Democrats of the old school" and its supporters as the "old enemies of Republicanism." Ransier was offended that the Germans supported a political party that was opposed to the civil rights of African Americans. Importantly, he believed that many Germans felt compelled to support the Citizens' Party due to community pressure. Perhaps most important, Ransier felt the Germans betrayed African Americans when he declared: "So far as the negro is concerned—let the Germans remember when they came here in their blue shirts—you patronized them, traded with them, and through your patronage they are enabled to-day to raise their heads and now desire to govern us" (*Daily Republican*, August 1, 1871).

White Charlestonians used the riot to draw centrist leaning voters into the Democratic fold. Frederick Porcher, a white Charlestonian, recalled that whites mobilized in response to the riot. Whites monitored voter registration, closed all of their stores on election day, and even assisted some African Americans in voting for Wagener (Frederick Adolphus Porcher to Miss Anne S. Porcher, August 12, 1871, Frederick Adolphus Porcher Papers, South Caroliniana Library, Columbia). Election officials distributed white ballots to Republicans and Citizens Conservatives brought blue ballots to the polls. The Conservatives, many of them business leaders and employers watched voters at the ballot boxes and intimidated Republicans (*Daily Republican*, August 5, 1871). The Conservatives used the riot to their advantage and called for the white community, including Germans, to vote for the Wagener ticket. The editor of the *Daily News* called for a force of white citizens equal to that of the African Americans at the polling places, and he condoned the use of violence at the polls if necessary, suggesting that whites arm themselves and prepare for conflict with the Republicans (*Charleston Daily News*, August 1, 1871, August 4, 1871).

John A. Wagener and the Citizens' Conservative Party soundly defeated the Republicans, and the Germans would continue to support the Democratic Party in future municipal elections. White southerners were pleased that the Germans had demonstrated a commitment to Democratic political ascendancy. The editor of the *Daily Republican* believed the riot probably cost the Republicans five hundred votes and helped consolidate the Democratic Party (August 4, 1871). One Democratic newspaper editor rejoiced, "Redeemed at Last! The day has been won by the united labors of white and black, rich and poor, adopted citizen and native Carolinian" (*Charleston Daily News*, August 4, 1871). The editors of the *Nation*, the *New York Daily Tribune*, and the *New York Times* all covered the election, suggestive of its national significance. The *New York Daily Tribune* reported the election was "one of the most exciting ever known" in Charleston (*Nation*, August 10, 1871; *New York Daily Tribune*, August 3, 1871, August 4, 1871, August 5, 1871; *New York Times*, August 3, 1871, August 5, 1871).

Following the election of Wagener, African Americans "declared war against the Germans generally" (*Daily Courier*, August 8, 1871). African Americans worked in groups of fifty to seventy-five people, patrolled the streets armed with pistols and sticks, and focused their efforts on the German storekeepers. They walked into their stores, ate and drank various goods without paying for them, and ran off with miscellaneous items. The editor of the *Daily Republican* appealed to African Americans to stop their attacks on Germans and their property, but he noted that white Democrats continued to provoke African Americans (August 7, 1871). Relations between African Americans and Germans continued to decline.

Conclusion

In conclusion, the community of Germans that settled in Charleston, South Carolina, during the antebellum period gradually developed a group identity as white southerners but they did not abandon their German cultural identity, and the community thrived into the late nineteenth century. Many of the Germans earned a living as traders and dealers—and they often dealt with free and enslaved African Americans. Some Germans elites—most of them successful businessmen—owned slaves, but the Germans as a whole were never identified with the institution of slavery. Importantly, dissenting German shopkeepers sold liquor to slaves and traded for merchandise requisitioned from slave masters in violation of the law, thereby undermining the rigid social control required to maintain a slave society. Economic interaction between Germans and African Americans increased during Reconstruction, but German business practices led to conflict with African Americans. In the social realm, German immigrants, both men and women, exhibited exceptional social relations with African Americans, sometimes even marrying and bearing children. In addition, the annual *Schutzenfest* provided a climate rife for sociocultural exchange—but soon the festival became a forum for white supremacy. Moreover, as the Germans became politically active on behalf of the Democratic Party after the Civil War, their relations with African Americans declined precipitously, especially following the municipal riot in 1871. The German experience in Charleston typifies the failure of Reconstruction—as the German community migrated into the white southern fold it did so at the expense of African Americans.

Works Cited

Baggett, James Alex. *The Scalawags: Southern Dissenters in the Civil War and Reconstruction.* Baton Rouge: Louisiana State University Press, 2003.

Barnes, Kenneth C. *Who Killed John Clayton?: Political Violence and the Emergence of the New South, 1861–1893.* Durham, NC: Duke University Press, 1998.

Bauman, Mark K. "Factionalism and Ethnic Politics in Atlanta: The German Jews from the Civil War through the Progressive Era." *Georgia Historical Quarterly* 82, no. 3 (Fall 1998): 533–58.

Bell, Michael Everett. "Regional Identity in the Antebellum South: How German Immigrants Became 'Good' Charlestonians." *South Carolina Historical Magazine* 100, no. 1 (1999): 9–28.

Bergquist, James M. "The Mid-Nineteenth Century Slavery Crisis and the German Americans." In *States of Progress: Germans and Blacks in America over 300 Years, Lectures from the Tricenten-nial of the Germantown Protest against Slavery,* ed. Randall Miller. Philadelphia: The German Society of Pennsylvania, 1989.

Callow, Jr., Alexander B. *The Tweed Ring.* New York: Oxford University Press, 1966.

Carter, Dan T. *When the War Was Over: The Failure of Self-Reconstruction in the South, 1865–1867.* Baton Rouge: Louisiana State University Press, 1985.

City of Charleston. *Census of Charleston, 1861.* Charleston, 1861.

Dailey, Jane. *Before Jim Crow: The Politics of Race in Postemancipation Virginia.* Chapel Hill: University of North Carolina Press, 2000.

Du Bois, W. E. B. *Black Reconstruction.* New York: Harcourt, Brace, 1935.

Faust, Albert Bernhard. *The German Element in the United States,* Vol. 2. New York: The Steuben Society of America, 1927.

Foner, Eric. *Reconstruction: America's Unfinished Revolution, 1863–1877.* New York: Harper & Row, 1988.

Formisano, Ronald P. "Analyzing American Voting, 1830–1860: Methods." In *Voters, Parties, and Elections: Quantitative Essays in the History of American Popular Voting Behavior,* ed. Joel H. Silbey and Samuel T. McSeveney. Lexington, MA: Xerox College Publishing, 1972.

Fraser, Jr., Walter J. *Charleston! Charleston!: The History of a Southern City.* Columbia: University of South Carolina Press, 1989.

Gilje, Paul A. *Rioting in America.* Bloomington: Indiana University Press, 1996.

Greenberg, Mark I. "Becoming Southern: The Jews of Savannah, Georgia, 1830–1870." *American Jewish History* 86, no. 1 (1998): 55–75.

Higham, John. *Strangers in the Land: Patterns of American Nativism, 1860–1925.* New York: Atheneum, 1975.

Holt, Thomas. *Black Over White: Negro Political Leadership in South Carolina during Reconstruction.* Urbana: University of Illinois Press, 1977.

Huger Smith, Daniel E. *A Charlestonian's Recollections, 1846–1913.* Charleston, SC: Charleston Art Association, 1950.

Jacobson, Matthew Frye. *Whiteness of a Different Color: European Immigrants and the Alchemy of Race.* Cambridge, MA: Harvard University Press, 1998.

Jenkins, Wilbert L. *Seizing the New Day: African-Americans in Post–Civil War Charleston.* Bloomington: Indiana University Press, 1998.

Kamphoefner, Walter D. *The Westphalians: From Germany to Missouri.* Princeton, NJ: Princeton University Press, 1987.

———. "New Perspectives on Texas Germans and the Confederacy." *Southwestern Historical Quarterly* 102, no. 4 (April 1999): 440–55.

Kantrowitz, Stephen. *Ben Tillman and the Reconstruction of White Supremacy.* Chapel Hill: University of North Carolina Press, 2000.

Keil, Hartmut. "Continuity and Change in the Transfer of Ideologies." Occasional Paper No. 7 Washington, DC: German Historical Institute, 1992.

Kleppner, Paul H. *The Third Electoral System, 1853–1892: Parties, Voters, and Political Cultures.* Chapel Hill: University of North Carolina Press, 1979.

Les Benedict, Michael. "The Politics of Reconstruction." In *American Political History: Essays on the State of the Discipline,* ed. John F. Marszalek and Wilson D. Miscamble. South Bend: University of Notre Dame Press, 1997.

Lesesne, Thomas Petigru. *History of Charleston County South Carolina: Narrative and Biographical.* Charleston, SC: A. H. Cawston, 1931.

Levine, Bruce. *The Spirit of 1848: German Immigrants, Labor Conflict, and the Coming of the Civil War.* Urbana: University of Illinois Press, 1992.

———. "The Migration of Ideology and the Contested Meaning of Freedom: German-Americans in the Mid-Nineteenth Century." Occasional Paper No. 7. Washington, DC: German Historical Institute, 1992.

Lonn, Ella. *Foreigners in the Confederacy.* Chapel Hill: University of North Carolina Press, 1941.

Miller, Randall M. "Introduction." In *States of Progress: Germans and Blacks in America over 300 Years, Lectures from the Tricentennial of the Germantown Protest Against Slavery,* ed. Randall Miller. Philadelphia: The German Society of Pennsylvania, 1989.

Page, Brian D. "'An Unholy Alliance': Irish-Americans and the Political Construction of Whiteness in Memphis, Tennessee, 1866–1879." *Left History* 8, no. 1 (2002): 77–96.

Perman, Michael. *The Road to Redemption: Southern Politics, 1869–1879.* Chapel Hill: University of North Carolina Press, 1984.

Powers, Bernard. *Black Charlestonians: A Social History, 1822–1885.* Fayetteville: University of Arkansas Press, 1994.

———. "Community Evolution and Race Relations in Reconstruction Charleston, South Carolina." *South Carolina Historical Magazine* 101, no. 3 (July 2000): 214–33.

Rabinowitz, Howard. Race Relations in the Urban South, 1865–1890. Athens: University of Georgia Press, 1996.

Rable, George C. *But There Was No Peace: The Role of Violence in the Politics of Reconstruction.* Athens: University of Georgia Press, 1984.

Ratzel, Friedrich. *Sketches of Urban and Cultural Life in North America,* trans. and ed. Steward A. Stehin. New Brunswick, NJ: Rutgers University Press, 1988.

Reinert, Gertha. "'Turning My Joy into Bitterness': A Letter from John A. Wagener." *South Carolina Historical Magazine* 100 (January 1999): 49–70.

Silverman, Jason H., and Robert M. Gorman. "The Confederacy's Fighting Poet: General John Wagener." *North & South* 2 (April 1999): 42–49.

United States Census Bureau. *The Eighth Census of the United States.* Washington, DC, 1864.

———. *The Ninth Census of the United States.* Washington, DC, 1872.

———. *The Tenth Census of the United States.* Washington, DC, 1883.

Williamson, Joel. *After Slavery: The Negro in South Carolina during Reconstruction, 1861–1877.* New York: Norton, 1975.

Newspapers

Daily Courier
Daily Republican
Daily News
New York Daily Tribune
New York Times
The Nation

Unpublished Sources

Federal Citizenship Rolls, City of Charleston, South Carolina Department of Archives and History, Columbia, South Carolina.

Frederick Adolphus Porcher to Miss Anne S. Porcher, August 12, 1871, Frederick Adolphus Porcher Papers, South Caroliniana Library, Columbia, South Carolina.

German Fourth Ward Democratic Club, Minutes, South Caroliniana Library, Columbia, South Carolina.

Jacob Schirmer Diary, South Carolina Historical Society, Charleston, South Carolina.

Sally DeSaussure to Mrs. Joseph Glover, 1863, DeSaussure Family Papers, Duke Special Collections, Durham, North Carolina.

Louis Douglas and the Weimar Reception of Harlemania

LEROY HOPKINS

In *Black People: Entertainers of African Descent in Europe and Germany*, Rainer E. Lotz reintroduces an African American performer who attained the status of a cultural icon in Weimar, Germany, only to be almost completely forgotten a generation later. Louis W. Douglas (1889–1939), a native of Philadelphia (Pennsylvania), had a remarkable show business career that over a little more than three decades took him to twenty-three countries in Europe, Africa, and Latin America. Although his career began before the First World War and ended with his untimely death just before the outbreak of the Second World War, Douglas enjoyed extraordinary success in Weimar, Germany, between 1925 and 1931.

During Weimar's "Golden Twenties" Douglas achieved iconic status as documented by his performances on radio, in music revues, and in three feature films. Images from two of his dancing performances were replicated on the popular tobacco cards of that period that featured the stars of stage and film to promote tobacco products.[1] Douglas's celebrity was symptomatic of what can be termed as "Harlemania," a receptivity for the cultural productions of African Americans connected to the movement known as the Harlem Renaissance.

The Harlem Renaissance was a singular eruption of creative energies that defined and, to a certain extent, legitimized African American arts and letters in an era of racism, discrimination, and frequent outbursts of mob violence taking the form of lynching. In recent years critical discussion of the period has been directed at reversing earlier judgments as to the efficacy of the movement. Notably, the late Nathan Huggins and the historian David Levering Lewis have been taken to task for their conclusion that the Harlem Renaissance was ultimately a failure.

To Huggins the failure was the result of the provincialism of the products and their inadequacy in terms of modernism. Lewis, however, saw the reason for the movement's failure in its unrealistic goal of trying to effect societal change. Both critics agreed that the advent of the Great Depression was the death knell of the movement. Huggins's and Lewis's global assessment of the Renaissance has been quite convincingly challenged by Houston A. Baker Jr. in his masterfully argued *Modernism and the Harlem Renaissance* (1987).

Baker invalidates both assessments by rejecting their starting point, the movement's failure. To describe an explicitly modern African American discourse he rejects the concept of "modernism" in its Western context which he exposes as grounded in terms and concepts not applicable to the realities of African American life and cultural production. Asserting the essential racist underpinnings of the Western expressive tradition, Baker posits a modern African American discourse that begins with Booker T. Washington, which he proposes as a tension between "mastery of form" and "deformation of mastery."

Baker's insightful deconstruction of Washington's *Up from Slavery* illustrates the concept of "mastery of form" by delineating how Washington adapted the then-prevailing discourse on race to create a strategy for group survival, or what Baker termed "[a] liberating manipulation of masks and a revolutionary renaming."[2] The full import of Baker's analysis becomes evident when he explains why he chose Booker T. Washington instead of Paul Laurence Dunbar as the starting point for African American modernism.

Although Dunbar's works exhibit a similar "mastery of form" in that Dunbar draws on the expressive tradition of minstrelsy by using the African American idiom in his texts, Baker insists that he was interested in

a definition of the mastery of form that renders it more than a strategy adopted for the aesthetic satisfaction of the individual artist. Indeed, I am interested in the strategy to precisely the extent that it ensures cognitive exploration and affective transformations leading to the growth and survival of a nation. Washington is "modern" in my view, then, because he earnestly projected the flourishing of a southern, black Eden at Tuskegee—a New World garden to nurture hands, heads, and hearts of a younger generation of agrarian black folk in the "country districts."[3]

The counterpoint to Washington's mastery of form is, according to Baker, W. E. B. Du Bois's "deformation of mastery" as expressed in *Souls of Black Folk*.

Classifying *Souls* as a "cultural performance"[4] Baker identifies "deformation of mastery," which is, in essence, a rejection of racist discourse or what Baker terms "a master's nonsense." In place of the master's discourse, the deformer resorts to the "common sense of the tribe."[5] This act of displacement or replacement differs, according to Baker, from mastery of form largely due to its relationship to masks: "The spirit house occupying the deformer is not minstrelsy, but the sound and space of an African ancestral past."[6]

Baker identifies Du Bois as the "most articulate adherent of African sound" at the beginning of the twentieth century because he discerns Du Bois's "phaneric" voice, a voice that describes instead of disguising,[7] in the use of the metaphor of the "Veil" and the appropriation of the African American musical tradition, specifically the spirituals, in *Souls of Black Folk*. The "Veil" represents, of course, the racial segregation oppressing African Americans. An emancipatory intent in this deformation of mastery Baker locates in the fourteenth chapter of *Souls* when the Veil is rendered as a result of an "Eternal Good" that compels American justice and liberates those imprisoned behind the Veil.[8]

Baker applies his dichotomy to the Harlem Renaissance and in the act liberates it from its temporal frame of the decade before the Depression. Instead, he subsumes it in what he terms "renaissancism," an expressive tradition beginning with Booker T. Washington and continuing to the present day. Within that context he perceives the black men and women associated with Harlem in the 1920s to be "national resources" and "audible signs of the human mind's masterful and insistent engagement with forms and deformation." From Baker's perspective, then, the Harlem Renaissance was a "resounding" success. Baker's theory on black modernism is an essential element in the theories of two critics who emphasize the importance of music in the Renaissance.

Samuel A. Floyd Jr. also challenged the emphasis placed by critics such as Huggins and David Levering Lewis on literary production as the essence of the Harlem Renaissance. Instead of literature, Floyd proposed music as the Renaissance's predominant feature and posits a musical genealogy that he identifies as a troika consisting of the "Group of Four," the "Jazzmen," and the "Pianists." The first group included Ford Dabney (1883–1958), James Reese Europe (1881–1919), Will Marion Cook (1869–1944), and William Christopher Handy (1873–1958). These men were both precursors as well as pioneers of the musical forms perfected by the "Jazzmen," Fletcher Henderson (1897–1952), and Edward Kennedy "Duke" Ellington (1894–1974), and the "Pianists," James P. Johnson (1894–1955), Willie "The Lion" Smith (1893–1973), and Thomas "Fats" Waller (1904–1943). Floyd is essentially positing a continuity between ragtime and jazz involving artists who were creative before, during, and after the 1920s. Floyd's hypothesis of the primacy of music in the cultural production of the Harlem Renaissance is adopted and expanded on by Jon Michael Spencer.

The title of Spencer's book, *The New Negroes and Their Music: The Success of the Harlem Renaissance* clearly indicates the import of his argument. Like Baker he judges the Renaissance a success and like Floyd he associates that success with the music of the period. Spencer appropriates Baker's dichotomy of mastery of form and deformation of mastery as an interpretative tool to measure the success of the Renaissance. His signposts are the many texts involving music beginning with James Weldon Johnson's *The Autobiography of an Ex-Colored Man* (1912) and continuing in texts created well after the Renaissance's purported demise.[9] Thus Spencer creates a different temporal frame for the Renaissance. Like Baker he subsumes it in an expressive tradition that extends from the beginning of the twentieth century and continues into the decades after the Second World War. The primacy of music in the Renaissance that both Floyd and Spencer assert provides a point of departure to consider how Louis Douglas became a representative of the "The New Negro" in Weimar, Germany.

Rainer Lotz's survey of African American performers is the ideal starting point for a study of Douglas's career in Germany (Lotz 1997).[10] Lotz presents in meticulous detail an account of almost all of Douglas's performances in Europe, Africa, and Latin America from 1903 to 1938. To evaluate Douglas's impact it is important to stress the fact documented by Lotz in his treatment of other black performers from the mid-nineteenth century to the mid-twentieth century that the black performer moving about the Atlantic world is not just a twentieth-century phenomenon. Ira Aldridge (1807?–1867) was lionized by European audiences from Ireland to Russia and the Ukraine in the three decades before the American Civil War. Eileen Southern documents one interesting aspect of Aldridge's European career.

According to Eileen Southern, Aldridge was responsible for preserving perhaps one of the earliest slave songs. Aldridge performed at New York City's African Grove Theatre and the English comedic actor Charles Mathews was present at one of his performances in the 1822–23 season. Mathews transcribed Aldridge's rendition of "Opossum up a Gum Tree" and adapted it for his own performances. Mathews's description differed from Aldridge's in that, instead of depicting an African as the protagonist who pulls the opossum out of the tree, Mathews replaces human agency with that of an animal, a sly raccoon. Southern terms this displacement from the human area to one of fable as a transformation from a slave to an Ethiopian song.[11]

Essential to this anecdote are the various means of representing blackness. Aldridge appropriated the black mask of the slave for his performance and thus put his own blackness on display. In Europe, by assuming the role of Othello, a character traditionally played by white actors in black face, Aldridge was clearly striving for what Houston Baker terms mastery of form. It is not clear, however, that this mastery served any but Aldridge's own personal aesthetic ambitions. But like many later African American entertainers, Aldridge used his race as an expressive element in his performances.

Notable in that context are the performances of the Fisk Jubilee Singers. Eileen Southern credits them with popularizing African American folksong in America after 1867.[12] Encouraged by the success at home, the Jubilee Singers went on tour in Europe, performing before royalty and commoners in Great Britain, Germany, and Switzerland. One measure of their success was in the area of fund-raising, the real reason for their tour. As Southern notes, within seven years the Singers were able to raise the remarkable sum of $150,000 for their institution.[13] This success spawned imitators and other struggling black colleges soon followed suit and sent their own groups on a concert circuit. The result was the introduction of African American folksong to a large part of the Western world.[14]

Louis Douglas's early career was nurtured by this lingering European interest in African American popular music and expressive culture. Plantation music had a significant role in his early repertoire and he apparently retained elements of it throughout his career. Lotz sets the beginning of Douglas's European career in 1903 when he arrived in Ireland on the SS *Belgenland* from Philadelphia as a member of a group of variety artists.[15] While uncertain as to the stage name utilized by the troupe, Lotz cites a reference to a performance at the Liverpool Empire on May 11, 1903, of "The Georgia Piccaninnies. Twelve in number, with their plantation songs and dances."[16] From January 1904 to November 1912 the troupe toured continental Europe beginning in the Netherlands. Of interest is that the troupe was featured in a film produced by the Bioscope Company in Berlin in 1908.[17] Lotz cannot, however, document Douglas's presence in the troupe with any certainty beyond May 1903 but surmises that he may have joined Belle Davis's group, "Belle Davis and her Picaninnies," as recalled by an informant, the African American trumpeter Arthur Briggs, who met Douglas after 1919.[18]

Douglas's career before the First World War is largely obscure except for the incredible detective work done by Lotz, who sifted through many sources, aided undoubtedly in no small measure by the information provided him by Douglas's daughter.[19] With the available information Lotz identified performances by Douglas possibly before October 1909 in Berlin, from June 16–30, 1909, in Vienna, and from October 16–31, 1909, again in Vienna, and from December 1–15 in Budapest.[20]

Lotz's assessment of Douglas's success in the years before 1914 is very interesting, especially in view of his later success in the Weimar period.[21]

> 1910 saw Douglas back in London where he played in Honi Soit at the Pavilion and at the Oxford in March. From London he went to St. Petersburg, where his success was such that he returned every year until war prevented this. Boldly headlined "the American king of dancers" and always well Reviewed, Louis Douglas crossed and recrossed Europe playing the leading theatres in major cities. Black dancers had been a staple ingredient in the theatrical diet of Europeans for two decades, who knew what to expect from "Nigger Dance" and "American Song & Dance" billed to appear at their local theatre. Yet the acclaim obtained by Douglas in the 1910s was despite the somewhat jaded nature of such acts. The novelty of African-descent performers had largely worn off, and the critics were often bored with the normal, almost traditional Black dance shows. At this time the Whites-in-black-face minstrel troupes, a part of Europe's entertainment world since the 1840's, also fell out of favour. So the critical appreciation of Louis Douglas indicates that he was different—in a class of his own.

Louis Douglas had, in fact, to cite Houston Baker again, achieved mastery of form. With his skills he was able to take the dance and musical forms Europeans had grown accustomed to as being specifically African American and present them in a new and appealing manner to critic and audience alike.

Douglas came in contact with what Samuel A. Floyd Jr. presents as the musical side of the Harlem Renaissance when some time in 1918–1919 he met, fell in love with, and married Marion Abigail Cook. Her parents, Will Marion Cook and Abbie Mitchell (1884–1960), were as Lotz terms them, "leading Afro-American theatrical personalities."[22] Will Marion Cook was a musical prodigy sent to Oberlin at the age of fifteen to study violin. Subsequently, with the help of local African Americans he studied at Berlin's Hochschule für Musik from 1887 to 1889. From 1894 to 1895, according to Eileen Southern, he attended the National Conservatory of Music, where his teachers included Anton Dvorak.[23]

With this formal training in European classical forms, Cook turned his attention to theater music. Southern notes that his first creative work was "Scenes from the Opera of Uncle Tom's Cabin" in 1893 for a performance on Colored American Day (August 25) at the Chicago World's Fair.[24] The performance never took place but it is significant that Cook then collaborated with Paul Laurence Dunbar to create the first black musical comedy sketch "Clorindy; or The Origin of the Cakewalk" (1898). Also then for a number of years Cook was in Southern's terms "composer-in-chief and musical director" of the George Walker and Bert Williams company.[25] Cook was therefore intimately connected to the late-nineteenth- and early-twentieth-century masters of form, Paul Laurence Dunbar and especially George Walker and Bert Williams, who took minstrelsy-based, blackface comedy to new heights.

Abbie Mitchell's résumé was equally interesting. She may have met Cook in 1898 when she performed in his musical comedy "Clorindy." Southern provides a brief sketch of Mitchell's career that features performance with groups such as "Black Patti's Troubadours," the Walker and Williams companies, and in the Cole-Johnson (Bob Cole and J. Rosamond Johnson with James Weldon Johnson) operetta "Red Moon."[26] Both Mitchell and Cook were involved with Walker and Williams's "Walker and Williams in Dahomey" (1903–1905), which Southern describes as "a satire on the American Colonization Society's 'back to Africa' movement."[27] Both Mitchell and Cook were associated with "In Dahomey" when it was performed in May 1903 in London for King Edward VII and for provincial audiences until January 1904.

Abbie Mitchell was again in London when her husband's Southern Syncopated Orchestra performed for, among others, King George V in 1919–1920. Louis Douglas clearly married into a family that was in the creative elite of African American musical life. Douglas's wife was not involved in his early performances after their marriage (their daughter was born in 1920). From 1920 to 1923 Douglas partnered with Sonny Jones and a group of twelve female dancers called the "Shurley Girls." As Lotz reports, from August 28 to September 3, 1922, the London Coliseum featured "Louis Douglas & Sonny Jones, Syncopated Black-faced Comedians."[28]

At various times in his career, as documented by numerous photos and sketches, Douglas performed in black face. This doubling of blackness emphasized race as a mask which he assumed to demonstrate his mastery of the various stereotypes associated with African Americans. By combining race with comedy he obviously hoped to communicate to his audiences in a nonthreatening manner and perhaps expose those lingering racial stereotypes that were used to oppress the race and which were in stark contrast with his technical virtuosity.

In 1924 Douglas joined his mother-in-law in the cast of "Negro Nuances," a Will Marion Cook production in New York City based on a book by Abbie Mitchell and Miller & Lyle using music and lyrics by Cook.[29] Though short-lived this production indicates that Douglas's in-laws considered him a worthy collaborator. The content of this short-lived production is instructive. Lotz reports that it "traced the musical history of Blacks starting in Africa, moving with slave ships, the lamentations of pre-civil war days to the reconstruction period as typified by the early minstrels of Jim Bland's day."[30] "Negro Nuances" was intended therefore to be a panorama of the African in America through the perspective of music; certainly a product of that era when the men and women of the Harlem Renaissance were exploring the roots of African Americans. Music was a very important part of that introspection.

Writing in *The New Negro*, the well-known anthology of voices from the Harlem Renaissance edited by Alain L. Locke, J. A. Rogers argued as cogently as Floyd seventy years later on the importance of music. Posing the rhetorical question: "What after all is taking this new thing, that, condemned in certain quarters, enthusiastically welcomed in others, has nonchalantly gone on until it ranks with the movie and the dollar as a foremost exponent of modern Americanism?"[31] Rogers states: "Jazz isn't music merely, it is a spirit that can express itself in almost anything. The true spirit of jazz is a joyous revolt from convention, custom, authority, Boredom, even sorrow—from everything that would confine the soul of man and hinder its riding free on the air."[32] Always the internationalist Rogers found kindred spirits to jazz among Native Americans, in Scotland, Ireland, among the Cossacks, in the Spanish fandango, the hula hula of the South Seas, gypsy music, and especially in ragtime.[33]

As was typical of the Harlem intellectuals Rogers stressed that jazz as a true art form was evolving from folk or popular forms which he obviously considered unrefined. As he stated: "Musically jazz has a great future. It is rapidly being sublimated. In the more famous jazz orchestras like those of Will Marion Cook, Paul Whiteman, Sissle and Blake, Sam Stewart, Fletcher Henderson, Vincent Lopez and the Clef Club units, there are none of the vulgarities and crudities of the lowly origin or the only too prevalent imitations."[34] Douglas was to become an important player in this confluence of music and racial history.

In 1925 Douglas's career entered a new phase when he arrived in Paris with the musical production "La Revue Nègre." The tour had been organized by Caroline Dudley Reagan and featured Douglas and his dancing partner, newcomer Josephine Baker. According to a handbill cited by Lotz, Douglas had written the seven-act production. The cast included Josephine Baker, Maud de Forest, Joè Alex, Louis Douglas, Honey Boy, and Marion Cook. Music was provided by the Charleston Jazz Band led by Claude Hopkins including Sidney Bechet. Other members of the cast were a dance ensemble, the Charleston Steppers, and the Bootleggers Quartette consisting of Spencer Williams, Sidney Bechet, Mercer Cook, and Louis Douglas.[35]

"La Revue Nègre" made Josephine Baker an instant star. When the show moved to Berlin, she received an apparently irresistible invitation to return to Paris and abandoned the show. The importance of the revue is, however, greater than an individual member, even one as charismatic as Josephine Baker. The significance of the revue was its ensemble. Claude Hopkins, Spencer Williams, and Sidney Bechet participated not only in the musical innovations that revolutionized American popular music in the first third of the twentieth century but also were connected to the musical history of the Harlem Renaissance and were bringing a radically new musical idiom to Weimar, Germany.

As we have already noted, Will Marion Cook was at the heart of the innovations that were changing American music before the First World War. He created the New York or Southern Syncopated Orchestra. In 1918 the orchestra toured the United States and before leaving for London for among others, a command performance before King George V, Cook encouraged a talented young clarinetist named Sidney Bechet (1897–1959) to join the orchestra. Bechet was probably one of the most idiosyncratic geniuses of the jazz age. His genius for performance was almost evenly matched by his volatile temper. Bechet performed with Cook's orchestra in London but soon left to join others. In 1923 he performed with Willie "The Lion" Smith and then in 1924 with Duke Ellington. Claude Hopkins, the band leader of "La Revue Nègre," had a similar pedigree.

A graduate of Howard University with a BA in music, Hopkins was influenced by the stride piano style of James P. Johnson and Fats Waller. Leaving his native Washington, D.C., Hopkins moved to Harlem and obviously gained enough notoriety to be included in the tour where he teamed with Spencer Williams (October 14, 1880–July 14, 1965) like Bechet a native of New Orleans. Williams is a rather mysterious figure about whom there are few facts in the standard reference works[36] but whom a no lesser figure than James Weldon Johnson considered one of the best African American writers of popular songs.[37] A sense of Williams's importance is given by Eileen Southern in her list of the "most enduring" black musicals on or off Broadway between 1921 and 1927. Williams was co-composer with Perry Bradford and Tim Brymm of "Put and Take" (1921) and with Eubie Blake in "Chocolate Dandies" (1924).[38] As early as 1918 he had also collaborated with Fats Waller.

"La Revue Nègre" brought with it a sample of the emerging jazz idiom and also the latest dance craze, the Charleston. The contents of the production were also familiar. The seven scenes were titled "Mississippi Steamboat Race," New York Skyscraper," "Louisiana Camp-Meeting, "Les Strutting Babies," "Darkey Impressions," "Les pieds qui parlent," and "Charleston Cabaret." As Rainer Lotz notes, the reception of Douglas's revue was mixed. Critics such as Alfred Polgar and Othmar Starke lauded the performances. In the magazine *Der Querschnitt* Starke noted that the musical production offered "an overview of Negro life in America, a 1925 version of the late Harriet Beecher Stowe's 'Uncle Tom's Cabin,' but *more conciliatory*" (italics mine).[39] Mastery of form but no apparent attempt to deform mastery, at least from Starke's perspective. Just as telling are his comments on Douglas and Baker.

As a couple he considered them clowns. Of Douglas he states: "In his black face (ihm zum Bilde, zum Bilde Gottes schuf er ihn) he paints a white target mark around his mouth, thus increasing his Negrodom."[40] Josephine Baker elicits even more revealing remarks from Starke:

Josephine Baker is a grotesque dancer, whenever she touches skin. Her backside, with all respect, is as flexible as a chocolate semolina pudding, and she is rightfully proud of this gift of nature. Her drolleries are, however, without much variation. All the time she shakes her various limbs, she has blank doubled-sized eyes, and she is incredibly (un)dressed. Her final Venus is of unmistakably callipygian nature, and that must make everybody happy.[41]

Douglas's mask which he assumed for his performance—as already noted he frequently performed in blackface and photos from the production of "La Revue Nègre" indicate that he did so then also—did not distract Starke from his virtuosity. The white circle drawn around Douglas's mouth, in Starke's own words, doubled his "Negrodom." That can be interpreted as Douglas punning as it were on his blackness. Here was a black man assuming a persona traditionally played by a white man impersonating a black one. For Starke the white target provided this doubling effect.

Josephine Baker's mask obviously distracted Starke. He focuses on her obvious display of sexuality and his description of her physiognomy along with the appellation of "bare-buttocked Venus" are reminiscent of the dehumanizing depictions of women of color in Western iconography. This was especially true of depictions of black women from the European colonies in Africa. As Jan Nederveen Pieterse has noted: "For many young men in the West pictures of scantily dressed native women, or African women with bare breast in decorative poses, brought them their first visual familiarity with female nudity, through magazines such as the *National Geographic* in the United States, illustrated encyclopedias and Postcards. The world of colonialism is a man's world."[42] Starke's comments on Josephine Baker border on the exploitative and reduce her performance to sexuality on display.

A conservative critic writing in *Das Theater* scoffed at "ugly physiogonomies" and "unaesthetic bodies" and claimed to be tortured by the noise of this "music." But again the critic was full of praise for the "fabulous dancer Louis Douglas who knows how to create veritable events with his feet."[43] A telling critique is found in Iwan Goll's review "Die Neger erobern Europa," which appeared in *Die literarische Welt* on January 15, 1926. Goll, a member of the German artistic avantgarde, perceived the revue as "an unmitigated challenge to Europe."[44]

That challenge Goll formulated in racialistic terms:

Negroes dance with their senses. (While Europeans can only dance with their minds.) They dance with their legs, breasts, and bellies. This was the dance of the Egyptians, the whole of antiquity, the Orient. This is the dance of the Negroes. One can only envy them, for this is life, sun, primeval forests, the singing of birds and the roar of a leopard, earth. They never dance naked; and yet, how naked is the dance. They have put on clothes only to show the clothes do not exist for them.[45]

Goll's emphasis on the vitalism that he perceived in African American dance echoes J. A. Rogers's arguments about jazz. Both perceived in the new forms an energizing force. While Rogers saw in jazz a manifestation of the New Negro's vigor, Goll recognized in it a challenge to the European status quo or as he put it: "the leading role belongs to Negro blood. Its drops are slowly falling over Europe, a long-since dried-up land that can scarcely breathe."[46]

In her essay "African-American Performers and Culture in Weimar Germany" Christine Naumann identifies a specific Weimar discourse that derived from the opposition between racialistic nationalism of the Right and Leftist escapism which perceived in Africans and African Americans an alternative to modernity.[47] Race was a contentious issue in Weimar Germany. Indignation over the use of African troops in the occupation of the Rhineland extended across the entire political spectrum. The children that resulted from the liaisons between the foreign troops and the indigenous population were pejoratively named "Rhineland bastards" and were registered by the government. In Nazi-Germany as these children approached puberty they were subjected to forced sterilization.

The loss of colonies as a result of the war did not lessen the impact of colonialism on Weimar's discourse on race. As Christine Naumann reports between 1925 and 1933 "no year passed without manifested nationalist opposition to African-American performers."[48] Four incidents illustrate her point. A member of the Sam Wooding orchestra related how an inebriated passerby assaulted him and objected to the presence of black people in the country: "During the war they cut off our noses and ears." In 1927 the mayor of Elberfeld prevented the performance of a revue called *Black People* because the Rhineland had already, in his words, endured "The Black Shame." As Naumann points out these two incidents were obviously grounded in misguided racist nationalism. The performers were after all African American and had had no connection to the colonial troops used by both sides during the war.[49]

The final two incidents cited by Naumann date from 1928 and 1930. In 1928 when Josephine Baker performed in the musical revue "Bitte einsteigen" a nationalist critic objected to the mixed cast which put the "beautiful blonde Lea Seidl" on the stage with a "negress." Racially tinged nationalistic indignation erupted on the opening night of Ossip Dymow's "Shades over Harlem" in Stuttgart in 1930. As Naumann notes, "Nationalists threw rotten eggs and spoiled vegetables on the stage and there were repeated cries of 'Germany wake up!'" Another source of this racialist nationalism is, of course, *Mein Kampf.*

Iwan Goll's review illustrates what Naumann terms Leftist escapism. To Goll Europe was an arid cultural wasteland devoid of the vitality he perceived in blacks. The performers represent for him a primitive life force, far superior to the overly cerebral European culture. His comments on the nakedness of the dance echo Starke's fascination with Josephine Baker's body. For both critics nudity equates with a lack of inhibitions, a display of primitive urges unfettered by the strictures of civilization. Both men invoke an almost Dionysian assault on European rationality.

Goll's critique can be considered escapist in that, like the European avantgarde at least since Gaugin, the non-Western world served as foil to industrialized Europe. Primitivism was coveted as the antidote to the ills of European civilization.

Concomitant with this rejection of European modernism was a development which Peter Jelavich terms the "Americanization of popular entertainment in Berlin," that is, a shift in popular music from the waltzes, polkas, mazurkas, folk songs, and marches that dominated German popular music before 1914 to the new forms emanating from America.[50]

Jelavich equates the change in taste not only to the sudden popularity of American music after 1920 but especially to the appearance of black performers after 1924. "Chocolate Kiddies" and "La Revue Nègre" are singled out by him as the catalysts for the Americanization process. Louis Douglas was clearly an integral part of that process and benefited from an important aspect of black performance in Europe. Cast members of the various troupes changed periodically. After Josephine Baker left "La Revue Nègre" the show continued with a new cast member.

Such cast changes are routine in the entertainment industry but this substitution process allowed European audiences to see a variety of African American performers. It was also apparently routine to borrow material from other sources. After Baker left Douglas's revue in early 1926 Maud de Forest replaced her and the show continued on to Vienna and eventually was terminated in April 1926.[51] In mid-1926 Douglas organized a new revue in Berlin called "Black People." As Lotz notes the Sam Wooding orchestra that had toured with the earlier revue "Chocolate Kiddies" had just returned from Russia and Douglas not only used trumpeter Tommy Ladnier and brass bass player John Warren in his new revue but also may have appropriated some of the material from "Chocolate Kiddies."[52]

"Black People" had two acts with five scenes. Douglas directed and Spencer Williams, of "La Revue Nègre" fame, provided the music. According to Lotz the cast also included Sidney Bechet and Arabella Fields, a veteran singer who had toured in Europe since the 1890s. From the information that Lotz provides on performances in Sweden and the Netherlands, Douglas did not perform in the troupe but directed instead. From a Dutch review cited by Lotz it is clear that Douglas recycled familiar themes from African American life to entertain his audiences. The scenes included a cotton plantation, a watermelon patch, a cabaret, and a street scene. As Lotz points out the material was not original but it is reminiscent of Williams and Walker's "In Dahomey."[53] Lotz does point out that this "plagiarism" did afford employment opportunities for black performers in Europe. It also demonstrates what tradition Douglas consciously placed himself.

"Black People" underwent an interesting transformation. After performances in the Netherlands, the troupe returned to perform in Berlin from July 13 to August 2, 1926. Douglas was busy preparing a new revue at the same time that "Black People" went on tour again. From Sweden to Hamburg, various stops in the Netherlands, and then Düsseldorf were on their itinerary. When the revue appeared in Munich from November 2–10, 1926, it was advertised as "Chocolate Kiddies by Louis Douglas" and continued under that name to Zurich. The confusion of names was most probably due to the similarity in content and the interchangeable performers.

While "Black People" was on tour, it was likely the show banned in Elberfeld in 1927 as noted by Christine Naumann, Douglas was busy in Berlin. He choreographed and debuted in "Von Mund zu Mund," an Erik Charell production. Charell was arguably one of the most important directors of musical revues in Weimar, Germany, and the entire revue was broadcast on the Berliner Funkstunde, Germany's pioneer radio station, on October 22, 1926. Besides Douglas the cast included a young Marlene Dietrich and established cabaret stars Curt Bois, Claire Waldoff, and Wilhelm Bendow. Douglas danced in two scenes of the revue, one with the memorable title "Kannst du Charleston, tanzst du Charleston (Go South)." Lotz indicates that this dance number was recorded by Bernard Ette's band and other Berlin bands as a "jazz number with hot solo choruses."[54] Lotz assumes that since Sam Wooding's orchestra was in Berlin at that time recording for the Deutsche Grammophon, it was likely that members of the band were used to record Douglas's number since German musicians apparently lacked the technical skills for improvisation.[55]

On February 6, 1927, Douglas and his wife, Marion Cook, starred in the "Ball der Funkstunde" held in Berlin's Marmorsaal. To advertise the event a full-length photo of Douglas in blackface playing a ukulele was published in the radio weekly magazine "Funk-Stunde" in January. At the Marmorsaal performance Alfred Braun, sometime announcer and program director of the Funkstunde, read a prologue written by Lion Feuchtwanger (1884–1958), one of Weimar Germany's most engaged political dramatists. A scene from "Mund zu Mund" was featured. Douglas performed a series of "Neger-Exzentrik-Tänze" and then, together with his wife and a dance ensemble, did the latest dance craze, the Charleston.[56] Later in February Douglas and his wife gave Charleston dance exhibitions at Berlin's Zoo restaurant. Lotz reports that in the possession of Douglas's daughter is a scrapbook that includes five photographs from this period on how to dance the Charleston.[57]

The Charleston was a key ingredient in Douglas's success and that success benefited other black performers, as Lotz indicates:

Blacks, even those from Guyana, Trinidad, Jamaica, Africa or—like Evelyn Dove who worked with Sam Wooding—of European birth, were taken to be Afro-Americans as opportunities for Black entertainers in Europe increased. Louis Douglas, with a quarter century of experience, was well placed to exploit such opportunities; indeed his efforts had paved the way to some Extent. By the time "Black People" played in Vienna in February 1927, there were twenty-five Black girls in the show.[58]

In 1928, after a brief sojourn the previous year in New York City where he had choreographed "Africana" starring Ethel Waters, Douglas got further exposure to appreciative Weimar audiences by appearing in "Es liegt in der Luft," a musical comedy in twenty-four scenes with music by Mischa Spoliansky, an Anglo-Russian composer deeply involved in Weimar cabaret (he set texts by Tucholsky, Klabund, and Ringelnatz to music). Besides Douglas the cast included Marlene

Dietrich, Margo Lion, Hubert von Meyerinck, and other star cabaret performers. The performance was held at Max Reinhardt's Komödie am Kurfürstendamm.

Douglas appeared in a revue titled "Wissen Sie schon?" which apparently was performed in Berlin in the summer of 1927 and then again in Breslau in August 1928.[59] From that point on he kept up a torrid pace. In October 1928 he was involved with a five-man group known as the "Douglas-Kappelles-Orchestra," and then in 1929 created yet another revue called "Louisiana" that played in Berlin (July 14–August, 1929), Barcelona (September 19, 1929), Hamburg (October 8–20), Paris (November 1929), Cairo (December 12–31, 1929), Budapest (February 1930), Paris (March 1930), Halle, Germany (January 30–March 30), Milan (March 21, 1930), Torino, Balbo (April 1, 1930), Rome (April 11, 1930), Paris, and then from April 30 to June 30 on tour in Greece, Turkey, Albania, and Yugoslavia before returning to Paris in June 1930.[60]

The cast of "Louisiana" included Douglas and his wife in leading roles but also featured the emerging Afro-British performer Mabel Mercer (1900–1984), whose career took her to the United States and stardom after the Second World War. The story line of the revue was familiar. Two locales are featured: a southern cotton plantation and the New York City theater scene. Unrequited love, separation, involvement in New York theater life (presumably in Harlem), reunion, and happy ending with a return to the South are the dramatic stops in the production. Once again Douglas drew on African American life for his inspiration.

As with his previous productions, Douglas's "Louisiana" also underwent changes in title as well as cast. Also known as "Black Flowers" or "Liza" the production toured Scandinavia, presumably in late 1929 and early 1930. Lotz quotes the memoires of a Douglas contemporary, Tommy Chase, a pianist who performed with his own group in Paris before joining Douglas and "Black Flowers" aka "Louisiana" on the first tour of the Baltic. Chase recalled that the troupe included Eddie Cole, older brother of Nat "King" Cole, and stated that starring in the production along with Douglas was Valaida Snow whom he characterized as "fabulous, a great entertainer who played excellent trumpet, sang contralto and danced marvelously on the stage."[61] Valaida Snow (1900–1956) was another of the superbly talented performers of the early jazz age whose life story and circumstances are both obscure and simultaneously tragic. She lived in Denmark and, according to varying accounts, spent either time in jail for drug possession or was a prisoner in a German concentration camp.

With the celebrity Douglas had gained performing with some of the leading African American and German entertainers of the day, it is not surprising that he should find his way to the film. In Weimar Germany film and radio enjoyed enormous popularity and afforded entertainers access to mass audiences. In just twelve months Douglas appeared in three feature films. His first film "Einbrecher" was a German-French project produced by Ufa, Germany's preeminent film studio and the source of a large number of German popular films in the 1920s and especially in Nazi Germany. A German version of the film premiered on December 16, 1930, in Berlin's Gloria Palast.

One of Germany's earliest speaking films, "Einbrecher" had a cast that included some of Weimar's most luminous star: Lillian Harvey, Willy Fritsch, Heinz Rühmann, and Kurt Gerron. The already famous Friedrich Holländer, who had earlier that year composed the immortal song "Ich bin vom Kopf bis Fuß auf Liebe eingestellt" for Marlene Dietrich in the "Blue Angel," had composed the film music and Sidney Bechet with his band performed in a scene located in a Parisian bar with a dance number by Douglas and two women.

This scene was the extent of Douglas's participation in the film. Neither he nor Bechet appear in the film credits. The plot line is predictable. A doll manufacturer (Ralph Arthur Roberts) neglects his young wife (Lillian Harvey) who begins to consider the advances of a lightweight lothario played by Heinz Rühmann. Their illicit rendezvous is, however, interrupted by a charming burglar (Willy Fritsch) who casts a spell on the frustrated wife. The alleged burglar then appears at the manufacturer's home and with the help of his accomplice, the butler, sends everyone away so he can arrange a late-night rendezvous with the wife at a black nightclub in Paris (Rue du Blonde 11). The wife arrives and she and her "burglar" are surprised by the husband. Instead of a burglar, the charming stranger turns out to be a dramatist looking for material who has been shadowing the wife for several months. Recognizing the bond between his wife and the dramatist, the husband leaves her to her newfound happiness.

Most interesting in this otherwise routine film is the cabaret scene. The dancers and lookers-on in the cabaret are mixed: interracial couples as well as same-race couples are found throughout the small room. A hint of primitivism is conveyed by two mechanical monkeys on poles that twirl as the small orchestra plays. Louis Douglas and two apparently African American women perform two dance numbers and at the end of the film when the lovers sing a final duet they are accompanied by the all-black jazz band. The film's subtitle is repeated in the last dialogue of the film when the false butler who is also a dramatist gets his notebook back. He had been spying on the members of the manufacturer's household to also find material for a drama. After retrieving the notebook he announces his intention to create "eine musikalische Ehekomödie." The real purpose of the film is to present a somewhat humorous plot supported by music.

A French version of the film entitled "Flagrant dèlit" premiered in March 1931. The cast was obviously changed to adapt to French tastes. Blanche Montel replaced Lillian Harvey; Ralph Arthur Roberts returned as the inattentive doll manufacturer, but his two rivals for his wife's affection were played by Charles Dechamp and Henri Garat. Music was again provided by Friedrich Hollaender but French lyrics were written by Jean Boyer. Sidney Bechet and Louis Douglas also reappear in the French version along with Franz Wachsmann, who for both versions is listed as a "schwarzer Musiker," an interesting designation for a native of Upper Silesia who became famous because of his work on "The Blue Angel" and then in America composed music for classic films such as "The Bride of Frankenstein," "Sunset Boulevard," and "Rear Window" under the name of Franz Waxmann. "Einbrecher" is typical of the light-hearted comedies so popular during the 1930s.

On October 22, 1931, Douglas was featured again as a dancer in the Allianz-Tonfilm production "Der brave Sünder," the directorial debut of well-known actor Fritz Kortner. The film was based on Alfred Polgar's theatrical adapation of Valentin Katajew's novel, starring Weimar favorites Max Pallenberg and Heinz Rühmann. They portray an inept duo, a head cashier and his assistant, who withdraw a large sum of cash for a client and then follow that client to Vienna to give him the money. Once in the metropolis the head cashier falls under the spell of gambling and the charms of a black jazz dancer named Kitty played by Rose Poindexter, the future wife of the African American novelist Ralph Ellison. Like "Einbrecher," "Der brave Sünder" resembles other Weimar productions that construct a conflict only to resolve it deus ex machina to supply the happy end that Depression-era audiences seemed to desire. A more significant production is the third film, which featured Douglas in the span of one year: the antiwar film "Niemandsland" that premiered in Berlin on December 10, 1931.

Russian émigré filmmaker Victor Trivas (1896–1970) was not only the director of "Niemandsland" but also wrote the scenario based on an idea by prominent pacifist Leonhard Frank. Hanns Eisler (1898–1962), collaborator with Bertolt Brecht and one of the leading advocates of "political" music, composed the music for the film whose international cast included actor/singer Ernst Busch, Hugh Stephen Douglas, and Russian émigré Vladimir Sokoloff. The international character of the film is especially evident in the sound track. Although a German production, French, English, and Yiddish were also spoken.

Louis Douglas's character had a central role. Five combatants, a Russian Jew, a German, an Englishman, a Frenchman, and a soldier from the French colonial army (Douglas) who had worked as an entertainer are trapped in no-man's land during World War I. Of the five only the black performer had the linguistic proficiency to interpret for the others—in his travels Louis Douglas had probably gained some proficiency in Russian, French, and German. The linguistic differences are mediated in order to demonstrate the absurdity and essential inhumanity of war.

By contrasting the idyllic scenes of their prewar lives with the chaos and destruction of the front, the personae in "Niemandsland" symbolically reject war and clear the way for peace by removing the encircling barbed-wire barriers. This pacifist message made the film controversial especially since it appeared just one year after the ultimate antiwar film "All Quiet on the Western Front" had angered nationalists in Germany and France. In the politically charged atmosphere of the Depression and amidst the rising tide of nationalism that was carrying the Right to power in Germany, the film was certain to elicit passionate responses.

At the Westdeutsche Kurzfilmtage held in Oberhausen from February 3–8, 1964, the film historian Enno Patalas cited a review of "Niemandsland" from the pen of no less a film critic than Siegfried Kracauer, who admired the artistic qualities of the film but deplored the naiveté of its political message. Most devastating was his judgment that the "German militarists did not have to fear the German pacifists."[62] The idea that good will and friendship could be a panacea for war was utopian at best. After Hitler became Reichskanzler the film was banned on April 22.

"Niemandsland" was released in the United States in early 1934 as "Hell on Earth" and a *New York Times* review of January 29, 1934, lauded the film and referred to the positive response it had received in several European countries as well as Germany before Hitler. Of the actors he stated: "Where the players are so good it seems almost out of place to select any particular one for especial mention, but, perhaps due to his role as the Negro international music hall artist who functions as interpreter for the German, Frenchman, and Englishman, the work of Louis Douglas is outstanding."[63] Once again Douglas received praise, this time for his acting skills.

"Niemandsland" marked the end of Douglas's involvement with German popular entertainment. As Lotz notes, between 1932 and 1938, he was based in Paris but complete details about his activities in those years are not yet available. Douglas may have spent some time in the United States. Tours of Italy and performances in Paris can be documented by Lotz in 1933, 1934, 1936, and 1937. In 1937 while in Italy his wife became ill and the Italian authorities stopped his tour. Stranded in Naples, deep in debt, and ill himself Douglas turned to his father-in-law for assistance. Cook wrote a letter to Alain Leroy Locke asking him to intercede with the U.S. Government to repatriate Douglas. Back in the United States in 1937 Douglas appeared at Harlem's Apollo Theater in the Razaf-Blake "Tan Manhattan" show and "Tan Town Topics" with the band of James P. Johnson.[64]

On December 29, 1938, a show titled "Policy Kings" opened. The music was created by James P. Johnson with lyrics by Douglas, who also directed the production. This was Douglas's last creative effort. On May 19, 1939, just five days after his fiftieth birthday, he died in New York. In assessing his impact on Weimar popular culture and, indirectly, the impact of the Harlem Renaissance on Weimar Germany, it is useful to revisit Peter Jelavich's analysis of Berlin popular culture of the 1920s.

In examining the phenomenon of Americanization Jelavich indirectly addresses the category of race. In Imperial Germany, popular composer Paul Lincke wrote an American cakewalk with what Jelavich terms the "unfortunate title" of "Coon's Birthday" (1903); but as Jelavich points out, "Niggersongs" were performed at the Hungry Pegasus in 1901.[65]

By way of explanation and, perhaps, apology, Jelavich continued:

Since the turn of the century, it had been common for Germans to refer to American blacks as "coons" and "niggers." Even the Dadaist verse of George Grosz and Walter Mehring was replete with those words, albeit apparently without any ill intent, since the terms were used in contexts that approved of blacks and their culture. Not only were seemingly well-meaning Germans insensitive to the denigration and abuse embedded in those words, they also failed to note the more fundamental problems in their disquisitions on the "Africanness" of American blacks. Many liberal German observers attributed a primitive spontaneity to blacks, whose blood supposedly boiled from the heat of the ancestral jungle.[66]

Jelavich's explanation is rather superficial. Well-intentioned epithets are still epithets and their use by "German liberals" exposes the ambiguity that is frequently found in contacts between black and white. Even alleged friends of blacks have not been completely free of racism. Latent racism can manifest itself in paternalism or a fascination for the black body as an exotic, that is, sexualized object.

Jelavich utilizes another strategy frequently used to rationalize the impact of racism: blaming the victim. As he points out black performers were also complicit: "'The Chocolate Kiddies' and the Baker-Douglas revue were commercial enterprises that toured Europe and presented clichés about America in general and American blacks in particular" (Jelavich 1993, 172).[67] Douglas, of course, appeared frequently in black face. Jelavich's assertion is not a new one. Similar charges have also been leveled against actors such as Lincoln Theodore Monroe Andrew Perry (Stepin Fetchit), Hattie McDaniels, or Butterfly McQueen for perpetuating racial stereotypes. Such accusations ignore the economics of the pre–civil rights era. Directors and most audiences were interested in seeing Africans or African Americans only in certain roles. Failure to satisfy expectations translated simply into unemployment. The independent films of pioneers such as Oscar Micheaux (1884–1951) are, of course, an exception but were certainly situated outside of the economic mainstream.

An interview with Douglas published in Dresden in 1928 indicates that he had reflected on the issue. He asserted:

> Negroes have always been associated with music hall entertainment, they have always been singers and jugglers, they were always a drawing card in our profession, but it appears that the Whites' desire to see the Negro as an artist has now changed . . . perhaps a desire to learn more about the Negro race through his art which is his gift of nature. The Race is no longer shown enmity but has achieved recognition in all areas, science, literature, medicine, painting, sculpture, technology.[68]

Here Douglas references not only the Harlem Renaissance and the higher profile achieved by African American intellectuals after 1919 but he is only indirectly defending his own art. During the majority of his career Douglas had used the African American experience as material for his productions. Lotz adds an interesting perspective by noting that Douglas had encountered discrimination during a visit to New York City, presumably in the early 1930s, and stated in a newspaper interview published in Brussels: "We should not exchange our former enslavement for a new form of semi- enslavement. Since we do have the intellectual and moral values of any American we should also enjoy the same advantages" (Lotz 1997, 376).[69] The militancy manifest in this statement puts Douglas's career as pickaninny and then black-faced performer in a new perspective. He obviously did not believe that his performances were demeaning or portrayed blacks in a negative light. Houston Baker's dichotomy of mastery of form and deformation of mastery is a useful tool for assessing both Douglas's perception of his art as well as his impact in Weimar Germany.

We have seen how Douglas repeatedly demonstrated his mastery of form and also his virtuosity in assuming the mask of blackness to present white audiences the stereotypes which they associated with people of color. The reactions to his performances exposed the racialistic and racist constructs that informed even those critics who commented favorably. Douglas's rationale for his presentations is not entirely clear. Baker posits an emancipatory intent for both of his rhetorical strategies and without more statements from Douglas himself it is not possible to say with absolute certainty that his mastery of form was intended for personal or group aims.

Douglas's role in "Niemandsland" certainly points in a new direction. The music hall performer cum soldier is clearly Douglas's alter ego if not his doppelgänger. Black cabaret performers were generally expected to represent blackness in their performances, as Douglas did with great success. That blackness elicited extremes of either a desire to shed the bonds of civilization and revel in sensual abandon or disgust at the primitive, oversexed individuals who posed an existential danger to Western (white) civilization. In general audiences expected only entertainment or a mild titillation from performances that presented the highs and lows of black life.

The black soldier in "Niemandsland" assumed a different role vis-à-vis white society. Here the black mask serves as an agent of conciliation between nations in a war that would undermine the colonial empires and nourish fears spread by Oswald Spengler and Lothrop Stoddard that the darker races were in ascendancy and posed a threat not just to Western hegemony but to civilization itself. Douglas's role represents an attempt at a deformation of mastery in that his character seems to call for a reevaluation of the role of race in modern society. Unfortunately, life did not imitate art. Weimar Germany was receptive to the "Harlemania," or to use Othmar Starke's term "Negrodom" that Louis Douglas masterfully represented but as the reviews document, even progressive critics of the Weimar cultural establishment were already thinking in biological categories that would acquire the force of law under the Nazis.

Notes

1. Rainer E. Lotz, *Black People: Entertainers of African Descent in Europe and Germany* (Birgit Lotz Verlag: Bonn, 1977), 3. Lotz mentions the series "Der künstlerische Tanz" in which Douglas was depicted on card #241. Josephine Baker was featured on numbers #242 and #243; Douglas was also featured on the Orami Serie F (1933) and his image was done by Photo-Jacobi, Berlin.

2. Houston A. Baker Jr., *Modernism and the Harlem Renaissance* (Chicago: University of Chicago Press, 1987).

3. Ibid., 37.

4. Ibid., 58.

5. Ibid., 56.

6. Ibid.

7. Ibid., 51.

8. Ibid., 57.

9. In his introduction Spencer establishes a link between W. E. B. Du Bois's *Souls of Black Folk*, James W. Johnson's *The Autobiography of an Ex-Colored Man* (1912), Alain Locke's *The New Negro* (1925) and *The Negro and His Music* (1936); he also points out that composers such as R. Nathaniel Dett and William Grant Still, as well as performers including Roland Hayes, Paul Robeson, Marian Anderson, and Jules Bledsoe all had careers that challenge the restriction of the Harlem Renaissance to the 1920s.

10. Lotz, *Black People.*

11. Eileen Southern, *The Music of Black Americans: A History*, 3rd ed. (New York: W. W. Norton, 1997), 120f.

12. Ibid., 227.

13. Ibid., 229.

14. Ibid., 231.

15. Lotz, *Black People*, 298.

16. Ibid., 299.

17. Ibid.

18. Ibid., 297–99.

19. Ibid., 386. Lotz acknowledges his debt to Eileen Southern, who introduced him to Marantha Quick, aka Marion Douglas.

20. Ibid., 300f.

21. Ibid., 301f.

22. Ibid., 307.

23. Southern, *The Music of Black Americans*, 272.

24. Ibid.

25. Ibid.

26. Ibid., 418. The Johnson brothers were, of course, the creative geniuses behind not just music hall music but also composed "Lift Every Voice and Sing!"

27. Ibid., 304. The American Colonization Society officially began operations in 1817 and sought through repatriation of enslaved and free Africans to "solve" the race problem in the United States. Their efforts met with great opposition in the free African community and subsequently inspired the creation of radical abolitionism under the leadership of William Lloyd Garrison.

28. Lotz, *Black People*, 309.

29. Ibid.

30. Ibid. James Bland (1854–1911) was the composer of over 700 songs and toured in a minstrel act throughout the United States and Europe extensively.

31. J. A. Rogers, "Jazz at Home," in *The New Negro*, ed. Alain Locke with an intro. by Arnold Rampersad (New York: Atheneum, 1992), 261f.

32. Ibid., 217.

33. Ibid., 221.

34. Ibid.

35. Ibid., 313f. Although not mentioned by Lotz, Mercer Cook, who performed with Douglas, was the son of Will Marion Cook and later became an eminent scholar specializing in French Language and Literature at Howard University.

36. Cf. Barry Kernfeld, ed., *The New Grove Dictionary of Jazz*, 2nd ed. (New York: Grove, 2002), in which two different dates for his birth are given, 1880 or 1889.

37. James Weldon Johnson, *Black Manhattan* (1930, repr.; New York: Arno Press and The New York Times, 1968), 115.

38. Southern, *The Music of Black Americans*, 437f.

39. Lotz, *Black People*, 318.

40. Ibid.

41. Ibid.

42. Jan Nederveen Pieterse, *White on Black: Images of Africa and Blacks in Western Popular Culture* (New Haven, CT: Yale University Press, 1992), 94.

43. Lotz, *Black People*, 315.

44. Iwan Goll, "Die Neger erobern Europa," in *The Weimar Republic Sourcebook*, ed. Anton Kaes, Martin Jay, and Edward Dimendberg (Berkeley and Los Angeles: University of California Press, 1994), 559.

45. Ibid.

46. Ibid., 560.

47. Christine Naumann, "African-American Performers and Culture in Weimar Germany," in *Crosscurrents: African Americans, Africa, and Germany in the Modern World*, ed. David McBride, Leroy Hopkins, and Carol Aisha-Blackshire Belay (Camden House, 1998), 96–112.

48. Ibid., 98.

49. Ibid., 98f.

50. Peter Jelavich, *Berlin Cabaret* (Cambridge, MA: Harvard University Press, 1993), 169.

51. Lotz, *Black People*, 321.

52. Ibid.

53. Ibid., 322.

54. Ibid., 332.

55. Ibid.

56. Ibid., 335.

57. Ibid., 333.

58. Ibid., 340.

59. Ibid.

60. Ibid., 341–47.

61. Ibid., 347.

62. Enno Patalas, Introduction to "Niemandsland" given on February 7, 1964, in Oberhausen. Text sent to me by the Deutsches Filmmuseum, Frankfurt/M.

63. Harry T. Smith, "An Anti-War Film," *New York Times*, January 29, 1934, 10:2.

64. Ibid., 381.

65. Jelavich, *Berlin Cabaret*.

66. Ibid., 170f.

67. Ibid., 172.

68. Lotz, *Black People*, 375f.

69. Ibid., 376.

Race in the Reich

The African American Press on Nazi Germany

LARRY A. GREENE

American entry into World War II heightened the already existing contradictions between America's democratic rhetoric and the reality of America's segregated society. It was that contradiction that initiated the modern African American civil rights movement led by an African American press, fully aware that these contradictions and the outbreak of World War II provided another opportunity in less than a quarter of a century to more forcefully continue the struggle for civil rights. An essential in that struggle involved drawing the parallel between Nazi Germany and the American South as two ideologically similar societies incompatible with America's values.

A sense of déjà vu permeated the early World War II writings of African American publishers and editors like Percival L. Prattis of the *Pittsburgh Courier*, John Sengstacke of the *Chicago Defender*, Fred Moore of the *New York Age*, and the editorial staffs of the *New York Amsterdam News* and the NAACP's *Crisis* magazine. Monroe Trotter in 1914, editor of the *Boston Guardian*, and a more diplomatic James Weldon Johnson of the NAACP and *New York Age* in 1918, had raised the question that if America was going to "make the world safe for democracy" by sending Americans abroad to die in European wars they should start at home. In both wars, the issues remained the same: antiblack pogroms and lynching in the South; political disfranchisement; de jure segregation in both civilian and military life; widespread violence against black soldiers in southern basic training camps; and pervasive employment discrimination.[1]

Despite the lack of change and unfortunate continuity with America's past, there was something more embittering about America's latest contradiction. America, even more than in World War I, emphasized the racism of their German opponents and their own commitment to democratic values. The *Pittsburgh Courier* in World War II more aggressively called for a victory over fascism abroad and racism at home, the "Double V" campaign was born in February 1942. In the black press, fascism was most clearly represented by Nazi Germany than any of the other Axis powers. Across the nation, black newspaper editors would pick up the phrase and the federal government would consider censoring and shutting down the African American press. African American admiration for Japan, the modern world's first nonwhite superpower and defender of oppressed darker-skin people, which appeared in the black press following the Russo-Japanese War of 1905 and in especially in the 1930s, became more subdued after Pearl Harbor. Germany will replace Japan as center of attention. Central to the Double V campaign was an emphasis on the similarity between the racial states of Germany under the Third Reich and that of the American South whose racial policies were permitted by the federal government. This ideological congruence between the racial states of Germany and the American South sparked the "Nazi–Jim Crow" analogy.

During World War I, the African American press made some sporadic attempts to turn the Wilsonian points of Germany's antidemocratic nature to their advantage in the struggle to influence black and white public opinion even if Wilson's views were inconsistent, naïve, and sometimes hypocritical. James Weldon Johnson, eventually to be the first black executive director of the NAACP, in his *New York Age* column, predicted that many of these atrocity stories would be proven false. Nevertheless, the black press would continue to make analogies between the atrocities in Europe and the 126 blacks lynched between 1914 and 1916 in ten southern states. As the *Chicago Defender* noted those killed in Europe were killed in wars involving national survival, blacks in the South are killed for "stealing a pig, for swearing in public or wanting to vote." James Weldon Johnson even compared antiblack violence to the Turkish treatment of the Armenians. Yet only a few blacks, like A. Philip Randolph and Chandler Owen, of the black socialist publication, the *Messenger*, took a militantly oppositional stance to black involvement in the Great War. The rhetoric of Du Bois in his famous "Close Ranks" editorial in the July 1918 issue of *The Crisis* reflected the more cautious and deferred quest for equal rights. However, the justification for the deferral by Du Bois was more suited for World War II rather than World War I: "That which the German power represents today spells death to the aspirations of Negroes and all darker races for equality, freedom and democracy . . . forget our special grievances and close our ranks shoulder to shoulder with our white fellow citizens and the allied nations that are fighting for democracy."[2] The reality is that all the nations fighting, including the United States, were indeed colonial powers at that time and not interested in extending "self-determination" to their colonized subject peoples.

The imperialistic and racist nature of fascism was clearly manifested in Germany's transformation by National Socialism, Japan's schizophrenic imperialist adventures and simultaneous self-proclamations as the anticolonial liberator of Asia from Euro-American hegemony, and Italy's invasion of Ethiopia in the mid-1930s. A confluence of domestic and international factors led to a new militancy among African Americans and the use of the Aryan supremacy component of German fascism to illustrate the analogy between Nazi anti-Semitism and American "Jim Crow." Japan, although engaged in its own imperialism in Asia, did not work as well as Nazi Germany as a mirror image of the American South which the African American press could hold up to white America. Pearl Harbor made the 1930s black press positive portrayals of Japan as an anticolonial liberator and

Fig. 1. "Twilight of the Gods," *The Crisis* (43), September 1936. Reprinted by permission of *The Crisis*.

the modern world's first major nonwhite superpower impracticable as a tactic for advancing civil rights in America and possibly exposing them to sedition charges.

During World War II, the African American press paid far greater attention to the racist nature of the Third Reich than they ever had in the 1930s and far more print space to the discriminatory treatment of black servicemen in southern basic training camps. Germany equaled and in many newspapers surpassed Japan as a focus of attention. The arrest of members of a small number of pro-Japanese organizations in 1942 and early 1943 further demonstrated the impracticality of using the Japanese model to attack American Jim Crow. The American government's refusal to aid Ethiopia against aggression by Italian fascists clearly demonstrated the racial bias of America's foreign policy. The black press, most notably the *Pittsburgh Courier*, continually characterized Hermann Goering and Governor Eugene Talmadge of Georgia as two racists cut from the same cloth as were Mississippi's racist U.S. senator, Theodore G. Bilbo, and Germany's Joseph Goebbels. The frustration level of African Americans had also increased as a result of the staggering economic deprivation of the Great Depression with American blacks experiencing unemployment rates as highs as 50 percent to 60 percent and the continuation of America's violent apartheid system. The black press found especially galling the continued refusal of the federal government to intervene in the South, which allowed the continuation of a "racial state" covering nearly a third of the United States. The Great Depression had unleashed many mass protests in the forms of public parades, local boycotts of businesses, and municipal governments engaged in employment discrimination in northern cities. A threatened march on the nation's capital in the summer of 1941 by tens of thousands of disgruntled blacks under the leadership of A. Philip Randolph's March on Washington Movement (MOWM) worried President Franklin Roosevelt. Antifascist, left organizations such as the Communist Party stepped up their recruitment of black intellectuals and workers with the call for aggressive mass action.[3] As the flames of war engulfed Asia and Europe in the late 1930s, African Americans prepared to go on the offensive to illustrate the hypocrisy of America's democracy and its need for reform.

Before America's entry into World War II, the black press proclaimed fascism a threat to the already precarious position of African Americans. David Pierce in a 1935 issue of *The Crisis* raised the question: "If a decaying capitalism sees fit to inaugurate a Fascist dictatorship in the United States, what will be the status of the Negro?" Pierce believed that if fascism took root in the United States it would be extremely brutal because it would face stiff opposition and would therefore "seek at once to divide the potential opposition. The dying middle class will be filled with the poison of race hatred . . . The fiction of Negro inferiority will be elevated to the status of a proved psychological and sociological law." A 1936 editorial in *The Crisis* asserted that black Americans were becoming more aware of the danger of fascism and compared Hitler's snub of Jesse Owens and the black athletes at the Berlin Olympics to the mindset of Mississippi. The editorial noted that Jesse Owens went with his track team to Los Angeles and was refused a room there. The NAACP's *Crisis* magazine carried a cartoon, "Twilight of the Gods," celebrating the victories of black track athletes at the Berlin Olympics and mocking the ideology of Aryan racial supremacy (Fig. 1). A Teutonic figure in a Wagnerian helmet with a swastika on his behind carried a sign, "We Aryans can lick anybody," is clearly left far behind in the race by a black sprinter. *The Crisis* in 1937 strongly noted the terrible similarity between the South's campaign to sterilize the infirm, the poor, and African Americans with the Nazi campaign of sterilization. Former Arkansas governor J. M. Futrell proposed sterilization of black and white tenants and sharecroppers was clearly used to depict the similarity between Jim Crow and Nazi ideologies. The author Elaine Ellis claimed the German Act on sterilization which became effective on January 1, 1934, influenced America and other countries.[4]

The similarity of American and Nazi sterilization policies were forcefully made in a July 1937 address by Langston Hughes before the Second International Writers Congress held in Paris. Hughes vigorously condemned the march of fascism in the world, the "sterilization of the Negro children of Cologne," and the "tyranny over the Jews." He also condemned Mussolini's "expedition of slaughter in Ethiopia" as well as the "Military Party in Japan" and their mistreatment of Koreans and Chinese. Hughes asserted that African Americans knew Fascism from experience: "We are the people who have long known in actual practice the meaning of the word Fascism—for the American attitude towards us has been one of economic and social discrimination; in many states of our country we are not permitted to vote or hold political office." Hughes spoke passionately about

America's segregationist laws in referring to the Nazi Nuremberg Laws: "All over America we know what it is to be refused admittance to schools and colleges, to theatres and concert halls, to hotels and restaurants." Hughes continued the Nazi–Jim Crow comparison throughout World War II in a series of columns for the *Chicago Defender.* Common comparisons were plentiful between Nazi racial laws and American "Jim Crow" statutes baring non-Aryans and blacks from politics, universities, professions, and intermarrying as in an article entitled "Nazi Plan for Negroes Copies Southern U.S.A." These comparisons between the Third Reich and Dixie proved too much to bear for some southern journalists as it did for the *Times-Dispatch* of Richmond, Virginia, which called such comparisons "'absurd.'"[5] The *New York Amsterdam News* raised the key question for those denying the comparison between Hitler's Reich and the Jim Crow South: "Now, what's the difference between Hitler and Talmadge?" The article noted that they both held racial superiority doctrines, considered blacks to be inferior, felt the so-called inferior races had to be separated from the superior races, and subscribed wholeheartedly to the maintenance of race purity. In two unflattering photos of Governor Talmadge and Adolf Hitler, the newspaper perceived the Talmadges to be the main beneficiary in America of Hitler's *Herrenvolk* ideology.[6]

Well-known black and liberal white personalities, who perceived the need for national unity with war on the horizon and the divisive persistence of American racism, began to publicly declare the immediacy of ending racism at "home" in order to combat fascist racism abroad. Mary McLeod Bethune, confidante of Eleanor Roosevelt and New Deal appointee to the National Youth Administration, told four hundred African American leaders in Washington, D.C., that Hitler and Hitlerism are threats to black hopes for a racially egalitarian America and "this is no time for quibbling or wavering. For the Negro it must be all out or it's all over." Bethune noted whatever progress blacks have made in America "such progress could not have been made under a Hitler regime." Civil rights activist and educator Mary McLeod Bethune reiterated this point in speeches in New York City and other cities. The popular *Pittsburgh Courier* columnist J. A. Rogers echoed the sentiments of Mrs. Bethune, observing that "Hitlerism . . . is a pernicious disease, which has been fostered and cultivated by the very nations that are now trying to get rid of it."[7] Internationally known and award-winning author Pearl Buck, in a letter to the *New York Times* and reprinted in the *Pittsburgh Courier* with banner headlines reading "Pearl Buck Denounces 'American' Brand of Democracy," made many of the points asserted by Bethune, Rogers, and other black newspaper columnists. In Pearl Buck's comparison of the Nazi racial state with that of the Old South, she noted Germany was less hypocritical about it while the Allies simultaneously retained their colonial empires while claiming to fight for "Democracy." She called upon the nation to live up to the egalitarian, but unapplied principles of the Constitution. Pearl Buck exclaimed: "With all the evils that Hitlerism has, at least it has one virtue, that it makes no pretense of loving its fellowman and of wanting all people to be free and equal." Ultimately, she perceived the fear of the loss of race purity and miscegenation behind race prejudice. She asked the question of white America; how long would they continue

DARK LAUGHTER · · · · · By OL' HARRINGTON

SAL DI TABACHI

"Whenever I go out with brown Americanos there are so many meelitary poleece. Thees ees a great complimento to the brown Americanos, yes?"

Fig. 2. "Dark Laughter," *Pittsburgh Courier*, May 19, 1945. Courtesy *New Pittsburgh Courier*.

to accept the "stupidities of race prejudice" and warned of an impending revolt against racism: "I know the oft-repeated wearisome defense. Intermarriage is the fearful specter behind everything. On that there is but one answer. Are we to deny to 12,000,000 Americans the rights and privileges of our country, and are we to risk our very democracy itself, by maintaining a determined ruler-subject relationship between white and colored, because some day a few white and colored individuals may choose to marry each other?"[8] Pearl Buck understood that a cornerstone of the Third Reich and the American South was racial supremacy and race purity.

The American preoccupation with racial purity and miscegenation phobias was mocked by well-known African American cartoonist and writer Ol' (Oliver) Harrington in his "Dark Laughter" series for the *Pittsburgh Courier* (Fig. 2). In a May 19, 1945, cartoon a Caucasian woman sitting at a sidewalk café in Italy with an African American GI comments: "Whenever I go out with brown Americans there are so many meelitary [military] poleece [police]. Thees [this] ees [is] a great complimento [compliment] to the brown Americanos [Americans], Yes?" Harrington's sense of irony is apparent. With World War II drawing to a close and the Axis powers defeated, America continued to hold onto its own racial purity and white supremacy doctrines. America entered the war with the need to control the behavior and sexuality of black troops in basic training camps, later in overseas theaters of operations, and will exit the war with a significant part of its population believing in the innate superiority and inferiority of races and the need to control black servicemen in postwar Germany and Japan.[9]

On Valentine's Day of 1942, the *Pittsburgh Courier* inaugurated its Double V campaign to great popular support in the black community. The paper over the next several months in a spirit of patriotism and self-defense against critics pledged along with other African Americans to support "the cause of freedom" as expressed by President Roosevelt and Prime Minister Churchill. Consequently, the paper "adopted the Double 'V' war cry—victory over our enemies at home and victory over our enemies on the battlefields abroad." The *Courier* said they would initiate a "two-pronged attack against our enslavers at home and those abroad who would enslave us. WE HAVE A STAKE IN THIS FIGHT . . . WE ARE AMERICANS, TOO!" Even with the patriotic caveat, the black press soon came under attack for the Double V from white newspapers columnists and the government. Westbrook Pegler, columnist for the *New York World-Telegram* and the Scripps-Howard newspaper chain, charged that black newspapers "'agitate violently . . . particularly in their appeal to colored soldiers whose loyalty is constantly bedeviled with doubts and with raceangling of news.'" Pegler failed to realize that blacks see American apartheid everyday in the South and most northerners have relatives or are themselves from the South. They know of the lynching, segregated underfunded black schools, and political disfranchisement.[10] African American newspapers did not create the discontent, but reflected it.

The black press noted these attempts at intimidation and repression and carried stories on them. The publisher of the black *California Eagle* newspaper, Charlotte A. Bass, stated that FBI agents visited her office and interrogated her about the possible reception of German or Japanese funds because her paper condemned color discrimination and segregation in institutions, agencies, or companies related to national defense. The *Courier* suggested that a better way to promote patriotism and national unity instead of trying to intimidate the black editors into silence: "we suggest that the FBI investigate those forces and institutions within America that are fostering and spreading fascism and disunity by treating Negroes as second-class citizens." The *Amsterdam News* considered Westbrook Pegler one who "assumed the role of advance man of an evidently near-at-hand program to deny the freedom of the press to Negro newspapers."[11] African Americans were not intimidated and turned out to show their support for the Double V campaign and civil rights at a massive rally in June 1942 at Madison Square Garden attended by twenty thousand people to bury "Uncle Tom."[12]

Although the U.S. Government and some elements of the white press may have perceived a contradiction between patriotic support of the war and aggressive advocacy for civil rights which pointed out the similarities between Nazi ideology and the South's Jim Crow philosophy, the vast majority of African Americans saw no contradiction and in effect believed it was the duty of the black press to illustrate just such contradictions. African American morale and lukewarm support for the war became a topic at a May 22, 1942, cabinet meeting along with the federal government's Office of Facts and Figures report charging the black press with lowering black morale by emphasizing racial discrimination

Fig. 3. "Arsenal of the Democracies," (New York) *Amsterdam News*, February 7, 1942.

in the armed forces and across the nation. The failure of the government to make a commitment, beyond the FEPC, to end American apartheid cost the government some support for the war effort in the black community. As the *New York Age* observed: "Negroes in America are not one hundred percent sold on the war effort of the nation and will not be until they are given some of their rights of democracy which have been denied them in the past." A meeting of the National Coordinating Committee, representing twenty national African American organizations and institutions, held at the Harlem Branch of the YMCA expressed just those sentiments.[13]

Visual expression is given to African American criticism in the form of cartoons attacking all aspects of American apartheid and illustrating the parallels between Nazism and Jim Crow. In an *Amsterdam News* February 7, 1942, cartoon a black figure chained to a post is being burned alive while Adolf Hitler in a Nazi uniform smiles at a Japanese figure in military uniform (Fig. 3). The caption above the cartoon reads "Arsenal of the Democracies." The white press and politicians often referred to America as the "Arsenal of Democracy." The two Axis figures are obviously taking a great deal of pleasure in observing the hypocrisy of the United States and probably relishing the propaganda value. Ted Carroll, cartoonist for *Amsterdam News*, placed a black soldier on a bench in an obvious pose, identical to Auguste Rodin's sculpture of "The Thinker," pondering the meaning of the war to African Americans (Fig. 4). The caption above the soldier reads, "Is it Worth It?" Under the caption is a "Colored" sign indicating the continuation of legally enshrined racial segregation. In the opposite corner of the

Fig. 4. "God's War," (New York) *Amsterdam News*, July 25, 1942.

cartoon is a battle scene. He is reading a newspaper with a headline: "Lynched," the persistence of "Jim Crow." This July 25, 1942, cartoon leaves little doubt about African American displeasure with the lack of equality and leaves the question open concerning black support for the war.

The African American press for the remainder of the war followed a two-prong strategy comparing treatment of blacks in the American South with Nazi Germany's treatment of Jews and quoting from official Nazi sources on the degraded nature of America's black population. P. L. Prattis quoted extensively from Hitler's *Mein Kampf* in his *Pittsburgh Courier* column with emphasis on the part attributing the rise of the first forms of civilization to "'where the Aryan came in contact with the inferior races, subjugated them and forced them to obey his command.'" Prattis quoted from *Das Schwarse [Schwarze] Korps* of November 21, 1940, which proclaimed that after the war when Germany needs foreign labor all the skilled jobs should be reserved for Germans while the Poles are given the unskilled manual labor jobs. Prattis cited other examples of similarities between Nazi law and Jim Crow ideology such as requiring Poles to give way to Germans on the sidewalks and in shops and markets: "'representatives of the German Forces and members of their families, as well as German nationals, must be served first.'" To African American readers, these racist practices were all too familiar and resembled the caste etiquette of the South. Prattis speculates on the fate of the blacks under Nazi hegemony for his African American readership, whom he asserts Hitler compared to apes: "I tremble to think of what would happen

to Adam Powell Jr., if this scourge reached Harlem." Would it be the extermina-
tionist fate of the Jews? Prattis points out to the newspaper's white readers and
monitors that America's "feeling of racial superiority won't help us to whip either
the Germans or the Japanese," but only contribute to the disunity that can lead
to defeat.[14] Clearly the impact of these columns was to increase black animosity
toward the Third Reich and increase black discontent with the American racial
status quo. The parallels drawn with American race relations convinced some
government officials of the need for censorship and the view that the black press
promoted disunity and lacked patriotism.

The *New York Age* also ran a number of stories describing the antiblack component of Nazi ideology. The *Age* noted that the anti-Semitic Nazi newspaper
Der Stürmer had in recent issues turned its attention to African Americans in a
most negative way: "For the last few weeks the Sturmer [Stürmer] has maintained
that the misfortunes befalling the Aryan nations were not caused by Jews alone:
both Jews and Negroes are guilty." The *Age* quoted Julius Streicher, editor of *Der
Stürmer* and friend of Hitler, in a speech to Nazi party friends in Nuremberg:
"'The emancipation of the Jews and the liberation of the black slaves are the two
crimes of civilization committed by the plutocrats in the last few centuries.'" The
Age proceeded to list six commands given by the General Staff governing blacks
within the German colonial empire that resembled in many respects southern
Jim Crow laws. This *Age* article is one of the few to discuss German colonial policies observing that colonial subjects have "no active or passive electoral rights in
the German colonial empire" and that interracial marriages between blacks and
whites and interracial sexual intercourse are prohibited by the Third Reich with
sanctions including the death penalty. Indeed "race intermixture with Negroes
was one of the chief factors in the French defeat" according to the courses for
German officers stationed in colonial territories organized by the General Staff.
The article made a rhetorical prediction, now more commonplace in the African
American press: "It is easy to imagine the fate of the colored people in a German
colonial empire, if the General Staff of the German army is already disseminating
these six commandments."[15]

African Americans perceived their own precarious position in the United
States as under siege not only from domestic racists, but also from their perceptions of collusion between domestic and foreign enemies of America. The
New York Age contended: "The majority of Negro people in America understand
that a victory for Hitler and his Axis partners in slavery, Japan and Italy, could
mean the complete extermination of Negroes as a people in the United States."
In this story, the *Age* asserted that Hitler's agents in America have used the Ku
Klux Klan, the Black Legion, and other pro fascist groups "to weaken our country from within by developing the myth of racial superiority." The *New York Age*
columnist George Murphy Jr. claimed American racists like the Lindberghs and
Talmadges obtained their racial instructions from the *Magazine Digest*, which
published an article entitled, "How to Wipe Out the American Negroes" by Heinrich Krieger in May 1936. The article represented a condensed version of the
original article taken from the German publication *Die Tat* published in Jena,

Germany, in February 1936. The article justified lynching and suggested ways to exclude blacks from the political processes that were already in effect. Whether these revelations are accurate remains to be seen, but clearly they were read by blacks and found plausible by many.[16]

Black newspapers carried many stories paralleling the Third Reich's commitment to racial purity and concerns over racial pollution with that of the American South. George Padmore, pan-Africanist and London correspondent for the *Pittsburgh Courier*, in an article entitled "Poison Minds of Hitler's Subjects Against Colored Minority Groups," accused Joseph Goebbels and Nazi racial expert Alfred Rosenberg of inciting Hitler's European victims and the German people against the Senegalese, Moroccan, Indian, Afro-American, and other nonwhite troops participating in the liberation of Europe "by describing them as savages whom the Allies intend using to pollute Nordic blood." Padmore blamed the Nazis for the deterioration of Germany and the rest of Europe by reducing "her to the lowest level of barbarism since the Dark Ages." The reference to blood/racial pollution was certain to have conjured up memories of Edmund Morel's post–World War I newspaper campaign, "Black Horror on the Rhine" and its recycling in the Nazi quest for power in the late 1920s and early 1930s. French Senegalese troops were falsely accused of raping thousands of German women. Padmore noted the irony that these very colored troops whom "Hitler describes as semi-apes have been called upon to help emancipate white folks from the yoke of Teutonic Kultur bearers." Rosenberg, according to Padmore, in an address before the Social Congress of International Union of Fascist Journalists in Vienna denounced FDR and General Eisenhower for allowing African American flyers, the Tuskegee Eagles, to operate "tomahawk bombers." The official organ of the United States Army, *Stars and Stripes*, reiterated quite closely Padmore's analysis which asserts that Nazis maintained that flying is "a privilege of the Nordic superior race."[17] *Das Schwarze Korps*, the weekly newspaper of the SS, invariably depicted allied flyers as black in cartoons despite the very small percentage of allied flyers who were black. Padmore did not note, nor did *Stars and Stripes*, the great difficulty black civil rights groups and white liberals like Eleanor Roosevelt had in obtaining admission of African Americans to the United States Army Air Force.

The similarities between National Socialist ideology and American racialist doctrine were personally observed by Ollie Harrington, a war correspondent for the *Pittsburgh Courier* in war-torn Italy. Harrington, like Padmore, describes the demonization of Allied "colored troops" as savages to bolster resistance against and prevent cooperation with allied military operations. Harrington described the collaboration between fascist propagandists and racist elements within the American military in Italy in the distribution of a leaflet throughout Italian towns occupied by Allied soldiers. The leaflet was allegedly the work of the Italian and American Committee for the Preservation of the Italian Race to prevent racial mongrelization in Italy. Strong condemnation was directed at elements in Naples who fraternized with African Americans, walked with them in the streets and invited them to their homes. The leaflet's authors assumed American miscegenationist phobias also characterized Italians: "'When will your honor, your pride in being Italian and white incite you to scorn justly the Negro.'" The leaflet proclaimed the inferiority of all blacks and foretold the coming day in Italy for "'vindicating this depravity. Then the machine gun will cut down the prostitute who sells the honor of her race and the people will seek revenge upon her and the black son whom this crime has brought forth to light.'" Harrington claims Italians from Sicily to Naples had received African American troops as just another group of Americans prior to this racist leaflet campaign. He notes fascist radio in Berlin and Rome concentrated on portraying blacks as "'bestial and rapacious.'" For the *Courier's* readership, the incident reinforced the necessity of the Double V campaign to combat not only foreign racism, but the globalization of American's home-grown racism.[18]

The southern obsession with miscegenation and interracial relationships were not only exemplified by the export of racism to Europe, but also by southern politicians on the home front recognizing that the Double V campaign was in effect the beginning of a national civil rights campaign aimed at overthrowing American apartheid. In language reminiscent of the 1960s, Governors Frank Dixon of Alabama and Eugene Talmadge of Georgia united in issuing statements that outside agitators were attempting to break down the principle of race segregation. Governor Dixon accused two federal agencies of adopting policies that would destroy segregation. Governor Talmadge warned all blacks not liking Georgia's racial segregation laws to stay out of the state. The southern political establishment and African American leadership were aware, more so than the general white public, that "Jim Crow" was coming under an assault greater than any since Reconstruction. The resort to playing upon America's centuries old interracial sexual phobias of black masculinity was an important part of countering that campaign.[19]

Mississippi United States senator James Eastland verbally attacked African American troops as an "'utter and abysmal failure'" that "'would neither work nor fight'" but would attack the families of French farmers. According to the *Pittsburgh Courier* Eastland not satisfied with demeaning African Americans claimed that black French troops raped five thousand German girls herded into a subway in Stuttgart, Germany. Eastland's notorious accusation coincides with efforts by southern Democrats to block any civil rights legislation emanating from the United States Congress which might change the *Herrenvolk* character of the South. Mississippi senators James Eastland and Theodore G. Bilbo engaged in a filibuster against the Fair Employment Practices Committee (FEPC) renewal bill. Establishment of the FEPC as a permanent federal agency, not simply a temporary wartime measure, could have weakened the economic pillar of white supremacy in both the North and the South. The FEPC was the first instance of federal government intervention to block employment discrimination in the private sector. A wartime measure created in response to the threatened "March On Washington Movement" in 1941, the FEPC was terminated at the end of the war despite efforts by civil rights organizations to make it permanent. Nearly twenty years would pass before the federal government would take a meaningful stand against employment discrimination with the passage of the 1964 Civil Rights Act. For the defenders of American apartheid, the images of blacks as militarily incompetent, lazy, and sexual predators were essential to the defense of the "racial state" in the American South. African Americans were not worthy of inclusion in the body politic, the secular covenanted community. Eastland and Bilbo did not derail the Double V campaign, but only intensified it. As African American columnists constantly illustrated, the southern defense of the racial status quo provided "the German and Japanese propagandists plenty of material which they have been quick to exploit."[20]

Despite the refusal of the federal government to take any action against segregation or political disfranchisement, the black press constantly ran stories on the mistreatment of African American servicemen whom they claimed were treated worse than German prisoners of war. In one of numerous examples of southern racialism encapsulating the Nazi–Jim Crow analogy that filled African American newspapers, nine sick black veterans were refused service in the local railroad station's dining room and looked on as twenty-four German prisoners of war came into the same lunchroom accompanied by two guards. The black soldiers were on their way from the hospital at Camp Clairborne, Louisiana, to the hospital at Fort Huachuca. Many articles of a similar nature including those citing attacks by white civilians on black troops in southern army camps were commonplace throughout the black press and served to fuel African American discontent.[21]

Despite the disillusionment of ever-present racism and racial inequalities, African Americans saw victory over the Axis powers, especially Germany, as essential to their racial progress within the United States. Dean William Pickens of North Carolina A and T College, a former NAACP field secretary, believed that African Americans had more at stake than any other racial group for "'the outcome of the war will control his destiny for hundreds of years.'" An Allied victory was mandatory for the expansion of black freedom in the United States. However, Pickens perceived the threat to future African American racial progress to emanate not only from foreign fascists, but also from the extreme racist right wing within the United States. Pickens claimed, "If the Fascist and dictatorial element in America ever gained control of the Government, the Jew would be placed at the bottom, but the Negro would be placed under the bottom." Pickens believed that racist and reactionary forces were so strong in America that they could even reverse the limited post–Civil War gains in civil rights (i.e., Fourteenth and Fifteenth Amendments) and establish an even more rigidly segregated and racially exclusionist society.[22]

Conservatives, fearing the march toward a more racially egalitarian society, and some liberal white Americans, fearing a weakening of unity and morale for the war effort, attacked the Nazi–Jim Crow analogy employed by the black press. Edwin R. Embree, liberal president of the Julius Rosenwald Fund, which contributed significantly to black social and educational causes, denied the comparison between German treatment of the Jews and American treatment of African Americans. While the Rosenwald Fund contributed to black education in the South, it also failed to challenge Jim Crow and black disfranchisement. Not surprisingly, southern politicians and southerners in the FDR administration sought unsuccessfully to have the black press censored, denied newsprint, denied second-class mailing privileges, or have the editors and publishers indicted for sedition. A story most ably explored in Patrick S. Washburn's excellent book, *A Question of Sedition.*[23]

The *Memphis Commercial Appeal*, one of the South's leading newspapers, in an attempt to distinguish southern "white supremacy" from Nazi Aryan supremacy justified American apartheid as a practice saving government and society from falling into the hands of persons "'who do not have the proper executive, cultural, philosophical, or educational background.'" In other words, Dixie's *Untermenschen* were just not ready for inclusion in the body politic. The *Commercial Appeal* further explained the positive benefits of white supremacy–based American apartheid structure to the maintenance of racial purity: "'It is a safeguard against the intermingling of black and white races. We have only to look at the progress of the Nation compared with Latin American countries where there is much miscegenation to realize the wisdom of this course.'" The Memphis newspaper suggested that Aryan supremacy was directed at the Jewish population that had reached cultural and educational maturity with the larger majority population. The *Commercial Appeal* in a fit of Orwellian "newspeak" and "doublethink" attempted to make a link between Nazi practices with those of northern carpetbaggers "'who instituted black supremacy during Reconstruction days in the South.'" Considering the South's history of grossly unequal expenditures on black and white schooling, exclusion of even educated blacks from voting, massive employment discrimination, antiblack violence, and the promulgation of biological inferiority racial doctrines, it was the height of hypocrisy to suggest that when African Americans reached parity with white Americans then "'white supremacy will evaporate.'"[24] Most southerners never expected the right level to be reached and southern state governments did everything in their power to make that level unattainable.

The outspoken Mississippi senator Theodore Bilbo, fighting in the postwar era to prevent the establishment of a permanent FEPC, to retain the poll tax, and to continue the literacy test, lost control of the perfunctory democratic rhetoric and made it all too clear of the desirability of a new southern idyll of a white, Christian Protestant America ethnically cleansed of blacks and Jews. He warned Jews, if they don't quit fighting for black rights, they might receive an "'invitation'" to resettle in Palestine. In a letter to Leonard E. Golditch, executive secretary of the National Committee to Combat Anti-Semitism, he warned: "'If Jews of your type don't quite fraternizing with the Negro race you are going to arouse so much opposition to all of you that they will get a very strong invitation to pack up and resettle in Palestine, the homeland of the Jews, just as we propose to provide a voluntary resettlement of the American Negro in West Africa, their fatherland.'" Bilbo was condemned by the Italian leftist congressman Vito Marcantonio and Jewish Democratic congressmen Samuel Dickstein and Emmanuel Celler. All were strong supporters of civil rights legislation in the post–World

War II era. Even some southern newspapers condemned Bilbo: the *Richmond Times Dispatch, Chattanooga Times,* and the *Macon News.*[25]

World War II and the holocaust created a more empathetic Jewish image in the United States making overt and blatant hyper-racist rhetoric too crude a violation of America's self-proclaimed democratic ethos, but it did not create a South ready to abandon apartheid. Bilbo's blatant demagogic racism was far more suited for the Reconstruction and late-nineteenth-century eras and not for a world shaken by the atrocities of World War II. As American apartheid came under increasing attack by African American civil rights groups, labor unions, liberals, and leftists, America's segregationists toned-down their racist rhetoric on the national stage, but not their fundamental opposition to racial equality, integration, or the inclusion of African Americans in the body politic. Their public face became one of promulgating segregation as a mutually harmonious system of race relations beneficial to both races and a separate system of mutual development well within the "states rights" tradition. They maintained their opposition to integration was not a sign of hostility to black southerners whom they loved and respected, but only to the communist agitators misleading the colored race and seeking to subvert America. As the flaming embers of World War II cooled, the Cold War began and the "Red" card will be played not only by segregationists, but also by integrationists proclaiming the loss of the "Third World" to communism if America did not end its racial albatross of Jim Crow.[26]

With the collapse of the Third Reich, but even before the final pronouncement of Hitler's death, a new image of Germany begins to emerge in the African American press, as black troops enter Germany in mid-1945 signaling the arrival of the postwar era. For black troops now on European soil, the real enemy is no longer Nazism or Hitlerism, but the American military transporting American racism and Jim Crow policies to Germany and infecting an entire continent.[27] The African American press will run many stories of how well black troops are received by the Europeans, including Germans, and the difficulties they encounter at the hands of white American racism. In William Gardner Smith's *Last of the Conquerors,* the protagonist, a black GI stationed in Germany a year or two after the end of the war talks with a fellow black GI as they prepared to ship back to the states. The black GI referred to as the Professor, because he was a college graduate, stated: "I'll go back, because it's the only place I know. But you know before I came here I just ignored the things that went on there [in the USA] . . . Now it's different. I've gotten away from that stuff and I'll never be able to take it calmly again. . . . I'll never take it the way I use to. It'll burn me up inside and might even fill me with hate. Because I'll always remember the irony of my going away to Germany to find democracy. That's bad."[28]

Notes

1. This essay is based on a paper entitled "The German Image in the African American Press: 1941–1955" that I presented at Sixth Biennial Collegium for African American Research Conference held at the University of Tours, Tours, France on April 22, 2005. The paper was later expanded and entitled "Race in the Reich" and presented at the Crossovers: African Americans and Germany Conference held at the University of Muenster, Muenster, Germany on March 22, 2006; William G. Jordan, *Black Newspapers and America's War for Democracy, 1914–1920* (Chapel Hill: University of North Carolina Press, 2001), 25–32. See, for key works relating to World War II African Americans and the black press: Patrick S. Washburn, *A Question of Sedition: The Federal Government's Investigation of the Black Press During World War II* (New York: Oxford University Press, 1986), 11–40; Brenda Gayle Plummer, *Rising Wind: Black Americans and U.S. Foreign Affairs, 1935–1960* (Chapel Hill: University of North Carolina Press, 1996), 83–124; Barbara Dianne Savage, *Broadcasting Freedom: Radio, War, and the Politics of Race, 1938–1948* (Chapel Hill: University of North Carolina Press, 1999), 63–153; Lee Finkle, "Forum For Protest: The Black Press During World War II" (Ph.D. dissertation, New York University, 1971), 139–78; Theodore Kornweibel Jr., *"Seeing Red": Federal Campaigns Against Black Militancy, 1919–1925* (Bloomington: University of Indiana Press, 1998), 1–75; Richard M. Dalfiume, "The 'Forgotten Years' of the Negro Revolution," *Journal of American History* 54 (June 1968); Glenda Gilmore's *Defying Dixie: The Radical Roots of Civil Rights, 1900–1950* (New York: W. W. Norton & Company, 2008) is an excellent study of the American left's influence on the southern civil rights movement in the first half of the twentieth century. The chapter on Nazis and Dixie is illuminating.

2. For a description of Germany as a racial state, see the work of Michael Burleigh and Wolfgang Wippermann, *The Racial State: Germany, 1933–1945* (Cambridge: Cambridge University Press, 1991), and Tina M. Campt, *Other Germans* (Ann Arbor: University of Michigan Press); Jordan, *Black Newspapers and America's War for Democracy*, 41, 42; James Weldon Johnson, "Weld Worth Thinking About," *New York Age*, February 15, 1917, 4; "How Much Longer," *Chicago Defender*, February 12, 1916, 8; W. E. B. Du Bois, "Close Ranks," *The Crisis* 16 (July 1918): 111.

3. Mark Naison, *Communists in Harlem during the Depression* (Urbana: University of Illinois Press, 1983), 31–165; Larry A. Greene, "Harlem, The Depression Years: Leadership and Social Conditions," *Afro-Americans in New York Life and History* 17 (July 1993): 42–45; Herbert Garfinkle, *When Negroes March: The March on Washington Movement in the Organizational Politics for FEPC* (Glencoe, IL: Free Press, 1959), 33–39; Jervis Anderson, *A. Philip Randolph, A Biographical Portrait* (New York: Harcourt, Brace, Jovanovich, 1973), 255–61; Joseph E. Harris, *African American Reactions to War in Ethiopia, 1936–1941* (Baton Rouge: Louisiana State University Press, 1994), 34–62. See for works on the Japanese use of race and anticolonialism: Gerald Horne, *Race War! White Supremacy and the Japanese Attack on the British Empire* (New York: New York University Press, 2004); John W. Dower, *War Without Mercy: Race and Power in the Pacific War* (New York: Pantheon Books, 1986); Marc Gallicchio, *The African American Encounter with Japan and China: Black Internationalism in Asia, 1895–1945* (Chapel Hill: University of North Carolina Press, 2000); and Reginald Kearney, "Afro-American Views of Japanese, 1900–1945" (Ph.D. dissertation, Kent State University, 1991). See for details on the raids in several cities of pro-Japanese black organizations: Dalfiume, "The 'Forgotten Years' of the Negro Revolution," 95, and *New York Times*, September 15, 22, 1942; January 14, 28, 1943.

4. David H. Pierce, "Fascism and the Negro," *The Crisis*, 42 (April 1935): 107; Editorial, "Fascism Now Means Something," *The Crisis* 43 (September 1936): 273; Elaine Ellis, "Sterilization: A Menace to the Negro," *The Crisis* 44 (May 1937): 137; "Twilight of the Gods," *The Crisis* 43 (September 1936): 272.

5. Langston Hughes, "Too Much of Race," *The Crisis* 44 (September 1937): 272; Christopher C. De Santis, *Langston Hughes and the Chicago Defender: Essays on Race, Politics, and Culture, 1942–62* (Urbana: University of Chicago Press, 1995), 78–85, 141–45; Editorial, "Nazi Plans for Negroes Copies Southern U.S.A.," *The Crisis* 48 (March 1941): 71; Editorial, "Nazis and Negroes," *The Crisis* 48 (May 1941): 151; Hughes was thrown out of Japan for meeting with Japanese writers opposing their government's militaristic aggression in Asia. See the Hughes autobiography, *I Wonder As I Wander* (New York: Hill and Wang, 1956).

6. "Talmadge Copies Hitler," *New York Amsterdam News*, October 4, 1941, 5.

7. "Blasts Adolf Hitler in Dynamic Address," *Pittsburgh Courier*, November 8, 1941; J. A. Rogers, "Hitlerism is a Disease Cultivated by His Present Foes," November 29, 1941, 7; "We Feel That Fight Against Hitler is Our Fight'—Bethune," *Pittsburgh Courier*, November 22, 1941, 9.

8. Pearl Buck, "New York Times 'Letter to the Editor' Dares to Tell the Truth," *Pittsburgh Courier*, November 29, 1941, 5; Burleigh and Wipperman identify race purity doctrines as a defining characteristic of the Third Reich. See their *The Racial State: Germany, 1933–1945*, 1–4, 304–8.

9. See for the post–World War II continuation of American and German fears concerning black soldiers and white women: Höhn, *GIs and Fräuleins*, 85–108 and Heide Fehrenbach, *Race after Hitler: Black Occupation Children in Postwar German and America* (Princeton, NJ: Princeton University Press, 2005), 1–45.

10. "Courier's Double 'V' For A Double Victory Campaign Gets Country-Wide Support," *Pittsburgh Courier*, February 14, 1942, 1; Editorial, "Muzzling the Negro Press," *New York Age*, May 9, 1942, 6.

11. Editorial, "Cowing the Negro Press," *Pittsburgh Courier*, March 14, 1942, 6; Editorial, "On Pegler's Attack," *New York Amsterdam News*, May 9, 1942, 6.

12. "20,000 Storm Madison Square Garden to Help Bury Race's 'Uncle Toms,'" *New York Amsterdam News*, June 20, 1942.

13. "Council of Negro Leaders finds Negroes Not Backing War Effort Fully, Due To Discrimination," *New York Age*, January 17, 1942, 1; Washburn, *The African American Newspaper*, 155, 156.

14. P. L. Prattis, "The Horizon: German Atrocities Confirm Merguson's Story, Indicate Nazis Can Teach Even Southern Whites A Few Lessons," *Pittsburgh Courier*, July 11, 1942; P. L. Prattis, "The Horizon: Our Feeling of Racial Superiority Won't Help Us to Whip Either the Germans or the Japanese," *Pittsburgh Courier*, August 8, 1942, 13.

15. Hans Mabe[?], "The Nazi Plan for Negroes," *New York Age*, November 22, 1941, 2; The newsprint is so unclear that the author's name is not clearly visible. The author noted that the *Illustrierte Beobachter*, a German illustrated weekly, had recently published a special issue devoted to the question of France's war guilt. His summary suggests that the focus was upon condemning France's liberal policies toward its colonial peoples such as the use of colored troops, assimilation of colored peoples into citizenship, and toleration of interracial mixing and marriages. All of these mistaken French colonial policies were stated to be incompatible with Nazi ideology and a German colonial empire.

16. George B. Murphy Jr., "Hitler's Instructions To Agents in America on How to Exterminate Negroes Published Here in 1936," *New York Age*, January 10, 1942, 2.

17. George Padmore, "Poison Minds of Hitler's Subjects Against the Colored Minority Groups," *Pittsburgh Courier*, July 24, 1943, 2; Edmund D. Morel, *The Horror on the Rhine* (London: 1921); Keith Nelson, "The Black Horror on the Rhine," *Journal of Modern History* 42 (1970): 606–27; Reiner Pommerin, *"Sterilisierung der Rheinlandbastarde": Das Schicksal einer farbigen deutschen Minderheit 1918–1937* (Düsseldorf: Droste, Verlag, 1979), provides the best study of the children born of those black-German unions and the Nazi propaganda against them and subsequent sterilization.

18. Ollie Harrington, "U.S. Takes Drastic Steps in Italy to Smash Nazi Race Hate Campaign," *Pittsburgh Courier*, September 9, 1944, 11. Harrington's opposition to American racism and leftist

views will lead him to defect to the GDR (East Germany) in the early 1960s. See the Schroeder essay in this volume.

19. "Segregation on Trial," *Pittsburgh Courier*, August 1, 1942.

20. Editorial, "Dr. Goebbels Rides Again," *Pittsburgh Courier*, July 7, 1945, 6; Marjorie McKenzie, "Pursuit of Democracy: Hitler's New Racial Theory an Insult to Many Whites," *Pittsburgh Courier*, October 3, 1942, 7; Editorial, "Dr. Goebbels Rides Again: The South Is in the Saddle," *Pittsburgh Courier*, July 7, 1945, 1; John H. Young III, "Eastland Insults 13,000,000 Citizens," *Pittsburgh Courier*, July 7, 1945, 1.

21. "Nine Sick Veterans Couldn't Believe It," *Pittsburgh Courier*, April 8, 1944, 1; see also: "What the Negro Soldier Thinks About the War Department," *The Crisis* 51 (1944); Lee Finkle, *Forum for Protest: The Black Press during World War II* (Cranbury, NJ: Associated University Presses, 1975); Jack Foner, *Blacks and the Military in American History: A New Perspective* (New York: Praeger, 1974); Ulysses Lee, *The Employment of Negro Troops: United States Army in World War II, Special Studies* (Washington, D.C.: Center of Military History, 1994); Bernard C. Nalty, *Strength for the Fight: A History of Black Americans in the Military* (New York: Free Press, 1989). See for an article that discounts the claim by some black newspapers that German prisoners of war were treated better than black soldiers: Matthias Reiss, "Icons of Insult: German and Italian Prisoners of War in African American Letters during World War II," *Amerikastudien/American Studies: A Quarterly* 49 (April 2004); 539–62.

22. "The Outcome of Conflict Will Control Negro's Destiny: Race Has Big Stake in the War," *New York Amsterdam News*, November 1, 1942, 11. See for similar African American expression of a positive belief in America's capacity for racial progress and fears of the immutability of America's racist attitudes: Editorial, "The South," *Pittsburgh Courier*, August 19, 1944, 6.

23. "'Nazi Treatment unlike U.S.' Embree," *Pittsburgh Courier*, February 28, 1942, 3; Washburn, *A Question of Sedition*.

24. "White Supremacy Will Evaporate When Negroes Reach the Right Level," *Pittsburgh Courier*, September 9, 1944, 3.

25. "He's Squirming: Bilbo Blasted for Attack on Jews, Negroes," *Pittsburgh Courier*, August 4, 1945, 1.

26. For an excellent analysis of the cold war, communism, and civil rights, see Mary L. Dudziak, *Cold War, Civil Rights: Race and the Image of American Democracy* (Princeton, NJ: Princeton University Press, 2000).

27. For a greatly informed discussion of American and German racial policies in postwar Germany, see Höhn, *GIs and Fräuleins*; Fehrenbach, *Race after Hitler*; Langston Hughes, "If Dixie Invades Europe," *Chicago Defender*, July 24, 1943.

28. William Gardner Smith, *Last of the Conquerors* (Chatham, NJ: Chatham Bookseller, 1948), 238.

Field Trip into the Twilight

A German Africanist Discovers the Black Bourgeoisie at Howard University, 1937–1939

BERNDT OSTENDORF

Anyone who is familiar with the economic and social structure of the U.S. must recognize that, particularly in times of crisis, the Negro problem is and will remain America's most pressing concern. In my view a solution within a capitalist system with its typical social and economic setup is impossible, and patchwork improvements which have been tried will be of small help. Only the removal of the racial and class divide, in other words the removal of capitalism itself would be the necessary first step for a solution of the negro problem. Only under a socialist system can this be achieved. (Lips 1950, 13)[1]

Thus ends the preface of a remarkable narrative entitled *Forschungsreise in die Dämmerung: Aus den Aufzeichnungen und Dokumenten des Professors Smith über sein Leben an einer Negeruniversität* published in 1950 by the Rector of Leipzig University, Julius Lips. Thirteen years earlier he had taught in the Social Science division of Howard University in Washington, D.C., in his area of specialization, African ethnology, and this book is, as the subtitle has it "a chronicle and documentation" of that unique experience. His colleagues at Howard University included Ralph Bunche, E. Franklin Frazier, Alain Locke, Abram L. Harris, Charles Wesley, and Emmet E. Dorsey. Howard University seemed the right place to be for a German *émigré* Africanist. By 1937 the university had become the intellectual nursery for the future architects of the civil rights movement whose activists may well have endorsed Lips's socialist take on racism as quoted above. Howard clearly was at the cutting edge of conflicting discourses regarding the interface of race and class and their combined effects on African American culture and society, positions that were controversially discussed in the context of the Frazier-Herskovits debates on African retentions or in Gunnar Myrdal's massive project *The American Dilemma* (Ostendorf 1975). In an ironic note to Boas, Lips described his sojourn at Howard as an "anthropological field trip" enabling him to study Washington's black bourgeoisie by participant observation (July 30, 1938). Howard represented for him a halfway house—hence twilight—to "his real Africa." Soon Lips found himself at the center of a racial politics of anthropological knowledge. As will become apparent in what follows his unique personality and his special version of African ethnology turned him into a loose cannon on campus. What story did he tell? His abiding interest was to document the pernicious impact of racism on individual black behavior and its baneful long-range effects upon the academic culture of "Hilltop University." (Lips used the name of the student paper *The Hilltop* as an alias for Howard University.) What did he object to? The wholesale aping of white ways on the part of students, faculty, and faculty wives and the paranoid color consciousness internalized by the victims of white racism. With sardonic insistence he dwells on individual and inter-group foibles and he finds the lack of a "cultural African identity" and of individual self-confidence in the black academic class deplorable. E. Franklin Frazier may well have agreed with him thus far; in fact, he may well have been an important source of information. But then Lips went one step further: Why would anyone want to acquire the norms of white America which he considered, from his European perch, somewhat shallow and wanting to begin with, when Africa had such a noble heritage. Who needed civilized alienation when there was primitive cultural authenticity? The time and place of this publication (Weimar 1950) were unusual and added an interesting political afterthought to his story. The author had just been appointed Rector of an old and distinguished university in the brand-new Socialist Republic of East Germany. In keeping with the socialist worldview of his employer, the German Democratic Republic, his prefatory note placed the blame for the colonial socialization squarely on white racist capitalism, a stance that would have found favor with current whiteness studies. However, unlike them he was not a radical postcolonial contextualist and would not let those black individuals off the hook who had made an art of blaming the system for their inadequacies and for their lack of personal achievement. In contrast to the preface which blames the system of racism, the main narrative analyzes content of character which adds up to blaming the victims. Thus at face value his chronicle seems to foreshadow E. Franklin Frazier's insider account of the black bourgeoisie, which appeared in 1957. Although Lips and Frazier identify the same pathological symptoms in the behavior of the black bourgeoisie, the latter sees the root causes in economic and social changes that are American made. Frazier's criticism denounced the lumpen bourgeoisie, whose collective interest made them accomplices of the racialized system that allowed them to exploit blacks without having to fear the competition of whites. Lips sees primarily treason to "his Africa." Thus his observations, while parading as ethnographic analysis, remained denunciatory and tacitly racist in intent.

In the main narrative Lips resolutely takes the outside point of view, that of a European Africanist, a cosmopolitan universalist, whose superior positionality is implied on both counts. From our perspective today the way he negotiates two epistemological barriers is most interesting: the American color line and the Atlantic divide in anthropological theory. This dual cognitive liability, to modify Ellison's trope of invisibility, generates its own set of erotoprimitivist essentialisms and neocolonial prejudices. His ethnographic descriptions of race relations at Howard are choreographed by tacit background assumption concerning race mixture, which, quite in line with classic eugenics, he considers pernicious. Last but not least, the book was a way of getting his own back by portraying in less than flattering terms those very colleagues who engineered his dismissal. His resentment added an element of backstage gossip to this complex tale and its multiple refractions.

How did this German armchair Africanist end up at Howard University? The historical contingencies of Weimar politics help to thicken the plot. His academic career began in Germany in 1919 with a doctorate in philosophy with minors in economics and anthropology. In 1923 he added a degree in law, but then he chose to make a career of his minor, anthropology. He worked as a graduate assistant with Willy Foy (1873–1929) and Fritz Graebner (1877–1934) at the Rautenstrauch-Joest Museum of Ethnology in Cologne. When Foy became incurably ill, Graebner briefly took over the directorship, but was prostrated by the same nervous illness as Foy. In a shrewd career move, Lips, who at the time was Graebner's research assistant, jockeyed himself into the position of director of the museum. At the same time, in 1929, he submitted his *Habilitation* and, after a controversial vote in the committee, was promoted to associate professor at the university in 1930. This promotion did not go unchallenged and triggered an academic scandal; for there were allegations voiced by his co-students Paul Leser and Martin Block that he had plagiarized the work of his predecessors at the museum and of other colleagues for his "Einleitung in die vergleichende Völkerkunde" (Leser 234–38). Due to the turbulent political times these claims were not dealt with or substantiated in court. But they occasioned a wild and denunciatory debate among anthropological colleagues (Fischer 1990, 184). The grand old man Leo Frobenius commented on the Lips fracas that professional standards had sunk to a deplorable level. Interestingly some of those very colleagues whose works Lips had plagiarized exonerated him in a series of letters which he and his wife wheedled out of them, yet in 1932 the ethics committee of the Federation of German Museums called his scholarship "borderline plagiarism." Soon thereafter, on March 12, 1933, Lips was dismissed by the new Nazi powers for reasons of "political unreliability," probably owing to his candidacy for the city council elections on the Social Democratic ticket in 1932. The Nazis took the allegations of plagiarism, though voiced by two Jews, seriously and made several house searches to retrieve stolen materials. Lips now threw himself at the feet of the Nazi mayor in Cologne in order to be reinstated as director and wrote him a letter that insisted on his excellent Aryan standing. Had not the "Marxist Jew" Honigsheim engineered his dismissal from the Social Democratic Party on the grounds that Lips had spoken up against "the class struggle and the internationalism of Social Democracy?" Had not his anti-Semitism been well known for years? Lips presented the very allegations of plagiarism by "Jewish slanderers" as proof of his anti-Semitic credentials. In his letter of April 1933 to the new Nazi mayor Lips writes: "Der marxistische Jude Prof. Honigsheim beantragte wegen meiner Stellungnahme gegen den Klassenkampf und die internationale Ideologie der Sozialdemokratie gegen mich den Ausschluß aus dieser Partei. Als weiteres Argument wurde mein seit Jahren gekannter Antisemitismus angeführt. Die Träger der gegen mich inszenierten Hetze waren jüdische Verleumder, deren Namen allein zu ihrer Kennzeichnung genügen: Honigsheim, Leser, Lehmann, Block, Vatter" [The marxist Jew Prof. Honigsheim called for my removal from the party in reaction to my statement against the class struggle and international ideology of the social democrats. To further this cause my well-known Antisemitism was cited. The instigators of this agitation against me were Jewish libelists, whose names alone serve as sufficient identification: Honigsheim, Leser, Lehmann, Block, Vatter.] (Pützstück 1988). But his groveling before the Nazi brass did him no good. His *venia legendi* was revoked and his salary discontinued. After persistent harassment by the Nazi powers he chose exile in France in March 1934. In the preface to *The Savage Hits Back* Lips claimed that the Nazis disapproved of the material he had collected for an exhibition at Cologne on the representation of whites in African art since it was "contrary to the racial theories of the Führer" (Lips 1937, xix–xxxi). It must have added insult to injury that Andreas Scheller, a mediocre, one-legged student, who was a member of the Nazi party, became his successor.[2] In May 1934 Lips was admitted to the United States on the basis of a letter of invitation by Franz Boas and he found a temporary academic home at Columbia University. In his request to Boas, Lips claimed not quite correctly that "he gave up his job voluntarily" because he could no longer live in "this prison house of the mind" (Lips to Boas, June 12, 1933, February 25, 1934). In the United States he became active in antifascist organizations: the American Committee for Anti-Nazi Literature, the German-American League for Culture, and the Council for a Democratic Germany. As may be expected his former colleagues in Nazi Germany denounced him as an enemy of the Third Reich and a professional fraud. In 1938 the Berlin anthropologist Walter Krickeberg calls him "den charakterlosesten und ketzerischsten deutschen Emigranten" (Diaz de Arce, 146). In the antifascist movement he formed a lasting friendship with Heinrich Mann and other exiled writers, a connection which stood him in good stead for the resumption of his career in Germany after the war. Quite obviously he possessed the cosmopolitan charm of a consummate trickster who never missed an opportunity for self-promotion. In keeping with his social democratic worldview Lips sought out white liberals of the day in the promotion of black civil rights. He claims in a letter to Boas that he socialized with justices Benjamin Cardozo, Irving Lehman, and Louis Brandeis, certainly not bad company. He clearly possessed charm and social graces that opened doors in liberal Washington.

In 1937, his book *The Savage Hits Back: Or The White Man Through Native Eyes* based on the exhibition he had planned in Cologne was published in London and by Yale University Press. Assuming a "native point of view" in the manner of Montesquieu's *Lettres Persannes* it dealt with the representation of the white man in African art. With this book Lips moved into the center of colonialism— that is, into its asymmetrical logic. In doing so he asserted his willingness to understand the African other from the native point of view. This *Lettres-Persannes*-optic may well be the origin of his construction of a Romantic *Afrique de l'esprit*. The book received a strong endorsement from Bronislav Malinowski, who praised its innovative, self-reflexive gaze. In an odd way Lips's book was postcolonial *avant la lettre* and therefore achieved quite a success in the field. After the war the same Walter Krickeberg strongly disagreed with Malinowski's positive assessment:

> Um den wahren Wert dieser unsympathischen Selbstverhimmelung zu erkennen, muß man allerdings näher über den Charakter Lips' als Mensch und Gelehrter informiert sein, und darüber hat bereits im Jahre 1931 der deutsche Ethnologe Dr. Paul Leser das letzte Wort gesprochen, als er nachwies, dass Lips ein elender Plagiator sei. Weitere Mitteilungen, die mir Leser über Prof. Lips machte, förderten so viele ungünstige Seiten an diesem Mann zutrage, dass mein Urteil über ihn schon vor der Nazizeit feststand und später auch nicht revidiert zu werden brauchte, zumal es auch von den meisten deutschen Ethnologen . . . geteilt wurde und noch heute geteilt wird. [To get at the true value of this unappealing self-aggrandizement, one has to know more about Lips' character as a human being and a scholar, about which the German ethnologist Dr. Paul Leser had the final say in 1931 when he exposed Lips as a shameless plagiarist. Further communications that I received from Leser about Prof. Lips brought forth so many unfavorable features of this man, that I had formed an opinion about him even before the Nazi period, which I did not have to revise later, especially as most German ethnologists were in complete agreement and continue to be today.] (Dias de Arce, 146–47)

But can we trust Krickeberg? He fails to mention that after the war he had problems shedding his reputation as a Nazi sympathizer. Before the war he had accused Malinowski of being a dyed-in-the-wool enemy of the Third Reich and he had a hard time to live down a series of anti-Semitic remarks in print. All the more ironic that he should call as his most important witness the Jew who had accused Lips of plagiarism (Fischer 1990, 190). Many years later the French anthropologist Pierre Centlivres, who had no particular ideological axe to grind, presented a positive assessment and a fair-minded review of the book's importance (Centlivres 1997). At the time Lips's sudden fame in the profession prompted the invitation from Howard University to set up the Department of African Anthropology. The shortness of his tenure there and the abrupt change in the estimation by his Howard colleagues are remarkable and give rise to further speculation. In 1937, three spokesmen of the Social Science division, among them E. Franklin Frazier, had emphatically endorsed him for the post. "The Division feels that Howard University can ill afford to present courses in this highly technical field except under the competent direction of Professor Lips's calibre and attainments." Yet his dismissal was demanded even more emphatically only two years later, this time signed by an even more powerful group in full academic regalia: "E. Franklin Frazier, Department of Sociology, Alain Locke, Department of Philosophy, Ralph Bunche, Department of Political Science, Abram L. Harris, Department of Economics, Charles H. Wesley, Department of History." Their controlled prose barely contains the profound contempt that this Africanist managed to shore up in less than two years:

> It is the considered opinion of the Division of the Social Sciences that instruction in Anthropology is a vital and desirable part of the college instruction in the social science field, and thus the Division has repeatedly urged its inauguration and expansion. However, this position is predicated upon the instruction in this subject constituting a program of standard courses of a type and sequence normally offered in American college. In reply to your letter of inquiry concerning the reappointment of Dr. Lips addressed to us as heads of the several social science departments concerned, we feel, with regret but upon the basis of concrete experience in the past, that Dr. Lips is unable by his background of experience and perhaps by temperament to participate effectively in the development of such a program. (Thompson to *Washington Daily*, June 1939)

In his letter to the *Washington Daily News* Dean Charles H. Thompson (who makes an appearance in Lips's book as Rockefeller Delirious Blockhead) spells out more specific details that lead to his firing. The paper had reported on the basis of an interview with Lips that he had quit Howard with the hope that there would be a "massive house-cleaning" after his departure.

> First, Dr. Lips possesses an unfortunate temperament and personality which make it extremely difficult, if not impossible, for him to get along amicably with his colleagues. At the present time his relationship with his colleagues in the social sciences is either one of polite indifference or suppressed hostility, so that any sort of real collaboration is highly improbable … Dr. Lips, for some reason, has attracted very few students to his courses, even after a two-year stay at the university. It will be observed that Dr. Lips has never had more than 38 students during any one of the five semesters he has been in the college, and during the current year he had only 15 students the first semester and 16 students are registered during the second semester. (Thompson to *Washington Daily*, June 1939)

Upon the request of a member of the board of trustees Lips was given the opportunity to resign before he was fired. In his letter to Boas, Lips stated that the "current views on aesthetics, ethics and morality within the staff are unbearable" and that the caterwauling between administration and faculty made daily work impossible both of which had rendered his resignation inevitable (Letter to Boas, July 23, 1939). What precisely happened between him and his colleagues is nowhere clearly spelled out and must be extrapolated from his skewed version of the story. But both his personality and his professional credo that he wore on his sleeve clearly had something to do with such abrupt changes of judgment. Rayford Logan makes no mention of Lips in his comprehensive history of Howard University, though he claims Lips's book *The Savage Hits Back* among the accomplishments of distinguished Howard University writers (Logan, appendix). Obviously the book, buttressed by the endorsement of Malinowski and published by Yale University Press, was significant enough to lift the veil of silence that had settled on the embarrassing Lips episode. In 1994, the university archivist at Howard mistakenly lists the self-declared Aryan Lips among the Jewish scholars at the university and in 2002 applauds his "long tenure" at Howard (Fischer 1990, 185; Moorland-Spingarn Research Center; Muse 2002). After his debacle at Howard, Lips returned to New York where he continued his journalistic work in antifascist organizations. By this time his relationship to Boas had cooled for several reasons. First, Lips had told Boas that he resigned from Howard voluntarily since he could not realize his academic goals under the given conditions. But Boas was informed by Dean Thompson about their true motives to fire Lips, that his qualifications as an Africanist were considered wanting and that he was impossible to work with. Second, Boas had asked Lips to contribute the entry on "government" to the encyclopedia *General Anthropology*. Lips gave Boas as editor a very hard time and exchanged acrimonious letters with him insisting that his text that Boas found problematic be printed as written. Third, Lips resigned in protest as honorary president of the German-American League for Culture, which in his view was "dominated by Communistic elements who misuse the League as a framework to foster Communistic politics and to indulge in propaganda for Sowjet [*sic*] Russia." Lips took particular umbrage at a resolution of the German-American League suggesting that the war between Hitler Germany and England was fought over natural resources and hence must be considered "imperialistic." Boas tried to calm things down, suggesting that membership in the League for Culture was at this time a question of strategy (fighting fascism) rather than of ideological fine tuning. "I do not believe in giving up a fight by resigning, but want to stand for my views inside the group as long as possible." Lips shot back testily that Boas was welcome to his political views or to his strategies, but that as far as he was concerned any cooperation with communists was out of the question. When in January 1941 Lips once again touched Boas for money and suggested he use his influence with Jewish donors to secure him some funding the eighty-three-year-old Boas slyly answered that the Jewish Committee had stopped their support because "my political views are too far to the left" (Lips to Sattler, December 7, 1939; Boas to Lips January 10, 1941).

Although Lips had conducted some fieldwork among Native Americans and although he lectured in anthropology at the New School for Social Research from 1944 to 1948, he had trouble resuming or advancing his career. Boas's support had become muted long before his death in 1942. Eminent American anthropologists such as Robert H. Lowie and A. L. Kroeber, whose recommendation Lips had solicited, found his talent "more literary than ethnological," which in retrospect seems a fair assessment, and finally the ghosts of the past came back to haunt him. That same Jewish doctoral student from Cologne, Paul Leser, who had made the allegations of plagiarism in the early thirties, raised this issue again when the New School offered Leser a position. Leser declined the invitation, arguing "that he would not be able to defend his scholarly honor while teaching in the same faculty with the plagiarist Lips." Lips had pleaded his version of the case in a letter to Franz Boas dated February 25, 1934, where he claimed that all allegations of plagiarism had been thrown out by courts in Cologne and Vienna. For the time being Boas seems to have accepted his version of the story. But within the academic grapevine Lips's scholarly standing as an anthropologist clearly had taken a beating by 1945. With his reputation in decline he made efforts after the war to return to Germany. First he gave his old university in Cologne a try. As a rule victims of Nazism and active antifascists were entitled to being reinstated as a full professor. Yet, older skeletons in the closet came back to haunt him. Upon the advice of a board member of the University of Cologne, Robert Görlinger, he was denied reinstatement in 1947. Although Görlinger was a Social Democrat and could be expected to favor the reappointment of a fellow party member, he had access to Lips's correspondence with the Nazi authorities. In a letter to Bruno Kuske of April 12, 1947, he stated that "Briefe von Prof. Julius Lipsius vom 19.4., 6.7., 19.7. 1933 vorlagen, in denen er sich geradezu in unwürdiger Weise dem Nationalsozialismus an den Hals geworfen hatte, nur um seinen Direktorposten am Museum und seine Lehrtätigkeit wieder aufnehmen zu können. Erst als das mißlungen war, ging er ins Ausland und wurde kämpferischer Gegner des Nationalsozialismus" (Pützstück 263). Lips then answered a Leipzig University advertisement for a politically untainted rector. His status as a Nazi victim, his American credentials, and his friendship with Boas made him look like the ideal candidate and he was chosen. It is odd that this staunch anticommunist and enemy of the Soviet Union would end up in the young socialist republic as rector of Leipzig University. In the preface to the novel he firmly embraced the Soviet worldview and blamed imperial American capitalism for slavery and its baneful long-range effects that he had witnessed at Howard University. In retrospect this preface appears as an opportunistic curtsy toward his communist employer.

In his application he made grandiose claims, which in the prevailing mood of quick restoration nobody was able to contest or inclined to question: Lips listed among his many achievements that he had coauthored Franz Boas's *General Anthropology* 1938 when in fact he only contributed one entry on government, a contribution that caused Boas endless editorial grief. He refers to extensive fieldwork in Africa, when in fact he never traveled much beyond Algiers. He had visited that city as a tourist on Mediterranean pleasure cruises in 1927 and 1932, which included stopovers and daily excursions, but clearly he had done no serious fieldwork anywhere in Subsaharan Africa. In terms of Africa he remained the armchair anthropologist who remained mired in the tacit assumptions of his discipline.

Lips died of colon cancer only a year after his inauguration as rector at age fifty-four. After his death his wife and fellow anthropologist Eva Lips saw to it that the self-congratulatory myths he had spun were not challenged, and over time she composed a hagiography to buttress his status as a near soteriological figure. In her book of 1938 Eva Lips claimed that Lips was accused not of plagiarism, but of sentiments "not worthy of a national socialist scholar," which was incorrect (Lips 1938, 310). By an act of creative translation the plagiarist Lips morphs into

an antifascist (Fischer 1990, 190–91). In her memories his wife portrays him as a
saintly figure with near superhuman talents. She calls him "a friend of Negroes
and Indians," "a great man and humanist," a universalist and no less than "a model
for mankind," and a "loving brother of humanity," in short, a veritable Mahatma
Ghandi of Anthropology (Fischer 1990, 188–89; Eva Lips 1965). While he clearly
had talent in impression management and cut a positive figure when appearing
in public, Lips was also a consummate opportunist endowed with a robust sense
of narcissism. He was a gifted raconteur who loved the twilight of half-truths
and half-lies and, last but not least, also an armchair anthropologist with a re-
markably creative narrative talent. Tricksters, as we know, are full of good stories
which need not be true. In 1983 the German original of *The Savage Hits Back* was
published simultaneously in the East and West. Eva Lips dropped Malinowski's
introduction and wrote a new one herself (Lips 1983). After Lips had died, his
wife managed to take over his professorship, from which she retired in 1966. She
died in 1988 at age eighty-two, a revered figure in Socialist anthropology. The
myriad contradictions of their career paths were first explored and researched at
greater length in a doctoral dissertation by Lothar Pützstück: *Symphonie in Moll:
Julius Lips und die Kölner Völkerkunde*. Lips's book on his experiences at Howard
was copyrighted in 1949 and published in Weimar at the founding of the German
Democratic Republic in 1950. Understandably, there was no substantial readership for a *roman à clef* about a black American university, and the book was
ignored in East Germany. Only a handful of West German libraries list a copy in
their holdings. After fifty years of neglect this remarkable document needs to be
rescued from oblivion.

At the time the book had less of an impact than its contents deserved. Gabrielle Simon Edgcomb mentions him in her book *From Swastika to Jim Crow* on
exiled Germans at black universities. She comments that Lips "portrays his Howard experience as a fascinating and moving sort of ethnographic field trip to explore the world of the African American bourgeoisie. Throughout his frequently
sardonic descriptions and his astonishing, unscientific conflation of biological
and cultural traits, he is the superior European, cultured and refined, generously
giving, while observing these unhappy folk" (Edgcomb 115). But she does not go
into greater detail.

The account is semi-fictional. Historical or living characters such as Frederick
Douglass, W. E. B. Du Bois, Roland Hayes, Claude McKay, and Langston Hughes
are mentioned or interact with invented *dramatis personae* at Howard. With the
exception of the president who is closely modeled on the original, the latter are
composite characters that Lips created bricolage fashion from recognizable traits
of his real-life colleagues. These rather graphic descriptions of daily academic
practice form the liveliest part of the story. It will be equally interesting to unpack
and study the epistemological filters through which he reads his African American data and how the libidinal economy of his anthropological knowledge plays
itself out in the text.

The story begins aboard the ocean liner *Ile de France* en route from Le Havre
to New York. The narrator and his wife, the anthropologists Peter and Pat Smith,

are of unidentified European origin (though with an English name) and introduce themselves as world citizens and cosmopolitans. One may speculate that
he chose an English point of view as a sort of visa of authenticity: first to disarm
any charges of prejudice against Anglo-Saxon America that an ethnic German
might harbor and secondly to add a touch of objectivity to his anthropological
judgments. Back from a research trip to England they are returning to their new
home in the United States. As anthropologists they love to observe people on the
world stage and they gaze upon the busy life on board with its myriad presentations of self as a sort of human zoo. This narrative stance of participant observation and quasi-ethnological evaluation is maintained throughout the book that
strings up a series of micro-events, of cultural vignettes, intimate portraits, and
social rituals. In the dining hall a "pale elegant" gentleman with short-cropped,
dark hair dines all alone. His solitude, they soon find out, is not voluntary. When
they invite him to join their table for a glass of *Veuve Cliquot*, which he readily
accepts, a white American couple next to them, after exchanging frantic whis-
pers, moves to another part of the dining hall. The gentleman turns out to be an
eminent black biologist, Dr. Parker, back from a research trip in Europe (probably modeled on the marine biologist at Howard, Ernest Just). Despite persistent
inquiries he refuses to tell them specifics about his profession or name the place
where he works. When in New York they suggest they should meet again, he
curtly refuses, dropping a loaded remark that he has "a profession, but not a position." Soon thereafter the narrator opens the letter that invites him to assume
a position at Hilltop University, a Negro university in Washington, D.C., and a
rash of memories overwhelms this "specialist of Africa." "For someone who knew
Negroes . . . instantly the old images returned: the moist damp jungle, the steppes
and deserts, sounds of drums, wood carvings documenting an age old tradition,
African metal work developed long before the white man invented foundries, the
dances, the rhythms, old tales, the respect of Gods, the dynamic power of proud
traditional tribes that, under the tutelage of chieftains, lived a primitive life that
brought home to the white man the emptiness of his own so-called civilization."
In that same erotoprimitivist vein the narrator makes frequent references to "real
Negroes" or to a pure "heart of Africa, where the noble and genuine children
of the continent maintain a sense of tradition, custom, safety, hospitality and
nurture. Here the negroes of Africa were masters of their realm" (22). Very different things he finds at Hilltop, "in the borderland between black and white:
a mongrelized crew, which combined the vices of both worlds without any of
their virtues" (22). He is both fascinated and horrified by race mixture and by
the effects of assimilation on "Africans" transported to the New World. On the
whole this specialist of "the real Africa" takes a dim view of hybridity thus echoing contemporary eugenic theory on both sides of the Atlantic. Add to that the
effects of social discrimination: while African blacks were proud tribesmen, new
world blacks had to work as subaltern lift boys, porters, Pullman staff, or jazz
musicians. They live in a twilight zone, neither here nor there.[3] "Anthropologi-
cally speaking they are not Negroes anymore. All their faces showed white blood.
How had the old traits mixed with the new? How had it affected their souls? Had

it turned them into denizens of a border world?" Hence the very notion of a "Negro University" that has to operate under these liminal conditions intrigues him. "Was there such a thing?"

Though many people warned him that Hilltop was faction-ridden, this "cosmopolitan" insists that he wants to go there "as a friend and helper," whereupon he is given the cynical insider advice: "At Hilltop there are no friends." And he is given to understand that his altruism will not be appreciated. His initiation to the reality of the color line begins as he rather naively tries to find lodgings in a racially territorialized city. Depending on where he looks in D.C., either no black visitors are allowed, or no white visitors will venture there. Therefore they move into a liminal space, a hotel. When he arrives at Hilltop, he is delighted to find that his office will be in Frederick Douglass Memorial Hall where his wife, to the chagrin of Hilltop janitors, commits the first breach of etiquette as she begins to clean and put order in his office, something unheard of among Hilltop's black faculty wives. Now begins the inventory of the *dramatis personae*, the strange types who people this twilight zone between the races. First Dr. Benjamin Jones, the chairman of the sociology department, is introduced, a character who is in all likelihood modeled on E. Franklin Frazier. The narrator quickly falls in line with the local color etiquette and sizes his characters up in the spirit of genealogical-cum-social ascription: "very dark, casually dressed, round forehead, broad nose, full mouth—bronze-Benin type." Then we meet President Obadiah Lamarquisde Wedlock (closely modeled on Mordecai Johnson), who is described as "light colored and as a cagey, shrewd operator with smooth hair, dark eyes. Nothing Negroid, more like a Jewish bandleader or a soft-featured Kapellmeister." This is Lips's least fictional figure; for Wedlock shares his looks, his leadership qualities, his rhetoric, and his controversial reputation with Mordecai Wyatt Johnson. The historian of Howard University, Rayford Logan, draws this portrait of the president: "Very few of those who have known President Johnson hold neutral views about him; the vast majority are fervent admirers or bitter critics . . . . There is however, one view about him on which friends, adversaries and neutrals tend to agree—that he possessed a 'Messianic Complex.' In certain 'Messianic Moments' he would tell the late E. Franklin Frazier the kind of sociology to write or the late Abram Harris the kind of economics to study . . . He was one of the great platform orators of his day. Practically never using a manuscript but relying almost entirely on an outline, his remarkable memory and his thorough 'homework,' he generally won the admiration of his audiences" (Logan, 249–50).

In the narrator's rhetoric and manner of description we detect that race mixture both fascinates and horrifies him—a belief that he may have brought with him from Germany. A philosophical source for his views of race mixture may have been Friedrich Nietzsche, who believed that race mixture led to mongrelization, to a decline of will power and life force (Nietzsche, 138). Miscegenation as a cause of genetic decline, this is also the *Leitmotif* in Faulkner's greatest novel *Absalom, Absalom!* published in 1936. In a textbook published on the other side of the Atlantic in the same year, anthropologist Wilhelm Mühlmann echoes the Nietzschean and Faulknerian caveats which dovetail with the ruling Nazi ideology on race mixture. He considered it the root cause of all social problems of the world, which are particularly visible in the United States (Mühlmann, 492–513).

The narrator encounters such race mixture not only in local black residents, but in people from all over the world, including Caribbeans, Asians, and Africans. All of them "exaggerate" their "pseudo-identities"—they are not balanced or well in their skins. He notes compulsive behavior and is amazed at the stand-offish student-teacher relations. Angus Hastings, dean of faculty and professor of German comes next, whose specialty are the medieval *Nibelungen* epics which he readily recites, which adds a moment of surrealism. Soon, another colleague, Dollar Grant McLee, a dark brown roundhead, head of economics (Abram Harris), who emerges as a gifted storyteller, along with Eusebius (Earl) Porter in Political Science, a forty-seven-year-old bachelor and closet Socialist, whose home is filled with portraits of Marx and Lenin and who receives "foreign visitors," a close portrait of Ralph Bunche. Porter, McLee, and Jones are drinking pals, known locally as "the thinkers and drinkers," and they welcome the chance to meet in the narrator's office for extended banter. They take the narrator along on their drinking binges when stories are told, gossip is exchanged, and particularly steam is let off against President Obadiah, whom all of them parody to great effect. Archibald Hume, who is part African and Asian and was educated in Europe, adds an intrigue-conscious denizen of the twilight zone along the color line. Then we meet Sidney Pretty, a Creole with straight hair who casually refers to his descent from Mexican forefathers, a claim which cuts little ice with his cynical colleagues. Dress-conscious, he remains a black Victorian with a vengeance. He particularly despises the coarse, uncultured presentation of self of his colleagues who love to tell off-color stories, and the mimetic talent of his colleagues, he says, reminds him more of monkeys. This may well be a partial portrait of Alain Locke. Enter Mr. Pradhana Tamil Grumukhi, disciple of Ghandi and dark Hindu who adds some caste condiment to the racialist gumbo. He is introduced as "different in many ways." Though blacker than most of his Hilltop colleagues and students, he turns out to run a caste-ridden New Age–type religious center that does not admit blacks. Enter Dr. George E. Parker again, the distinguished scholar, biologist, and embryologist, specialist of sea mollusks, who greets Smith with "You don't belong here." The narrator comments: "On board he had been a cool, solitary and bored gentleman, on Hilltop campus he appeared as an ice cold, solitary and mute misanthrope." He is characterized as the only true cosmopolitan who, though he moves in the best circles in Paris, Germany, and Austria, is thwarted by the academic situation at Hilltop. We also meet Mr. Quivers, a black Bostonian who is keeper of materials, a charming family man whose children do performances of Shoeshine Boy. These people represent a more genuine folk. The narrator praises the talent for mimicry and performance and cheers the "curious moment when the compulsively bourgeois mannerisms are thrown overboard . . . When the special talents of their race become visible." In a way he preaches the valorization of a black oral tradition and its rules of performance long before this became a rallying cry of black cultural nationalism (Ostendorf 1975). He comments on the compulsively neutral housing and dress codes and on racial gendering. Enter Puma, a passablanc art historian who feels like a pariah and who marvels at white matrimonial habits. She finds it odd that Smith's wife, Pat, should do the cleaning, plus secretarial and other service work for her husband. "No black woman would help her husband like you do, she would make him work for her." Cauli Jones, wife of the department chairman, is described as a high yeller Venus of the "Willendorf type." The negro problem is the only topic she is interested in, which weighs down every conversation. When Pat protests that she is not color conscious, she is reminded by Cauli that in the United States there is a culture of mutual hatred between black and white. She is given a lesson in cross-racial etiquette: "When we meet a white person who does not behave in accordance with the color line, we are puzzled and confused." The narrator comments on the paradox situation that the Smiths may be invited by blacks to their homes, but they cannot reciprocate; for no black visitors will be let into their hotel by the black doormen. Therefore they institutionalize a common room afternoon tea at 4 P.M. in Douglass Hall, and this venue becomes a favorite exchange on the problems of the color line and of Hilltop University. Permanent topics are the South, the color line, and President Obadiah. The narrator marvels at the use of "debasing" language, the use of the term "Nigger" is to him astonishing, as is the prevailing cynicism. When one of the protagonists, Jones alias Frazier, picks up a German edition of "Afrika singt" and reads Langston Hughes *I too sing America* in German, the trio chimes in like a Greek choir and disses on Hughes's "dream." Clearly their dreams are already deferred. Topics like "good hair" are prominent; the problem of cutting black hair is raised. One of them relates that in London only Jews can do it well. A storytelling session is devoted to dissing Anabel, who is introduced as the author of a book entitled *Black Man and White Lady*, a white do-gooder and "niggerlover," perhaps a caricature of Nancy Cunard.

As a teacher of ethnology and hence as a "specialist" on race relations, the narrator breaks many tacit rules of academic etiquette. He lets his students articulate their "broken" sense of self and invites essays on an anthropological archeology of their own situation, which brings forth surprisingly honest answers. He makes the observation that all students report on the experience of coming of age, of becoming conscious of the color line (107). He also notes that complaints about racism are strongest from the academically weakest (109). The practice of color coding among student fraternities gets commented upon, as do the popular genealogical family myths of having descended from free blacks (110). "These sounded like answers to questions nobody had asked" (110). His description of fraternity and sorority life turns into a scathing caricature and he invites those students not admitted to critique these initiation rites. He includes a long list of rules for admission to three of the most popular sororities which one of his most intelligent students does not meet due to her skin color. Repeatedly he praises the musical and mimic talents of his students. To him moments of pure joy occur when the choir sings *Ave Verum*: "Could this exist: that perfect charm of color should pair with perfect charm of harmony" (119). But he finds the talent most evident when they perform black music: "Rhythm, tricksters, magic, exuberance and music triumphed" (120). He notes with surprise that divinity students tend to be darker, and he attributes their choice of a religious career to the fact that they did not get into a fraternity of social climbers. Describing a Roland Hayes concert, he notes with astonishment that the bourgeois audience seems to prefer the classics on the program to the Negro spirituals which Hayes gives as encores. The latter draw muted applause at best. "Yes, this true artist did not find an echo amongst the brethren of his race that he would have encountered in the great concert halls of this world." The same effect is observed at a folk life concert where a black group does work songs and draws criticism from Hilltop faculty wives: "Africans." "Those with us had forgotten their simple origins, were trying to move from the swamps to the salon" (169). In their eagerness to assimilate, they had lost their ability to appreciate their own true folk art. But there is also insurgent political consciousness. A black militant student of Jamaican extraction explodes: "These know-it-alls here at Hilltop, the entire bastardized society, which is neither black nor white, will certainly not be the leadership in the fight toward the emancipation of blacks. We hate them, we despise them." Even Afrocentrism makes an appearance. The narrator mentions a black professor of religion who is an advocate of Afrocentrism, a theory that the narrator outs as nonsense. "The achievements of African blacks are important enough not to call for absurdities." Most puzzling to Smith is the power of the president and his ability to control the seething cauldron of discontent and to choreograph what Thorstein Veblen called "the conscientious withdrawal of efficiency." When Smith proposes to do a public lecture on "the white man in primitive art," the postcolonial topic creates such a sense of panic at Hilltop that the first attempt is tacitly boycotted by everyone including the janitors. The slide projector does not work, nobody shows up since someone forgot to hang the posters. Only when the narrator insists on going through with his lecture does the event finally happen. There is a mixed-race audience, which at Howard means courting danger. The atmosphere is tense. A white American visitor comments: "Only your naiveté brought us together."

As part of a project Smith asks his students to do an anthropological study of black religion in the city. We get a fairly accurate description of the singing preacher Elder Lightfoot Solomon Michaux and his "Happy Am I" congregation, and we learn about the charitable institutions of Daddy Grace, also about his powers over his detractors. Two of his students, who are attuned to religious sentiments, introduce him to the denominational differences between rocking storefront churches and the more bourgeois congregations. He comments on a lengthy radio sermon by Elder Lightfoot Solomon Michaux rather positively, but finds the interruption by a commercial for a laxative shocking, a typical example of the pernicious effect of American capitalism on black life. A much-advertised scientific conference set up by the Social Science Division turns into a major disaster: nobody at Hilltop or of the city shows up or is interested. In fact there is a total lack of interest on the part of the student body, the other faculty, and the surrounding white world. The small group that attends decides to adjourn to a student bar where they are treated to a blackface minstrel performance got up by the students. The final two chapters deal with the secret powers and leader-ship talents of Obadiah Wedlock. There seems to be a revolution afoot to upset and demote the president. This corresponds to one of several attempts to oust President Johnson, who ran Howard like an autocrat. The case against Johnson was raised by the General Alumni Federation, which issued a special issue of its journal in winter of 1937–1938 (Logan, 338). How does the president deal with it in Lips's account? First he dresses down his staff by telling them what he thinks of their academic qualification and what they owe to him. His criticism is that they have failed to improve the race. He particularly lambastes the stupid mimicry of pure science—an area of inquiry where they with their strictly limited talents would never make it anyway. In fact pure science is a mere veil for their incompe-tence. Instead, they should have strengthened the applied sciences and contem-plated their services to the race, a sentiment in line with Booker T. Washington. All those "performers" who had been so brave in combating Obadiah by parody or "putting pressure" on him are now mute and subdued. "Putting pressure on the president is dangerous." When McLee tries to get a pay raise, the president outfoxes him. When Dean Hastings passes away, the president appoints a non-entity in education, Rockefeller Delirious Blockhead (Dean Thompson), who en-ters the fray with a "Ten Year Plan." Intriguing are the author's remarks on the treatment of white staff. Either they are superheroes like Smith who are above the caterwauling and cabals, or they are subaltern staff who have to be doubly subservient and are doomed to play white Uncle Toms (272). Often they are from the American South and are made to pay for the sins of their fathers. But there are also those who cynically exploit this niche in the racialized system. One Dr. Hail, a biologist who studies "roots" is known on campus as the hyena and root doctor (276).

The penultimate chapter is entitled "The Seven Sermons of Obadiah" where the latter is introduced as a consummate performer and orator. Again Lips stays very close to the original Mordecai Johnson. Like him Obadiah pulls all registers in his commencement speech on "The Achievement of the Black Race." Logan writes about Johnson: "He exploited his commanding physical presence and res-onant voice which ran the gamut from an overpowering crescendo to almost a whisper . . . Few persons who heard him were left unmoved, although many lis-teners had later reservations about the intellectual content of some of his public addresses" (250), and he adds that regrettably Johnson left no paper trace of his oratorical abilities for he never wrote his speeches down. In two chapters Lips gives a detailed rendering of two speeches which correspond in manner of de-livery and radical content to Logan's description of Johnson. The final chapter is entitled "Homecoming" and ends on a note of hope. The blind emeritus Homer Anderson wants to set up a museum of the American Negro. The final scene brings Parker and Anderson together. In Smith's estimate they are the finest specimen of the university. With obvious disgust Parker pulls out of his pocket a letter by the student union propagating, "The James Weldon Johnson Social Reg-ister" of Hilltop University. The narrator ends his survey of Hilltop mores with:

"Everything is enveloped in the feeling of a great and unspecified sadness." The dedication of the book reads: "I dedicate this book to the liberation of the Negro race from its black and white oppressors."

Lips assumes the position of the cosmopolitan, enhanced by a self-aggrandizing personality, but he is a steadfast universalist and critic of racism. As has become evident there is quite a bit of ironic potential in the point of view of the German exiled Africanist who considers his African American colleagues legitimate objects of his ethnographic scrutiny and who is forever in search of the true African soul behind the façade of intellectual mimicry and social pretensions. His observations, though choreographed by his overarching worldview, are quite trenchant. Clearly his critique of Howard social life is based on intimate knowledge. This allows him to satirize the dilemma of these doubly alienated scholars and blame it on their inability to accept their true "Negroness."

Lips remains a staunch Eurocentric universalist and thus an opponent of racism, but also a romantic Africanist, a defender of primitive culture against "effete American civilization," of cultural purity against the hybridity of mulatto twilight. This combination of attitudes made him highly suspect at Hilltop and perhaps a bit of a loose cannon for his colleagues who were trying to cope in a racialized world. A white innocent abroad at Howard would have been enough of a liability, but Lips clearly intended to "help" and ended up as an elephant in a porcelain shop. Unfortunately we have no evidence of what went on behind the scenes, whether his previous history as a confidence man or plagiarist was ever revealed to his colleagues at Howard, whether Boas was involved as much in his dismissal as in his hiring, or whether it was his professional incompetence as an Africanist or indeed his constant breach of racial etiquette which made his stay at Hilltop a liability for his colleagues and for the president. These are questions that need further research.[4]

Notes

1. Author's translation.

2. Andreas Scheller (1894–1977) was succeeded in 1940 by Martin Heydrich (1889–1969), a fervent Nazi, who in accordance with the Nazi outreach for new Lebensraum founded the "neo-colonial movement." Despite this Nazi mortgage Heydrich received "denazification papers" in 1948, was reinstated in his position, and ultimately became one of the leading post–WWII ethnologist in Germany. In his letters Lips names the Nazi restoration as his main reason for not returning to Cologne after the war and for trying his luck in Leipzig.

3. The twilight metaphor is well established in the black tradition. W. E. B. Dubois used it repeatedly. So do Derek Walcott, *What the Twilight Says* (1970), and Cornel West, "Black Strivings in a Twilight Civilization," in *The Future of the Race* (New York: Vintage 1996).

4. This article draws on a short previous version: "Forschungsreise in die Dämmerung: The Strange Transatlantic Career of Julius Lips between Howard University Washington D.C. and Leipzig University," *Transatlantic Cultural Contexts: Essays in Honor of Eberhard Brüning*, ed. Hartmut Keil (Tübingen: Stauffenburg, 2005), 115–27.

Works Cited

Centlivres, Pierre. "Julius Lips et la riposte sauvage." *Terrain* 28. *Miroirs du colonialisme* (Mars 1997). Online version: //terrain.revues.org/documents3172.html.

Diaz de Arce, Norbert. *Plagiatsvorwurf und Denunziation: Untersuchungen zur Geschichte der Altamerikanistik in Berlin 1900–1945.* Freie Universität, Berlin. Dr. phil. Diss, 2005.

Edgcomb, Gabrielle Simon. *From Swastika to Jim Crow: Refugee Scholars at Black Colleges.* Malabar: Krieger Publishing, 1993.

Fischer, Hans. "Der Fall Julius Lips." *Völkerkunde im Nationalsozialismus: Aspekte der Anpassung, Affinität und Behauptung einer wissenschaftlichen Disziplin.* Berlin: Dietrich Reimer Verlag, 1990. 181–91.

Frazier, E. Franklin. *Black Bourgeoisie: The Rise of a New Middle Class in the United States.* New York: Macmillan, 1957.

Leser, Paul. Review of Julius Lips. *Einleitung in die vergleichende Völkerkunde.* In *Ethnologischer Anzeiger* 2 E. G. Weimann Verlag Leipzig (1929–32): 234–38.

Lips, Eva. "Vom Ursprung der Dinge." *Zwischen Lehrstuhl und Indianerzelt: Aus dem Leben und Werk von Julius Lips.* Berlin, 1965. www.jadu.de/jadukids/ursprung/index.html.

Lips, Eva. *What Hitler Did to Us. A Personal Record of the Third Reich.* London, 1938.

Lips, Julius. *The Savage Hits Back.* Introduction by Bronislaw Malinowski, translated by Vincent Benson. New Haven, CT: Yale University Press, 1937. xix–xxxi.

Lips, Julius. *Forschungsreise in die Dämmerung: Aus den Aufzeichnungen und Dokumenten des Professors Smith über sein Leben an einer Negeruniversität.* Weimar: Kiepenheuer, 1950.

Lips, Julius. *Der Weiße im Spiegel der Farbigen.* Introd. Eva Lips. Leipzig: VEB E.A. Seemann Verlag and München: Carl Hanser Verlag, 1983.

Logan, Rayford W. *Howard University: The First Hundred Years, 1867–1967.* New York: New York University Press, 1969.

Mühlmann, Wilhelm. *Rassen- und Völkerkunde.* Bielefeld: Vieweg & Sohn, 1936.

Muse, Clifford L., Jr. "Howard University and U.S. foreign affairs during the Franklin D. Roosevelt administration, 1933–1945." *Journal of African American History* 87 (Fall 2002): 403–15.

Nietzsche, Friedrich. *Jenseits von Gut und Böse.* Sechstes Hauptstück: Wir Gelehrten, 1885. 207–208. München: DTV, 1988.

Ostendorf, Berndt. "Black Poetry, Blues, and Folklore: Double Consciousness in Afro-American Oral Culture." *Amerikastudien* 20 (1975): 209–59.

Ostendorf, Berndt. "Celebration or Pathology? Commodity or Art? The Dilemma of African American Expressive Culture." *Black Music Research Journal* (Fall 2000): 213–33.

Pützstück, Lothar. *Symphonie in Moll: Julius Lips und die Kölner Völkerkunde.* Pfaffenweiler: Centaurus Verlag, 1995.

Pützstück, Lothar. "Von Dichtung und Wahrheit im akademischen Lehrbetrieb. Die Entlassung des Völkerkundlers Julius E. Lips durch die Nationalsozialisten in Köln 1933." In *Nachhilfe zur Erinnerung—600 Jahre Universität zu Köln*, ed. Wolfgang Blaschke et al. Köln: 1988.

Miscellaneous Sources

Franz Boas Papers. American Philosophical Society, Philadelphia. The generous help of Curator Robert S. Cox is gratefully acknowledged.

Lips to Boas. June 12, 1933, February 25, 1934.

Lips to Sattler. December 7, 1939. Lips to Franz Boas, July 31, 1936, July 30, 1938, December 12, 1939, and January 8, 1941. Boas letter to Lips, January 10, 1941.

Clifford L. Muse. Moorland Spingarn Research Center, letter of May 18, 1994.

Thompson, Dean Charles H. June 13, 1939, to the *Washington Daily News.*

Love across the Color Line

The Limits of German and American Democracy, 1945–1968

MARIA HÖHN

For many decades, research on the American military occupation in West Germany and the more than sixty-year lasting military presence has been concerned with high politics, the economy, and denazification.[1] It was not until the 1990s that a new generation of scholars turned to the social consequences of the U.S. presence. This more recent research has also raised the important issues of gender and race by exploring the sexual relationships between GIs and German women, and by incorporating African American GIs into the narrative of the U.S. occupation.[2] Some of that research is also concerned with how German debates on race after 1945 were transformed in the encounter with American racial assumptions. In my own work, *GIs and Fräuleins*, I have shown how German notions of race and proper female sexuality were informed by the daily observance of, and interaction with, American forms of racial boundaries in the U.S. military. Thus, while the Americans brought democracy to Germany, the nature of that democracy was compromised by *de jure* racial segregation of the military during the years of occupation when U.S. influence on German society was most pronounced. Integration of the U.S. military forces in Europe was not accomplished until 1953, but even after integration, Germans were able to observe on a daily basis the social segregation that remained the norm in the military. Until the American civil rights revolution of the 1960s came to U.S. military bases in Germany, Germans could assume that their alliance with America was an alliance between two white nations, and that West Germany's new democracy was, just like America's, fully compatible with the social exclusion of racial minorities.[3]

The thorough exploration of the transnational transfer of American racial assumptions has only just begun and will have to go beyond the limited focus on Germany, since the American military has had a substantial troop presence in many other countries since 1945.[4] This transnational approach will also need to focus more closely on how American debates on race and the American civil rights struggle were impacted by the experience of the military abroad, and will need to attend specifically to the experiences of African American GIs. In my new research, which explores the grievances of African American GIs over discrimination in U.S. military bases in Germany, and within German society, I argue that African American GIs expanded the American civil rights movement beyond the physical boundaries of the United States.[5] One of the first instances that allowed them to do so, as I argue in this essay, was their experience of being able to enter into intimate relationships with German women after America's victory over Nazism.[6]

By looking at the intersection of American and German forms of racism expressed over these romantic relationships, and by exploring interracial marriages between black GIs and white German women, I uncovered a fascinating cross-cultural and cross-national learning experience. For the Americans, this learning process was initiated by African American GIs who compared the relative freedom they experienced in postwar Germany to indict the absence of that same tolerance and freedom in the United States.[7] The soldiers' freedom to associate with white German women also generated a sustained debate about the propriety of racial mixing in Germany despite the country's constitutional commitment not to discriminate on the basis of race. The German and American debates on interracial relationships after 1945 reveal a separate but also simultaneous learning process, in which the American and German understanding of the meaning of democracy was vastly expanded. By the mid- to late 1960s, democracy was no longer understood to mean merely constitutional government, free elections, and equal opportunity in jobs and education, but also the right of racial minorities to social equality. As my essay will show furthermore, in both the United States and Germany the German Nazi past served as a background against which discussions about the propriety of interracial love and marriage were conducted.

Black GIs and Germany

As scholars of the civil rights movement have shown, WWII invigorated the cause of civil rights in the United States significantly. The so-called Double V (Double Victory) campaign, endorsed by the National Association for the Advancement of Colored People, envisioned the participation of African American soldiers in the struggle against fascism as bringing about a world without racism at home or abroad. The NAACP's publication, *The Crisis*, enunciated those goals in January 1942 when it insisted that "for 13 million of American Negroes that means a fight for a world in which lynching, brutality, terror, humiliation and degradation through segregation and discrimination shall have no place—either here or there."[8] To drive home the point that racism was not merely a scourge to be defeated in Europe, *The Crisis* insisted that the "fight against Hitlerism begins in Washington D.C., the capital of our nation, where black Americans have a status only slighter above that of Jews in Berlin."[9]

While service in the wartime military had already stoked the desire of African American GIs for greater political and social rights, it was their experience of serving in the occupation in Germany gave that desire even greater urgency.[10] Recollections of African American GIs show that they tended to experience their time in Germany as a moment of liberation. Black GIs had come as conquerors and wore the uniform of victors, but their experience as second-class citizens in the occupation army softened their attitude toward the vanquished. German society was hardly free from racism, but lacking in the encounter between Germans and African American GIs was the institutionalized and legal racism of the Jim Crow South and the deeply entrenched traditions of segregation that prevailed in much of the rest of the United States.[11]

Prominent in the recollections of black soldiers and in the African American press coverage on the GIs' experience in Germany was the fact that black GIs could date white women. It would be a mistake, however, to argue that these interracial romantic and sexual relationships were the only, or even the most important, interactions with Germans that convinced African American GIs that their experience in Germany was a moment of liberation.[12] What is important about these relationships is that for black GIs they presented the collapse of the very foundation on which the elaborate system of American racial segregation and racial domination was built.[13]

The centrality of the prohibition against romantic and sexual relationships in the elaborate system of American racial boundaries, and the existence of miscegenation laws in thirty of the states of the United States, induced the African American press to stress that the ultimate taboo was broken in the very land where, as *Ebony*, put it, "Aryanism" had "ruled supreme." By linking images of German women and black GIs with a commentary on the presence of democracy in Germany and a lack thereof in the United States, *Ebony* argues that the soldiers' "freedom" to associate with a white woman was about more than just sexual relations. The magazine also contrasted those experiences with the reality of black life in the United States. The magazine informed its readers in 1946 that "Negroes are finding more friendship, more respect and more equality than they would back home—either in Dixie or on Broadway." While providing a wide selection of photos of interracial fraternization, *Ebony* concluded that "many of the Negro GIs . . . find that democracy has more meaning on Wilhelmstrasse than on Beale Street in Memphis."[14]

Because of this extensive coverage in the African American press, the "freedom" that African American GIs experienced in post-Nazi Germany also reverberated powerfully back home. Male readers of *Ebony* responded to the stories from Germany by also connecting the GIs' experience of loving and being loved by a white woman with democracy, a democracy that was missing in their own lives. One reader wrote in 1947,

Your pictures and articles on . . . "GIs in Germany" were great, because . . . they gave undeniable proof that the Negro is a human being, a creature who loves and is loved . . . As a free people we Negroes want the right to live wherever we choose and can pay the rent; to associate with, court or marry whomever we choose . . . If a Negro boy and a white girl find things in common and desire to associate with each other, we as believers in democratic freedom should support their democratic right to do so.[15]

As Renee Romano has argued in *Race Mixing*, until the rise of black nationalism in the second half of the 1960s, *Ebony* and *Negro Digest* were exuberant
in their support of interracial relationships and marriages, believing that such
unions could overcome the American "race problem." Throughout the 1950s and
into the 1960s those two magazines as well as newspapers such as the *Pittsburgh
Courier* reported approvingly on the rare occasions when such marriages did
take place. In the United States, those marriages usually involved movie stars, or
the occasional marriage between a black artist and a "society girl." The coverage
in the African American press on such relationships in Germany was remarkable
because it was not concerned with celebrities whose way of life was unattainable,
but with "regular people" who had fallen in love and were willing to defy long-
established prohibitions.

What also stands out in the coverage of the African American press on black
GIs in Germany is that throughout the years of occupation, the black press insisted that American servicemen and officers were acting like Nazis, while Germans
were treating black GIs kindly. Headlines such as "Found Freedom in Germany.
Few GIs Eager to Return to States" and "American Officers Abroad Propagating
Race Hatred" powerfully conveyed the disappointment of black Americans over
their own country's shortcomings to a broad African American readership. In
that coverage, the African American press was also not afraid to print headlines
such as "Nazi Attitudes of White Soldiers" to bring home the message that the
U.S. victory over Nazism had done little to defeat "Hitlerism" at home in the
United States.[16] Another headline in the *Pittsburgh Courier* "War's End Left Untouched Nazi Race Ideas in Midst of Army," put forth that the problem African
Americans faced was not just racism from individuals, but also a larger institutional one.[17]

Such explicit comparisons between U.S. racism and Nazi racism disappeared
in the African American press once the Cold War heated up and black civil rights
leaders saw their best strategy in aligning themselves with Cold War liberals in
the common struggle against communism. That struggle forced white America to
make serious civil rights concessions at home if the country wanted to maintain
its self-proclaimed position as the leader of the free world.[18] At the same time, the
Cold War also severely limited the scope of that struggle because opponents of
civil rights regularly framed the demands of African Americans as part of a communist plot aimed at undermining the moral fiber of America.[19] Under that logic,
all civil rights legislation had one aim—namely, the destruction of the color line
that protected white women from the sexual advances of black men and assured
white supremacy rule. These kinds of arguments were not limited to uneducated
racists, and held wide sway. As Lee Nichols has shown, during debates on the
integration of the military, officers "always rang in a bedroom scene" to make the
case that integration would weaken, not strengthen the nation.[20]

The anxieties of white supremacists, in combination with those of Cold War
liberals who insisted on restrained white female sexuality as an antidote to overcome the gender upheaval of the war and to contain Cold War *angst*, left little
room for tolerating interracial love and marriage.[21] Black civil rights leaders

understood this constellation of forces as well, and they were extremely anxious not to endorse interracial marriage for fear of being accused by white racists that this was their sole agenda. Throughout the 1950s, the NAACP practiced "firm abstention" from the issue, and Thurgood Marshall pleaded with the ACLU not to challenge the antimiscegenation laws in the courts.[22] Martin Luther Kings's famous statement from 1958 that he wanted to be the "white man's brother, not his brother-in-law," expressed powerfully those anxieties. In private, it should be noted, King railed against the "cruel and silly forces in life that were keeping two people from doing what they most wanted to do."[23]

White America Responds

Outside of the black community, the topic of romantic love between white European women and African American GIs also attracted attention. Already during the staging phase for D-Day in Great Britain, the military worried that pictures and stories of African American GIs dancing with English women would undermine support for the mission at home. To ensure that such photos would no longer appear in the press, the military had them stamped for "private use only."[24] The occupation in Germany did not alleviate those concerns because black occupation soldiers were now also in a position to exercise power over a white population. Not surprisingly, southern segregationists were appalled at what was happening in Germany, and they threatened that African Americans would have to be reined in upon their return to the United States. Former head of the American Legion Alvin Owsley felt compelled to inform General Eisenhower in 1946 that the black GIs who had experienced new freedoms in Germany, "likely [were] on the way to be hanged or to be burned alive at public lynchings by the white men of the South."[25] Numerous returning GIs were in fact lynched as white southerners tried to reverse the empowerment African American men had gained abroad. Hate groups like the Columbians were adamant that the new freedoms black GIs had experienced abroad ought not reverberate in the United States because "Americans who had died in Europe had not given their lives so that niggers could marry white American women."[26]

It is hardly surprising that racist segregationists opposed interracial relationships, but the overwhelming majority of white civil rights supporters also did not endorse romantic relations between blacks and whites, let alone interracial marriage. For much of the 1940s and 1950s, their focus was first and foremost on assuring the formal rights of democracy, not social equality.[27] An American officer, speaking for many progressive Americans after WWII, reveals the gender conservatism and the limited vision of social equality for minorities that defined the 1950s civil rights agenda:

Even I am not sure how far I would go to insure that democracy. I want my colored friend to vote; I want him to be free from prejudice in the courts; I want him to go to college; . . . I want him to know and enjoy the four freedoms. I will work hard to see that he—or his sons—get these things, but—I do not want him to live next door to me; I do not want him to be my houseguest; and I do not want him to dance with my daughter.[28]

Harry Truman, the president who had used the prerogative of the Executive office to force the integration of the military in 1948, one of the landmark developments in the advancement of civil rights, echoed many of those same convictions in a 1963 interview. When a reporter asked the former president if he thought school integration would lead to intermarriage, he answered, "I hope not. I don't believe in it. The Lord created it that way. You read your Bible and you'll find out."[29]

Just how sensitive the topic of intermarriage was in even the most progressive circles of American society can be seen in the uproar over Hannah Arendt's essay "Reflections on Little Rock" published in *Dissent* in 1959. In her essay, Arendt argues that "with respect to constitutional legislation, the Civil Rights bill did not go far enough, for it left untouched the most outrageous laws of Southern States—the law which makes mixed marriage a criminal offense. The right to marry whoever one wishes is an elementary human right." The editors of *Dissent* distanced themselves from her argument, assuring the readers that "we publish [Arendt's article] not because we agree with it—quite the contrary!—but because we believe in freedom of expression even for views that seem to us entirely mistaken." To drive that point home, *Dissent* offered two rebuttals, one of which actually supported legal restrictions on interracial marriage.[30]

The philosopher Sidney Hook, one of New York's most distinguished intellectuals, even went so far as to accuse Arendt of being more interested in equality in the bedroom than in the classroom.[31] A shocked Arendt responded by asserting the moral high ground and referring to her background as a German-born Jew. She pointed out the limits of Hook's liberal vision of civil rights, which, in her eyes, was only concerned with "social opportunity" but paid little attention to "human dignity."[32] Arendt lambasted her American liberal colleagues for insisting that, "Negroes themselves have no interest in this matter." She also reminded Hook of the "embarrassment" suffered by liberal America for tolerating "what the whole world knows to be the most outrageous piece of legislation in the whole western hemisphere." To emphasize her point, Arendt reminded Hook and his liberal colleagues of the shameful episode of the twenty-seven African American soldiers who had returned to the United States with wives from Germany in 1957. The soldiers could not be stationed at a military base in Texas because their marriage to a white woman made them "guilty of a crime in the eyes of Texas legislation." While she did not say so explicitly, Arendt clearly wanted to drive home her outrage that this humiliation of black servicemen and their white German wives was possible in the very country that defeated Nazism twelve years prior. Arendt concluded her response to Hook by reiterating that "it was not discrimination and social segregation, in whatever forms, but racial legislation [that] constitutes the perpetuation of the original crime in this country's history."[33]

The outcry over the Hannah Arendt comments illustrate that the overwhelming majority of white Americans assumed that their democracy was compatible with the legal prohibition against interracial marriage. If civil rights were to be fought for, the focus would be on assuring the formal rights of democracy, the right to vote, the right to a job, the right to equal access to education, or to rent an apartment. Love between the races was not on the agenda as the first national poll on that topic revealed. The Gallup poll of 1958 showed that 95 percent of white northerners and 99 percent of white southerners disapproved of interracial marriage. African Americans were not asked what they thought, so the *Pittsburgh Courier* conducted its own poll, which showed that African Americans did not share the sentiments of white America; 70 percent would not object if their children married a white person.[34]

Despite America's victory over fascism and Nazi racism, change was slow to come in the United States, and when it came it was against overwhelming public opposition. Supported by the Catholic Interracial Council of Los Angeles, a couple, which had been denied the right to marry in California, took their case in 1948 to the state's supreme court. The court voted in their favor, ruling that the existing miscegenation laws were unconstitutional because "marriage was a fundamental right of free men." Interestingly enough, the case was decided by the plaintiff's argument that those laws violated the couple's free exercise of religion. Because both of them were Catholics, the deciding vote (4 to 3) was cast by a California supreme court justice who defended their rights as Catholics (rather than their equal rights as American citizens). Still, the recent victory over Nazism clearly influenced how the judges voted. The couples' lawyer repeatedly made his argument by comparing the state's miscegenation laws and the arguments of the State of California in defense of those laws with the racist rants of Adolf Hitler in *Mein Kampf.* Those arguments impressed the justices who made repeated reference to the victory over Nazism and America's failure to live up to its own creed of equality at home.[35] After that 1948 ruling, Oregon, Montana, North Dakota, South Dakota, Colorado, Idaho, and Nevada quietly abandoned the laws between 1951 and 1959, often because white American veterans who had served in Japan or Korea complained that those laws violated their civil rights because they also forbid marriage with Asian partners.[36]

By the early 1960s, the ACLU and the American Jewish Congress, who had championed the struggle so far, were finally joined by the NAACP, the National Catholic Conference, and the General Assembly of the United Presbyterian Church.[37] As the pressure was growing, five more states (Arizona, Utah, Nebraska, Indiana, and Wyoming) abandoned the laws before the 1967 Supreme Court decision in *Loving versus Commonwealth of Virginia* declared miscegenation laws unconstitutional, thus forcing the remaining fifteen states in the South to take them off the books. The 1960s also saw a vigorous return to the strategy of the 1940s, when civil rights activists equated the spirit of the U.S. miscegenation laws with those of Nazi Germany. When making their case, the lawyers for the couple drew comparisons between Virginia's policy of "racial integrity" and "Hitler's dream" of a "super race."[38] In their landmark ruling, the judges concluded, that "marriage is one of the basic civil rights of man, fundamental to our very existence and survival . . . under our constitution, the freedom to marry or not to marry a person of another race resides with the individual and cannot be infringed upon by the state."[39] With that decision, the principal and most enduring underpinning of Jim Crow America was abolished.[40]

The Court's ruling was truly revolutionary given that in 1965, 72 percent of white southerners and 42 percent of white northerners still rejected interracial marriage and insisted on the validity of such laws. Disapproval numbers were even higher when people were asked how they felt about such a marriage for somebody in their own family. Ninety percent of white Americans and 97 percent of white southerners were opposed. These numbers stand in stark contrast to those of black Americans: 80 percent of African Americans questioned would approve if their child married a person of another race, and those who were not in favor mostly feared the hardship that their children would have to endure.[41]

Interracial Love and Marriage—Debates in Germany

While American civil rights activists struggled until 1967 to convince the U.S. Supreme Court to overturn the still-existing miscegenation laws, the U.S. military government in Germany was able to declare null and void all Nazi racial laws. With a stroke of the pen, the Allied Control Council invalidated the infamous 1935 Nuremburg Race Laws that had declared "miscegenation" (*Rassenschande*) a crime against the *Volk* that could be punished by death.[42] That purge of Germany's racial laws was followed up with an effort at reeducation that enlisted the soldiers and their families serving in the occupation. Just how successful the military was in conveying this message is highly debatable, given that the occupation was conducted with a strictly segregated and stridently racist military.[43] Be that as it may, the 1948 Basic Law of the Federal Republic was a self-conscious expression that the lessons of the past had been taken to heart. The *Grundgesetz* enshrined that discrimination based on race or religion would not be tolerated in the new democracy.

Thus, in postwar West Germany, racial categories with regard to black and white relationships and marriages were legally irrelevant, but as we will see in the discussion below, they were nonetheless important social markers.[44] While concerns over interracial relationships arose as soon as the first African American soldier set foot into Germany, *public* debates on that topic were not to be found during the years of occupation because Germans were not allowed to criticize the occupying powers. After the establishment of the Federal Republic, the debates on interracial relationships in West Germany's garrison towns hosting American troops became much more vocal; at times they also became hostile. What marks the debate on the propriety of interracial love and marriage in the 1950s is that Germans distanced themselves from Nazism when voicing their opposition.[45] They did so by drawing on racial hierarchies that long predated the

Nazi regime, and in doing so, they sounded very much like American opponents of such marriages. These Germans did not regard their convictions as residual racism inherited from Nazism, but understood them as "natural" or "God-given" notions fully compatible with Western tradition and their new democracy. A 1952 essay published by a Protestant minister in the *Pfälzische Volkszeitung* is a typical example of that strategy. The author warned that "the racially mixed marriage presents a danger . . . and that God has made the different races and wants them separate accordingly."[46]

German commentaries expressing opposition to interracial marriage reveal that in the garrison towns of Germany, local officials and the population were aware of the existing miscegenation laws in the United States. Germans were also fully cognizant of the fact that most military commanders did everything in their power to prevent such marriages.[47] The German officials who conducted the marriages of GIs and German women, for example, could only marry the couple after the military commander had given his permission. The *Standesbeamte* also had to keep the marriage laws of all states in the United States on record so that they could inform the German partner of what awaited them in the United States. Thus, when Germans expressed their opposition to interracial relationships during the 1950s, they often suggested that nobody could fault the Germans for wanting to look to the American model of racial segregation as a guide for German behavior in this question.[48] Observing the American military's vehement opposition toward interracial marriages convinced these Germans that at least some aspects of Nazi racial segregation, codified in the 1935 Nuremberg Laws, were not an aberration but instead were wholly compatible with Western democracy.

Even progressive voices that called for "racial tolerance" drew the line when it came to interracial relationships, and in doing so they also very much echoed the convictions of American liberals at the time. A typical example of that attitude can be found in a 1957 newspaper essay that admonished Germans to treat all Americans "with the same courtesy—no matter what their skin color may be— as long as [they] conform to local morality standards" (*sich wie gesittete Menschen benehmen*). The essay included two photographs to illuminate what was considered proper and improper behavior for American GIs. The first picture showed a black soldier in the arms of a white woman. The other picture showed three black soldiers who were sitting by themselves, drinking beer. The writer suggested that it was no wonder that the "local population was tired of seeing the shameless next steps of the embracing couple," but that nobody minded when "dark-skinned young men" come into the city of Kaiserslautern and "peacefully drink their beer" (by themselves, one should add).[49]

As I have argued in *GIs and Fräuleins*, postwar Germans hardly needed the Americans to teach them how to be racists. Still, in their day-to-day encounters with the American military it was easy enough for Germans to assume that their alliance with America was an alliance between two white nations, and that their new democracy was, just like America's, not compromised by their objections to interracial sexuality and marriage. Because Germans could observe the widespread opposition toward the social implications of integration, and especially interracial marriage within the U.S. military, Germans could also insist that their own opposition to such marriages should not mark them as Nazis. Interacting with American racism thus allowed Germans to revive pre-Nazi models of racial exclusion that they based in immutable laws of nature or understood as being tied firmly to the Western liberal tradition.

Winds of Change: Germany in the 1950s and 1960s

In Germany, as in the United States, attitudes toward interracial relationships were slow to change and it was not until the mid-1960s that a new consensus toward an expanded understanding of democracy emerged. For the German side of my story we do, of course, not have the extensive legal record and the society-wide debates on such relationships that we have for the United States. Still, during my research in German garrison towns hosting American troops, I have come across a number of court cases that show that as late as the 1960s legal rulings involving romantic relationships with people of color were deeply pervaded by race. My findings also suggest that a dramatic transformation was underway by the late 1950s and early 1960s in terms of how Germans thought about interracial relationships, and how the country's Nazi past was framed when debating those relationships.[50]

A 1956 ruling of the Amtsgericht Baumholder reveals just how much race informed German justices at a time when race was no longer considered a legally relevant category. In 1956 a young woman, identified only as Dagmar, was arrested for prostitution in the small town of Baumholder when German and American police officers picked her up in a so-called Negro-Bar (Negerbar). Tracking down alleged prostitutes in this manner was standard procedure in Germany's garrison communities, since both the German police and American military police officers assumed that any woman in the company of a black man could be nothing but a prostitute. Thus it was in the daily praxis of how German police and American military police conducted their combined vice raids in West Germany's garrison towns that the boundaries of proper German female sexuality were negotiated. At a time when no more than 13 percent of the U.S. soldiers stationed in Germany were African Americans, almost 80 percent of the women indicted for prostitution in Baumholder were charged because they were arrested in the company of a black GI.[51]

Despite the nationally known severity of the Baumholder court, Dagmar got off in the most unusual circumstances: the same court that regularly and ruthlessly condemned women to jail and the workhouse for being picked up in the company of a black man, showed mercy in her case, because the woman in question was an Afro-German, born in 1934. Giving voice to widespread objection to racial mixing, the judge argued that she should not be punished as a prostitute since only a black man would be an appropriate partner for her. Unfortunately, the state archive no longer held the proceedings of the trial, only the judgment, but the newspaper coverage of the trial is illuminating. The woman is described as a "young colored German, who combines favorably the two races in her person." The paper continues that "for the 22-year old Dagmar from Saxony, only a husband of the same color would be appropriate. As a *Mischling* (mixed race) she never had a very rosy youth, so that it is understandable that she searched for the love of a Negro soldier—and found it." The paper praises the judge for recognizing "immediately that Dagmar does not belong to the usual sort of girls." Dagmar was also helped by the fact that she was able to show a letter from her future mother-in-law, who "expressed her happiness that her son will marry a dark-skinned girl."[52]

A ruling of Bavaria's highest court, the *Oberlandesgericht*, Nürnberg in 1960 revealed that the chambers of provincial *Amtsgerichte* were not the only places where race informed the rulings of judges. In this case, the *Oberlandesgericht* affirmed the 1957 ruling of a lower court that had assigned sole blame for a divorce to the wife. The judges ruled in this manner, because the woman had allegedly failed to tell her husband when she married him in 1951 that a black occupation soldier had sired her illegitimate son (born in 1946). The woman appealed the decision, arguing that her husband had always known that the father of the child had a "dark complexion" (*dunkler Teint*). Defending her former lover, but also her choice of him as a partner, the woman argued that she had never considered him a "Negro." She stressed his European roots by describing him as a descendent of a French woman in New Orleans. It was not due to the mixed-race child that her husband had left her, the woman argued, but because of another woman. Her husband had been fully aware when they got married in 1951 that the child was of "foreign ethnic stock" (*fremdstämmiger Herkunft*).

During the review process for the new trial, the woman's German husband died and the appeal case now also posed the question of whether the woman's son was eligible for an inheritance. The *Oberlandesgericht* decided against any sort of inheritance right for the child and reaffirmed the earlier ruling, arguing that the man would have never married the woman had he known the truth "about the descent (*Abstammung*) of her child."

> The fact that the illegitimate son of a woman was not sired by a white man but by a member of the Negro race, is, in light of the appropriate dignity of the essence of marriage (*richtiger Würdigung des Wesen der Ehe*) of such a significant circumstance, that it can prevent a man from marrying such a woman.[53]

Thus, in 1960, when German "racial liberals," pleased with their efforts of integrating the children born of German mothers and African American fathers, declared that "race" was no longer a valid category in Germany,[54] the judges at the Nuremburg state court had no qualms about insisting on the centrality of such categories in their rulings. What had changed, however, by 1960, was the public response to that ruling, which was not approval for reining in interracial sexuality, as was the case for most of the 1950s, but outright consternation. Germany's left-liberal magazine, *Der Spiegel*, for example, mocked the court's ruling in an article entitled, "Racial Segregation: Colored Fathers Not Allowed" (*Rassentrennung: Farbige Väter verboten*). *Spiegel*'s coverage indicates that change was in the air and that Germany's Nazi past was finally being debated more publicly. The magazine expressed its outrage, writing that the "judges jerry-rigged a decision that puts the relationships with dark-skinned lovers under special law (*Sonderrecht*)"; and this, *Der Spiegel* continued indignantly, "in the very city that gave its name to the Nazi racial laws" (which had prohibited marriage between "Aryan" Germans and German Jews, Gypsies, as well as people of color).[55]

The critical coverage of *Der Spiegel* reflected a broader trend under way. Beginning in the later part of the 1950s, liberal newspaper coverage of incidents of racism stressed that decent Germans spoke up, and that they protested on behalf of the victims of racist incidents. Newspapers often used humor or mocking in urging Germans to contemplate how deep-seated racism was in German society.[56] Much more research is needed to explore how this important shift came about, but I suspect that the desecration of the newly reopened Cologne synagogue with Swastikas on Christmas Day 1959 played a significant role in bringing about serious soul searching about the limits of racial tolerance in West Germany. Germans at the end of the 1950s and in the early 1960s were also for the first time facing more assertive African American GIs who refused to budge when they were denied service in restaurants or bars that catered to GIs. That greater assertiveness emerged at the same time that African students, brought to study at German universities, faced discrimination from Germans, and at times violence from white American military personnel, who mistook them for "uppity [American] blacks" who did not know their place and tried to enter establishments "reserved" for white GIs only. While German officials in the federal government all too quickly concluded that racist discrimination aimed at black GIs and African students was imported from America, because white GIs pressured German owners to keep people of color out, the public at large as well as the media began to stress German roots of these prejudices.[57]

The uproar caused by the actions of health workers in the town of Giessen in 1968, who harassed a young German student in the company of a black GI, reveals just how much attitudes had changed since the late 1950s. In terms of exploring how race played out in postwar Germany, Giessen is an interesting case study. Approximately seven hundred students from Africa studied as guests of the Federal Republic in the university's departments of medicine, veterinary medicine, and agriculture. A significant number of African American GIs also made their home in Giessen, which was host to a large U.S. military base. The public outcry caused by the case and the legal proceedings that followed show that an increasing number of Germans no longer believed that opposition and condemnation of interracial relationships was compatible with their democracy. Indeed, the public discourse surrounding this case shows that a growing number of Germans argued that opposition to such relationships proved that Germans had not overcome their Nazi past.

At the health office of the city of Giessen, an overzealous civil servant named Bernhard made it a practice to arrest and force gynecological exams on young women who were observed in the company of black GIs or African students. In October 1968, this happened to a young medical student who was walking in the company of a black GI after visiting a popular student pub. Bernhard, who was accompanied by two police officers, asked for her ID card (which he pocketed), and then told her that she would be taken to the local health office. Once there, and under substantial amount of duress, she submitted to a gynecological exam for venereal disease. Bernhard told her that failure to have the exam could result in her arrest. He also pressured her by saying that should she resist, her parents and the university would be notified that she was picked up for suspicion of prostitution.

The practice of the local health worker was highly improper and, as was later exposed, did not comply with existing laws on combating venereal disease. After overcoming her initial shock, the woman informed the *Frankfurter Rundschau*, a left of center, liberal newspaper. The newspaper wrote a scathing exposé of the incident; that story, in turn, attracted newspapers and magazines from across Germany to Giessen. *Bild Zeitung, Quick, Constanze, Vorwärts*, and *Konkret*, as well as television and radio stations, all reported on the incident. The *Frankfurter Rundschau* led the charge by condemning the fact that in Giessen, young women were afraid to show themselves in public with people of color.

In the 1950s this kind of story would have brought on swarms of voyeuristic reporters and streams of moralistic commentaries deploring the fact that black GIs could enjoy the company of a white woman in one of the "Little Harlems" of Germany's garrison towns.[58] The reaction in 1968 was decidedly different. Even *Quick*, one of Germany's more racy tabloid magazines, reported with outrage on "methods that reveal racial hatred and misogyny."[59] While plenty of Germans still agreed that women in the company of men of color were loose at best and prostitutes at worst, they kept such comments to themselves, indicating their disapproval through dirty looks or dispensing their objections anonymously. *Konkret*, as part of its coverage of the Giessen story, for example, printed a couple of letters from young women who had found hostile comments such as "Negro Whore" left anonymously on their car window or encountered dirty looks in restaurants.[60]

The students' reaction to the whole affair and the coverage within the media confirms Heide Fehrenbach's contention that discussions of "race" *within* German society had been silenced by the 1960s.[61] Never once did Germans responding to the events in Giessen point out that such racist policies might also victimize Afro-Germans who resided in Giessen. Their numbers were not large, but they were also not invisible given that Giessen had been home to a considerable number of black military units after the war, and a number of babies had been born to German women and African American soldiers. The protest expressed first and foremost outrage over the humiliation that had been inflicted on German female students and the "foreigners" they associated with. But the students' reactions, and those of some faculty and administrators at a series of teach-ins at the university, also show that a more engaged and public reckoning with Germany's Nazi past, as evidenced by the commentaries of *Der Spiegel* in the Nuremburg case, was underway. In flyers that were passed out to students and the citizens of Giessen, the students argued that racism was a home-grown problem with deep roots in German history: "As things stand, it would be a mistake to see the missteps of the health worker (Bernhard) in isolation, indeed they must be seen against the background of an unbroken continuation of racial ideology from the Third Reich."[62] AStA, the student council, brought this message to an even wider audience in letters to the editor of the *Frankfurter Rundschau* and the *Giessener Anzeiger* in which they argued that "beliefs about pure blood and racial disgrace (*Rassenschande*) that we thought were long overcome, seem to be celebrating a happy revival" (*Urständ*) in Giessen.[63]

Outrage about what happened in Giessen could also be found in letters to the editor of the *Frankfurter Rundschau*, local newspapers, and in editorials of newspapers in neighboring communities and cities. Letter writers expressed dismay that the young women were only picked up "because they were walking with men of color."[64] A somber editorial in the *Wetzlaer Zeitung* reiterated that such vice controls of women cannot be conducted out of sheer suspicion, and especially not simply because of the fact that the "woman was seen walking with a Negro."[65]

The aftermath of the incident suggests that the students and the sympathetic coverage in liberal newspapers gave voice to a broader consensus of how the German understanding of their democracy had been transformed. The courts in Giessen found the health worker Bernhard "guilty of illegally depriving the young woman of her liberty" and "punished him accordingly."[66] Even more important, when Bernhard sued the student and the *Frankfurter Rundschau* for libel for having called him a racist, the state's attorney office in Frankfurt rejected his suit. The office ruled in that manner because the civil servant's behavior and his attitudes were not just a "private concern" to be endured by the injured parties. Instead, they argued that "the critical coverage of the events described by the newspaper" needed to be aired because these issues were in the "interest of society at large" (*Interesse der Allgemeinheit*).[67] With this ruling, the judges gave voice to a much more inclusive understanding of democracy that also insisted on ensuring the rights of racial minorities.

The affair also had some bitter lessons for the city of Giessen. The young woman sued the city for compensatory damages and was awarded 1,000 DM (her attorney had asked for 5,000 DM but suggested that any favorable decision would send the correct message). In their verdict, the judges found Bernhard guilty of a number of inappropriate actions, but they also insisted that the mere fact that the woman was in the company of a "colored American" in the vicinity of the train station (a favorite pick-up location for prostitution) did not justify the suspicion against her.[68]

Conclusion

As the German and American debates on the propriety of interracial sexuality and marriage show, until the mid-1960s most Germans, like most white Americans, believed that their democracy was fully compatible with the social exclusion of racial minorities. For postwar Germans in the Federal Republic, the road to a more instinctive but also more inclusive democracy was—and continues to be—a long and drawn-out learning process. That learning process entailed a growing trust in pluralist-liberal values, but also involved challenging centuries of Eurocentric racism that has its roots in the Western liberal tradition. Significantly, the process of maturation was not a one-way street, with Americans bringing democratic values to the vanquished Germans. Instead, by bringing democracy to Germany, Americans themselves were forced to confront the limits of their own democratic model. African American GIs, their civil rights advocates in the United States, and the much-maligned German women who associated with the soldiers exposed the hypocrisy and limits of both the American and German visions of democracy. Neither the United States nor West Germany, nor any other Western country for that matter, was ready to acknowledge before the mid to late 1960s that democracy also entailed full social equality of racial minorities. Even when the demand for racial equality finally came to the forefront in the 1950s with the American civil rights movement, the debates were mostly limited to assuring the formal or "public" rights of democracy: the right to vote, equal access to jobs, or integrated education, rather than "private" rights, such as the right to choose one's spouse.

In both Germany and the United States, the conviction that democracy was possible without full social equality for minorities would not change until the emergence of the "rights revolution" of the 1960s that called for not only legal but also social equality.[69] We have seen how in the United States that shift was accompanied by the reemergence of a tactic that equated U.S. race laws with those of Nazism, a tactic that of civil rights activists had been silenced by the Cold War. In Germany, a similar shift was observable. Germans, who had been assured by their Cold War alliance with the United States during the 1950s that their opposition to interracial relationships should not mark them as Nazis, were no longer so certain. As I have shown, the debates about interracial sexuality led many Germans to acknowledge that racism had not been overcome and that their democracy was lacking because of that failure. For younger Germans who came of age after the war, taking on the Nazi past often merely meant an indictment of the "old Nazis" who still hung on for dear life. Older Germans were less harsh in their rhetoric; they often framed their stance against racism by pointing out that Germans have a special obligation to speak out given the country's Nazi past.

I do not want to suggest that racism was overcome in the 1960s or that everybody came around to supporting interracial unions. Indeed, a worldwide Gallup poll conducted in 1968 reveals that in both Germany and the United States large numbers of people remained deeply ambivalent about, if not hostile to interracial unions in the period discussed here. In that 1968 poll, 72 percent of Americans and 47 percent of Germans still did not approve of such marriages.[70] Racism is alive and well, both in Germany and the United States, as both African Americans and Afro-Germans can attest to in their daily encounters with white society. But the mid- to late 1960s were, in both the United States and West Germany, an important turning point that prepared the way for the long road ahead for a more inclusive society.

Notes

1. The essay presented here is an expanded and revised version of "Ein Atemzug der Freiheit: Afro-Amerikanische GIs, deutsche Frauen und die Grenzen der Demokratie," in *Demokratiewunder: Transatlantische Mittler und die kulturelle Öffnung Westdeutschlads 1945–1970*, ed. Arnd Bauerkämper, Konrad Jarausch, and Marcus Payk (Göttingen: Vandenhoeck & Ruprecht, 2005). For histories of the years of the United States military government, see, for example, Earl Frederick Ziemke, *The U.S. Army in the Occupation of Germany 1944–46* (Washington, DC: Center for Military History, 1975); Harold Zink, *The United States in Germany, 1944–1955* (Princeton, NJ: Van Nostrand, 1957); Edward Peterson, *The American Occupation: Retreat to Victory* (Detroit: Wayne State University Press, 1977); Eugene Davidson, *The Death and Life of Germany: An Account of the American Occupation* (New York: Knopf, 1959); Rebecca Boehling, *A Question of Priorities: Democratic Reforms and Economic Recovery in Early Postwar Germany* (New York: Berghahn, 1996); Klaus Dietmar Henke, *Die amerikanische Besetzung* (Munich: Oldenbourg, 1995).

2. Maria Höhn, "GIs, Veronikas and Lucky Strikes: German Reaction to the American Military Presence in Rhineland Palatinate" (Doctoral dissertation, University of Pennsylvania, 1995); Johannes Kleinschmidt, *"Do not fraternize": Die schwierigen Anfänge deutsch-amerikanischer Freundschaft 1944–1949* (Trier: WWT, 1997); Annette Brauerhoch, "Schwarzes Kind und weiße Nachkriegsgesellschaft in Toxi (BRD 1953)," *Frauen und Film* 60 (1997): 106–30; David Braden Posner, "Afro-America in West German Perspective 1945–1966" (Doctoral dissertation, Yale University, 1997); Timothy Schroer, "Race After the Masterrace: Germans and African Americans" (Doctoral dissertation, University of Virginia, 1998); John Willoughby, *Remaking the Conquering Heroes: The Social and Geopolitical Impact of the Post-War American Occupation of Germany* (New York: Palgrave, 2001); Heide Fehrenbach, "Of German Mothers and 'Negermischlingskinder': Race, Sex and the Postwar Nation," in *The Miracle Years: A Cultural History of West Germany 1949–1968*, ed. Hanna Schissler (Princeton, NJ: Princeton University Press, 2001); Maria Höhn, "Heimat in Turmoil: African-American GIs in 1950s West Germany," in *The Miracle Years*, and Maria Höhn, *GIs and Fräuleins: The German American Encounter in 1950s West Germany*, ed. Schissler (Chapel Hill: University of North Carolina Press, 2002); Petra Goedde, *GIs and Germans: Culture, Gender, and Foreign Relations* (New Haven, CT: Yale University Press, 2003); Yara Collette Lemke Munzia de Faria, *Zwischen Fürsorge und Ausgrenzung: Afro-deutsche Besatzungskinder im Nachkriegsdeutschland* (Berlin: Metropol, 2002); Heide Fehrenbach, *Race after Hitler: Black Occupation Children in Postwar Germany and America* (Princeton, NJ: Princeton University Press, 2005); Tim Schroer, *Recasting Race after World War II: Germans and African Americans in American-Occupied Germany* (Boulder: University of Colorado Press, 2007); Höhn, "'We will Never Go Back to the Old Way Again': Germany in the African American Debate on Civil Rights," *Central European History* 41, 4 (December 2008): 605–37.

3. Höhn, "Heimat in Turmoil," *GIs and Fräuleins* and "Ein Atemzug." Fehrenbach's *Race after Hitler* on the German debates on mixed-race children reiterates my findings that American opposition to interracial sexuality enforced the German conviction that their new democracy was fully compatible with the social exclusion of minorities, but she also illustrates that the transnational transfer of American racial assumptions was not limited to interactions with the U.S. military. German debates on how to integrate the children born of African American fathers and German mothers evolved in an exchange of ideas between American and German social scientists, and close collaboration between the German and American branches of such organizations as the National Council of Christians and Jews and the National Council of Churches.

4. See, for example, Maria Höhn and Seungsook Moon, eds., *Over There: Living with the U.S. Military Empire* (Durham, NC: Duke University Press, 2010). The essays gathered there also address how U.S. racial boundaries impacted gender and race in Japan and Korea.

5. For example, see Höhn, "We Will Never Go Back."

6. See Höhn, "Ein Atemzug," and my essays, "The Black Panther Solidarity Committees and the *Voice of the Lumpen*," *German Studies Review* 31, no. 1 (February 2008): 133–54, and "The Trial of the Ramstein 2 and German Debates on Race," *Changing the World, Changing Oneself*, ed. Belinda Davis, Wilfried Mausbach, Martin Klimke (Berghahn Press, 2010), 376–416. Also see the Web site and digital archive, *The Civil Rights Struggle, African American GIs and Germany*, that I am building with Martin Klimke from the Center for American Studies at the University of Heidelberg: aacvr-germany.org.

7. Mary Dudziak, *Cold War Civil Rights: Race and the Image of American Democracy* (Princeton, NJ: Princeton University Press, 2000); Thomas Borstelmann, *The Cold War and the Color Line: American Race Relations in the Global Arena* (Cambridge, MA: Harvard University Press, 2001); Brenda Gayle Plummer, *Rising Wind: Black Americans and U.S. Foreign Affairs, 1935–1960* (Chapel Hill: University of North Carolina Press, 1996), have shown how the competition for the de-colonizing powers in the Third World gave impetus to the civil rights movement. Their research ignores, however, how the creation of the worldwide U.S. military base system after 1945 expanded the boundaries of the civil rights movement beyond the United States.

8. "Now is the Time Not to be Silent," *The Crisis*, January 1942, 7. For a stunning portrayal of how deeply wounded black GIs were by the continuing racism in the military, see "Jim Crow in the Army," *New Republic* 110, no. 11, March 13, 1944.

9. "Now is the Time Not to be Silent," *The Crisis*, January 1942, 7.

10. On the struggle to connect civil rights with America's military mission abroad, see Höhn, "We Will Never Go Back" and "The Black Panther Solidarity Committees." On the African American struggle to connect their fight for democracy with the fight against racism and imperialism in the non-Western world during WWII, see Walter White, *A Rising Wind* (Garden City, NY: Doubleday, 1945); Plummer, *Rising Wind*; and Russell Buchanan, *Black Americans in World War* (Santa Barbara: Clio Books, 1978). On the army's abysmal record toward African American GIs during WWII, see Morris McGregor, *Integration of the Armed Forces 1940–1965* (Washington, DC: Center for Military History, 1980), and Ralph Ellison, "In a Strange Land," in *I have Seen War*, ed. Dorothy Sterling (New York: Hill and Wang, 1960), 103–10.

11. Höhn, *GIs and Fräuleins*, chapter 3, and "Ein Atemzug."

12. Höhn, "We Will Never Go Back," for a detailed discussion of the many interactions between Germans and African Americans. Also, Fehrenbach, *Race after Hitler*, and Schroer, *Recasting Race*.

13. It should be stressed here that sexual relations between slave owners and their female slaves were the norm in the South. The prohibition against marriage ensured that children of such relationships were always illegitimate and thus could not inherit. For a history of miscegenation laws, see Martha Hodes, ed., *Sex, Love, Race: Crossing Boundaries in North American History* (New

York: New York University Press, 1999); Paul Spickard, *Mixed Blood: Intermarriage and Ethnic Identity in Twentieth-Century America* (Madison: University of Wisconsin Press, 1989); Werner Sollors, *Interracialism: Black-White Intermarriage in American History, Literature, and Law* (Oxford: Oxford University Press, 2000); Kevin Johnson, *Mixed Race America and the Law* (New York: New York University Press, 2003); Renee Romano, *Race Mixing: Black-White Marriage in Postwar America* (Cambridge, MA: Harvard University Press, 2003.

14. "Germany Meets the Negro Soldier: GIs Find More Friendship and Equality in Berlin than in Birmingham or Broadway," *Ebony* 2, no. 10, October 1946, 5–11 and *Pittsburgh Courier*, February 22, 1947, "Found Freedom in Germany. See also Schmundt-Thomas, "America's Germany," 73–74 on how Germany became a sort of "racial utopia" for African American GIs. .

15. Letters to the editor section, *Ebony*, March 1947, 2, no. 5. African American women were far more guarded, if not critical in their response to such stories. One woman expressed the feelings of many women, who did not object to these relationships *per se*, but saw themselves "victims of progress" because the arrival of each new "war bride" means "one less brown man" in the marriage market. Neither did all African Americans women agree that interracial love was an integral expression of democracy. One black woman expressed disappointment that *Ebony* associated the achievement of equality for black men with their ability to associate with white women. She raised a valid point, since this vision of democracy ignored the aspirations for full citizenship of black women. See "Are White Women Stealing Our Husbands?" *Negro Digest*, April 1951, 55 and Letters to the Editor section, *Ebony*, November 1947.

16. "Found Freedom in Germany. Few GIs Eager to Return to States," *Pittsburgh Courier*, February 22, 1947; "American Prejudice Rampant in Germany," March 1, 1947; "American Officers Abroad Propagating Race Hatred," June 8, 1946; and "Nazi Attitudes of White Soldiers," September 29, 1945. William Gardner Smith wrote many of these articles for the *Pittsburgh Courier* while serving as a GI in Germany. In his widely read novel, *The Last of the Conquerors* (New York: Farrar, Straus, 1948), which was at the time hailed as one of the most important texts coming out of the war, Smith reiterated powerfully the liberation and freedom that black GIs experienced in Germany. See also Azza Salama Layton, *International Politics and Civil Rights in the United States* (Cambridge: Cambridge University Press, 2000), 40.

17. "Three Die in France Because War's End Left Untouched Nazi Race Ideas in Midst of Army," *Pittsburgh Courier*, November 3, 1945.

18. Dudziak, *Cold War;* Borstelmann, *The Cold War;* and Plummer, *Rising Wind.*

19. See Penny von Eschen, *Race against Empire: Black Americans and Anticolonialism 1937–1957* (Ithaca, NY: Cornell University Press, 1997), and Carol Anderson, *Eyes Off the Prize: The United Nations and the African American Struggle for Human Rights, 1944–1955* (Cambridge: Cambridge University Press, 2003).

20. Cited in Lee Nichols, *Breakthrough on the Color Front* (New York: Random House, 1954), 180.

21. For the connection between gender conservatism and racial boundaries and the Cold War, see Elaine May, *Homeward Bound: American Families in the Cold War* (New York: Basic Books, 1988), and Ruth Feldstein, *Motherhood in Black and White: Race and Sex in American Liberalism, 1930–1965* (Ithaca, NY: Cornell University Press, 2000).

22. Phyl Newbeck, *Virginia Hasn't Always Been for Lovers: Interracial Marriage Bans and the Case of Richard and Mildred Loving* (Carbondale: Southern Illinois Press, 2004), 90.

23. Cited in Jonathan Zimmermann, "Crossing Oceans, Crossing Colors. Black Peace Corps Volunteers and Interracial Love in Africa, 1961–1971," in *Sex, Love, Race: Crossing Boundaries in North American History*, ed. Martha Hodes (New York: New York University Press, 1999), 516. For African American intellectuals on interracial marriage, see Werner Sollors, "Of Mules and Mares in a Land of Difference; or Quadrupeds All?" *American Quarterly* 42, no. 2 (June 1979): 189 n. 18.

See also, Spickard, *Mixed Blood*, 298–302. A letter from a woman commenting on *Ebony*'s coverage of interracial relationships in Germany illustrates how anxious African American civil rights advocates were, that an endorsement of interracial relationships might threaten the larger struggle for civil rights: "These pictures seem to uphold the timeworn contention of the bigoted enemies of our race who reiterate that all the Negro means by social equality is association with white women." See "Are White Women Stealing Our Husbands?" *Negro Digest*, April 1951, 55 and Letters to the Editor section, *Ebony*, November 1947.

24. George Roeder, "Censoring Disorder: American Visual Imagery of World War II," in *The War in American Culture*, ed. Lewis Erenberg and Susan Hirsch (Chicago: University of Chicago Press, 1996), 56.

25. Owsley letter cited in Richard Dalfiume, *Desegregation of the U.S. Armed Forces: Fighting on Two Fronts, 1939–53* (Columbia: University of Missouri Press, 1975), 133.

26. J. Wayne Dudley, "'Hate' Organizations of the 1940s: The Columbians, Inc.," *Phylon* 42, no. 3 (1981): 268. See Schroer, *Recasting Race*, and Willoughby, *Remaking*, for the military's effort to exclude black GIs from the occupation of Germany.

27. Layton, *International Politics and Civil Rights in the United States*, 108, cites a Justice Department memo during WWII that defines safe and unsafe areas for federal intervention in race matters. At the top of the unsafe category was "intimate relations with the Negro."

28. Cited in Spickard, *Mixed Blood*, 290. Interestingly enough, even opponents of integration realized that the practice was hardly democratic. The former secretary of the navy, Frank Knox, for example, concluded in 1941 that refusing to "admit Negroes to intimate family relations leading to marriage" is "not truly democratic" but he doubted that even the most "ardent lovers of democracy" would agree with such unions. Cited in Lee Nichols, *Breakthrough on the Color Front*, 180. Knox made that comment in 1941, when he explained why black sailors should be employed only in the mess on navy ships.

29. *Chicago Daily Defender*, September 12, 1963.

30. Hannah Arendt, "Reflection on Little Rock," *Dissent* 6, no. 1 (Winter 1959): 45–56. See responses by David Spitz and Melvin Tumin in *Dissent* 6, no. 1 (Winter 1959): 56–71.

31. On this incident, see David Hollinger, "Amalgamation and Hypodescent: The Question of Ethnoracial Mixture in the History of the United States," *American Historical Review* 108, no. 5 (December 2003): 1363–65; Werner Sollors, "Of Mules and Mares," 167–90.

32. For the exchange between Hook and Arendt, see *Dissent* 6, no. 2 (Spring 1959): 203–5.

33. *Dissent* 6 no. 2 (Spring 1959): 181.

34. Renee Romano, *Race Mixing: Black-White Marriage in Postwar America* (Cambridge, MA: Harvard University Press, 2003), 100, 191, 196. As Romano has shown, in the 1950s and 1960s only very few people in the African American community argued that these relationships "betrayed the race." Most objections were based on the reasoning that approval of such relationships would make life even harder for African Americans. Romano, *Race Mixing*, 89.

35. Peter Wallenstein, *Tell the Court I Love My Wife: Race, Marriage and the Law: An American History* (New York: Palgrave, 2002), 193–97.

36. Phyl Newbeck, *Virginia Hasn't Always Been for Lovers: Interracial Marriage Bans and the Case of Richard and Mildred Loving* (Carbondale: Southern Illinois Press, 2004), 100. See also Werner Sollors, *Interracialism: Black-White Intermarriage in American History, Literature, and Law* (Oxford: Oxford University Press, 2000); Kevin Johnson, *Mixed Race America and the Law* (New York: New York University Press, 2003).

37. Newbeck, *Virgina Hasn't Always Been for Lovers*, 118.

38. Newbeck, *Virgina Hasn't Always Been for Lovers*, 157.

39. On the history of the miscegenation laws, see Werner Sollors, *Interracialism*, 5–11, and Spickard, *Mixed Blood*, 292–93.

40. For a good overview of the repeal of the legislation prior to 1965, see William Zabel, "Interracial Marriage and the Law," in *Atlantic* 216, no. 4, October 1965.

41. See the 1964 study of 700 African American families in Chicago in Romano, *Race Mixing*, 89.

42. Aside from the Nuremburg Race Laws, German society had experienced periods of prohibition against interracial marriages in the colonies. Decrees were passed in German Southwest Africa in 1905 (followed by East Africa 1906 and Samoa 1912) to prevent marriages between Germans and colonial inhabitants. However, these decrees conflicted with Imperial Law and the Reichstag's ratification of the 1913 Citizenship Law again affirmed the legality of mixed-race marriages. But the debates around the 1913 citizenship law also make clear that racial mixing was viewed, in Tina Campt's words, with "ambivalence and foreboding." See Tina Campt, *Other Germans: Black Germans and the Politics of Race, Gender, Memory in the Third Reich* (Ann Arbor: University of Michigan Press, 2004), 49. On the 1912–13 debates, see Pascal Grosse, *Kolonialismus, Eugenik und bürgerliche Gesellschaft in Deutschland 1850–1918* (Frankfurt: Campus, 2000), 162–92; Lora Wildenthal, *German Women for Empire 1884–1945* (Durham, NC: Duke University Press, 2001), 131–70.

43. See Höhn, "We Will Never Go Back," for how the black press and civil rights groups again and again pointed out this contradiction to push forward their struggle for civil rights at home.

44. Although Germany did not produce the same sort of rich collection of sources as the United States, a rich and at times strident public discourse on the propriety of interracial love and marriages emerged where these unions were most prevalent—namely, in the garrison towns that hosted U.S. troops. The other places where these sorts of relationships were a focus of interest are Germany's port cities like Hamburg and German university towns, where, beginning in the 1960s, an increasing number of students from the non-Western world came to study as guests of the German government.

45. Höhn, *GIs and Fräuleins*, chapters 3 and 4.

46. "Wie ist heute die Ehe möglich?" *Pfälzische Volkszeitung*, July 11, 1952. See also "Letter to the editor," *Pfälzische Volkszeitung*, March 10, 1953, and "Leserbrief: Rassentrennung," *Rheinpfalz*, April 3, 1954.

47. See Höhn, *GIs and Fräuleins*, chapter 3, for a more detailed discussion on how the military tried to stop marriages between black GIs and German women. In my interview with the *Standesbeamte* in Baumholder, he stated that it was almost impossible for black GIs in the 1950s to get marriage permits.

48. "Der Mensch zwischen Freiheit und Verantwortung," *Rheinpfalz*, February 24, 1953. See also "Hautfarbe, ein echtes Problem?" *Pfälzische Volkszeitung*, March 10, 1953. See also Video collection of IANAS, at the Johannes Gutenberg Universität, Mainz. Videos 37 and 38. One man recalled that people "adopted the official attitude [of race segregation] of the United States towards the blacks."

49. "Steinstrasse-Viertel 'off-limits'/Ab heute für Amerikaner gesperrt," und "Jetzt müssen die Behörden zupacken," *Pfälzische Volkszeitung*, September 7, 1957.

50. These findings conflict with Heide Fehrenbach's conclusion that the West German public discourse declared the "postwar period of racial reexamination and reeducation closed" by the early 1960s. See Fehrenbach, *Race after Hitler*, 174.

51. See my chapters 7 and 8 in *GIs and Fräuleins* for a detailed discussion of how German and American racism interacted in the prosecution of alleged prostitutes in the garrison communities of Baumholder and Kaiserslautern. The same patterns can be found in other garrison towns, no matter the size of the community.

52. "Dagmar führte die Starparade an," *Rheinzeitung*, May 17, 1956.

53. "Rassentrennung. Farbige Väter verboten," *Der Spiegel*, Juni 15, 1960, 27–28.

54. Fehrenbach, *Race after Hitler*, 174.

55. "Rassentrennung. Farbige Väter verboten," *Der Spiegel*, Juni 15, 1960, 27–28. Unfortunately, despite vigorous efforts I have not been able to locate the files for this court case.

56. Posner, "Afro America," 42, puts that shift in the early 1960s, but I found evidence in the late 1950s. In 1958, twenty-three female employees of the Kaiserslautern Post Exchange wrote a letter of protest to the tabloid *Neue Illustrierte* to express their dismay that the magazine had serialized a novel in which a black GI kills his German girlfriend. The women rejected the portrayal of black soldiers in the novel, defending them as decent and polite human beings. They also accused the magazine of inciting racial hatred. See Rosemarie Lester, *Trivialneger: Das Bild des Schwarzen im westdeutschen Illustriertenroman* (Stuttgart: Akademischer Verlag H.-D. Heinz, 1982), 82. For an even earlier example of protest against racial discrimination against white women and black soldiers, see "Gerechtigkeit schielt nicht," *Mannheimer Morgen*, June 6, 1956.

57. See, for example, Archiv des Auswärtigen Amtes, B 86/937, for a 1963 document that argues that German pub owners kept African students out of their establishments because white GIs pressured the owner that they would boycott the place if he allowed people of color. German officials insisted on that explanation until the 1970s, and the Americans, for the most part, confirmed that conviction for them.

58. Höhn, *GIs and Fräuleins*, chapter 8, where I describe the voyeuristic and racist coverage concerning an incident in 1957 in Kasiserslautern.

59. Stadtarchiv Giessen, Gesundheitsamt, "Durchführung von GK-Kontrollen." *Quick*, nr. 19, "Moralhüter macht Jagd auf Mädchen."

60. Stadtarchiv Giessen, Gesundheitsamt, "Durchführung von GK-Kontrollen." *Konkret*, no date, "Eine deutsche Frau tut das nicht," and "Du Negerhure, du Sau . . . Augenzeugenberichte von Giessener Mädchen und farbigen Studenten."

61. Fehrenbach, *Race after Hitler*, 174.

62. Stadtarchiv Giessen, Gesundheitsamt, "Durchführung von GK-Kontrollen," AStA flyer November 8, 1968. See also "Gesundheitspflege. Laufend Männer," *Der Spiegel*, November 25, 1968. For other examples where they draw connections to Nazism, see *Giessener Wochenspiegel*, November 15, 1968, "Wir fragen die Staatsanwaltschaft" and Staatsarchiv Hessen, 461/31251 Staatsanwalt gegen Marlies Nehrstede, "Mediziner und Farbige Geschlechtskrank!" AStA flyer of November 7, 1968. For the views of the faculty, see "Rassendiskriminierung und Vorurteile," *Giessener Allgemeine Zeitung*, November 23, 1968.

63. *Frankfurter Rundschau*, November 11, 1968.

64. *Frankfurter Rundschau*, November 11, 1968.

65. "Zum Tage," *Wetzlaer Zeitung*, November 13, 1968.

66. Staatsarchiv Hessen, H 12 Gießen Nr. 76, Landgericht Gießen, 3. Zivilkammer—Bürgerlicher Rechtsstreit, Mäckel, Annegret / Stadt Giessen, 4.

67. Staatsarchiv Hessen, 461/31251 Staatsanwalt gegen Marlies Nehrstede, 93.

68. Staatsarchiv Hessen, Landgericht Giessen, 3. Zivilkammer, Mäckel, Annegret vs Stadt Giessen, H 12 Giessen Nr. 76, 49.

69. Romano, *Race Mixing*, chapter 6, for the United States.

70. Hazel Erskine, "The Polls: Interracial Socializing," *Public Opinion Quarterly* 37, no. 2 (Summer 1973): 293–94.

The Erotics of African American Endurance, Or: On the Right Side of History?

White (West)-German Public Sentiment between Pornotroping and Civil Rights Solidarity

SABINE BROECK

This article first wants to zoom the reader back into the year 1974. Picture the Vietnam War, international student rebellion, the burgeoning of a radical white women's movement, heated controversies about the validity and/or ethics of what called itself revolutionary violence, the beginnings of the green movement, and, on the other side: militant clashes between police forces and mass demonstrations, a massive push for the expansion of state executive power over and against democratic transparency, an intense step-up of federal state security. Picture the cold war still on its peak. Then look again. Picture West-Germany, without hip-hop being the backbone of kiddie ads, without Naomi Campbell doing H&M lingerie on bus stops, without African immigrants in the street, clubs, restaurants, and supermarkets, without black students in seminars, without black kids in every kindergarten, at least one or two; without Danny Glover, Eddie Murphy, Bill Cosby, Denzel Washington on the silver screen, without Tiger Woods hitting the course for everybody's Sunday afternoon entertainment. Picture a Germany before *Roots*, without Toni Morrison publicly reading for Rowohlt, without *The Color Purple*, in German, making it to the bestseller list. Picture the loneliness and singularity of a Martin Luther King, Sammy Davis Jr., a Harry Belafonte, an Ella Fitzgerald, a Muhammad Ali, in the representational orbit of blackness for West Germans. James Brown for a handful of soul fanatics; Jimi Hendrix for Woodstock hippie types; no Michael Jackson on radio channels. No Will Smith. No 50 Cent, Queen Latifah, or Missy Elliott, anywhere. Picture the proverbial German heart of whiteness. Then put the writer of this piece in the picture, at age twenty: a small white brunette-haired German with a big permed "Free Angela Davis"–afro head of hair. In her spare free time, when she is not being a dutiful student, or running around some demonstration, she is reading George Jackson's letters from jail, a step into militancy from having gotten to James Baldwin's *Tell me How Long the Train's Been Gone* first, on the heels of a diary entry of hers, deeply shocked out of teenage complacency, in 1968: "Martin Luther King Shot. How can I ever trust the world again?"

This anecdotal entry shall serve as a kind of guiding light through the following scenarios. The enthusiasm for the icons of black articulation, contained in the permed afro, combined with actual political efforts at radical international solidarity, will be read as emblematic for the political and cultural effects African American articulation and militancy called forth at the time in Germany. The interaction between white Germans, and African American culture and politics for a long historical phase—roughly encompassing the 1950s, 1960s, and 1970s, to a certain extent the 1980s—was characterized by practices and discourses of white adoration of black endurance, and black moral power, of an eager immersion in black rhetoric and posturing, including body speak (as in "permed hair"), and of a rather sentimental take-on of black suffering and resistance to conceptualize and formulate specifically local political and cultural desires. These practices and discourses either went openly hand in hand with, or in rather unacknowledged fashion underlay explicitly political campaigns and activities that did indeed serve to champion the cause of first, the civil rights movement, and later black power, in Germany.

In cold war Germany there was neither a strong African American presence which might have reined in, or at least counterpointed the white romanticism of demonstrators rallying the German public with their "We are all black" war cries, nor were those practices and discourses in any way connected to an acquisition of knowledge about the historical, cultural, and political facets of the black struggle, and how Europe, or even Germany might have been implicated in it. Which is to say, not only is Sander Gilman's coinage "blackness without blacks" appropriate, but one could even turn it around to descriptive effect. "Blacks without blackness" could quite succinctly capture the relationship between the German "scènes engagés" and representatives of African America: a willful, and sometimes very self-serving identification without any context of blackness: the history of the slave trade, slavery, reconstruction, and the long century of the aggressive and violent color line missing almost entirely. African Americans had been and were the victims of United States betrayal of democracy, or of imperialism in more radical books; thus, siding with them warranted the reward of seeing oneself a priori on the right side of history. One "knew" about systemic, and endemic racism, but only just so: slavery existed as an unexamined given, its paradigmatic *American* evil a foil before which one's own righteousness could freely unfold.

It is only in the 1990s that this began to change to a certain degree, largely due to four factors:

1. African American Studies' growing international visibility and black accumulative control over the discourses which frame the Middle Passage and the transatlantic black experience; the wide dissemination of texts like Paul Gilroy's *Black Atlantic* which called for an awareness of the slave trade, and slavery as a modern phenomenon of global impact which postmodernity should own up to—taking interested circles in and beyond white academia beyond guilt-ridden, but self-serving empathy;

2. the growing black disapora immigrant community which has demanded public acknowledgment;

3. a push for postcolonial paradigms which has been slowly leading to a critical rereading of Germany's colonial past,

4. (no system in the order here): the media-visible self-articulation of black Germans, for which African American agency in the person of Audre Lorde, and others, turned out to be crucial.

This article will pass through scenarios that mark the interaction between various segments of the West-German public and African Americans in the cold war decades. These scenarios are situated in different historical frames; they also represent different moments of public cultural inscription and of performative practices. What unites them is a discursive interest in the African American plight which—across the divides of generation, gender, and political priorities, has been cast in terms which U.S.-American abolitionism prefigured over a century ago. That is to claim that liberal and progressive West German interaction with African Americans has largely been characterized by a "Stellvertreter"— abolitionism; German progressives did not devise a critical epistemology which could have taken German antiblack racism, Germany's role in the history of the slave trade and colonialism, actual German implications in an international black diaspora, and a self-critical reading of white hegemony into account.

The respective political contexts: cold war, Vietnam, 68 Rebellion, RAF, the women's movement cannot be addressed here extensively. Instead, I will reconsider the appropriation of African American blackness in those various contexts, which has taken different shapes, but has maintained its pornotroping features, above and beyond their differences. The critical instrumentarium here will be "borrowed," from Hortense Spillers, whose work on U.S. abolitionism has enabled me to begin theorizing this field of observation which, in both the disciplines most immediately at hand—that is, German Studies and African American Studies—has not become an object of extended scrutiny so far.

One needs to look, then, at the cultural environment of African American "bodies" in Germany. "Bodies" appears here advisedly, because the contention is that it was a distinct fascination with the black *embodiment* of suffering, rather than an actual acquaintance with African American knowledge that led the liberal West German public into identification with spokespeople like Martin Luther King, James Baldwin, or Alice Walker, for that matter, with various degrees of emotional charge. Campaigns of political solidarity with black liberation were thus oftentimes predicated on rather vague kinds of emotional "elective affinity" with black humanity suffering at the hands of white U.S.-American bigotry. This characterizes the practices of intellectuals, church groups, and liberal media, as well as the rather preposterous self-blackening slogans of the radical student movement a few years later.

That kind of imaginary ersatz-suffering did valuable work in German postwar intellectual and public cultures:

1. It allowed German progressive intellectuals a fascination with the "other America," as it was called—while positioning themselves at an intellectually and aesthetically productive skeptical angle vis-à-vis the United States.

2. It helped the liberal—church and otherwise 1950s—German public, in a convenient circumvention of a disturbingly close memory of the Shoah, to turn a critical lens on "the hypocritical Americans."

3. By using African American masculinity for a negative foil, even though "black men clearly inhabit their bodies more sensuously"—as in the feminist bestseller *Häutungen* of 1975—it defined white radical feminists' very own collective voice against overpowering male leftist mental hegemony: "Sexism is more fundamental than racism, and capitalism!" . . . as author Verena Stephan proclaimed, under massive applause from the newly burgeoning white women's movement. A slogan which might, for the historically minded ear, recall not only a faint echo of the late-nineteenth-century U.S. women's movement's emancipatory desire for themselves which also took them beyond antiracism for decades to come.

4. It served—as in the case of bestseller stardom for *The Color Purple*—white German women-identified women to satisfy both their aesthetic desire and their political need for an articulation of embodiment.

Few of these gestures, however brought forth a sustained interest in antiracist cooperation beyond the particular receptive moment, or in acknowledging African Americans, let alone other black people living in Germany, as agents of a dialogue which might have an impact on the world larger than attracting and echoing the respectively involved white egos.

Next you will be asked to "click" back a few decades: 1952 is the year of the first UNESCO declaration against racism. Seen in light of this declaration, the liberal German postwar discourses on "the negro" and "race"—as opposed to the rampant racism also very much active at the time—were characterized by a strange form of productive amnesia, not to say bigotry. As noted in disgust by Americans, Germans immediately after their liberation, in face of the Shoah, could be quite adamant in their moralistic rejection of racism as America's evil; it was not such a rare experience in Germany to meet people who performed as negrophiliacs while at the same time being more or less openly anti-Semitic. This public sentiment resulted in official U.S.-American answers like a brochure on "Der Neger im amerikanischen Leben," printed and distributed for the U.S.-Archiv Dienst Frankfurt in the early 1950s. At best, these admonitions reproduced classical Yankee ideology, to teach the Germans that yes, slavery was horrible, but must be understood within its time, and that in having destroyed the "old" South and its system in the Civil War, the North may legitimately lay claim to a moral superiority that outshines occasional lapses into racism in northern cities.

Those debates prefigured the mass enthusiasm for the civil rights movement a decade later. Cultural figureheads of the African American civil rights movement, like Sidney Poitier, Harry Belafonte, Sammy Davis Jr., even jazz icon Ella Fitzgerald, but above all Martin Luther King as spiritual leader arrived at a public notoriety that went much beyond their coveted status as U.S.-American politi-cal/religious spokespeople. A widespread pro–civil rights sentiment in those decades functioned like a self-realignment of the liberal German public with state-of-the-art international humanism in the UNESCO vein, while it had the added benefit to keep the same circles afloat in a legitimately outspoken critique of United States policies—serving purposes that oscillated between downright anti-Americanism and militant anti-imperialist skepticism.

A short essay by Max Frisch—one of the most internationally respected criti-cal literary voices in the German language at the time—entitled *Begegnungen mit Negern* (Meeting Negroes[1]) from 1954, functions here as a paradigmatic "high end" version of this pro–civil rights public sentiment. Frisch, as a Swiss writ-er, may, of course, not be read as a postwar *German* author; however, since his work was so widely read, and canonized in German high school curricula at the time, and because of that it poignantly fostered the intellectual atmosphere of the generation of young intellectuals coming of age in the 1960s and 1970s, his essay may serve my purpose to examine a certain strand of progressive *Weltan-schauung*, and cosmopolitanism at the time. The autobiographical text recalls a series of occasions of meeting African Americans in New York, Negroes in the parlance of his time. Frisch stages these meetings as random occasions, as when he "stumbles" into a quasi-clandestine meeting of an African American Com-munist Party section in a big New York hotel. In its insistence on the sporadic character of those "Begegnungen" the text allows for no other agency than the narrating I's curiosity; it comes to us as a protocol of the intellectual in search of authentic observation. Frisch—and his reader—makes his acquaintance with a Negro singer, with a church community at an active sermon, with one young ambitious Negro professional, with Negro communists. The haphazard assem-bly of contacts haunts the skeptical reader with Frisch's distinctly subjectivist voice; unsuspecting readers are invited to gaze, with Frisch's discerning eyes, in a manner of quasi-anthropological truth-finding, on his object in question: *the American Negro*, about whom even these scattered impressions seem to enable Frisch to talk in rather authoritative fashion. What is most disturbing about the essay—apart from Frisch's reckless self-empowerment to *know the American Ne-gro* by having observed a few members of the "species"—is its combination of an emphatic voice with an aggressive exoticist and Africanist, even downright rac-ist tone of what passes as "description"—a paradigmatic abolitionist repertoire. Frisch obviously feels completely confident to line up the topoi of a white mind-set vis-à-vis the "African" object, half child, half jungle witch animal—never mind he is not dealing with anything, or anyone African at all. This does not keep him from alluding to U.S. slavery, and a racist economy as the source of the Negro's persistent victimization, which his empathy is meant to deplore. His construc-tion—in its apparent paradox—thus strikingly recalls the abolitionist "urtext"; it mirrors *Uncle Tom's Cabin's* proclamations to the letter.

Uncle Tom's Cabin, in German *Onkel Tom's Hütte*, has had an awesome pub-lication history in Germany; the first edition registered in the online catalogue of *Die Deutsche Bibliothek*, certainly by no means the first edition available in

German, is from 1908 in Berlin. The catalogue documents hundreds of thousands of sold copies in about at least a hundred different editions, published annually in new editions, and all through the 1930s, oddly and disturbingly so; those numbers being complemented by versions as plays, as radio plays, as children's books, on disc, cassette, and recently, DVD. In the postwar years, the first edition is with Kiepenheuer & Witsch, one of the larger German publishers, in 1948; followed by two editions, the second one of 25,000 copies, by Neubau Verlag, Munich, in the same year. In the 1950s and 1960s, the sales do not abate. In 1966, Fischer Verlag brings out a new edition of 60,000, and so it continues in like dimensions until 2006, with an announcement in the *Deutsche Bibliothek* catalogue of a new edition.

Here is Beecher Stowe, with all her antislavery goodwill, laying down the gospel truth about "the race": "The Negro, it must be remembered, is an exotic of the most gorgeous and superb countries of the world, and he has, deep in his heart, a passion for all that is splendid, rich, and fanciful; a passion which, rudely indulged by an untrained taste, draws on them the ridicule of the colder and more correct white race" (Harriet Beecher Stowe 1966, 180). And to flesh out the object under the abolitionist gaze, the "African personality's sensations and impressions are very vivid, and their fancy and imagination lively. In this respect, the race has an oriental character, and betrays its tropical origin. Like the Hebrews of old and Oriental nations of the present, they give vent to their emotions with the utmost vivacity of expression, and their whole bodily system sympathizes with the movement of their minds . . . . They incline much toward outward expression, violent gesticulations, and agitating movements of the body. . . . They will laugh, weep, and embrace each other convulsively; and sometimes become entirely paralyzed and cataleptic . . . . (They are) believers in spells, in 'fetish and obi,' in the 'evil eye' and other singular influences, for which probably there is an origin in this peculiarity of constitution" a peculiarity that is, "of nervous condition quite different from those of the whites" (Harriet Beecher Stowe n.d., 45).

Frisch's essay resonates impressively with the closeness to Stowe's mid-nineteenth-century argument, not just in terms of a general mental affinity, but in terms of the almost literal repetition of topoi and tropes. Frisch establishes himself as a benevolent authority at the outset of his essay. With an air of understood importance, which assumes immediate complicity between his essayistic voice and his presumably all-white readers about the necessity of such a defensive, and at the same time self-righteous gesture, he assures us that he can "understand" that the Negro slums look the way they do: neglected, dirty, rotten, unfit for human habitation. Because he knows about U.S. racist social and economic structure, his empathy is with its victims. The gist of his essay, however, lies not in an analysis of the history of U.S. racism, and African American resistance to it—as one might expect from those self-assured pronunciations of empathy, but in transmitting to the titillated white reader Frisch's insight into the African American psyche. For that purpose, in elegantly spare, engaged, but nonpathetic, rather pleasingly aloof prose he takes us readers to meet Negroes. (*Quotations can be found in my own translations.*)

Frisch sees Negroes dancing: "To see Negroes dancing, not only for the first time, but still for the 10th time, forces us to stand paralyzed in surprise, feeling bliss and sadness at the same time; an emotion as if one has been expelled from paradise, but is allowed to watch this paradise, feeling the fascination of a painful joy, a joy about the human creature, painful because such congruence with oneself, such unity and harmony with oneself one will never again be permitted. [. . .] They dance, to represent something. Their movements are not Ersatz, but expression . . . . Without touching each other, the sexes woo and fight each other. [. . .] both have this air of unrelated wistfulness of kids at play [. . .] Eros as ecstasy of a double loneliness."

Next, here is Frisch, observing a black religious congregation in a storefront church in Harlem. The episode is introduced with a simple tell-it-all one-word fix: Africa. Then follow his observations in duly picturesque details; the following passages are selected from a host of rather similar ones almost at random:

> Everything appeared somewhat kindergarten-like, or better, it had an air somewhere between cooking school, and witch Sabbath. On a podium sat Mother Earth, more immediately personal than I have ever seen her, a matron fat beyond expression, with a white cap, and shirt, her black hands resting on the chair's arms. Everybody spoke at the same time [. . .] For the audience, who do not shy away from encouraging laughter, the bottle, the flour, and the sugar (all in commercial packaging!) are not at all ciphers of allegory, they experience sign and meaning in perfect congruence, it appears, like only children do with us. [. . .] Suddenly, without any recognizable reason, there they went again—we are, you have to know, with the so-called shakers, that kind of sect where they work themselves into a trance by way of rhythmic hopping and trampling, until Jesus Christ himself talks through their mouths, and then, as I said, the room is full of shouts as if one were in the stock exchange. An old hag gestures witch-like with her black arms, cap askance, telling people how Jesus came to her, nobody listens to her. A young girl runs around as if she were in a burning house, shreaking to God, foam coming out of her mouth. [. . .] All this accompanied by jazz. Finally they are all stranded in the pews, gasping with ecstasy [. . .] one is getting up for a last flickering dance, until she, too, leans against the wall like a tumbling drunk. Africa ebbs away. (248, 249)

He criticizes an internationally known Negro singer for her lack of authenticity. She lives in an apartment that looks like a corny realization of Salzburg baroque, complete with bits and pieces of "old world culture." They have a conversation in which he assures her, that even if she could pay for a building of her own, he would not agree with her taste: "She wished for, if she could own her house, a little palace like George Washington's. Only to picture themselves (falsely) equal with their white oppressors, the Negroes remain—even on this intellectual level—on the developmental backseat of imitation" (255). He talks about middle-class blacks at some dinner function: "The men in correct dark attire, the women, however, as is so often the case with Negresses, appeared to be grandiosely and pompously overdressed, decolletés and rustling evening gowns made from cheap artificial silk, and, on top of that, colorful like an exotic bird cage" (251). He observes his neighbor's quite uneventful anniversary party, invisible himself behind his living room window curtains (252): "Nothing much happened, seen from our perspective: the boringly conventional, a white bourgeois lifestyle as its own copy cat caricature, which does not have the faintest idea of Africa, and the unalienated life, *that* made, I think, the event for them." He searches and does not find any "remarkable Negro theatre, simply because they do not attend as an audience. The average Negro does not want to be Negro, attending a Negro performance is beneath him." This is because, as Frisch knows, it is "so difficult, under these circumstances, to be a Negro, without cursing white skin, or denying one's own Negro skin, and both do not redeem anything."

There is also a political side to the Negro, which, however, seems to interest Frisch only to the extent that it marginalizes himself. One day Frisch hears that Paul Robeson, "now communist" is holding a meeting in Frisch's hotel in Manhattan. "Curiously" as he says, he sneaks into the meeting, undisturbed, and overhears the comrades organizing a demonstration in solidarity for the "Negro pundit Du Bois": "They stood up, taking turns, Negroes and Whites, and discussed how to raise the money for the demonstration [. . .] Only I [. . .] had nobody to represent other than myself. [. . .] without ever being asked, I listened to their war palaver to the very end." Eventually, Frisch leaves, not without disappointment at not having been registered: "Then I left [. . .] a human being without a voice." He ends his observations with a coda on another sermon—the encounter which touched him the most:

> With a triumphant air, as if the lord had just solved all racial problems, it began, piano jazz of the very best kind, then the voices: low first, humming like a hot summer field, trembling like the heat burnin down on a cotton plantation, as if from afar one heard the age old stream of lament, dull and monotonous as the rolling of loam waves, a slow swelling which suddenly flooded everything, an orgy of anger and joyful shrieks, a violence of song, to scare you, slowly sinking without ending, endless like a river, wide as the Mississippi, [. . .] then only the strange humming . . . the heat, the dancing dust flakes in the sun, the stink of gasoline, of sweat, of perfume.

This long passage culminates in an ominous phrasing, with the words "—the slum."

Directly after those sentences, like a political afterthought, Frisch attaches a summarized version of political demands from an older essay by Langston Hughes, reprinted in *What the Negro Wants*, a 1944 anthology by Rayford W. Logan, which he might have come across in New York. He does not reference the first publication of the essay, nor does he give the correct title of the 1944 anthology,[2] let alone name its editor; it appears rather out of the blue as one of the New York findings he happened to come across, like the Negro singer, or his next-door neighbors. The passages seem significant mostly for the fact that Frisch feels compelled to explicate, and thereby himself authenticate the Negro's demands, as in "6. Wir verlangen Höflichkeit)." (*Höflichkeit* means politeness, and one wonders, if the whole issue was not about respect, rather than politeness, but I haven't been able to check a copy of the anthology yet.) Frisch explains: "He protests against the fact that the Negro will not be called Miss, Mister, or Mistress, but only by their first names, Jim and Mary" (259). The extent to which Frisch remains stuck in his abolitionist fantasies is all the more troubling, if one realizes at the very end of his text that he must have actually read—without acknowledging it—an array of African American intellectual contributions to the "race question," all assembled in the mentioned volume, among others Du Bois, McLeod Bethune, Schuyler, and Wilkins. His studied innocence in "meeting" Negroes appears to be quite an ingenious narrative fiction to keep his anthropological, abolitionist gaze in place, complete with its intriguing combination of sentimental pity, contempt, exoticist desire, and his gesture of care-taking.

Frisch's prose oeuvre is what our student rebellion trained teachers and high school generations in the late 1960s and 1970s still and again read voraciously, for its uncompromised intellectual presence of mind, and its appealing modernist aesthetics. That Frisch also underwrote a white sign system which lasted throughout the cold war decades, and to a large extent is still operative today, was a feature of his work we, and our teachers, clearly missed. Even in responses to *The Color Purple* its elements reverberate: the persistent white fascination with the heady magic mix of black spirituality and sensuality, with the "Deep South" appeal of poverty, endurance, and righteousness, works as a static, frozen abolitionist cluster of reception across and against more than two centuries of black self-articulation.

This rather willful politics of abolitionist reception functioned well not only in intellectual discourses, but also in the realm of liberal mass media production. A visit to the magazine's archives enabled me to peruse a few decades of journalistic engagement with African American people and issues in the German magazine *Stern*, a politically respected, glossy, high-end biweekly quite catholic in its political and cultural "tastes," characterized by its singular combination of print and photo essays, which has been in business from the late 1940s to today. The *Stern*'s moral preoccupations, topical selections, and political loyalties best capture the Zeitgeist mood of the enlightened, educated segments of the German public in the Cold War decades; the magazine faithfully covered and accompanied the crucial political, social, and cultural controversies of those decades with a keen eye for marketable publicity, it also effused—to the extent possible for such a publication—a liberal ethos.

The 1960s had seen the African American civil rights movement come alive in Germany in ways that matched, sometimes maybe even outdid its home popularity among white people. In 1964, Martin Luther King, the movement's most cherished living symbol, gave a speech in Berlin for an audience of over 60,000; his sermons, speeches, and essays (in German translation) were circulated widely in repeated editions of thousands of copies. The *Bertelsmann* Lesering, a well-established commercial German book club, selected *Why We Can't Wait* for its paying members in 1964. James Baldwin's novels, too, found a wide readership; the Wollschläger translation of *Another Country* sold 57,000 copies in the first-year edition and was reedited four times until 1988; the same translation sold in the GDR, to similar success, by the way. *The Fire Next Time*, or in German *Hundert Jahre Freiheit ohne Gleichberechtigung: Eine Warnung an die Weißen*, signaling the threatening transition to black militancy, sold 40,000 copies between 1964 and 1968. (This is NOT a comprehensive list!) The abolitionist drive manifested itself most visibly in features like German translations published complete with white German authorization, thus obviously copying an American nineteenth-century modus white authorization of African American slave narratives and other texts without any apparent reason for this kind of framing: *Freiheit! Der Aufbruch der Neger Nordamerikas: Die Thesen der Gewaltlosigkeit exemplarisch ausgesprochen von dem großen Negerführer selbst und in den aktuellen Zusammenhang gestellt durch einen historischen Überblick "Amerika und seine schwarzen Bürger" von Hans Dollinger* is the cover title of a paperback by Heine Verlag, 1968 (*Freedom! North America's Negroes On the Move: The Theses of Non-Violence Spoken By the Great Negro Leader Himself, Put in Historical Context By An Essay By Hans Dollinger, "America and Its Black Citizens"*). The *Stern* articles of the 1960s and 1970s should be read within this mental environment of a German public deeply disturbed by and moved to emulate the civic lessons of the civil rights movement's nonviolence campaigns: church groups and neighborhood streets were renamed after MLK; teaching *I have a dream* became canonical in high schools; grass-roots activities were designed according to civil rights movements' examples; and adults and teenagers eventually mourned King's death in wild outrage.

As a reading of *Stern* articles will show, this empathy, again, was tenable only within an abolitionist framework; its fragility became visible at the precise moment when militant, radical black self-articulation, and violent resistance appeared on the 1960s scene. White empathy, even at the German distance, seismographically caught the signs of a threat to white cultural and political hegemony, and showed its janus face of white contempt and racist ignorance. An erosion of discursive control becomes visible in the bizarre and quite helpless narrative strategies of containment with which the *Stern* covered post-1968 black militancy, as in their features about Angela Davis; it also shows up in the *Stern*'s ambivalent fascination with Muhammad Ali (or Cassius Clay, in the early years) whose grandiose but unpredictable performance in and out of the boxing ring merited several large, high-class photo essays by star *Stern* reporters like Eva Windmöller. Commentary ranges from anxious pity for *"Die armen Neger"* (*the poor negroes*) to the baffled, and quite self-deconstructive phrasing in one of Eva Windmöller's articles about a Cassius Clay who does not pay attention to white women (meaning, also, he did not court her!). It is hard to miss the disappointment of white benevolence and the shift to a racist leave-taking from a claim on white solidarity which would have to be predicated on African American terms in those passages.

In 1958, the *Stern* offers a title cover with a half-naked Harry Belafonte in a beach cocktail bar chair; the caption is: "The curse of black skin," because *inside* the magazine, there is an article about the racist discrimination against "the poor Negroes." Between 1963 and 1968 there follows a series of articles that try to discursively prepare the readers for a social explosion in the United States and at the same time keep themselves at a safe intellectual distance from that explosion; headings in the series run like "America's Negroes at the end of their patience," "Hatred tears America apart," "City in Fear," to culminate in a big photo story about the death of Martin Luther King, in which terrible snapshots of the assassination are captioned by sentences like: "The murder will give the signal for the cruelest Negro riot in the US"—which, in their book, does seem to be the gravest problem. In that same issue, a reporter observes the riots—his benevolence collapsing because "No, they did not mourn, they ran amok. They were not organized, and they were not interested in political organization. They only wanted to enjoy those hours, those singularly ecstatic, trancelike hours, rob, steal, plunder, loot, in the face of the police burn, call officers out of their names, humiliate the established order, and be the masters of Harlem."

Abolitionist goodwill slides into contempt as soon as the object of its empathy does not behave within the rules of the game, which even white subjects as remote as the *Stern* was in 1968 from ghettos burning in the United States, implicate themselves in without prompt. It seems as if a pre-patterned narrative script for *how to read Negroes* is always already in place, even for liberal Germans who are not at all in the center of attack; irreverent of specific time, location, actors, reasons, explications, interests.

The last example will be the *Stern* reportage about Angela Davis, who in a series of articles published between 1970 and 1972 figures as the incomprehensible Amazon.[3] She is mostly severed of her biography except for the juicy piece of her studies in Germany with the Frankfurt School, which appears, too, mostly by way of stunned remarks about "how she could read so much, and so well," and how she taught herself German by reading German plays, with a dictionary. In the articles, Davis is always "beautiful," "the young woman with the ample afro-head, the sensuous lips, and the nicely curved neck," she is "slender," humbly but tastefully dressed, displaying a "fantastical grace, this harmony of brain and body, intellect and sensuality"—attractive, in other words, as a female can be, if it weren't for her "extraordinary sharp intelligence," and, even more so, for her utter impracticality: "she could not keep her room tidy, and kept losing her purse," plus, significantly, she "did not have an idea of time." She was courageous, but nervous; intellectually trained but disorganized, and—one learns for good measure—traumatized by racism. Which is what made her in the prominent leftist spokesman Oskar Negt's words, the "incarnation of a revolutionary," complete, if one wants to follow the *Stern*, with "suede leather mini skirt, silk blouse, silver ear loops, and a coral necklace." If she committed a crime—which remains unclear in the articles for a long time—it may just be one of "female passion," because she fell in love with George Jackson, to some audiences' eager delight, and other people's racist anger.

Angela Davis—cast as an overdemanding strange cross breed of Harriet Beecher Stowe's slovenly mammy, the courageous Eliza, and a hitherto unconceptualized extravagant jungle fighter—came unto the German scene with a vengeance of her own. As the previously absented black woman who did not figure in the triangular representational orbit of white men, white women, and black men—which must be seen as a sine-qua-non constellation of abolitionist attachments—she burst on our imagination from the wings as it were. She had to be either *unmade* as a woman: revolutionary, super intellectual, a fighter, a black sister—or *overdone* as a sexy female: appearing as the "elegant Negress"—which, given all the previous stories about "poor Negroes," analphabetic women and children, or tasteless, cheaply dressed females, seems to have been quite an over-the-top oxymoron for white audiences at the time. Again, what is most mind-boggling in this textual construction is the self-assuredness and the air of understood knowledge of white Germans taking on the preconditioned script, without modifications, without ever having been spoken to, learned from, argued with a black person, or even having lived in any geographical proximity to them.

Apart from arresting readers with its unabashed exoticism and reckless racist presumptions, what are the theoretical implications this material invites one to trace? And why would an in-depth reading of those instances—forty to fifty years after the fact—still be useful and productive? The latter question may immediately be answered with a nod toward the German media campaign surrounding Hurricane Katrina, and the black neighborhoods of New Orleans; it has been quite amazing to see how both, the double-faced trope of "the poor Negroes," in tandem with its perfect match, the "negro out of control"—give and take a few variations in vocabulary—were put in recirculation at a moment's notice. Even the liberal and progressive German public has largely been ill equipped to formulate a response to the racist disaster beyond pity. Thus, the need for disseminating new epistemology within and beyond institutions of high education seems, still and again, a pressing urgency. How, then, to create interventions on the scenes of theory and advance those insights in, for example, German Humanities' departments, is a challenge to live up to.

This article's excursion into theory will use Hortense Spillers's work as a base of some Germanized speculations—it starts with a longer passage quoted from "Mama's Baby, Papa's Maybe," one of her groundbreaking essays originally published in 1987. Spillers describes the black body's "meaning and uses" for white discourses as follows: (1) the captive body (is) the source of an irresistible, destructive sensuality; (2) at the same time—in stunning contradiction—it is reduced to a thing, to *being* for the captor; (3) in this distance *from* a subject position, the captured sexualities provide a physical and biological expression of "otherness"; (4) as a category of "otherness," the captive body translates into a potential for pornotroping and embodies sheer physical powerlessness that slides into a more general "powerlessness," resonating through various centers of human and social meaning" (Spillers 206).

In keeping with this argument Spillers provocatively marks the abolitionist script as one of "the ubertas, of the appetites generally" (177), and speaks of a white "metaphysical desire" for abolitionism's "most coveted body" (178). These passages refer not only to sexually charged scenarios between black and white individuals; and not exclusively to clearly pornographic representations of African American bodies in white representations, either. The notion of pornotroping entails, also, human negotiations on various mundane levels; said troping obscenely overwrites the black person with his or her assumed bodily "gestalt": an overwhelming yet powerless presence and its assumed visceral, charismatic energies. In the same move, however paradoxical it may sound, the trope invariably glues black personhood to its mythical history as a movable body-thing that white people have been able to transgress against without reprimand; a work of voyeuristic troping, and re-troping which casts the African American human being always already in the representational shape of a body at disposal, for a variety of services depending on the given historical situation and its agents. This pornotroping as the key element of white abolitionist responses to and assumptions of blackness then works as a protean palimpsest—an ever-changing configuration.

Abolitionism has traveled amazingly well to the German context—without a clear focus, or discursive need for it—and survived even, and especially so, into a social and cultural realm characterized by a lack of an agenda-setting black presence. A nineteenth-century local narrative configuration has actually set the parameters not only for national (as Baldwin and others have amply observed) but also for international discourses; after more than 150 years of active service, it still holds sway over our transatlantic symbolic order of race relations. The dissemination of abolitionist sentiment as one particular feature of U.S.-Americanization, in recurring waves of discursive constellations certainly deserves further examination. The fact of it appears banal to the point of invisibility, since it has been so much taken for granted over so many generations, but I want to argue that it is not. Just imagine for a moment how different race relations could be had white people in the transatlantic realm—for example, Germans—decided to create their own tropes to come to terms with the black diaspora. That this did not happen, I suspect, is due to an extremely persistent hold the legacy of the slave trade and slavery has had not only on New World peoples but also on white European modernity, and postmodernity. In order to surpass abolitionist pornotroping as the hegemonic representation of African Americans as well as other black peoples, European intellectual Weltanschauung needed to first come to grips with their pervasive denial of slavery's constitutive function for the Enlightenment. The palimpsest that slavery and abolition wrote in the nineteenth century fixed a segregated symbolic pertaining not only to the place of black people within it, but even more so—as it turns out today—it inscribed white people within an extremely limited array of subject positions. Looking at abolitionism thus becomes important all over again, not so much because of whatever more or less racist things it had to say about its script's black characters, which has been thoroughly deconstructed for centuries, but because of its fixation of white subject positions in Western modern collective memory and imagination. As long as white people in Germany create no scripts for themselves other than accepting the choice between the die-hard racist, the benevolent, emphatic, self-reflexive good white man, the white plantation bitch, the stern moralizing and authoritarian do-gooder, or, as the feminine role of choice, sweet little Eva who may desire the black person in all presumptuous innocence, be it as mother, sister, lover, redeemer, or omnipotent healer of wounds, their "readings" of and more importantly their relations with African Americans and other black people will not get beyond the prototypical "peep at Uncle Tom" which Spillers scathingly interrupts with her argument.

The *Stern*'s "arme Neger"—a German phrase that semantically oscillates all too obviously between pity and contempt—and Max Frisch's naïvely rendered episode of how he stood behind the window curtains in his own living room, himself invisible to others, and literally sneaked looks on black bodies (his neighbors having an anniversary party)—those pornotropic moments will recur. I am thus interested in a critique of "travelled" abolitionism mainly because—as a paradigmatic, and static script—not only does it freeze the reception of African Americans and other black diasporic groups in racist terms, but also it frees white people at whatever historical remove from the Middle Passage from the responsibility to reflect on their respective particular implications in the black diaspora and allows them a false empathy stimulated by "ersatz" guilt which structurally does not require a critique of their respective racist history, and presence.

Looking at race relations in Germany and Europe today, this reassessment will be of crucial importance, and it might hold great potential. Political/cultural elites in Europe today more or less explicitly belong to the very generation of intellectuals who had let themselves be "moved" by the civil rights movement and by radical black articulation, in their pre-professional formative years as younger adults. Have they become aware of the ambiguities of their attachments? And how would bringing that cultural memory to the forefront of attention sharpen our sense of civil rights' challenges for Europe, in that one could possibly build on a reconstructed, post-abolitionist eye-to-eye negotiation with black agency which could be made productive in the contemporary moment?

The issue of civil rights has become, and will remain, a tantamount issue for Europe, particularly because new discourses around civil rights, at the crossroads between ethnic conflicts, race hierarchies, women's rights, and religious freedom have emerged in the process of Europeanization. To what extent could one reactivate a retinue of an impact of the post-sixties African American civil rights movement in those European discourses in various national incarnations? How has this post-sixties impact become modified and further developed by the present transcultural negotiations of various ethnic, including white, mostly youth subcultures? How does a knowledge of those transatlantic civil rights exchanges become integrated into the most recent discourses about civic life and values in Europe that over and again—what with all its nods toward multiethnicity and diversity—recasts itself as white, somehow devoid of colonial history and slavery, and absolutely untouched by blackness in the political sense? All these are the forward-looking questions that could be drawn out from a self-critical analysis of the quasi-abolitionist history of German contact with African Americans, and one is optimistically looking forward to the terms and substances of address that will be found in response to go beyond the safe grammar of myth, of attachments and disavowals that has remained understudied. How the African American civil rights movement, in its various phases and incarnations, has worked within and against this abolitionist script in their transnational and transatlantic alliances with various European communities remains a challenging question for research, which also awaits critical attention.

Notes

1. All translations in the following are my own.

2. He mentions a "small, highly recommendable "Anthology of American Negro Literature," published in the "Modern Library" (New York: Random House, 1944) as his source for Langston Hughes's demands.

3. These are the articles: *Stern* 1970, 43:68–70, "Die Jagd auf Angela Davis"; 1971, 20:145–49, "Liebesbriefe voller Haß, Rache und Verzweiflung"; 1972, 13:155–59, "In Frankfurt war kein Zimmer frei"; 1972, 17:148–53, "Das Tatmotiv soll Liebe sein"; 1972, 44:214–22, "Die Rebellin wurde linientreu."

Works Cited

Beecher Stowe, Harriet. *The Key to Uncle Tom's Cabin.* London: Clark, Beeton and Co., Foreign Booksellers, n.d, quoted in Spillers.

Beecher Stowe, Harriet. *Uncle Tom's Cabin.* New York: New American Library, 1966.

Frisch, Max. "Begegnungen mit Negern. Eindrücke aus Amerika." In *Gesammelte Werke in zeitlicher Folge, 1949–1956*, Vol. III. SuhrkampVerlag: Frankfurt am Main, 1976.

Spillers, Hortense. *Black, White and in Color: Essays on American Literature and Culture.* Chicago: University of Chicago Press, 2003.

Logan, Rayford W., ed. *What the Negro Wants.* New York: Random House, 1944.

"Nazi Jim Crow"

Hans Jürgen Massaquoi's Democratic Vistas on the Black Atlantic and Afro-Germans in *Ebony*

FRANK MEHRING

Let America be the dream the dreamers dreamed—
Let it be that great strong land of love
Where never kings connive nor tyrants scheme
That any man be crushed by one above.
　　LANGSTON HUGHES, "Let America Be America Again" (1938)

Introduction

Like Hughes's evocation of European immigrant dreams about a democratic haven of freedom across the Atlantic, Hans Jürgen Massaquoi's writings are crossovers in more than one sense. He grew up in Hamburg during the tumultuous years of the Weimar Republic as the son of a Liberian consul and a German mother. Having survived the terror of National Socialist persecution, he moved to Liberia in 1948. Later, Massaquoi forged a career in journalism and became the managing editor of *Ebony*, the most influential African American magazine in the United States. His tricultural background has made him particularly sensitive toward patterns of racial discrimination in Western democratic societies. Massaquoi's first encounters with Americans immediately after WWII in occupied Germany were marked by both enthusiasm and disappointment. He realized the one-sidedness of his German notion of American democracy when black GIs were treated like second-class citizens in segregated military units. Massaquoi's work is marked by his commitment to reveal discrepancies between democratic ideals and practices on both sides of the Atlantic. It was not before the 1960s that he faced the Afro-German past to critically evaluate his new sociopolitical role in the United States. This process of ethnic self-examination was triggered by a series of articles in *Ebony* on Afro-Germans and his growing interest in Malcolm X's endorsement of violence as the appropriate answer to "white supremacy" in the American South.

In 1966, Massaquoi returned to his German roots to raise similar questions about Nazi and postwar Germany. His two articles, "A Journey into the Past (Part I and II)," reveal both drastic changes and subtle continuities in the standing of minorities in Germany and the challenges of a multiethnical democratic society. "Nazi Jim Crow," Massaquoi's special term to describe the traumatic events on both sides of the Atlantic, connects fascist political strategies of racial superiority with the reality of racial segregation in the southern parts of the United States. What are the differences between the Afro-German and African American struggle for recognition? How did the Third Reich experience shape Massaquoi's identity as an Afro-German and later as an African American? What are the repercussions for Massaquoi's democratic vistas on the black Atlantic? This article contextualizes Massaquoi's democratic visions of the United States and postwar Germany to shed new light on the search for recognition of Afro-Germans.

Democratic Vistas in Nazi Germany: Triple Consciousness

The Afro-German history and the presence of blackness in Germany have largely been marked by denial and almost complete ignorance.[1] As metaphors, terms such as *Neger* or *schwarzer Mann* have been prominent in the socialization of many generations. The song *"Zehn kleine Negerlein"* ("Ten Little Negroes"), the children's game *Wer hat Angst vor'm schwarzen Mann?* ("Who's Afraid of the Black Man," the children's call *Neger, Neger, Schornsteinfeger* ("Negro, Negro, Chimney Sweep"), and chocolates such as *Negerküsse* ("Negro Kisses") or *Mohrenköpfe* (Moors' Heads) underline a racial discourse that connotes the African presence as culturally inferior, threatening, or make it the butt of jokes. As the preceding chapter on black portraiture showed, the visual narrative of German poster art had established color codes and stereotypical postures that placed dark-skinned people either in the role of servants or exotic commodities.

It was not before the 1980s that Germans of African or African American descent began to articulate their experience as a minority by utilizing a discourse of victimization. In their efforts to discuss the challenges, meanings, and consequences of growing up black in Germany, the preferred medium was the genre of autobiographical writing. This mode of expression resembled the discursive strategy that had been successfully employed by African Americans from Frederick Douglass via Sojourner Truth to Langston Hughes and Malcolm X in order to find one's voice, to raise racial consciousness in the United States, and to gain recognition. The collection of autobiographical accounts of Afro-Germans in *Farbe bekennen* from 1986 brought the black experience in German cultural history to public attention.[2] These testimonies broke with the assumption that Germany had been an ethnically homogenous country. It brought into perspective processes of transformation emphasizing multicultural, multiracial, and multiethnic tendencies, particularly after 1945. These essays and oral histories mainly addressed the experience of so-called brown babies, the *Besatzungskinder* (other terms include *Mischling, Mulatto*, or the derogative *Neger*), during the

American occupation in Western Germany. Thus, the issue of racism had been catapulted from the Third Reich to an unexpected period in post–World War II Germany, albeit without the totalitarian framework sanctifying political persecution. Addressing the everyday experience of discrimination, Ika Hügel-Marshall, for example, recounts in her autobiography *Invisible Woman: Growing up Black in Germany* (2001) the traumatic suffering produced by being identified as an exotic outsider during her childhood and adolescence in postwar Germany.

Despite extensive reports on "Brown Babies" on both sides of the Atlantic in the 1950s, comparatively few scholars have addressed the black presence in Germany and the ensuing transcultural confrontations.[3] Since the late 1990s, academics have applied postcolonial and poststructuralist theories to approach questions of cultural hybridity and identity formation.[4] In Germany, *Weißsein* has become a term differentiated from American whiteness studies in order to specify the cultural parameters of monocultural constructions in Western Germany.[5] With the publication of *Destined to Witness* by Hans Jürgen Massaquoi in 1999, a new facet of German history came to the attention of a transatlantic audience.

Massaquoi's narrative is a particularly striking case in point to address various forms of intercultural racism in Germany, imaginary concepts of American democratic culture, and transcultural confrontations in the United States. At the same time, his account hardly fits in the general experience which Afro-Germans shared. The corner stone of Massaquoi's life is the struggle of coming to terms with what the philosopher and sociologist Axel Honneth describes as the feeling of social disrespect. Social recognition is the guiding principle for a successful development of one's personality. The neglect of social recognition or even outright disrespect can lead to a loss of personality (Honneth 1994, 53). In the system of critical theory, Honneth argues that recognition is based on three key elements: first, emotional care within intimate social family ties; second, jurisdictional recognition as a moral rational member of society; and third, social respect for individual achievements. Massaquoi's autobiographies *Destined to Witness* (1999) and *Hänschen Klein, Ging Allein . . .* (2004) deal with his struggles to achieve jurisdictional and social recognition. His tricultural background, his racial encounters in Nazi Germany, Liberia, and the United States have made him deeply suspicious of the American dream of liberty, equality, and opportunity. Tracing back his quest for recognition is closely linked to the question of how to make democratic societies live up to their creed.

The cover images on Massaquoi's two autobiographies convey the dilemma of Afro-Germans who grew up during the twelve-year period of Nazi rule. The first part, *Destined to Witness*, deals with Massaquoi's youth in Germany, his passage to Africa, and his emigration to the United States. The follow-up publication, which up to this point has appeared exclusively in German translation, *Hänschen Klein, Ging Allein . . .* , tells the success story of becoming an American citizen. The photos chosen for the book covers summarize the psychological struggle that Massaquoi as an Afro-German had to come to terms with. *Destined to Witness* shows the Afro-German as a young eight-year-old schoolboy surrounded by his peers. His skin color and curly black hair mark him as the "other" among the blond boys and girls. His looks are sad if not skeptical. On his vest, the black boy displays a swastika button, possibly to match the proud attitude of the boy standing next to him. The image captures the identity dilemma Afro-Germans faced during the Third Reich. Identity, according to Charles Taylor, is shaped both by recognition or its absence (Taylor 1992, 25). To overcome his self-depreciation produced through the oppressive racial politics of the Nuremberg Laws, Massaquoi tried to overwrite racial difference through a surplus of patriotism. However, he is not only destined to witness but also destined to be denied social recognition. The dilemma becomes clear: The more Afro-Germans tried to conform to Nazi German standards of recognition, the more they advocated their own destruction.

The image on the second book on Massaquoi's career in the United States shows a young black man standing full of pride at Times Square, suggesting relaxedness, independence, pride, and optimism. The immigrant will seamlessly blend into his new cultural environment. A visual clue is given by the three black women who cross the street behind him.[6] The text authenticates these sentiments. "As we strolled through Manhattan, I immediately felt at home" (Massaquoi 1999, 413). At the same time, Massaquoi sensed that the feeling of belonging was still far ahead in time.

Massaquoi's German experience is one of double consciousness in the Du Boisian sense. Growing up black in Nazi Germany he experienced the peculiar sensation "of always looking at one's self through the eyes of others, of measuring one's soul by the tape of a world that looks on in amused contempt and pity. One ever feels his two-ness" (Du Bois 2003, 9). Before Massaquoi begins his autobiographical account chronologically, he jumps ahead in time to retell an incident that left one of the most striking marks in his memory: the visit of Adolf Hitler in Massaquoi's hometown Hamburg in the summer of 1934.

> The "biggest moment in our lives" for which Principal Wriede had prepared us had lasted only a few seconds, but to me they seemed like an eternity. There I was, a kinky-haired, brown-skinned eight-year-old boy amid a sea of blond and blue-eyed kids, filled with childlike patriotism, still shielded by blissful ignorance. Like everyone around me, I cheered the man whose every waking hour was dedicated to the destruction of "inferior non-Aryan people" like myself, the same man who only a few years later would lead his own nation to the greatest catastrophe in its long history and bring the world to the brink of destruction. (Massaquoi 1999, 2)[7]

This short paragraph introduces the reader to a double perspective, that of the naïve child and the wise narrator who in retrospect contextualizes the innocent cheers of the little boy. The narrative shifts its perspective, thereby introducing ambiguous notions of belonging and unbelonging. The encounter with Massaquoi's childhood hero signifies the futility of his efforts to erase the racial differences in Germany.[8]

Fig. 1. Cover page of *Destined to Witness* and *Neger, Neger Schornsteinfeger.* Reprinted by kind permission of F. Fisher Verlag.

Within the discourse of recognition, Massaquoi received positive feedback on the intimate sphere; namely, the continuing loving support of his mother. However, on the second level, the public sphere, where the formation of identity and the self is marked by forms of dialogue and struggle with what George Herbert Mead called "significant others" (Mead 1934, yx), Massaquoi is stigmatized as a second-class citizen and ultimately denied the status of a dignified citizen in Nazi Germany.

Massaquoi's account of his life repeatedly creates crossovers from Germany to the United States via references to Jim Crow. In the chapter "Paradise Lost" in *Destined to Witness* he outlines both feelings of admiration and fear regarding the Nazi ideology. The sign on a Hamburg playground made young Massaquoi aware of his racial identity and difference in comparison to his friends. The sign read: "Non-Aryans are sternly prohibited from entering this playground" (Massaquoi 1999, 47). A few pages later, the author explains his fascination with American movies, particularly *The Littlest Rebel* from 1935 with child star Shirley Temple. Being a great admirer of her singing and dancing, he interviewed his former idol forty years later for *Ebony.* Due to Jim Crow laws, Temple's black co-star and dancing partner Bill Robinson was not able to stay at the same Florida hotel (Massaquoi 1999, 51). In addition, the restricting rules of the Production Code of the Motion Picture Producers and Directors of America prohibited intimate contacts on screen between (adult) whites and blacks during the 1930s (Sollors 1997, 5). These painful proofs of racial discrimination in the United States remain uncommented by Massaquoi. However, the literary technique of juxtaposing the playground sign in Nazi Germany with racial segregation in Miami hotels serves as a grim reminder that Massquoi's dream of the Fox newsreel "land of unlimited opportunities" would hold major disappointments. Instead of psychological introspection and analytical deconstructions of the promise of American democracy, the author's narrative remains on the descriptive surface. This technique

Fig. 2. Cover page of *Hänschen Klein, Ging Allein* . . . Reprinted by kind permission of F. Fisher Verlag.

allows Massaquoi to authenticate his story while leaving the obvious conclusions regarding similarities between the National Socialist race regulations and United States Jim Crow laws to the reader.

During the Nazi regime, Massaquoi continually battled with opposing sentiments: his disgust of National Socialism and his wish to become part of the German social system. One way of coping with this troublesome state of limbo was the creation of a dreamland where blacks were both popular and successful. During the summer of 1936, modern mass media provided a new means to imagine an identity distinct from his white German peers. Radio and newspaper reports on Joe Louis's achievements as a boxer and his fight against Max Schmeling in the New York City's Yankee Stadium offered the young black boy a "ticket to prestige and respect" (Massaquoi 1999, 117). Fellow schoolchildren compared him immediately to the so-called brown bomber from the United States. This newly earned respect showed Massaquoi the way out of his racial loneliness. "I became obliged to forgo my local patriotism [for Max Schmeling] and come out for my black brother from the States" (Massaquoi 1999, 115). Despite Louis's defeat against Schmeling on June 19, 1936, a new opportunity of reinscription would soon arise with the Olympic Games in Berlin. Massaquoi felt that victories of black athletes resembled victories of his own battles in the racialized schoolyard. "I immediately felt a surge of pride over the very special kinship that linked me with these men from America" (Massaquoi 1999, 122). Among the new heroes was the Alabama-born runner Jesse Owens. With Leni Riefenstahl's visual homage to athletic features of Owen's black body in *Olympia—Festival of the Nations and Festival of Beauty* (1938) Massaquoi became proudly identified as "Jesse's little brother" (Massaquoi 1999, 124).[9]

In the following years, Massaquoi actively fashioned himself into an ideal American. Modern mass media like film and radio served as powerful agents of cultural transfer. In 1938, Massaquoi entered the "fantasy realm of the 'swing boys'" (Massaquoi 1999, 159). This group resisted the conformist military agenda of the Hitler Youths by wearing long hair with sideburns, dressed in exaggeratedly neat manners while listening to (forbidden) American jazz music. At the same time, Massaquoi started learning to play the trumpet. The goal was to imitate his musical idol, the world-famous jazz musician Louis Armstrong. Later, Massaquoi switched to the iconographic instrument of jazz: the saxophone.

His efforts of gaining recognition are quite different compared to those of W. E. B. Du Bois, who fashioned himself into a German in terms of looks, manners, and language during his academic year in Berlin (Du Bois 1968, 126). While Massaquoi repeatedly draws on scenarios of exclusion and stigmatization, Du Bois reported as late as 1936 during his trip from the Alps to the North Seas that he enjoyed his five-month stay in Germany. "I have been treated with uniform courtesy and consideration. It would have been impossible for me to have spent a similarly long time in any part of the United States, without some, if not frequent cases of personal insult or discrimination. I cannot record a single instance here" (Du Bois 1995, 734). As Sieglinde Lemke points out, in Germany Du Bois considered himself living on the civilized side of the world. His foreign sojourn provided him with a vantage point from which to criticize white Americans and emphasize superior cultural expressions of black Americans (Lemke 2002, 214). Such an account of racial tolerance three years after Hitler's rise to power and one year after the Nuremberg Laws, the restrictions of black jazz musicians, and instances of ethnic cleansing might seem startling. Nevertheless, it is in line with many accounts of African Americans who have continually reported on the warm and open-hearted reception in Germany from Frederick Douglass to Alain Locke (Paul 2005, 303).

Despite this preference for becoming an American, Massaquoi also continued his efforts to fit into German society and erase racial boundaries. In 1943, he even considered serving in the Nazi army. "Once in uniform, I was certain that I would prove beyond a doubt that I was as good as anyone else" (Massaquoi 1999, 193). Massaquoi developed a sense of triple consciousness oscillating between wanting to be accepted as a German, being identified as an African, and dreaming about becoming an African American. A crucial change in his quest for recognition was triggered during the phase of American occupation and his encounters with African American soldiers.

Between Totalitarianism and Democracy: Occupied Germany

The National Socialist vision/nightmare of an elitist Aryan monocultural society produced the illusion that being black meant at the same time being an (inferior) outsider. During the first three decades of the twentieth century, black people in Germany were mostly recognized as exotic curiosities displayed in ethnic shows called "Afrika-Völkerschauen" in zoos (Thode-Arora 2004, 26) or demonized for propaganda purposes in the context of the French Rhineland occupation (Campt 2004, 33). In their historical overview of Afro-German culture, Patricia Mazón and Reinhild Steingröver remark that the German society continues to recognize those citizens of mixed German and African or African American parentage as "foreigners," that is, not German (Mazón and Steingröver 2005, 2).

Nevertheless, in the immediacy after World War II, the majority of newly recruited black GIs emphasized the warm-hearted German responses regarding the presence of black GIs and a surprising lack of racist attitudes. Under the headline "Germany meets the Negro Soldier" *Ebony* magazine featured an article on the notion of racial equality in occupied Germany in 1946.

> Strangely enough, here where once Aryanism ruled supreme, Negroes are finding more friendship, more respect and more equality than they would back home—either in Dixie or on Broadway. [. . .] Today in Berlin the common people of Germany, minus uniforms and no longer goose-stepping, are meeting black Americans face-to-face after lifting of the U.S. ban against fraternization. Race hate has faded with better acquaintance and interracialism in Berlin flourishes. (*Ebony* 1946, 5)

The general notion was summed up in the impression that democracy had more meaning in the former capital of Nazi fascism than in the American South. In 1947, the *Pittsburgh Courier* ran similar articles announcing on the front page that few GIs were eager to return to the United States. Compared to their white fellow occupation forces, African American soldiers developed a special sensitivity regarding the respect they received from German people. The appreciative responses from German people, who seemed to downplay racial differences in favor of racial tolerance,[10] reaffirmed not only their American identity but also generated a new sense of self-respect. This experience would later activate a more critical and active response to Jim Crow once they had returned to the United States.

The sensitivity developed by a Massaquoi growing up black in Nazi Germany produced a racial narrative that turned the experience of black American soldiers upside down. Massaquoi's story of postwar encounters with African American and white American soldiers adds a fascinating facet to the patterns of recognition. Like a trickster figure, he plays with cultural expectations, undermines, and exploits them. In order to survive in the hunger-stricken years of 1945–1948, Massaquoi used his skin color to move—more or less—freely between the lines of restricted zones of the allied forces and the German population. The adventurous accounts of "passing" in *Destined to Witness* foreshadow tales of an American hero. Massaquoi does not represent himself as a victim of the Holocaust but as a cunning agent between two worlds.[11]

[At the beginning of the American occupation] I underwent an amazing physical as well as psychological transformation [. . .] . I learned to eat the American way, with only a fork in my right hand, instead of the European way, fork in the left hand and knife in the right hand. Werner also helped me Americanize my rapidly expanding English vocabulary by making me discard British terms such as petrol, leftenant, bloke, and lorry in favor of gas, lieutenant, guy, and truck, respectively. What we didn't know about the States, its customs, and speech habits, we learned from watching American movies. (Massaquoi 1999, 305)

In economic terms, this meant moving "from rags to riches" (and back again). Massaquoi's motivations were two-fold: first, to serve the basic need of getting food from the American occupiers; second, to interact with those people he imagined in his dream about "America." The account of Massaquoi's first encounter with an African American is remarkable as far as the creation of a nexus regarding race, nation, and cultural identity is concerned. Due to his racial features, the black GI immediately identifies him as a "brother" and inquires skeptically: "What in the world are you doing here among these Krauts?" (Massaquoi 1999, 270). The underlying assumption holds that no black person could ever be part of everyday German life, not to mention being a German citizen. Massaquoi was convinced that his future must lie in the land where the liberators of Nazi Germany and the representatives of democracy roam freely. "It was during those few minutes that I first was struck by the sentimental notion to leave Germany and to get to know 'my people' in the United States" (Massaquoi 1999, 271). The word "sentimental" functions as a signifier for the double-edged sword of being a second-class citizen without being accepted as a person with equal rights.[12]

Massaquoi learned to disguise himself under a false banner to attract the attention of African American GIs. When being asked about his parents, he invented a back story regarding his identity. Instead of explaining the African background of his Liberian father, he referred to himself as the son of an American citizen. He discovered that such a connection with the United States "could make the difference between cordial acceptance as a brother and cold rejection as an unwelcome stranger" (Massaquoi 1999, 316). References to Africa were considered backward and associated with that part of American history of which black GIs did not want to be reminded. Despite the artistic reevaluation of the African heritage in the United States during the Harlem Renaissance, social recognition among black GIs could only be gained by claiming to be an African American.

Massaquoi was confronted with the disenchantment of his dream when he recognized the racially segregated units of American soldiers. These obvious contradictions with his American fantasy created points of cultural friction. How could an army with racial segregation fight for "the stated purpose of making the world free for democracy"? (Massaquoi 1999, 318). Massaquoi quickly realized the American dilemma; namely, the gap of the creed regarding "liberty and justice for all" and the political practice of segregation. The experience that racial discrimination was not only condoned but, as the military occupied forces demonstrated, practiced and enforced by the U.S. Government, proved all the more shocking to Massaquoi.

> As much as I hated the Nazis for it, somehow, their overt racism and refusal to accept me in their military ranks seemed more honest to me than the United States' lip service to democracy and eagerness to recruit blacks while keeping them at arm's length in segregated, low-status service units commanded primarily by whites. (Massaquoi 1999, 319)

His high expectations of the American way of life were again shattered when he actually arrived in the United States in 1950. He encountered "racism American style, in the reputedly racially liberal North" at his job and later as a GI himself during the Korean War. When conversations came to the issue of Jewish holidays, one of the white soldiers in Massaquoi's basic training camp complained in harsh language about the standing of Jewish people in the United States. In particular, the GI criticized that Jewish soldiers enjoyed more holidays than non-Jewish recruits. In a cynical manner, the Holocaust was evoked as an event to be lauded.

> I couldn't believe what I had just heard. I had always assumed, quite naively, that the reasons America went to war against Hitler were to stop aggression, wipe out totalitarianism and racism, re-establish democracy, and free the Jews. Now an American used the same language of hate and intolerance that I knew so well from Nazi Germany. Anti-Semitism, I reluctantly concluded, was alive and well in the good old U.S.A. (Massaquoi 1999, 421)

What is the function of Massaquoi's repeated attack on American religious and racial prejudice and questionable democratic attitudes? I can think of two reasons. Massaquoi underlines his sensitivity regarding parallel patterns of racial discrimination in democratic and totalitarian systems. At the same time he emphasizes his willingness to become part of U.S.-American culture despite repeated instances of political—that is, democratic—failures. Massaquoi was determined to make the United States live up to the creed of freedom and equality. One way to overcome racial stereotypes and fight Jim Crow legislation was to embrace mass media as a powerful agent of sociopolitical reform.

Transatlantic Vistas in *Ebony:* Resistance, Reform, Representation

When Massaquoi entered journalism, he inscribed himself consciously into the African American literary topoi mentioned at the beginning of *Destined to Witness.* Massaquoi evoked Frederick Douglass as a precursor repeating the pattern of bondage, flight, escape, conversion, upward mobility, and ultimately of testifying. The African American magazine *Ebony* offered a chance to gain recognition, economic wealth, and to tell his own (spectacular) story of survival. The magazine proved to be a perfect vehicle for Massaquoi to fight for more democracy in the United States. The experience of being an Afro-German in the American occupation zone turned out to be vital for his struggle with what he called Nazi Jim Crow.

Like Massaquoi's own search for recognition, the magazine's success story began shortly after WWII when thousands of black GIs returned from their military service and fight against the enemies of democracy. Now, they had to come to terms with the harsh reality of segregation, racial inequality, cultural misrepresentation, and the democratic gap in their home country. John H. Johnson, a twenty-seven-year-old black businessman from Chicago, set out to respond to these discrepancies. One of the means was to counterbalance journalistic representations of African Americans largely controlled by a white media empire. In the autumn of 1945, he launched *Ebony* magazine whose credo involved providing positive black images by highlighting political, social, economical, and cultural achievements. The magazine introduced models of African Americans who triumphed not only over poverty, but also racial and ideological barriers. Johnson's journalistic vision of reporting about success, however, tended to blend out issues of radical dissenters in black communities and fails to critically address aspects of violence to overcome racial barriers.

When Massaquoi joined the *Ebony* staff writers in the late 1950s, journalists covered a broad spectrum of topics ranging from the civil rights movement, religion, and politics to sports, music, television, films, fashion, and the arts. The articles were designed to generate a new sense of self-respect among the readers. Reports on the freedom movement of the 1950s and 1960s culminated in the magazine's coverage of the famous March on Washington on August 28, 1963, when Johnson activated his entire editorial force of writers and photographers to document the historic event. Dr. Martin Luther King Jr.'s prayer-like proclamation "I have a dream" also represented the dream of *Ebony*. Johnson formulated a declaration of independence for African American media calling for the so-called *Ebony* revolution (Bennett 2005, 74). This led the magazine to become a close observer of the freedom movement in Africa. Together with its sister magazine *Jet*, *Ebony* started to cover regularly African Independence ceremonies starting with Ghana in 1957. It remained for a long time the only major American magazine to report extensively on the progress of African struggles for independence.[13] The political and cultural evolution regarding racial tolerance became a focus early on.

A special transatlantic connection was forged by Massaquoi, whose career from staff writer to managing editor successfully integrated his tricultural background. Massaquoi's prime focus concerned aspects of ethnic tolerance, subtle forms of exploitation, racism, sociopolitical inequality, and the promise of democracy inside and outside the United States. He interviewed leading politicians around the world and wrote against racial stereotypes in Africa, Europe, Asia, and the Caribbean. His diverse assignments included interviews with presidents of Nigeria, Botswana, Liberia, and Namibia; civil rights activists like Dr. Martin Luther King Jr., the Reverend Jesse Jackson, and Malcolm X; as well as icons of American culture such as singer Diana Ross, actor Richard Roundtree, writer Alex Haley, or boxer Muhammad Ali. Massaquoi confronted what he called "the ugly side of America." His transcultural perspective on issues regarding human rights became an important source of inspiration for other colleagues on both sides of the Atlantic.[14]

The credo of *Ebony* was to report on the contributions of blacks to American culture and to shed light on the positive sides of African American's lives. The popular ongoing series on "black pioneers" introduced the first black judge in the Supreme Court, the first walk on the moon by a black astronaut, the first black winner of the Nobel Peace Prize, and so forth (Bennett Jr. 2005, 76). To a certain degree, Massaquoi himself belonged to this category. *Ebony* introduced him as the "first" Afro-German who survived Nazi terror to become an influential model African American journalist documenting "Germany's New Way of Life" (Massaquoi 1966, Part II, 102).

These tactics were publisher Johnson's response to the impression that white magazines and newspapers focused on blacks only with references to criminal activities. After close analysis, Massaquoi agreed that in terms of racial equality the American news market left a lot to be desired. Instead of objective journalism, white publishers tended to condone racially manipulative articles undermining democratic ideals of freedom of speech (Massaquoi 2004, 47). *Ebony*, however, became also biased by neglecting to provide an objective platform for African American matters. Articles on blacks were equally one-sided emphasizing exclusively positive aspects of African American cultural expressions. Even worse, the magazine's aesthetics were often dominated by white preferences. Most of the photos of models printed in *Ebony* showcase their mulatto skin color. Not surprisingly, the magazine was in favor of product advertisements that promised "a glamorous new you with a lighter, clear skin" with Dr. Fred Palmer's Skin Whitener (*Ebony* 1966, 96). These aspects seem to support the argument that the sociologist E. Franklin Frazier sketched out in his essay "Black Bourgeoisie" roughly a decade earlier. Frazier argued that middle-class[15] African Americans became culturally rootless since they were driven by feelings of inferiority, insecurity, and estrangement from black traditions. Detecting a mask behind talk of racial pride, the African American middle class might, according to Frazier, complain about discrimination. Ultimately, however, the argument goes, they wished to be accepted by whites and feared direct competition. This, as Frazier explains, is the reason for the extreme exaggerations regarding the success of African American achievements.[16] While Massaquoi was also interested in emphasizing accomplishments of black intellectuals and artists, his interracial background helped him to create bridges across color lines.

The task of democratizing post-fascist Germany brought into question American political legitimacy in reference to Jim Crow laws. *Ebony* had been a close observer of racial discourses in postwar Germany early on. The general tone was optimistic foregrounding the liberal attitude of West Germany. Only one year after the German capitulation, a seven-page article entitled "Germany Meets the Negro Soldier" stressed that racial tensions could be found not so much among Germans but within the American camps. The former political enemy became a model for tolerance in the African American press. Referring to McNarney's remark about the inferiority of blacks as "it will be one hundred years before the Negro will develop to a point where he will be on a parity with white Americans," *Ebony* concluded:

> To Germans, that kind of talk is familiar; it echoes the shrill hysterics of Hitler only a few short years back. They listened to the Nazi boss and paid with blood and tears. Some wonder if America will not pay the same price in heeding the racist doctrine spread by men like General McNarney. (*Ebony* 1946, 11)

Themes of racial tolerance and multiethnic integration continue to play an important role in black press reports about Germany. In the following years, the fate of about three thousand occupation children conceived by African American GIs and German women shifted the focus to American concerns of moral responsibility. Articles such as "German War Babies" (1951), "Germany's Tragic War Babies" (1952), "We Adopted a Brown Baby" (1953), or "Should White Parents Adopt Brown Babies" (1958) focused on the need to help these children in their uncommon living situation abroad. The legal challenges of incorporating "brown babies" in the United States was reported widely and in many cases celebrated as a "triumph of American democracy" (*Ebony* June 1958, 28). Later articles created sites of cultural contrast to question American racial politics. In "Brown Babies Go to Work," *Ebony* ran an extensive article on what appeared to be a frictionless move for fifteen hundred Afro-Germans to assume their place as equal citizens in democratic Western Germany. "As a whole, the country has risen to the challenge posed by its newest minority and is eagerly seizing the opportunities to erase the stigma which Hitler's brutal enforcement of his 'super race' schemes attached to the nation" (*Ebony* November 1960, 97). Despite these positive accounts, many Germans continued to reject black Germans as foreigners or sociopolitical outsiders from the United States or Africa. As the foundational anthology of Afro-Germans history *Farbe bekennen: Afro-deutsche Frauen auf den Spuren ihrer Geschichte* (1986), autobiographies, essays, and memoirs like those of Ika Hügel-Marshall or May Ayim aptly document, Germans of African or African American descent suffered from being identified as outsiders despite their German citizenship.[17] Why does Hans Jürgen Massaquoi follow along the lines of earlier reports in *Ebony* to paint a more optimistic image of Western Germany and the citizens of this newly formed democratic nation? I can think of two reasons: Although Maria Höhn and Heide Fehrenbach suggest that German attitudes toward African American GIs and "German Brown Babies" were more nuanced, varied, and not quite as positive as some of the *Ebony* articles on Germany imply, Massaquoi emphasizes the positive effects of public diplomacy and the way young people in particular embrace American popular culture.

While Maria Höhn has shown that "Amerikanisierung" and "Coca-Colonization" aroused fear, worries, and suspicion among conservative clergy, church-affiliated social welfare workers, and bourgeois observers in Western Germany, *Ebony* and Massaquoi chose to blend out elements of transcultural frictions in favor of reporting on successful practices of appropriating the "American way of life."[18] It is likely that Massaquoi with his fascination of American culture and his warmhearted embrace of his new homeland believed that a similar positive attitude would ultimately be beneficiary to Germans who decided to stay in their home country, as well. In addition, Massaquoi believed in the cause of the European Reconstruction Program to integrate Western Germany successfully into what was then envisioned to be a united "New Europe." Massaquoi emphasized the German population's willingness and ability to renounce ill-fated chauvinistic fanaticism of the past in favor of accepting the opportunities of a democratic reeducation and political renewal American style.

With Massaquoi's competent evaluation and representation of Germany's democratic development, the post-fascist success story of racial tolerance became an explicit foil for the civil rights movement in the United States. The magazine's readership in the sixties, the times of most radical changes within black communities and the emergence of aggressive civil rights activists, was mostly conservative. Massaquoi used *Ebony* as a platform to address the Afro-German history from the "Rhineland Bastards" to "Brown Babies" and "Coca-Colonization" of Western Germany.[19] He contextualized his reference to Nazi Jim Crow by questioning the homogeneous image of Nazi Germany as a thoroughly intolerant society. At the same time, he outlined chances and shortcomings, moments of resistance and venues for reforms to create democratic societies without racial prejudice both in Europe and the United States.[20]

Democracy and "Nazi Jim Crow": Massaquoi and Malcolm X

In a two-part *Ebony* article on racial tolerance in post–World War II Germany, Massaquoi coined the term "Nazi Jim Crow." The linkage of these two terms is both suggestive and problematic. The striking compound intertwines segregation of African Americans during national socialist rule Germany and the United States. Massaquoi's examples strike a familiar chord on both sides of the Atlantic by drawing on scenarios of exclusion and stigmatization: being refused admittance to a public building, being asked to leave a seat on a bus to a white person, or being insulted in public due to the color of one's skin (Massaquoi 1966, 94). However, the linkage erases the lines between different political systems. While the United States is a democratic country based on the political assurance of basic human rights as proclaimed in the Declaration of Independence and inscribed in the Constitution, the Third Reich represents a totalitarian system in which racial differences are politically cemented with far-reaching jurisdictional consequences. The alleged equation of Nazi racism with Jim Crow rules elevates the fight for democracy of black GIs abroad into a test case for American democracy at home.[21] What are the particular cultural connotations of this compound and what is the function of the linkage in Massaquoi's work?

A comparison of both the cover image and the opening chapter provide clues for the shifting notion of Nazi persecution and Jim Crow laws. The image that conveys this doubleness is printed on the cover of Massaquoi's autobiography. An eleven-year-old black boy proudly presents the emblem that makes him feel he is a well-accepted person among his white peers from second grade in the year Hitler came to power. More than thirty years later, the kinky-haired, brown-skinned eight-year-old boy returned as an accomplished citizen of the United States. "A Journey into the Past" from 1966 opens with a familiar scenario, but twists the situation for his American audience by blurring the boundary between enemy and friend, between the stereotype of white Germans and black Americans. The large photograph on the first page of the article brings together the Old and the New World. The black American citizen poses in a relaxed manner in front of the Hamburg town hall. He is well dressed in a long coat, tie, and shirt, relaxing on the Elbkanal rail. His facial features suggest a meditative mood. At the same time, he seems relaxed and self-confident. The first striking feature at the center of the page is the gothic lettering evoking immediately old-fashioned German writings and, particularly in the United States, an allusion to iconographic inscriptions of the Nazi terror regime. The "Nazi" reference is explicitly mentioned in the second headline. *Ebony* is linked with German history in the syntax: "*EBONY* staffer visits his native Germany; recalls bomb horrors and Nazi persecution" (Massaquoi 1966, 91). Thus, "Nazi Jim Crow" is evoked both syntactically and visually.

Massaquoi relives the last years of total war in Hamburg when about forty thousand people died under Allied bomb attacks. It is a scene not so much marked by "childlike patriotism" and "blissful ignorance" of a black German schoolboy. Rather, Massaquoi becomes the victim of misidentification, of racial and national hatred. References to explosions and bombings instantly evoke significant moments of the civil rights movement in the 1960s and before. The race riots in Detroit and Harlem in 1943 come to mind as well as to the sixteen unsolved bombings in Birmingham in the early 1960s, the Harlem riot of 1964, or the attack on Martin Luther King Jr.'s home.

> The pounding of bombs had stopped and an eerie silence had settled over what was left of Hamburg, Germany. Dazed and choking, I stumbled over smouldering debris, past burning buildings and twisted streetcar rails while trying hard not to look at the corpses that lay scattered in my path. Suddenly, a scream pierced the smoke-filled air. "There's one of those murderers! Kill that American swine! Let's show him how it feels to burn alive!" Shrieking hysterically at the top of her voice, a large, buxom woman pointed straight at me. Within minutes I was surrounded by a wildly cursing and gesticulating mob.
>
> As I looked down at my grease-splattered overalls and felt the welding goggles around my neck, the ironic truth dawned on me: they were mistaking me for a shot down U.S. pilot.

There was no point in explaining that, although my skin was dark, I was a German myself—the son of a German mother and a Liberian father, and the grandson of Liberia's former consul-general to Germany; that because a bomb had razed the nearby plant where I was employed as a machinist, I had been obliged to walk home in my work clothes. In their blind rage over the destruction around them, they were demanding their pound of flesh. Obviously they were in no mood to listen to an unlikely story such as mine. (Massaquoi 1966, 91)

These multilayer confrontations develop into a tricultural story about switching nationalities and finally coming to terms with his vision of a "model American." Structurally, Massaquoi's report does not unfold in chronological order. Rather, his article jumps back and forth in time thereby reflecting the constant confrontation of different patterns of identification and national associations. The next paragraph pulls the narrator back into the present, in this case the plane from Chicago to Frankfurt, when the flight attendant of the Lufthansa flight asks him if he was feeling all right. Again, he is identified as an American. This time, however, Massaquoi is more comfortable. After answering in English, he switches to German to challenge the linguistic expectations of the flight attendant. Massaquoi's trip to Germany authenticated earlier reports by *Ebony* suggesting that West Germany might function as a model for American racial integration politics.[22] In 1960, the magazine quoted Dorothea Struwe, Nuremberg youth office official, who argued that through the special support of "our colored children" can Germany help to "make good some of the guilt we have laden upon us in the past" (*Ebony* 1960, 97–108).

One of the challenges Massaquoi tackled were questions regarding appropriate means to change the legal standing of what Alain Locke identified as the "sick man American Democracy" (Locke 1925/1972, 578). Massaquoi's activities overlap with those of one of the most influential thinkers of the 1960s: Malcolm X. Many of his speeches and essays utilized references to Germany's Nazi history not only to criticize "white supremacy" (Malcolm X 1965, 245) but also the "Gestapo-type police force" within the ranks of the black Muslim movement (*Ebony* 1964, 40). Despite being the hottest topic in public racial discourse during the early 1960s, *Ebony* avoided and to a certain degree neglected reporting on the former leader of the black Muslims. Massaquoi recognized this questionable practice and actively confronted it. Johnson did not want to irritate his conservative subscribers and, even worse, "scare his conservative clients from the ad industry away" (Massaquoi 2004, 8). Nevertheless, Massaquoi convinced the editor that the magazine could not afford to avoid the issue of violence in the civil rights movement. Consequently, he accompanied Malcolm X for two days in the summer of 1964 to report on his life, philosophy, and the changes after his exclusion from the black Muslims. However, by the time Massaquoi brought the controversial figure to the attention of *Ebony* readers, many of his most radical statements had already been modified.

In an almost prophetic manner, the article opens with an iconic photography of Malcolm X holding out his hands toward his audience while the captions address the means to bring about social justice for African Americans. "Whether you use bullets or ballots, you've got to aim well. Don't strike at the puppet; strike at the puppeteer" (Massaquoi 1964, 38). The image at the end of the article shows Malcolm X with a gun at his window—this time not aiming at the "white puppeteer," but—in an attitude of self-defense—at an unknown enemy that might well be positioned within the African American lines. The threat of assassination was real. It seemed as if the kind of violence that Malcolm X had promoted, returned with a vengeance. During the interview with Massaquoi, Malcolm X explained that the black Muslims, the Mafia, or the CIA planned to murder him.

In retrospect, Massaquoi explained in *Hänschen Klein, Ging Allein . . .* that despite initial hesitation he had found a "real friend" in Malcolm X during the two-day encounter (Massaquoi 2004, 88). However, the title "Mystery of Malcolm X" of the article published forty years earlier clearly shows that the author distanced himself from the solutions offered by the aggressive civil rights activist. While Massaquoi expressed empathy for his latest program to form a new nonreligious and nonsectarian Organization of Afro-American Unity to set up a constructive program toward attainment of human rights, he remained critical about his inherent racism, his notions regarding armed guerrillas to protect civil rights workers from the Ku Klux Klan, his position on violence, and demand for "back pay for 400 years of slave labor" (Massaquoi 1964, 46). After a description of Malcolm X's sophisticated rhetoric and an overview of black and white responses, Massaquoi provides a detailed account of his adventurous biography. In the end, Massaquoi harks back to the title of the article and withholds a personal statement. "[Malcolm X] makes it abundantly clear that he still hates, but says that his hatred is now confined to those who hate blacks. Until put to a real test, the true intentions of Malcolm X—like the man himself—will remain shrouded in speculation and mystery" (Massaquoi 1964, 46).

How could somebody who had experienced the violence of the Nazis and the (much-delayed) counterviolence of the allied forces to break the fascist agenda of the Holocaust remain puzzled by the outrage of Malcolm X? Although Massaquoi stated in his 1964 article that nobody knew whether Malcolm X was "a charlatan or saviour, an opportunist or sincere leader dedicated to the liberation of his race" (Massaquoi 1964, 40), he clearly was skeptical regarding his sincerity. In contrast to Malcolm X, Massaquoi was willing to compromise for the sake of getting a share of the proverbial American dream. Having been raised as an Afro-German who desperately wanted to fit in the cultural surroundings and be respected as an equal among his peers, the United States offered not only a different political system, but also a different group feeling. Massaquoi could identify with 30 million African Americans. His efforts to blend in an economic, social, and aesthetic system based on white parameters brought self-confidence and success. After all, one of the first public responsibilities he was asked to fulfill in the United States meant going abroad to fight a war in the name of a democracy he hardly knew anything about. In 2004, he summarized his success story in terms of being a model American.

> Looking back, I can say that so far my "marriage" with the United States might not have been perfect, however, it has been a good one. Here, too, I had become a victim of discrimination due to my skin color. The bottom line, however, is that America has been good to me and I have also been good for America. We have, so to say, both made a good deal. This country opened up new opportunities and chances of upward mobility which would have been inconceivable elsewhere. And therefore I continue to be a loyal and law-abiding citizen who casts his vote at every local and national election (hoping that it will be counted), who pays his taxes, who recycles his trash, and generally acts in an environmentally conscious way. (Massaquoi 2004, 61, translation by the author)

In his most recent autobiography, the term "Nazi Jim Crow" has vanished from Massaquoi's vocabulary. However, the second last chapter revisits the transcultural link with references to 9/11. The military actions in the Middle East are contextualized with Hitler's war on Poland. In retrospect, President Bush's preemptive strike appears to be even less justified than the attack on Poland. Massaquoi is concerned about the growing anti-Americanism and the loss of international recognition. The charge behind "Nazi Jim Crow" has not lost its critical appeal. Massaquoi has, however, become more careful in its usage.

Conclusion

During the U.S. occupation in Germany, the public display of antiblack racism at home and abroad became a watershed for the success of America's mission: to denazify Germany, to initiate the process of political democratization through social, economic, and ideological reconstruction, and ultimately to establish cooperative allies at the heart of Europe. Moral superiority was a key factor to persuade the former enemy to adopt the model of democracy American style. African American GIs and Jim Crow segregation, white American hostility regarding interracial relationships between African American troops and German women produced a space of ideological friction which Afro-Germans like Hans Jürgen Massaquoi felt deeply. The expression "Nazi Jim Crow" captures the blurry contact zones between racism in democratic and fascist societies. Instead of abandoning the dream of a new and better world across the Atlantic, Massaquoi was determined to make the United States live up to the creed of freedom and equality. One way to overcome racial stereotypes and to fight Jim Crow legislation was to embrace mass media as a powerful agent to bring about sociopolitical reform. Massaquoi's articles on post–World War II Germany in the 1960s were designed as a reminder that Germany and the United States had many things in common as far as chances and shortcomings of democracy are concerned. "A Journey into the Past, Part II" ends with an optimistic outlook on aspects of reorientation, friendly persuasion, and racial tolerance within democratic societies.[23]

Massaquoi successfully came to terms with his dilemma of triple conscious-ness. As an Afro-German, National Socialist racial politics denied him recognition in the public sphere. The United States offered not only a different political platform, but also an open socioeconomic environment to gain recognition beyond intimate family ties. Here, he was legally recognized as an intelligent member of society and received encouragement to earn (self-)respect through his achievements as a journalist. Massaquoi fashioned himself into a transatlantic ambassador of racial tolerance. With his key term "Nazi Jim Crow" he reported on the process of democratization, Americanization, and self-Americanization of Germany. His transatlantic vistas served as a mirror for the United States to contextualize racial segregation at home. Referring to "Nazi Jim Crow" Massaquoi reminded his fellow citizens that "America" should be in the words of Langston Hughes the land "where never kings connive nor tyrants scheme" (Hughes 1938/2004, 5). Thereby he activated and reshaped the cultural memory of the black Atlantic to foster democratic environments that live up to their promises of freedom and equality.

Notes

1. For a critical assessment, see Fatima El-Tayeb, *Schwarze Deutsche: Der Diskurs um Rasse und nationale Identität 1890–1933* (Frankfurt am Main: Campus Verlag, 2001).

2. Public attention increased particularly after the republication by a major German publishing house in 1992. In a similar vein, the publication edited by Gisela Fremgen, Cathy S. Gelbin, Kader Konuk, and Peggy Piesche entitled *AufBrüche: Kulturelle Produktionen von Migrantinnen, Schwarzen und jüdischen Frauen in Deutschland* (Königstein: Helmer, 1999) offers accounts of Afro-German women in postwar Germany.

3. Among the few descriptions of black children in postwar Germany are Klaus Eyferth, Ursula Brandt, and Wolfgang Hawel, *Farbige Kinder in Deutschland. Die Situation der Mischlingskinder und die Aufgaben ihrer Eingliederung* (München: Juventa.-Verlag, 1960). From a historical perspective, Reiner Pommerin approached the neglected chapter of the so-called Rhineland Bastards in *Die Sterilisierung der Rheinlandbastarde. Das Schicksal einer farbigen deutschen Minderheit 1918–1937* (Düsseldorf: Droste, 1979). Rosemarie K. Lester opened a new discursive field by analyzing the representation of blacks in popular magazines. See *Trivialneger: Das Bild des Schwarzen im Westdeutschen Illustriertenroman* (Stuttgart: Heinz, 1982).

4. Among the most prominent publications on the black presence in Germany are Paulette Reed-Anderson, *Rewriting the Footnotes: Berlin and the African Diaspora* (Berlin: Ausländerbeauftragte des Senats, 2000). Fatima El-Tayeb, *Schwarze Deutsche: Der Diskurs um Rasse und nationale Identität 1890–1933* (Frankfurt am Main: Campus Verlag, 2001). Yara-Colette and Lemke Muniz de Faria, *Zwischen Fürsorge und Ausgrenzung: Afro-deutsche Besatzungskinder im Nachkriegsdeutschland* (Berlin: Zentrum für Antisemitismusforschung, 2002). Michael Schuberts Studie *Der Schwarze Fremde: Das Bild des Schwarzafrikaners in der Parlamentarischen und Publizistischen Kolonialdiskussion in Deutschland von den 1870er bis in die 1930er Jahre* (Stuttgart: Steiner, 2003). Peter Martins and Christine Alonzos (eds.), *Zwischen Charleston und Stechschritt: Schwarze im Nationalsozialismus* (Hamburg: Dölling und Galitz, 2004). Heide Fehrenbach, *Race after Hitler:*

Black Occupation Children in Postwar Germany (Princeton, NJ: Princeton University Press, 2005). See also Michelle M. Wright's chapter on "Black Subjectivities in Berlin, London, and Paris," in *Becoming Black: Creating Identity in the African Diaspora* (Durham, NC: Duke University Press, 2004), 183–228.

5. The following publications have addressed the black presence in postwar Germany from the perspective of *Weisssein:* Maureen Maisha Eggers, Grada Kilomba, Peggy Piesche, and Susan Arndt, eds., *Mythen Masken und Subjekte: Kritische Weißseinsforschung in Deutschland* (Münster: Unrast, 2005). Susan Arndt, ed., *AfrikaBilder: Studien zu Rassismus in Deutschland* (Münster: Unrast, 2001). Eske Wollrad, *Weißsein im Widerspruch: Feministische Perspektiven auf Rassismus, Kultur und Religion* (Königstein: Helmer, 2005). Moritz Ege, *Schwarz Werden: "Afroamerikanopholie" in den 1960er und 1970er Jahren* (Bielefeld: Transcript, 2007).

6. Massaquoi's account of his experience as a black growing up in Nazi Germany has been marketed in the United States as a Holocaust narrative. His account, however, does not only show how a racial outsider in Nazi Germany could be mesmerized by Adolf Hitler and, at the same time, take issue with his racial politics. It also tries to come to terms with the promise of American freedom and the dream of acquiring citizenship in the alleged land of the free. Thus, the book also resembles the format of a slave narrative with its theme from slavery to freedom. Not surprisingly, Massaquoi opens his "Prologue" with a quotation by Frederick Douglass and a reference to *My Bondage and My Freedom* from 1855. The Afro-German writer creates a link between the "great abolitionist" (xi) and his own biography, which has far-reaching consequences for the political trajectory of his book. In contrast to the majority of Holocaust memoirs from Eli Wiesel's *Night* (1960) to Peter Gay's *My German Question* (1998), Massaquoi has cherished a lifelong commitment and positive attitude toward both German culture and its people.

7. This passage is quoted almost verbatim from the 1966 *Ebony* article "A Journey into the Past (Part I)." There is, however, a slight difference in chronology. In the article, Massaquoi refers to a spring morning in 1935. In addition, he provides more details regarding the emotional impact of Hitler's appearance on the crowd (Massaquoi 1966, 99).

8. Heike Paul rightfully identifies young Massaquoi's fascination with Hitler and the masculine representation of national socialist troops as a psychological substitute for the lack of a father in his intimate social environment (Paul 2001, 9).

9. The victory of American athletes in general and that of Jesse Owens in particular also pushed the self-esteem of other victimized minorities in Germany. For example, it propelled the longing for becoming "Americans" for the Jewish historian Peter Gay. However, he criticized the U.S. acceptance to not send Jewish athletes to Berlin. "I am glad in retrospect that I knew nothing of this in 1936. It would have tarnished my unqualified idealization of the United States" (Gay 1998, 83).

10. Heide Fehrenbach emphasizes that Germany had not become a "racial paradise." Rather, the elevated economic status and sociopolitical power of the occupational forces determined responses of respect and (relative) friendliness among Germans (Fehrenbach 2005, 37).

11. Heike Paul recognizes in these literary moments of passing new formulaic codes for "writing the Holocaust from the perspective of an African American." Familiar literary patterns of the American hero create a space for African American readers to empathize with unfamiliar cultural and political circumstances (Paul 2001, 13).

12. While Massaquoi stresses the ambiguities of his notions regarding living in Germany, Liberia, and the United States, Ralph Giordano tells in his epic family chronicle *Die Bertinis* about a young black man called "Mickey" whose character is modeled after Hans Jürgen Massaquoi. In Giordano's memoirs, Mickey lost all his emotional connections with his life in Hamburg and favored early on the idea of emigration. For Mickey, the United States had, according to Giordano, become the only escape channel to become a wholesome person. "Denn Mickey erging sich in dichten und blühenden Zukunftsvisionen; plastisch als seien sie greifbar nahe, fast schon verwirklicht, so inbrünstig beschwor er sie, und sie alle bündelte er in drei Buchstaben—USA! Dorthin

wollte Mickey, gleich danach wenn alles vorbei sein würde. Mit dem ersten Schiff, lieber aber noch mit dem Flugzeug, weil das schneller ging über den Großen Teich, und gleich tief hinein in den Kontinent [. . .] hin zu seinem Volk, den Schwarzen Nordamerikas" (Giordano 1985, 115) ("Because Mickey entertained rich and colorful visions of the future; three dimensional as if they were in close reach, almost real. He summoned on them with such dedication and condensed them all into three letters—USA. That was where Mickey wanted to go, immediately after everything was over. With the first ship, or even better with an airplane because that took less time to cross the "big pond" and right away deeply into the continent [. . .] to his people, the blacks of North America.") Translation by F. Mehring.

13. Among the many talents of writers were executive editors Herbert Nipson, later Era Bell Thompson and the historian Lerone Bennett Jr. The latter produced an impressive series of influential articles on African American cultural history. In addition, Bennett published more than twenty books, among them the seventh edition of *Before the Mayflower: A History of Black America* (2003), which appeared originally in 1962; *The Shaping of Black America* (1975); *Pioneers in Protest* (1968); or *Confrontation: Black or White* (1965). Many of his books evolved from articles he contributed to *Ebony*.

14. Particularly German journalists found in Massaquoi a firsthand informer on civil rights issues in the United States. In addition to its staff writers, *Ebony* has provided a platform for internationally renown poets and novelists such as Maya Angelou, Gwendolyn Brooks, James Baldwin, Alex Haley, or Langston Hughes. Other leading figures in African American culture include Supreme Court justice Thurgood Marshall, former first lady Eleanor Roosevelt, educator Mary McLeod Bethune, the Reverend Jesse Jackson, or Dr. Martin Luther King Jr. The visual representation plays a crucial role in the magazines aesthetic design complementing the informative texts. For his photo of the grieving Mrs. Coretta Scott King and her youngest daughter, Bernice, at Martin Luther King Jr.'s funeral, *Ebony* photographer Moneta Sleet Jr. was awarded the Pulitzer Prize.

15. Frazier uses this term as a reference to urban professionals and business people including upper-class African Americans. The usage of "middle class," however, lacks differentiation and would have benefited from a stronger sense of gradations within the groups analyzed in the book.

16. August Meier has aptly pointed out the limitations of Frazier's generalizations in his book *A White Scholar and the Black Community 1945–1954*. See in particular 94–96.

17. See in this context Katharina Oguntoye, May Opitz, and Dagmar Schultz, eds., *Farbe bekennen: Afro-deutsche Frauen auf den Spuren ihrer Geschichte* (Berlin: Orlanda Frauenverlag, 1986). Ika Hügel-Marshall, *Invisible Woman: Growing up Black in Germany*, trans. Elisabeth Gaffney (New York: Continuum, 2001). May Ayim, *Grenzenlos und Unverschämt* (Berlin: Orlanda Frauenverlag, 1997).

18. See in this case Maria Höhn's chapter on "Keeping America at Bay" in *GIs and Fräuleins: The German-American Encounter in 1950s West Germany* (2002), in particular pages 155–56. In his excellent analysis on *Coca-Colonisation und der Kalte Krieg* (1991), Reinhold Wagnleitner has documented a similar tension of attraction and repulsion in the 1950s in Austria. In this case it is important to remind oneself of the complex ways in which cultural exchange processes are structured. Winfried Fluck emphasizes that the phenomenon of cultural Americanization "cannot be analysed by merely identifying economic or political interests" (Fluck 2005, 222). Different contexts produce different and often unpredictable effects. See Rob Kroes, "Americanization: What are we talking about?" In *Cultural Transmissions and Receptions: American Mass Culture in Europe*, ed. Rob Kroes, Robert W. Rydell, and Doeko F. J. Bosscher (Amsterdam: VU University Press, 1993), 302–18, 313.

19. The multiethnic background of American society created a specific form of popular culture which appealed not only to audiences inside, but also outside the United States. In the early 1920s, the still young Weimar Republic experienced a cultural phenomenon that could be described

as Germany's first "American season." American culture had a similar impact on the art scene in France, Italy, or Austria. Under the popular catchword "Amerikanismus" Germans turned to a utopian notion of America. The new twist on transatlantic vistas served as a looking glass for the hopes and dreams of a generation that had to deal with the traumatic aftermath of WWI. The New World represented a young and innocent culture without the burden of tradition, a boundless country where new technological inventions created better social and economic environments. Entertainment, luxury, and mobility offered a better way of life—the "American way of life." See Rudolf Kaiser, "Amerikanismus," *Weimarer Republik: Manifeste und Dokumente zur deutschen Literatur 1918–1933*, ed. Anton Kaes, 265–69 (Stuttgart: Metzler, 1983). Jazz, Afro-American musicians, and dancers became a hyperbolic cipher of American "otherness," initiating a process that can be described as "Afro-Americanization" of popular culture. See Kaspar Maase, *Bravo Amerika: Erkundungen zur Jugendkultur der Bundesrepublik in den 50er Jahren* (Hamburg: Junius, 1992), 23.

20. The Marshall Plan film program and documentaries produced with the help of the U.S. Information Service had focused on similar transcultural issues at the beginning of the 1950s. For example, when the Vienna-based international Lycée Français moved to a new building in 1954, Austrian director Georg Tressler realized the potential for a narrative of democratic progress in both national as well as universal terms. The story of "Wie die Jungen Sungen" (1954) about an innocent newcomer to the school system celebrates multiethnic, multinational, and multilingual diversity of future European citizens. By including a child from Africa and North America, the film ultimately argues for a new generation of citizens who hopefully will act and think in global terms. Unlike Robert Stemmle's highly successful feature film "Toxi" (1952), which rendered the integration of Afro-Germans both as a political and humanitarian problem, Tressler does not address multicultural interactions as a problem for society; he goes one step further. The perspective of children is turned into an aesthetic and a didactic tool. By learning how to cope with one another's different national backgrounds children become role models for their parents, showing them how to make a multicultural and multinational society work. Tressler's film suggests that the new European experiment in democracy will be able to overcome the very discrepancies of American ideals and shortcomings in everyday life such as racial segregation of the Jim Crow laws. See in this context my article "From a 'New Europe' to a 'New Middle East': Propaganda for Democracy and Authoritarian Tendencies in Film," *Conformism, Non-Conformism and Anti-Conformism in American Culture*, ed. Antonis Balasopoulos, Gesa Mackenthun, and Dora Tsimpouki, 259–85 (Heidelberg: Winter, 2008).

21. The *Pittsburgh Courier* repeatedly referred to National Socialism in order to contextualize undemocratic occurrences within the United States particularly in relation to activities of the Ku Klux Klan. "In the first 'incident'—highly reminiscent of the staged 'incidents' of Nazi Germany, which provoked the calling in of Hitler's troops 'for protection'—the Negro Methodist Church was burned to the ground" (*Pittsburgh Courier*, December 6, 1947, 1). On the changing functions of Germany as a "signifier" on America's own domestic racial conditions and the Third Reich/Jim Crow analogy in the African American press, see Larry A. Greene's article in this volume.

22. In her revealing and insightful account on what she calls the "impossible minority" of Afro-Germans in her book *Becoming Black: Creating Identity in the African Diaspora* (2004), Michelle Wright repeatedly cites Massaquoi's first autobiography *Destined to Witness* as an example that supports to the outsider status described by other black Germans such as May Ayim, Helga Emde, Astrid Berger, Miriam Goldschmidt, Laura Baum, Ellen Wiedenroth, Raya Lubinetzki, or Ika Hügel-Marshall. However, my close reading of Massaquoi's text shows that despite patterns of misrecognition, he emphasizes changes in the thinking of Germans in regard of tearing down racial boundaries and rethinking what it means to be German.

23. "'Get a load of how these cats are digging the sounds; you'd think you're in one of them Harlem joints,' remarked a Negro soldier in civvies as we peeped through the door of a jam-packed

Munich discothèque. For several minutes I watched the enraptured young faces of this new breed as they frugged, swam, and monkeyed to Basie beat. Remembering the rigid, goose-stepping brown shirts of my childhood days, I suddenly felt very hopeful for the country of my birth" (Massaquoi 1966, 2:111). This passage is reprinted almost verbatim in his autobiography thirty-three years later (Massaquoi 1999, 435–36).

Bibliography

Anonymous. "Brown Babies Go to Work." *Ebony* (November 1960): 97–108.

———. "Two Schools, Church Burned. Klan Blamed for Nazi-Like Tactics." *St. Louis Edition of Pittsburgh Courier*, December 6, 1947, 1 and 5.

———. "German War Babies." *Ebony* (January 1951): 38–45.

———. "Germany meets the Negro Soldier." *Ebony* (October 1946): 5–11.

———. "Should White Parents Adopt Brown Babies?" *Ebony* (June 1958): 26–30.

Arndt, Susan, ed. *AfrikaBilder: Studien zu Rassismus in Deutschland*. Münster: Unrast, 2001.

Ayim, May. *Grenzenlos und Unverschämt*. Berlin: Orlanda Frauenverlag, 1997.

Bennett, Lerone Jr. "The *EBONY* Revolution." *Ebony*. (November 2005): 74–79.

Campt, Tina. *Other Germans: Black Germans and the Politics of Race, Gender, and Memory in the Third Reich*. Ann Arbor: University of Michigan Press, 2004.

Douglass, Frederick. *My Bondage and My Freedom*. New York: Miller, Orton, and Mulligan, 1855.

Du Bois, W. E. B. *The Autobiography of W. E. B. Du Bois: A Soliloquy on Viewing My Life from the Last Decade of Its First Century*. New York: International Publishers, 1968.

———. "Germany and Hitler." *W. E. B. Du Bois. A Reader*, ed. David Levering Lewis. New York: Henry Holt and Company, 1995. 734–38.

———. *The Souls of Black Folk*. New York: Barnes and Nobles, 2003.

Ege, Moritz. *Schwarz Werden: "Afroamerikanopholie" in den 1960er und 1970er Jahren*. Bielefeld: Transcript, 2007.

Eggers, Maureen Maisha, Grada Kilomba, Peggy Piesche, and Susan Arndt, eds. *Mythen Masken und Subjekte: Kritische Weißseinsforschung in Deutschland*. Münster: Unrast, 2005.

El-Tayeb, Fatima. *Schwarze Deutsche: Der Diskurs um Rasse und nationale Identität 1890–1933*. Frankfurt am Main: Campus Verlag, 2001.

Eyferth, Klaus, Ursula Brandt, and Wolfgang Hawel. *Farbige Kinder in Deutschland: Die Situation der Mischlingskinder und die Aufgaben ihrer Eingliederung*. München: Juventa.-Verlag, 1960.

Fehrenbach, Heide. *Race after Hitler: Black Occupation Children in Postwar Germany and America*. Princeton, NJ: Princeton University Press, 2005.

Fluck, Winfried. "California Blue: Americanization as Self-Americanization." *Americanization and Anti-Americanization: The German Encounter with American Culture After 1945*, ed. Alexander Stephan, 221–37. New York: Berghahn Books, 2005.

Frazier, Edward Franklin. *Black Bourgeosie*. New York: Free Press, 1965.

Fremgen, Gisela, Cathy S. Gelbin, Kader Konuk, and Peggy Piesche, eds. *AufBrüche: Kulturelle Produktionen von Migrantinnen, Schwarzen und jüdischen Frauen in Deutschland*. Königstein: Helmer, 1999.

Gay, Peter. *My German Question; Growing up in Nazi Berlin*. New Haven, CT: Yale University Press, 1998.

Giordano, Ralph. *Die Bertinis*. Frankfurt: Fischer, 1985.

Gould, Allan. "Germany's Tragic War Babies." *Ebony* (December 1952): 74–78.

Höhn, Maria. *GIs and Fräuleins: The German-American Encounter in 1950s West Germany*. Chapel Hill: University of North Carolina Press, 2002.

Honneth, Axel. "Die soziale Dynamik von Missachtung. Zur Ortsbestimmung einer kritischen Ge-sellschaftstheorie." *Gesellschaft im Übergang: Perspektiven Kritischer Soziologie*, ed. Christoph Görg, 44–62. Darmstadt: Wissenschaftliche Buchgesellschaft, 1994.

Hopkins, Leroy. "Writing Diasporic Identity: Afro-German Literature since 1985." *Not So Plain as Black and White. Afro-German Culture and History, 1890–2000*, ed. Patricia Mazón and Rein-hild Steingröver, 183–208. University of Rochester Press, 2005.

Hügel-Marshall, Ika. *Invisible Woman: Growing up Black in Germany*. Translated by Elisabeth Gaffney. New York: Continuum, 2001.

Hughes, Langston. *Let America Be America Again* (1938). New York: Vintage Books, 2004.

Kaiser, Rudolf. "Amerikanismus." *Weimarer Republik: Manifeste und Dokumente zur deutschen Literatur 1918–1933*, ed. Anton Kaes, 165–69. Stuttgart: Metzler, 1983.

Kroes, Rob. "Americanization: What are we talking about?" *Cultural Transmissions and Recep-tions: American Mass Culture in Europe*, ed. Rob Kroes, Robert W. Rydell, Doeko F. J. Bosscher, 302–18. Amsterdam: VU University Press, 1993.

Lemke, Sieglinde. "The German Du Bois." *German? American? Literature? New Directions in Ger-man-American Studies*, ed. Winfried Fluck and Werner Sollors, 207–15. New York: Peter Lang, 2002.

Lester, Rosemarie K. *Trivialneger: Das Bild des Schwarzen im Westdeutschen Illustriertenroman*. Stuttgart: Heinz, 1982.

Lissner, Erich. "We Adopted a Brown Baby." *Ebony* (May 1953): 38–45.

Locke, Alain. "The New Negro" (1925). *Black Writers of America: A Comprehensive Anthology*, ed. Richard Barksdale and Keneth Kinnamon, 575–81. New York: Macmillan, 1972.

Maase, Kaspar. *Bravo Amerika. Erkundungen zur Jugendkultur der Bundesrepublik in den 50er Jah-ren*. Hamburg: Junius, 1992.

Malcolm X. *The Autobiography of Malcolm X*. New York: Grove, 1965.

Massaquoi, Hans Jürgen. *Destined to Witness: Growing up Black in Nazi Germany*. New York: W. Morrow, 1999.

———. *Hänschen klein, ging allein . . . Mein Weg in die Neue Welt*. Bern: Scherz, 2004.

———. "A Journey into the Past. Part I." *Ebony* (February 1966): 91–99.

———. "A Journey into the Past. Part II." *Ebony* (March 1966): 102–11.

———. "The Mystery of Malcolm X." *Ebony* (September 1964): 37–46.

———. *Neger, Neger, Schornsteinfeger. Meine Kindheit in Deutschland*. München: Knaur, 2001.

Mazón, Patricia, and Reinhild Steingröver, eds. "Introduction." *Not So Plain as Black and White. Afro-German Culture and History, 1890–2000*. University of Rochester Press, 2005. 1–23.

Mead, George Herbert. *Mind, Self, and Society*. Chicago: University of Chicago Press, 1934.

Mehring, Frank. "From a 'New Europe' to a 'New Middle East': Propaganda for Democracy and Authoritarian Tendencies in Film." *Conformism, Non-Conformism and Anti-Conformism in American Culture*, ed. Antonis Balasopoulos, Gesa Mackenthun, and Dora Tsimpouki, 259–85. Heidelberg: Winter, 2008.

Meier, August. *A White Scholar and the Black Community, 1945–1965: Essays and Reflections*. Am-herst: University of Massachusetts Press, 1992.

Oguntoye, Katharina, May Opitz, and Dagmar Schultz, eds. *Farbe bekennen: Afro-deutsche Frauen auf den Spuren ihrer Geschichte*. Berlin: Orlanda Frauenverlag, 1986.

Paul, Heike. *Kulturkontakt und Racial Presences: Afro-Amerikaner und die deutsche Amerika-Literatur 1815–1914*. Heidelberg: Winter, 2005.

———. "Racialized Topographies of the New and the Old World: Jeanette Lander's Atlanta and Hans J. Massaquoi's Hamburg." *Working Paper No. 127*. Berlin: John F. Kennedy-Institut für Nordamerikastudien, 2001.

Pommerin, Reiner. *Die Sterilisierung der Rheinlandbastarde: Das Schicksal einer farbigen deutschen Minderheit 1918–1937*. Düsseldorf: Droste, 1979.

Sollors, Werner. *Neither Black Nor White Yet Both: Thematic Explorations of Interracial Literature.* Cambridge, MA: Harvard University Press, 1997.

Taylor, Charles. *Multiculturalism and "The Politics of Recognition."* Princeton, NJ: Princeton University Press, 1992.

Thode-Arora, Hilke. "Afrika-Völkerschauen in Deutschland." *AfrikanerInnen in Deutschland und schwarze Deutsche—Geschichte und Gegenwart,* ed. Mariann Bechhaus-Gerst and Reinhard Klein-Arendt, 25–40. Münster: Lit, 2004.

Wagnleitner, Reinhold. *Coca-Colonisation und Kalter Krieg: Die Kulturmission der USA in Österreich nach dem Zweiten Weltkrieg.* Wien: Verlag für Gesellschaftskritik, 1991.

Wiesel, Eli. *Night.* New York: Hill and Wang, 1960.

Wollrad, Eske. *Weißsein im Widerspruch: Feministische Perspektiven auf Rassismus, Kultur und Religion.* Königstein: Helmer, 2005.

Wright, Michelle M. *Becoming Black: Creating Identity in the African Diaspora.* Durham, NC: Duke University Press, 2004.

A Raisin in the East

African American Civil Rights Drama in GDR Scholarship and Theater Practice

ASTRID HAAS

While the official image of the United States propagated in the GDR was that of a stronghold of political reaction and center of imperialist aggression, East German popular and intellectual images of America were more complex and diversified (cf. Schnoor 2001a, passim; Schnoor 2001b, passim). Based on Lenin's dictum that each society contains two cultures, a reactionary one and a progressive, proletarian, socialist culture (cf. Lenin 1960, 209), even the official political doctrine differentiated between the United States as the key embodiment of capitalist reaction and imperialism on the one hand and the American people as containing, besides the "bourgeois" mainstream, a second culture of oppressed masses on the other hand (cf. Schnoor 1999, 35; Schnoor 2001a, 936, 941–42).

As part of this "other America" considered to be in opposition to the dominant culture, African America enjoyed a certain political acceptability in GDR cultural politics, whereas the connection of black culture to America at large stirred the fascination of the East German people (cf. Schnoor 1999, 38–39; Schnoor 2001a, 940). The traditional socialist concern with the American "Negro question" but especially the African American struggle for political equality and social justice in the Black Civil Rights and Black Power movements moreover enabled artists and intellectuals in the GDR to critically and creatively approach black literature, music, politics, and scholarship within the framework of the state's socialist cultural policy (cf. Frenz and Hess 1973, 190).

Major African American novels, stories, and plays were published by leading GDR publishing houses (cf. Brüning 1980, 308–9; Frenz and Hess 1973, 189–92), and even more were discussed in scholarly studies. However, within the field of black drama, only a few plays connected to the ideas of the African American civil rights movement were given productions in East German theaters. Against the backdrop of Americanist scholarship as well as theater practice in the GDR, my essay will analyze the East German reception of the major two among these works: Lorraine Hansberry's 1959 play *A Raisin in the Sun* and James Baldwin's 1964 drama *Blues for Mister Charlie* (cf. Baldwin 1969, passim; Hansberry 1987, passim). Two lines of reception will form the pillars of my analysis: the scholarly research of these works within GDR Americanist academic discourses in comparison with Western European and American scholars' assessments of the two plays on the one hand and the GDR stage productions of Hansberry's and Baldwin's dramas as well as their reception in the East German press on the other hand.

GDR Americanist Scholarship

Since the late 1940s, American literature, linguistics, and civilization were researched and taught at seven universities in East Germany. While usually remaining a part of joined *Anglistik-Amerikanistik* programs, the field of American Studies evolved as a distinct and fully-fledged regional studies subject of research and teaching in the course of the 1960s. Throughout the existence of the socialist German state, Americanist scholarship operated under the premise of dealing with the culture(s) and society of the "class enemy" scholars and teachers were supposed to fight against. Since the late 1950s, institutional reforms and the radicalization of GDR cultural politics, especially the denunciation of nonrealist art, tightened the political grip on the East German academe; the erection of the Berlin Wall in 1961 further limited personal and institutional ties to the West (cf. Brüning 1999, 74–78; Schnoor 1999, 30–39; Schnoor 2001a, 932, 940–42). Ten years later, Erich Honecker's assumption of political power in 1971 was followed by a partial and limited liberalization of academic and cultural policy. Together with the American diplomatic recognition of the GDR in 1974, this new policy enabled the East German *Amerikanistik* to broaden its activities and partially break out of its isolation from the West (cf. Brüning 1999, 77–85; Schnoor 1999, 39–47, Schnoor 2001b, 775–79, 783–84).

East German Americanists responded to the political limitations of their field by emphasizing the difference between GDR *Amerikanistik* and Western American Studies in their writing, by stressing the integration of their discipline into Marxist-Leninist scholarship, and by underlining its role in strengthening the socialist state against Western imperialism. If the ideological race for advancement over capitalism was to be won, they argued, the East German populace had to know Western languages and cultures (cf. Brüning 1970, 177, 184; Hofmann 1960, 176, 183–84; Scheffel 1972, 371–73; Schönfelder 1959, 54). By constantly and explicitly invoking these causes in all public utterances, the GDR Americanists, consciously and deliberately or not, served the political system; yet without at least paying lip service to the rhetoric of the anti-imperialist struggle of the GDR, academic work on American literature and culture would have been impossible to carry out (cf. Brüning 1999, 73, 76). Sometimes, the critical appreciation of American literature in Soviet scholarship was put forth to justify the East German academic study of the field (cf. Manske 1974, passim; Riese 1985, passim).

Literary scholars largely concentrated on the one hand on the canonical works of "mainstream" American literature, drawing especially upon the theses, articulated first in Soviet scholarship, of America's democratic revolutionary beginnings or its progressive development during the nineteenth century. On the other hand, GDR scholarly endeavors focused on the proletarian and leftist bourgeois writing as well as the social protest and ethnic minority literatures representing the "other America." Since the late 1960s, East German Americanists mapped new opportunities and directions for their work by arguing that their political function made it imperative to observe current developments in Western scholarship and American literature, and that the now higher developed socialist consciousness in the GDR enabled people to critically evaluate formerly rejected strains of literature (cf. Brüning 1970, 175–78, 184–85; Scheffel 1972, 373–75, 381, 386–87; Wirzberger 1968, passim; Wirzberger 1969, 343; see also Brüning 1999, 70–75; Neubauer 83; Schnoor 1999, 34–37).

The political situation during the Honecker era further allowed scholars to present a more differentiated image of the United States. Americanists increasingly reevaluated "bourgeois" writing, both established works and the emerging postmodernist literature. They emphasized the role of literature within a dialogic process of social communication or elements of nonconformism and progressive political critique within "mainstream" American letters (cf. Brüning 1980, 293–94, 318; Schönfelder 1984, 247–48; Weimann 1980, passim; see also Brüning 1999, 70–75; Neubauer 1997, 83–84, 101–6, 134–40; Schnoor 1999, 41–42). Nevertheless, as Rainer Schnoor observes, GDR Americanist scholarship failed to make full use of the possibilities the tentative political liberation offered them, especially during the 1970s (cf. Schnoor 1999, 42).

Owing to the importance accorded to the political struggles of African Americans, East German scholars presented black American culture as one of the central and most productive parts of the "other America." In their analyses of the black experience, GDR Americanists foregrounded the elements of social class struggle inherent in the black fight against slavery, segregation, and urban ghettoization, and they credited Marxist political consciousness alongside the example of African colonial liberation movements with the most formative influence on the African American civil rights and black power movements from the 1950s through the 1970s. In line with Marxist-Leninist doctrine, scholars praised these black political movements and their literary manifestations as such but scrutinized what was at odds with class consciousness. However, the way either "bourgeois" liberal or ethnic nationalist positions were scrutinized in the reading of African American writing revealed a nuanced assessment of black literature that was partially ahead of West German scholarship in the field (cf. Brüning 1970, 182–83; Brüning 1977, passim; Brüning 1980, 307–9; Frenz and Hess 189–92; Hajek 1978, passim; Hajek 1984, passim; Ihde 1975, passim; Ihde 1985, passim; Schönfelder and Wirzberger 141–48, 174–79, 410–15, 495–500; Wirzberger 1967, passim; Wirzberger 1968, 17–20; Wüstenhagen 1965, passim).

American Drama in GDR Stage Repertory and Scholarship

Promoted by the American military administration in occupied Germany as a means of educating the German populace in the democratic tradition and offering the much sought-after popular entertainment at the same time, American drama reentered the German stages only a few months after World War II. The increasing political tensions between the occupation powers soon led to a separate theater policy in the different occupation zones. East German theaters became state-owned venues operating under the control of the Soviet military administration and later the ministry of culture of the GDR. All employees were made subject to ministerial control; all seasonal repertories as well as each play-script and the conceptualization for its mise-en-scène had to be submitted for approval to the ministry before rehearsals could begin (cf. Hammerthaler 1994, 163–210; Stuber 1998, 12–253).

Among the American plays available for productions in Germany, only those pieces considered politically relevant and pedagogically worthwhile remained in the repertory of the East German stages, a practice that was taken over into the GDR after the foundation of the state in 1949. These plays included especially socially critical drama written in a realist mode that met the thematic and formal tastes of the political decision makers as well as many spectators. Clifford Odets's *Golden Boy* (1937) or Arthur Miller's *All My Sons* (1947), for instance, were widely staged throughout East Germany, whereas productions of Eugene O'Neill's *Mourning Becomes Electra* (1931) in the late 1940s were received so poorly and scrutinized as nihilistic and decadent that the play was not restaged until the early 1970s (cf. Brüning 1959, 246–51, 258; Brüning 1983, 306–7; Frenz and Hess 1973, 182–89; Scheller 1975, n.p.).

Being part of the press, theater criticism was subjected to close political surveillance. To avoid censorship, reviewers tended to make judgments in conformity with cultural political directions: plays were expected to be evaluated for their capacity to promote socialist persuasions and behavior, and mise-en-scènes should articulate a productive commitment to the common good. Theater critics therefore had to argue for the partisan political value of a given production before they could positively assess aesthetic matters. Moreover, many of them understood themselves as partners of the playhouses rather than as mediators between theater and society. As a consequence, GDR drama criticism largely failed to carry the discourses dramatic productions inspired among audiences to a larger public beyond the playhouses (cf. Hammerthaler 220–24).

Owing to the more lenient political control of Americanist scholarly publications, the academic assessment of American drama in the GDR was ahead of theater practice and criticism. Drama had been playing a small but secure part in East German Americanist research and publishing projects, even though the two fields focused primarily on socially critical, especially explicitly leftist political plays (cf. Brüning 1980, 295–307, 310–13; Brüning 1983, 305–7; Frenz and Hess 1973, 172–82, 192–99; Schnoor 2001b, 778, 781). Both theater practice and Americanist drama scholarship profited considerably from the tentative liberalization of GDR cultural policy since the mid-1960s that allowed formerly rejected playwrights like Eugene O'Neill or Thornton Wilder as well as new "bourgeois" works, such as the plays of Neil Simon, to (re)enter university curricula and stage repertories (cf. Brüning 1980, 314–18; Brüning 1983, 306–11; Frenz and Hess 1973, 186–89).

The scholarly reception of African American drama in the GDR mirrors the East German Americanist assessment of black literature in general: black writing from the United States was seen as almost unanimously a literature of protest, born out of the experience of racial exclusion and by necessity contributing to the ongoing African American political fight for freedom, equality, and "revolutionary" social change. GDR scholars primarily read the history of black drama as a struggle for an adequate representation of the black experience on an American stage that operates as capitalist enterprise and thus depends on catering to the tastes of white clients and sponsors. Tracing the development of African American "legitimate theater" and "serious" drama during the twentieth century, East German Americanists emphasized especially the role leftist white dramatists played in creating more "realistic" images of black life in their writing that replaced the traditional exoticizing representations of African Americans since the 1920s. Moreover, scholars noted the emerging tendency to dramatize actual political incidents, for instance the Scottsboro murder case indicted for its racist implications in Langston Hughes's *Scottsboro, Limited* (1931) and John Wexley's *They Shall Not Die* (1934) (cf. Brüning 1972, 46–48, 57–58; Brüning 1977, 214, 216f., 222–29).

Following World War II, GDR Americanists pointed out, the theater and drama of the "other America" entered a new stage, and now black drama was central to it as never before, as the black civil rights and black power movements of the 1950s and 1960s provided a strong impetus for an aesthetically innovative theater committed to a topical political cause. On the grounds of their racial experience, black writers were depicted in GDR scholarship as "writers of the people," as conscious educators and agitators of the black masses against racial discrimination and the capitalist exploitation of the black underclass. Employing a wide range of dramatic narrative forms, current African American drama was considered to follow along two major lines: on the one hand plays that sought to confront white America with its racism and articulating black determination to fight against it and on the other hand works which, by turning the gaze on black life itself, aimed to educate and strengthen the black community. While the former group of plays—most prominently the works of James Baldwin, Lorraine Hansberry, and Alice Childress—particularly scrutinized self-appointed white liberals for lacking the will to radical action against racism, the latter set of dramas tended to critique moderate, assimilationist segments of the black populace for striving for white acceptance and middle-class respectability. The simplified reversed racial binaries of much theater affiliated with the black power and black arts movements cut across the communist doctrines of the primacy of the class struggle and of international socialist solidarity across racial or national lines. Echoing their Marxist-Leninist assessment of African American writing at large, East German scholars accordingly criticized the black nationalist tendencies inherent especially in the black Revolutionary Theater of Amiri Baraka / LeRoi Jones and the Street Theater of Ed Bullins (cf. Brüning 1972, 51–57; Brüning 1977, 223–24, 245–48; Hajek 1977, 257–58; Hajek 1978, 113–14, 117–18; Hajek 1984, 31–36, 90–92; Schönfelder and Wirzberger 1977, 495–500).

Black Civil Rights Drama on Stage and Page: *A Raisin in the Sun* and *Blues for Mister Charlie*

Given these political inhibitions against black nationalism, it is no surprise that the two African American plays receiving the greatest attention in GDR scholarship articulated a rather liberal, racial integrationist position: Lorraine Hansberry's *A Raisin in the Sun* (1959) and James Baldwin's 1964 drama *Blues for Mister Charlie* (1964). These were also the only black-authored dramas to be produced professionally on the East German stage (cf. Brüning 1980, 317; Brüning 1983, 310; Frenz and Hess 1973, 191–92). *A Raisin in the Sun* had already written theater history in the United States as one of the longest-running black-authored works on Broadway, the first play by a black woman to be produced there, and the first drama by an African American to win the prestigious New York Drama Critics' Circle Award.

Hansberry's realist family drama depicts the lives and dreams of the members of a poor African American family in Chicago's black Southside community, as they await the life insurance money from their deceased patriarch Walter Lee Younger Sr. Committed to offering her family a better life, Walter Lee's widow, Lena, intends to use the money to buy a house in a "better"—and white-populated—neighborhood, for which she already paid a deposit, as well as to enable her daughter Beneatha to study medicine. Beneatha herself wants to go to Africa with her Nigerian boyfriend Joseph after medical school. Her brother Walter Lee Jr., a chauffeur, dreams of his own car and liquor store to gain independence from white employers and a higher social standing as a black patriarch in the African American community, whereas his pregnant wife, Ruth, supports the plans of her mother-in-law. When Karl Lindner, a representative of the white neighborhood, offers the Youngers a large sum of money if they abandon the plan to move there, Walter Lee is tempted to agree, as his plans for the liquor store have been thwarted and he is now in debt. However, realizing that accepting the money would turn him into an accomplice of the white dominance over black lives and black dignity he and his family try to escape from, he rejects the offer, and the play ends with the Youngers being about to move to their new home (cf. Hansberry 1987, passim).

Conflicts arise among the family members in particular from the diverging concepts that underlie their different plans for the use of the insurance money: the desire for racial integration clashes with housing segregation and the claim to a place in white America with both the struggle for social rise within the black community and a pan-African consciousness that seeks a future for black Americans in Africa. Lena and Ruth's "motherly" concern with the living conditions of the entire family is set against Walter Lee's striving for individual "male" respectability, and the dream of material success against that of universal human dignity. Taken from a line of Langston Hughes's poem "Harlem" (1951)—"What happens to a dream deferred? / Does it dry up / like a raisin in the sun? / . . . / or does it explode?" (quoted in full in Hansberry 1987, 5)—, the title of the drama powerfully captures the situation of the Younger family as representatives of civil rights–era black America that was growing ever more restless to realize its dream of a life in human dignity, social equality, and material security.

A Raisin in the Sun met with critical praise on both sides of the Atlantic, especially among white liberals, but was also harshly criticized for its racially integrationist perspective. Especially, the play's ending with the Younger family moving into a white neighborhood was widely perceived to be catering to (black and white) bourgeois sensibilities, and radical black intellectuals scrutinized the playwright as supporting the white power system (cf., for example, Bigsby 1985, 274; Breitinger 1976, 154–56; Brüning 1977, 230–33; Hajek 1977, 258–60; Hajek 1984, 32). Scholarly analyses of the drama generally pointed out its racial political context but also its concern with the struggle for personal dignity independent of color lines. American and Western European Americanists from the 1960s through the 1980s tended to foreground the psychological implications of the characters' individual choices, their striving for social rise, and the typological and artificial qualities of the play (cf. Ashley 1990, 151–52; Bigsby 1985, 381–85; Breitinger 1976, 154, 156–66; Scanlan 1978, 196–200; Sollors 1978, 139–42).

In contrast to them, GDR scholars not only stressed the working-class setting of the play and the elements of social class conflict the drama addresses but also put particular emphasis on the wider disruptive political potential of *A Raisin in the Sun* (cf. Brüning 1977, 233–35; Brüning 1980, 309; Hajek 1977, 259–63; Hajek 1978, 111–13; Hajek 1984, 32–34; Schönfelder and Wirzberger 1977, 495; Wirzberger 1968, 19). In doing this, they prefigured the Western reassessment of Hansberry's drama since the 1980s as being more radical in its political assumptions than many formally and thematically less conventional and "bourgeois" works from the black arts period (cf. Baraka 1987, passim; Nemiroff 1987, ix–xiv; Wilkerson 2001, 40–47).

As Friederike Hajek pointed out, *A Raisin in the Sun* establishes connections to viewers' own lives. By calling especially white spectators to rethink their personal actions with regard to the rights and dignity of their black fellow citizens, she argued, the piece becomes particularly relevant for and more easily accessible to the largely white East German audiences. When the action breaks off at the end of the drama,

> it immediately links up to life, is brought further and to an end in a way by spectators in their daily life practice; because the African American family moving out here (in the theater) in fact directly moves toward them, the (white) spectators. Hereby, play and reality finally and immediately confront each other, and the play becomes potentially productive in the mediation of an alternative society. (Hajek 1978, 112, translation mine; cf. also Hajek 1977, 261)

Hajek moreover contended that, rather than subscribing to the American dream of material success, Hansberry's characters come to gain self-esteem and mutual respect by interrogating this myth, and the drama's Broadway success allowed the play to challenge American mainstream society from within one of its most established cultural institutions (cf. Hajek 1977, 259–63; also Brüning 1977, 233–34; Hajek 1978, 111–13; Hajek 1984, 32–34).

In a similar vein, Eberhard Brüning read *A Raisin in the Sun* as centrally depicting the interconnection between racial and class struggle:

> As the personal decision [of Walter Lee to reject Karl Lindner's offer] and the character development in their preconditions and effects are in a close relationship to fundamental social problems, they step out of the narrow individual realm and become representative of the black proletarian masses in the U.S.A. per se. (Brüning 1977, 234, translation mine)

He further argued that the decision of the Youngers to move to a "better" and "white" neighborhood already antagonistic to them represents an act of determination to fight, which explicitly sets the play in the context of the wider African American political struggle. Not bourgeois black respectability but challenging a social system based on (informal) racial segregation and racialized class difference is what *A Raisin in the Sun* fights for (cf. Brüning 1977, 233ff.; Brüning 1980, 309; also Hajek 1977, 262f.; Schönfelder and Wirzberger 495). Moreover, by depicting Karl Lindner not as the stereotype of a white racist, as similar figures were often portrayed in many "radical" African American plays from the period, but as a "well-meaning citizen who is willing to negotiate [. . .] ," Brüning wrote, the "inhumanity and amorality of his concern are shown in their true light" (Brüning 1977, 234, translation mine).

At the same time as the drama is linked to the black civil rights movement, GDR Americanists emphasized the fact that *A Raisin in the Sun* addresses the issues of universal human dignity and material living conditions in a manner that transcends the racial political realm to include elements of social class conflict imperative to a critical appreciation of American literature in East German scholarship. Friederike Hajek tellingly argued:

> The appellative and even suggestive effect of Hansberry's play is *not* based on a pronounced black-white confrontation but on the author's presenting the specific racial problem in its at first generally human perspective as a problem of (coincidentally black) people that seek to realize their claim to a dignified existence. (Hajek 1978, 112, translation mine, emphasis in the original; cf. also Brüning 1977, 233f.; Schönfelder and Witzberger 495)

And "especially in Lena's, the Black Mama's, becoming the Great American Mama to audiences, including the white ones among them, lies the extraordinary artistic achievement" (Hajek 1977, 260, translation mine) of *A Raisin in the Sun.*

Mounted at East Berlin's Maxim-Gorki-Theater under the direction of Hans-Dieter Mäde for the celebration of "World Theater Day" on March 28, 1963, Hansberry's play received favorable reviews from East Germany's theater critics. Although they scrutinized the drama for its sentimental moments and "bourgeois" political orientation, the reviewers almost unanimously praised *A Raisin in the Sun* for scrutinizing white American racism and black capitalist business dreams as well as for ending on an optimistic, politically activist note (cf. Ebert-Obermeier 1963; Funke 1963; Gersch 1963; Kerndl 1963; Nössing 1963; *Sehnsucht* 1963).[1] As Elvira Mollenschott noted in *Neues Deutschland:* "Even though the author does not yet clearly show the way that leads to ultimate liberation—the optimistic tone, the conviction that people will learn to let their good dreams come true cannot be overheard" (Mollenschott, translation mine).

Anticipating Eberhard Brüning's argumentation, the reviewer for the *Neue Zeit* applauded *A Raisin in the Sun* for unmasking both capitalism and pan-Africanism as illusions: "Wanting to become rich does not help the poor Negro. The romantic flight to the African past does not help. Only the fight for equal rights helps, and this fight for equality goes together with the [fight] for better living conditions" (*Was aus Träumen wird* 1971, translation mine). And like GDR Americanists later, Peter Edel's review in *BZ am Abend* emphasized the universal appeal of the drama and its suitability for reception in a white-populated Socialist European country:

> That the plot of this play is set among Negroes only aggravates the general validity of the conflicts of the Younger Family, only elucidates that the author Lorraine Hansberry wants to not only denounce racial discrimination in the U.S.A. but also, hereby posing the class question at the same time, but also illustrate the hardships of many thousands of such "ordinary people" dreaming in the capitalist world—whether of black or white skin color. (Edel, translation mine)

The contemporary international political agenda also informed the second GDR production of Hansberry's piece, a Sorbian version staged by Beno Sram with the Deutsch-Sorbisches Volkstheater, which premiered on May 5, 1971, at the Bautzener Kammerbühne. The theater program provided the East German audiences with political background information, including photographs and texts pertaining to the later phase of the black civil rights movement in the United States. The reprint of Langston Hughes's "Harlem" poem next to a photograph of the Lincoln Memorial on the Washington Mall further put both the play and the civil rights movement into the larger historical context of the African American "deferred dream" of political and material equality since slavery and emancipation. And an image of contemporary black poverty, accompanied by a quote from Lenin, finally connects the American racial conflict to the global socialist concern with class struggle (cf. *Rózynka w s»óncu* 1971, passim). By proclaiming that "with this mise-en-scène, the Bautzen artists also confess their solidarity with Angela Davis" (*Was aus Träumen wird* 1971, translation mine), the reviewer for the *Nationalzeitung* even tied the production to the most topical global leftist affair of the day, the international campaign to free Davis, an African American leftist political activist, from political imprisonment in the United States.

The reception of James Baldwin's *Blues for Mister Charlie* in East German media and scholarship was more complex than the perception of Hansberry's drama. Inspired by the brutal murders of Emmett Till, a black boy, and the black civil rights activist Medgar Evers, the play captures the moment of budding militancy in the fight for African American equality through depicting how a racially mixed but segregated small town in the South deals with a racial murder, its aftermath, and the ensuing trial. The drama tells the story of Richard Henry, a black minister's son recently returned from a long stay in the North, who is shot by the poor white store owner Lyle Britten for allegedly attempting to rape his wife. Using a free form which integrates numerous flashback scenes to unravel the events that lead to the murder, *Blues for Mister Charlie* explores the racial attitudes prevailing in American society and elucidates the socioeconomic and psychic anxieties that underlie them: Lyle's blunt racism here mixes with his fear of social decline, and Richard's provocative rebelliousness as an end in itself is scrutinized while the rightness of his claim to racial equality is put forward. In a similar manner, the play reveals how the liberal racial attitude of the white journalist Parnell James is firmly grounded in both his secure economic position and in the moderate political agenda of the local black civil rights activists: once Lyle is acquitted in court and the African American community turns to a more radical political agenda and strategy in their fight for civil rights, Parnell's belief in a smooth racial rapprochement process is suddenly challenged, and he is forced to decide between the loyalty to his white friends and the black political cause he wants to support (cf. Baldwin 1969, passim).

Blending elements of agit-prop theater and psychological realism, Baldwin's drama was received controversially along both racial and ideological lines in the United States as well as abroad. *Blues for Mister Charlie* premiered in the GDR at the Großes Haus of the Volkstheater Rostock, directed by Hanns Anselm Perten, on January 11, 1969. Only three months later, the play was staged to open the Kellertheater Leipzig on April 13, 1969, under the direction of Karl Kayser. The programs of both productions contextualized the drama for its East German spectators through essays on African American history and the civil rights movement, on Baldwin, his play, and on the blues as a genre of black protest music. In the Rostock program, explicit connections were established between the social pressures of capitalism and white American racism, presenting the former as offering a fertile ground for the latter. A text on African American communism here and a quote by Bertolt Brecht on the black political struggle in the Leipzig playbill further connected the African American civil rights movement to international socialist concerns (cf. Perten 1969, passim; *Blues* 1969, passim). The Leipzig production was further flanked by a series of well-received "club talks," in which spectators could discuss the play with theater practitioners involved in the production and scholars (cf. *Diskussion um "Blues"* 1969; Brüning 1980, 317; Brüning 1983, 310).

Writing in the Rostock program, Karl-Heinz Schönfelder poignantly captures what were to become the main lines of the critical and scholarly reception of Baldwin's play in the GDR:

> [*Blues for Mister Charlie*] is characterized by its militant message as well as the author's deep understanding of social contexts [. . .] . Although Richard's individual rebellion remains unsuccessful, resignation and despair do not dominate here. Baldwin rather shows an alternative and a perspective: the organized battle of the Negroes within the Civil Rights movement. He especially lets the colored minister recognize that this battle must be led no longer with the Holy Scriptures but with the Bible AND with arms. The optimistic basic tendency of the drama is enforced by the ending, in which Baldwin lets the white liberal [. . .] find his way to the Negroes. He [. . .] hereby indicates for the first time that he considers a coalition of colored people and progressive white forces possible and desirable. *Blues for Mister Charlie* bespeaks Baldwin's having gained considerable insight in the nature and function of the machinery of state power in the South of the U.S.A. (Schönfelder 1969, n.p.)

Like *A Raisin in the Sun*, *Blues for Mister Charlie* met with favorable reviews in the GDR press. While some theater critics complained about the political limits of the drama they attributed to Baldwin's ignorance of "the world-changing power of socialism" (Antosch, translation mine), reviewers echoed Schönfelder's assessment of the play in praising its political critique of white racism and support of black civil rights activism. As Jürgen Grambow put it in *Der Demokrat*, Baldwin's drama "introduced us to the intellectual climate which enabled the unpunished murder of a president, a presidential candidate, and a Nobel laureate within a brief period of time [and] the daily humiliation and physical threat to thousands of colored citizens" (Grambow 1969, translation mine). Reviewing the play for *Neues Deutschland*, Rainer Kerndl argued that, with *Blues for Mister Charlie*, "Baldwin becomes an unambiguous fighter against racial discrimination" (Kerndl 1969, translation mine). In line with communist doctrine, the GDR theater critics particularly hailed the play for its depiction of the white racists as complex characters and for its ending with a racially integrationist vision that retained a place for progressive whites within the black political movement (cf. Bankel 1969; Funke 1969; Grambow 1969; Kerndl 1969; Krecek 1969; Zelt 1969, 25). The reviewers praised the two productions for turning what they considered a compromising work of bourgeois consciousness into an artistic and social experience: the emphasis on the aspects of class struggle inherent in the drama in Rostock and Leipzig, they argued, met the aesthetic and political expectations of their Marxist-educated GDR audiences, and by foregrounding Parnell's role as an identification figure for white supporters of the black political struggle, the two productions underlined the relevance of an African American play to the East German Socialist experience (cf. Antosch 1969; *Blues als Protestsong* 1969; *Diskussion um "Blues"* 1969; Kerndl 1969; Krecek 1969; Zelt 1969, passim).

Many reviews stressed the impact of the theatrical mise-en-scènes in Rostock and Leipzig in conveying the African American experience to GDR audiences. Stylized sets, costumes, and make-up not only avoided the pitfall of blackface performance by the all-white casts—an aspect that Bernhard Scheller would later foreground in his scholarly analysis of the two productions (cf. Scheller 1977, 258–59)—but also visualized the political aspect of *Blues for Mister Charlie*. According to the critics, especially the use of black gloves to identify the African American characters in Rostock interacting powerfully with the backdrop image of the final scene of the production, the widely medialized documentary footage of Tommy Smith's and John Carlos's raising their fists in support of the black power movement during their victory ceremony at the 1968 Mexico City Olympics. Through this reference, reviewers argued, the black gloves of the players extended the function of a dramaturgically necessary racial marker to signify "the accumulating resistance of the black U.S. citizens" (Kerndl 1969, translation mine; cf. also Grambow 1969; Rieger 1969; Timm 1969; Zelt 1969, 28).

In Leipzig, the actors wore gloves and white facial masks, respectively, to identify the black and white characters in the play. The use of ghost-like "toothpaste-white" (Krecek; translation mine) masks to visualize whiteness reversed the tradition of white blackface performance and hereby signified upon its racist implications. Moreover, it served as an alienation device, whereas the natural— and white—facial appearance of the black characters facilitated audiences' identification with the black American experience. As Werner Krecek wrote in the *Leipziger Volkszeitung:* "Thus, the Negro figures are brought closer to the spectator [whereas] their opponents are given a typological character" (Krecek 1969, translation mine; cf. also Antosch 1969; *Blues als Protestsong* 1969; Funke 1969).

Reviewers of the Rostock version further hailed the way the mise-en-scène reinforced the class-focused interpretation of Baldwin's race drama. "By refraining from using Negro masks," Jürgen Grambow wrote, "the director reveals the deeper nature of racial discrimination: it is part of the social sphere [and] thus finally a class question" (Grambow 1969, translation mine). And Rainer Kerndl pointed out the political function of the costumes: While all black characters unanimously wore blue jeans and white T-shirts—clothes then associated with physical labor—, "the suits and costumes of the whites, kept equally uniform, indicated their better social position" (Kerndl 1969, translation mine; cf. also Timm 1969).

The East German reviewers especially scrutinized the psychological explanations and sexual undertones of *Blues for Mister Charlie*. While Christoph Funke noted Baldwin's concern with the psychological bases for white racism in the United States in a neutral tone in his review of the Leipzig version (cf. Funke 1969), several critics applauded the "justified strong reduction of erotic motives for the actions of the figures" (*Blues als Protestsong* 1969, translation mine) in both GDR productions, which strengthened the politically desired element of "active solidarity with the rightless" (Zelt 1969, 26, translation mine) of Baldwin's drama. In Rostock, Rainer Kerndl argued, "for instance in the figure of Richard, the references to his drug and sexual experiences were reduced; important here is the young man who has decided to no longer turn the other cheek but to hit back" (Kerndl 1969, translation mine).

Reviewing the Rostock production in the West German *Frankfurter Rundschau*, Manfred Rieger critically evaluated the political bent of the mise-en-scène and its pitfalls: While "it was foreseeable that racial differences were

comprehended in Rostock as class differences" (Rieger 18), the "tame" representation of the character of Richard through the suppression of the sexual psychological elements of Baldwin's text seriously limited the political militancy
the production aspired. As Rieger admitted, the Rostock version nevertheless
positively differed from previous West German and Austrian productions of the
drama, which had "resulted in emptiness and resignation, as the Black Power
consequence was received with reservation" (ibid. 18).

Most scholarly evaluations of Baldwin's play stressed the interconnectedness
of the personal and collective experiences in *Blues for Mister Charlie* as well as
how racism shapes and threatens humanity on either side of the color line. Yet,
Western scholarship from the 1960s through the 1980s tended to criticize both
the sentimental and agit-prop-like qualities of the drama as well as its militant
racial political agenda (cf., for example, Bigsby 1985, 387–91; Bruck 1975, 74–94;
Macebuh 1973, 172; Schwank 170–83). Echoing the GDR press reviews of the Rostock and Leipzig productions of *Blues for Mister Charlie*, East German Americanists praised the social political critique of the play and its use of documentary
and agit-prop elements (cf. Brüning 1977, 243; Hajek 1978, 114–15; Hajek 1984,
35–36; Scheller 1975, n.p.; Scheller 1977, 258–64). Friederike Hajek stressed that
"the confrontation of black and white masses is a new element in African American drama which took the counter-public as it emerged through the civil rights
movement into account" (Hajek 1978, 115, translation mine). She went on to suggest that, with this mode of presentation, *Blues for Mister Charlie* points to the
relevance of the social class struggle for the African American movement: "Baldwin refers to the fact that the relations between black and white individuals in
the U.S.A. are determined by social conditions far more complex than the 'color
line' or the racial barrier and which urgently need a fundamental change" (ibid.,
115, translation mine). As Bernhard Scheller wrote, the two GDR productions did
particular justice to the "necessary conclusion" from the historically materialist
"recognition" (Scheller 1977, 264, translation mine; cf. also ibid., 258–64) of the
class struggle underlying the racial conflict of *Blues for Mister Charlie*. In line
with the Marxist doctrine of interracial solidarity of progressive forces, Scheller,
Hajek, and other East German scholars further followed GDR theater reviewer-
ers in emphasizing the importance of Baldwin's at least somewhat differentiated
picture of white American society—especially in the character of Parnell, the key
identification figure for liberal white audiences—and its optimistic conclusion
with the hope for an ongoing joint black and white fight against racism (cf. Brüning 1977, 244; Hajek 1978, 114–15; Hajek 1984, 35–36; Scheller 1977, 251, 258–64).

The East German academic reception of the play occurred in the context of a
larger scholarly uneasiness about Baldwin's work. The perception of his novels,
essays, and plays in the GDR was marred until the 1970s by the apparently apolitical stand of the writer and his "bourgeois" psychological and sexual explanations for the actions and attitudes of his fictional characters (cf. Frenz and Hess
1973, 192). In an analysis of Baldwin's essays and novels, Heinz Wüstenhagen,
for instance, reproached the writer's "reduction of his characters to the sexual
sphere" through which his "subjectivism and individualism" (Wüstenhagen 1965,

155, translation mine) manifested themselves. It is this "philosophical-aesthetic modernism," Wüstenhagen concluded, "[. . .] which finally both neutralizes and paralyzes the social critical aspects" (ibid., 157, translation mine; cf. also Brüning 1980, 308) of Baldwin's work. GDR Americanist assessments grew more balanced and appreciative when Baldwin became more explicitly political in his literary writing and public commentary, especially after he wrote a widely publicized open letter to the imprisoned Angela Davis in 1970 (cf. Brüning 1980, 308; Schönfelder and Wirzberger 1977, 413–14; see also Frenz and Hess 1973, 192). Nevertheless, in his review of an East German scholarly edition of Baldwin essays, Hans-Jochen Sander criticized the "complicated blending of recognized social laws and psychologizing, individualist conceptualizations" (quoted in Brüning 1980, 308, translation mine) of their author.

Like the GDR theater critics, East German Americanists found particular fault with the sexual-psychological explanations of white racism in *Blues for Mister Charlie*. Eberhard Brüning criticized that Baldwin, as he saw it, presented a white male sexual inferiority complex as the origin of antiblack racism in the United States. The drama, he claimed,

> reveals the fragility of the material as well as the intellectual claim to power of the white middle-class world but attempts to shift what is concretely socially motivated to what is sexually psychological and to shock the white middle-class as incarnation of the impotence of a whole race and civilization whose only way out is brutality and terror. (Brüning 1972, 5, translation mine; cf. also Brüning 1970, 184; Brüning 1980, 317)

Consequentially, Brüning and other GDR scholars hailed the reduction of psychological interpretations and sexual references in their discussion of the two East German stage productions of the drama. As Bernhard Scheller wrote, "the reduction of the sexual psychological element [. . .] proved to be an enlargement of the play, which does justice to the conceptual concern to show active solidarity with the rightless" (Scheller 1977, 262–63, translation mine; cf. also ibid., 258–64). And according to Brüning, "only a sensitive and consequentially Marxist-Leninist mise-en-scène—such as the one by Karl Kayser at the Leipzig 'Kellertheater'—can, by cutting the hypertrophy of the sex-related vocabulary, lead toward the actual social basic concern of the play and turn it 'into an artistic and social experience at once'" (Brüning 1970, 184, translation mine).

In line with the generally changing attitudes of East German Americanists to Baldwin's works in the 1970s, Karl-Heinz Schönfelder and Karl-Heinz Wirzberger, on the other hand, argued that *Blues for Mister Charlie* "refers to sexuality only to the degree to which it is necessary for a comprehensive characterization of the characters and social conditions" (Schönfelder and Wirzberger 1977, 413, translation mine). But even this more differentiated assessment crucially missed the point of the meaning of Richard's sexual affairs for the play: Baldwin's drama evokes the black man's sexual adventures with white women to scrutinize the racist double standard of white men, which rejects black male–white female miscegenation and grants white men full sexual access to black women. Rather than deflecting from the subject of the black political struggle, as the East German scholars saw it, Richard's affairs function here as an act of black male resistance to a sexualized system of racial hierarchy. The black power movement of the 1960s even propagated the claim to black male equality through the (sexual) "possession" of white women that had been denied to African American men under Jim Crow laws in the American South (cf. Hine and Jenkins 1999, 38–39).

Western intellectuals and political activists sympathetic to the black power movement have often failed to acknowledge the fact that this practice precisely mirrors the equally racialized and sexist notion of white masculinity through the "availability" of black mistresses it claims to undermine (cf. Hine and Jenkins 1999, 38–39). In contrast to them, GDR Americanists and theater reviewers rightfully criticized the cynic misogyny of Richard's self-definition through his past sexual affairs with white women in the North. However, they dismissed the political implications of both Richard's boasting of his interracial sexual adventures and Lyle's murderous reaction to Richard's macho role play on the grounds of Baldwin's lack of Socialist class consciousness. This pinpoints to yet ultimately fails to articulate the crucial difference between the African American civil rights movement on the one hand and the Marxist-Leninist concern with class conflicts on the other: where Baldwin's drama explicitly cuts across social class lines— especially the group of white characters, including both poor men like Lyle and modestly wealthy ones like Parnell—in its depiction of the central, racial political conflict between blacks and whites, the East German reception of the play fiercely struggled with and fundamentally failed in pressing *Blues for Mister Charlie* into the scheme of a social class struggle between black workers and their white capitalist oppressors that was politically demanded in both theater criticism and scholarship in the GDR.

Conclusion

Americanist research in the GDR moved between the poles of political doctrine demanding ideological distance to its subject of study and the personal freedom of the inventive scholar. Lenin's doctrine of the two cultures not only provided a framework for the appropriation and appreciation of ever-growing segments of American literature but also led East German scholarship to often-pioneering treatments of aspects of American culture neglected to a smaller or larger degree in Western Americanist studies. The political limitations and performance of conformity of GDR Americanists become obvious most prominently in their standard framing of the United States as an imperialist power, their depiction of African American political consciousness in terms of anticolonial and class struggles, and in the emphasis they placed on interracial solidarity of "progressive" forces. Reading between the lines of the Marxist-Leninist standard formulae, East German scholars dealt with American, especially African American, literature in a similarly differentiated manner as their Western colleagues operating under much less restrictive political conditions.

Advocating the fight against black political and economic inequality without rejecting white America altogether, African American literature connected to the black civil rights movement of the 1950s and early 1960s. It also offered itself for a political perception that could connect the struggle against racial discrimination with a socialist emphasis on class conflict. Embodying the black civil rights movement's agenda of racially integrationist activism and touching upon the black American economic struggle in a model manner, Lorraine Hansberry's *A Raisin in the Sun* and James Baldwin's *Blues for Mister Charlie* tellingly remained the only African American stage plays from this era to be produced on professional stages in the GDR. Given the limitations placed especially upon theater practitioners and critics, East German stage productions and press reviews provided a comparatively differentiated reading of the two works. Hansberry's and Baldwin's dramas moreover featured prominently among the black plays of the period GDR Americanists addressed in their writing, which, corresponding to the greater freedom they enjoyed, usually exceeded the stage productions and press reviews in complexity and depth. As time has shown, these scholarly interpretations have proven their validity alongside the perceptions Western academics have offered.

Note

1. Except for Manfred Zelt's review of Baldwin's drama, all press reviews and theater programs pertaining to the GDR productions of *A Raisin in the Sun* and *Blues for Mister Charlie* quoted here have been retrieved from the productions' clipping/program files at the Stiftung Archiv der Akademie der Künste, Berlin.

Works Cited

Antosch, Georg. "Zeugnis von der Macht der Liebe: 'Blues für Mister Charlie' in Leipzig." *Neue Zeit*, April 27, 1969.

Ashley, Leonard R. "Lorraine Hansberry and the Great Black Way." In *Modern American Drama: The Female Canon*. Ed. June Schlueter, 151–60. Rutherford: Fairleigh Dickinson University Press, 1990.

Baldwin, James. *Blues for Mister Charlie*. 6th printing. New York: Dell, 1969.

Bankel, W. "Appell und Requiem für Schwarz und Weiß." *Leipziger Volkszeitung*, April 12, 1969.

Baraka, Amiri [LeRoi Jones]. "A Critical Evaluation: *A Raisin in the Sun*'s Enduring Passion." In *A Raisin in the Sun: Expanded 25th Anniversary Edition* and *The Sign in Sidney Brustein's Window*. By Lorraine Hansberry. Ed. Robert Nemiroff, 9–20. New York: Plume, 1987.

Bigsby, Christopher. *A Critical Introduction to Twentieth-Century American Drama*. Vol. III: *Beyond Broadway*. Cambridge: Cambridge University Press, 1985.

"Blues als Protestsong: Erste Premiere in Leipzigs 'Theater im Keller.'" *Mitteldeutsche Neueste Nachrichten*, April 16, 1969.

Blues für Mister Charlie. Theater program. Leipzig: Kellertheater Leipzig, 1969.

Breitinger, Eckhard. "Lorraine Hansberry: *A Raisin in the Sun* (1959)." In *Das amerikanische Drama der Gegenwart*. Ed. Herbert Grabes, 153–68. Kronberg: Athenaeum, 1976.

Bruck, Peter. *Von der 'Store Front Church' zum 'American Dream': James Baldwin und der ameri-kanische Rassenkonflikt.* Bochum Studies in English, 2. Amsterdam: Grüner, 1975.

Brüning, Eberhard. "Die Amerikanistik an der Universität Leipzig (1950–1990)–40 Jahre Gratwanderung eines ungeliebten Faches." In *Amerikanistik in der DDR: Geschichte—Analyse—Zeitzeugenberichte.* Gesellschaft—Geschichte—Gegenwart, 19, 67–85. Berlin: Trafo, 1999.

———. "American Drama in the German Democratic Republic: Some Facts and Problems." *ZAA* 31, no. 4 (1983): 305–13.

———. "Amerikanische Dramen an den Bühnen der Deutschen Demokratischen Republik und Berlins von 1945–1955." *ZAA* 7, no. 3 (1959): 246–69.

———. "'The Black Liberation Movement' und das amerikanische Drama." *ZAA* 20, no. 1 (1972): 46–58.

———. "Probleme der Rezeption amerikanischer Literatur in der DDR." *Weimarer Beiträge* 16, no. 4 (1970): 175–87.

———. "Schwarze Befreiungsbewegung und afroamerikanische Dramatik." In *Studien zum amerikanischen Drama nach dem zweiten Weltkrieg.* Ed. Eberhard Brüning, Klaus Köhler, and Bernhard Scheller, 214–48. Neue Beiträge zur Literaturwissenschaft, 39. Berlin (East): Rütten & Loening, 1977.

———. "US-amerikanische Literatur in der DDR seit 1965." *ZAA* 28, no. 4 (1980): 293–319.

"Diskussion um Blues." *Leipziger Volkszeitung,* May 23, 1969.

Ebert-Obermeier, Gerhard. "Amerikanische Dramatik heute." *Sonntag,* May 5, 1963.

Edel, Peter. "Die Träume der Familie Younger: 'Eine Rosine in der Sonne'—Zur Erstaufführung des amerikanischen Schauspiels im Maxim Gorki Theater." *BZ am Abend,* April 3, 1963.

Frenz, Horst, and John Hess. "Die nordamerikanische Literatur in der Deutschen Demokratischen Republik." In *Nordamerikanische Literatur im deutschen Sprachraum seit 1945: Beiträge zu ihrer Rezeption.* Ed. Horst Frenz and Hans-Joachim Lang, 171–99. Munich: Winkler, 1973.

Funke, Christoph. "Theater im Opern-Keller: Karl Kayser inszenierte 'Blues für Mister Charlie' in Leipzig." *Der Morgen,* May 9, 1969.

———. "Was wird aus einem vertagten Traum? 'Eine Rosine in der Sonne' von Lorraine Hansberry im Maxim-Gorki-Theater erstaufgeführt." *Der Morgen,* March 29, 1963.

Gersch, Wolfgang. "Die Youngers suchen das Glück: Deutsche Erstaufführung von 'Eine Rosine in der Sonne' im Berliner Maxim Gorki Theater." *Tribüne,* April 6, 1963.

Grambow, Jürgen. "Der Rassenhaß und die weiße Anmaßung—Teil der imperialistischen Lebensform." *Der Demokrat* 14 (January 17, 1969).

Hajek, Friederike. "Die afroamerikanische Befreiungsbewegung der sechziger Jahre in den USA und Aspekte ihrer Literatur." *Weimarer Beiträge* 24, no. 12 (1978): 104–31.

———. "Lorraine Hansberry und ihre Kritiker: Zur Rezeption von Lorraine Hansberrys Stück *A Raisin in the Sun.*" *Wissenschaftliche Zeitschrift der Pädagogischen Hochschule 'Karl Liebknecht' Potsdam* 21, no. 1 (1977): 257–64.

———. *Selbstzeugnisse der Afroamerikaner: Black Liberation Movement und Autobiographie.* Berlin: Akademie-Verlag, 1984.

Hammerthaler, Ralph. "Die Position des Theaters in der DDR." In *Theater in der DDR: Chronik und Perspektiven.* Ed. Christa Hasche, Traute Schelling, and Joachim Fiebach, 151–273. Berlin: Henschel, 1994.

Hansberry, Lorraine. "*A Raisin in the Sun.*" In *A Raisin in the Sun: Expanded 25th Anniversary Edition* and *The Sign in Sidney Brustein's Window.* Ed. Robert Nemiroff, 1–151. New York: Plume, 1987.

Hine, Darlene Clark, and Earnestine Jenkins. "Introduction: Black Men's History—Toward a Gendered Perspective." In *A Question of Manhood: A Reader in U.S. Black Men's History and*

Masculinity. Vol. I: *"Manhood Rights": The Construction of Black Male History and Manhood, 1750–1870.* Ed. Darlene Clark Hine and Earnestine Jenkins, 1–58. Bloomington: Indiana University Press, 1999.

Hofmann, Christa. "Die Anglistik-Amerikanistik in der Deutschen Demokratischen Republik." *ZAA* 8, no. 2 (1960): 171–85.

Ihde, Horst. *Von der Plantage zum schwarzen Ghetto.* Leipzig: Urania, 1975.

———. "Die zweite Kultur der Afroamerikaner und der antiimperialistische Kampf um die Jahrhundertwende." *ZAA* 33, no. 4 (1985): 310–23.

Kerndl, Rainer. "Blues gegen Mister Charlie: DDR-Erstaufführung eines Baldwin-Stückes in Rostock." *Neues Deutschland,* January 26, 1969.

———. "'Eine Rosine in der Sonne': Zur Inszenierung eines amerikanischen Stückes." *Freie Presse,* Zwickau, April 20, 1963.

Krecek, Werner. "Exemplarischer Beginn: Erstes Ereignis im Leipziger Kellertheater: 'Blues für Mister Charlie.'" *Leipziger Volkszeitung,* April 17, 1969.

Lenin, Vladimir I. "Aus: Kritische Bemerkungen zur Nationalen Frage." In *Über Kultur und Kunst.* Berlin (East): Dietz Verlag, 1960. 204–19.

Macebuh, Stanley. *James Baldwin: A Critical Study.* New York: Third Press, 1973.

Manske, Eva. "Amerikanische Gegenwartsliteratur im Urteil sowjetischer Literaturkritik." *ZAA* 22, no. 3 (1974): 362–70.

Mollenschott, Elvira. "'Eine Rosine in der Sonne': Deutsche Erstaufführung zum Welttheatertag im Maxim Gorki Theater." *Neues Deutschland,* March 31, 1963.

Nemiroff, Robert. Foreword to This New Edition. In *A Raisin in the Sun: Expanded 25th Anniversary Edition* and *The Sign in Sidney Brustein's Window.* By Lorraine Hansberry. Ed. Robert Nemiroff, ix–xviii. New York: Plume, 1987.

Neubauer, Paul. "The Academic Reception of Postmodern American Literature in Germany." In *"Closing the Gap": American Postmodern Fiction in Germany, Italy, Spain, and the Netherlands.* Ed. Theo D'haen and Hans Bertens, 69–147. Postmodern Studies, 20. Amsterdam and Atlanta: Rodopi, 1997.

Nössing, Manfred. "Des Menschen Würde bewahrt: 'Eine Rosine in der Sonne' im Maxim-Gorki Theater." *BZ,* April 2, 1963.

Perten, Hanns Anselm, ed. *Blues für Mister Charlie.* Dialog-Blätter des Volkstheaters Rostock, 74. Spielzeit (1968/69). Rostock: Volkstheater Rostock, 1969.

Rieger, Manfred. "Black Power in Rostock: Hanns Anselm Perten inszenierte die DDR-Erstaufführung von James Baldwins 'Blues für Mister Charlie.'" *Frankfurter Rundschau,* January 18, 1969.

Riese, Utz. ""Zur amerikanischen Literatur der siebziger Jahre aus sowjetischer Sicht." *ZAA* 33, no. 3 (1985): 258–61.

Rózynka w s»óncu. By Lorraine Hansberry. Theater program. Bautzen: Deutsch-Sorbisches Volkstheater / Bautzener Kammerbühne, 1971.

Scanlan, Tom. *Family, Drama, and American Dreams.* Contributions in American Studies, 35. Westport, CT: Greenwood Press, 1978.

Scheffel, Werner. "Zu einigen Aufgaben der Amerikanistik im Kampf gegen die ideologische Diversion des USA-Imperialismus." *ZAA* 20, no. 4 (1972): 370–91.

Scheller, Bernhard. "Die Gestalt des Farbigen bei Williams, Albee und Baldwin und ihre szenische Realisierung in DDR-Aufführungen." In *Studien zum amerikanischen Drama nach dem zweiten Weltkrieg.* Ed. Eberhard Brüning, Klaus Köhler, and Bernhard Scheller, 249–64. Neue Beiträge zur Literaturwissenschaft, 39. Berlin (East): Rütten & Loening, 1977.

———. *Notizen zur Rezeption englisch-amerikanischer Gegenwartsdramatik.* Diskurs: Texte zur Theaterarbeit, 5. Rostock: Volkstheater Rostock, 1975.

Schnoor, Rainer. "Amerikanistik in 40 Jahren DDR: Eine wissenschaftshistorische Skizze." In *Amerikanistik in der DDR: Geschichte—Analyse—Zeitzeugenberichte*. Gesellschaft—Geschichte—Gegenwart, 19, 29–50. Berlin: Trafo, 1999.

———. "Das gute und das schlechte Amerika: Wahrnehmungen der USA in der DDR." In *Die USA und Deutschland im Zeitalter des kalten Krieges 1945–1990*. Vol. I: *1945–1968*. Ed. Detlef Junker, 932–43. 2nd ed. Stuttgart: DVA, 2001. (=Schnoor 2001a).

———. "Zwischen privater Meinung und offizieller Verlautbarung: Amerikabilder in der DDR." In *Die USA und Deutschland im Zeitalter des kalten Krieges 1945–1990*. Vol. II: *1968–1990*. Ed. Detlef Junker, 775–85. 2nd ed. Stuttgart and Munich: DVA, 2001. (=Schnoor 2001b).

Schönfelder, Karl-Heinz. "Amerikanische Literatur in Europa." *ZAA* 7, no. 1 (1959): 35–57.

———. "James Baldwin." In *Blues für Mister Charlie*. Ed. Hanns Anselm Perten. Dialog-Blätter des Volkstheaters Rostock, 74. Spielzeit (1968/69). Rostock: Volkstheater Rostock, 1969.

———. "Strömungen der neueren US-amerikanischen Literatur im Urteil von Amerikanisten der DDR." *ZAA* 32, no. 3 (1984): 247–56.

Schönfelder, Karl-Heinz, and Karl-Heinz Wirzberger. *Literatur der USA im Überblick: Von den Anfängen bis zur Gegenwart*. Reclams Universal-Bibliothek 373. 2nd rev. and enl. ed. Leipzig: Reclam, 1977.

Schwank, Klaus. "James Baldwin, *Blues for Mister Charlie* (1964)." In *Das amerikanische Drama der Gegenwart*. Ed. Herbert Grabes, 169–84. Kronberg: Athenaeum, 1976.

"Sehnsucht nach einem besseren Leben: Erstaufführung des amerikanischen Stückes 'Eine Rosine in der Sonne' in Berlin." *Neue Zeit*, April 2, 1963.

Sollors, Werner. "The New Black Theatre." In *Theater und Drama in Amerika: Aspekte und Interpretationen*. Ed. Edgar Lohner and Rudolf Haas, 136–53. Berlin (West): Schmidt, 1978.

Stuber, Petra. *Spielräume und Grenzen: Studien zum DDR-Theater*. Berlin: Links, 1998.

Timm, Werner. "'We Shall Overcome': Packende DDR-Erstaufführung 'Blues für Mister Charlie.'" *Norddeutsche Neueste Nachrichten*, January 14, 1969.

"Von Träumen zum Kampf: Lorraine Hansberrys 'Eine Rosine in der Sonne' in der Bautzener Kammerbühne." *Sächsisches Tageblatt*, May 6, 1971.

"Was aus Träumen wird: 'Eine Rosine in der Sonne'—Maxim Gorki Theater." *Nationalzeitung*, March 29, 1963.

Weimann, Robert. "Literaturwissenschaft und historisch-materialistische Theorie: Aktuelle Fragen der Entwicklung der Literaturtheorie und Methodologie in der Anglistik-Amerikanistik." *ZAA* 28, no. 1 (1980): 12–31.

Wilkerson, Margaret B. "Political Radicalism and Artistic Innovation in the Works of Lorraine Hansberry." In *African American Performance and Theater History: A Critical Reader*. Ed. Harry J. Elam and David Krasner, 40–55. Oxford: Oxford University Press, 2001.

Wirzberger, Karl-Heinz. "'Great Tradition' oder Episode? Nonkonformismus, Protest und Engagement in der amerikanischen Gegenwartsliteratur." *ZAA* 16, no. 1 (1968): 5–24.

———. *Probleme der Bürgerrechtsbewegung in der amerikanischen Prosaliteratur der Gegenwart*. Sitzungsberichte der Deutschen Akademie der Wissenschaften zu Berlin, Klasse für Sprachen, Literatur und Kunst 2. Berlin (East): Akademie-Verlag, 1967.

———. "20 Jahre Deutsche Demokratische Republik, 17 Jahre *Zeitschrift für Anglistik und Amerikanistik*." *ZAA* 17, no. 4 (1969): 341–43.

Wüstenhagen, Heinz. "James Baldwins Essays und Romane: Versuch einer ersten Einschätzung." *ZAA* 13, no. 2 (1965): 117–57.

Zelt, Manfred. "Ein Stück Amerika: Zur Rostocker Erstaufführung von Baldwins 'Blues für Mister Charlie.'" *Theater der Zeit* 24, no. 4 (April 1969): 25–28.

Ollie Harrington

His Portrait Drawn on the Basis of East German (GDR) Secret
Service Files

ARIBERT SCHROEDER

Oliver Wendell Harrington was a major black American leftist writer, journalist,
and cartoonist with the leading African American newspapers. After his self-
imposed exile in Paris, he lived in the German Democratic Republic (GDR) from
1961 until his death in 1995. Harrington was a pioneer African American cartoonist whose social and political commentary was widely read in the 1940s.[1]

Harrington was born in Valhalla, Westchester County, New York, on February
14, 1912. Though he later tried to present himself differently, at least in the United
States in 1991,[2] Harrington was raised by an African American middle-class family under relatively privileged circumstances. After having attended the famous
DeWitt Clinton High School in the South Bronx, New York City, from which he
graduated in 1929, he went to the National Academy of Design. Later on, he also
attended the School of Fine Arts of Yale University from 1936 until 1941.

During those years, Harrington had made his way to Harlem, where leftists
and communists like Langston Hughes, Richard Wright, Henry Winston, James
E. Jackson, and John Pittman became his friends. The last three of them rose to
high positions within the Communist Party of the United States (CPUS). Harrington made his living mainly as a caricaturist. But for a short period he also
worked for the NAACP as a "public relations director in the national office of
the NAACP," which at that time was led by Walter White as general secretary.[3]
He is best known for the creation of his comic character "Bootsie," which was
first published in the *New York Amsterdam News* and later also printed in other
widely read African American newspapers, like the *Pittsburgh Courier*, the *Chicago Defender*, and the *Baltimore Afro-American*. The *People's Voice* published
his political caricatures during World War II.

In the latter part of 1951, Harrington left the United States and went to Paris
where he lived and worked as a caricaturist and writer. He became one of the African American "exiles" who moved in the circle of Richard Wright. After Wright's
mysterious death on November 28, 1960, Harrington went to (East) Berlin in
November 1961. When he died there at the age of eighty-four, on November 2,

1995, the popular African American periodical *Ebony* dedicated an obituary to him.[4]

Throughout his lifetime, Harrington was a committed African American communist with an independent mind who was widely respected beyond CPUS circles among African Americans in and outside the United States, and even among Africans. He steadfastly held on to his friends, communist or other, even if some of them like Richard Wright or Langston Hughes had distanced themselves from the communist world movement. Harrington participated in a number of important international discourses.

From the beginning Harrington used his caricatures and writings to fight against racism and colonialism worldwide. He also followed this strategy in the GDR, where he continued to raise his voice in support of equality for black Americans and African liberation movements, particularly South Africa. In this period, his articles and cartoons were mainly published in American and British communist periodicals, and in papers printed in the GDR. His cartoons, in which he criticized "capitalist systems of government and exploitation," appeared in the periodical *Magazin*, for example. "Oliver Harrington's Actual Gallery" was regularly given space in the weekly *Der Eulenspiegel*.

Harrington was a loyal foreign visitor to the GDR. But he was one who kept his eyes wide open on developments in the communist world movement. Among the theoreticians he studied were the writings of "Abweichler" (deviants), like those of the Austrian communist cultural philosopher Ernst Fischer,[5] whom Sozialistische Einheitspartei Deutschland (*SED* or *Socialist Unity Party*) functionaries and the *Stasi* regarded as a "*Revisionist*": his thesis concerning the leading role of artists and the intelligentsia was anathema to them because one of their dogmas clearly stated that the avant-garde role exclusively belonged to "the Party."

With an eye on achieving constructive change in the "socialist country" where he had chosen to live, Harrington did not hesitate to initiate, or participate in, several national discourses with international dimensions. In order to have the living and working conditions of *Kulturschaffende und Intellektuelle* (cultural workers and intellectuals), ameliorated, for example, Harrington and his artist friends openly offered resistance to the dogma of so-called *realistische Kunst* (realistic art) imposed on them by communist functionaries of the *SED*.[6] The *Stasi* files focusing on Harrington's international and national discourses are especially revealing about the manner in which Harrington became of concern to the Stasi and why he deserved their attention.

Harrington stated in a public speech given in Detroit in 1991 and later published in his book *Why I Left America* that he went to communist East Berlin in August 1961 in order to discuss with publishers the possibility of illustrating the works of classic American and English writers there. Harrington claimed that due to a military confrontation, the so-called tank crisis between the Soviets and the Americans, and personal visa problems emanating from this situation, he practically had become "a virtual prisoner." He later noted that he was occasionally tempted to leave the GDR, but that he had stayed on because his work there had pleased him.[7]

This version, in which Harrington partly presents himself as a victim to his mostly African American listeners, and later to his readers, is not confirmed by what the *Staatssicherheitsdienst* (*Stasi*) of the GDR reports about him in his so-called *Ausländerakte* (i.e., a type of files which were specially kept on foreigners). According to these files Harrington arrived in East Berlin as late as November 5, 1961, and that he intended to stay there for a year upon invitations extended to him by the publishing house *Aufbauverlag* and the *Staatliches Rundfunk-komitee*[8] (i.e., the directorate of the National Broadcasting Service). Also, the so-called tank crisis already occurred on October 27, 1961, and the construction of the Berlin wall, as is well known, was begun as early as August 13, 1961. Both events therefore occurred before Harrington's arrival in the GDR. And finally the point must be made that Harrington, being a citizen of the United States of America, could have left East Berlin whenever he wished by going to West Berlin via Checkpoint Charlie, which was the transit point for American, British, and French military personnel and citizens. Throughout his sojourn in East Germany Harrington had seen to it that his American passport was renewed regularly.[9]

Interestingly, another *Legende* about Harrington, as this type of text is called in German secret service terms, also appears in his *Stasi* files of July 1985. This legend would make him a deserter from the United States Army: it says that both he and one Billy Mullis deserted from the United States Army and went to (East) Berlin together. But this story is not confirmed in respective secret service materials, either. Mullis, for example, had already become a deserter on December 5, 1959. Harrington, therefore, could have met him at the earliest only after his own arrival in East Berlin. But he certainly did, when he, too, had started to work for *Radio Berlin International* (*RBI*).

As far as Harrington's military service is concerned, which would certainly gain him sympathy among African American readers or listeners and increase his popularity in certain circles of the GDR, he himself remains ambivalent. Thus with an eye on the draft after Pearl Harbor he once writes: "I saw one brother face his moment of truth at Camp Patrick Henry, our embarkation center."[10] Regarding his meeting with Walter White, general secretary of the NAACP, in Italy, it could only be established that White had indeed visited that country in World War II as a member of an American commission. It was to examine the fighting morale of African American soldiers in African and European war theaters.[11] And that Harrington, on his part, had been sent to North Africa and Europe in World War II as a war correspondent by the *Pittsburgh Courier*, but not as a fighting soldier.[12]

It was perhaps in this context that Chester Himes believes to have seen Harrington in an officer's uniform in Harlem toward the end of World War II.[13] This seems probable because correspondents active in the different U.S. war theaters were most probably put into uniforms. In Harrington's *Ausländerakte* "North Africa, Sicily, Italy, and France" are cited only as "addresses" for the years 1942–1945, but nothing appears in these pages concerning a possible military service or even a desertion.

Harrington and the Stasi

The East German secret service made a special effort to obtain something on foreigners living in the GDR in a routine way. This was done for the purpose of better controlling them or, even worse, in order to win them over as informers known as *Informelle Mitarbeiter* (unofficial collaborators), or even spies. In Harrington's case these attempts were given up, and he eventually in 1968, became categorized as an *"unsichere Kontaktperson"* (a contact who could not be trusted). Nevertheless, Harrington had already, knowingly or unknowingly, taken a first step in the direction of binding himself when he submitted to the East German authorities an *Antrag für die Einreise in die DDR* (entry application) dated January 3, 1962. Harrington also took, or was obliged to take, another step binding himself, when he joined the *nordamerikanische Redaktion* ("North America Editorial staff") of *Radio Berlin International.* According to his file, this assignment began in October 1961. If this date is correct, it would suggest that Harrington had perhaps worked for *RBI* already, while he was still in France. Harrington's engagement with *RBI* officially ended late in December 1962, when he became a *freier Mitarbeiter* (freelancer). He kept this status until 1972. In a *Stasi* report dated February 28, 1968, Harrington is mentioned as working for the *Abt.[eilung] Außen-politik* (Foreign Affairs Department) of the *Staatliches Rundfunkkomitee der DDR.*

Harrington's activities at *RBI* included his participation in the production of secret propaganda broadcasts called *OPS.*[14] The purpose was to entice defections and/or sow discord in the ranks of the American military. These programs were aimed at American GIs stationed in West Berlin and the Federal Republic of Germany. They were broadcast around midnight on the *Berliner Welle* (i.e., the medium wave [band] of *RBI*). A *Stasi* officer states about Harrington in one of his reports dated June 24, 1964: "[He] now works for OPS only occasionally. He has written, and above all does write, short stories for OPS-programmes, which are aimed at American citizens [living] in Western Europe."

As an editor, Harrington also made contributions to a number of news and propaganda radio programs at later dates. As mentioned above, he became a member of the *Abt.[eilung] Außenpolitik* des *Staatlichen Rundfunkkomitees der DDR.* And in December 1979, the note was entered into Harrington's files that he had achieved the special status of *Fremdsprachenkader* (foreign language cadre). There is evidence enough, therefore, that he gradually rose in his career at *RBI* through his work for this radio station.

The *Stasi* seems to have tried to control Harrington by taking persons close to him, at least temporarily, as "hostages": on one occasion, for example, his wife and their son, Oliver, were under rather flimsy pretexts prevented from leaving the GDR together with Harrington. This situation occurred in 1968, when he had been offered the position of director of a communist publishing house in France. In 1984 though, Mrs. Harrington and her son were allowed to visit with her mother-in-law in the United States without problems. Harrington himself had already been given permission to travel to Paris by plane on December 12, 1973.

Harrington and his American colleagues at *RBI/OPS* like Bert Pierce (aka Billy Mullis) apparently gave support to one another for the purpose of strengthening, or ameliorating, their position against the *Stasi*. Consequently, in July 1963 Harrington informed Billy Mullis that the latter was under observation from an American car. This was partly confirmed by one of their colleagues. Mullis reported this to the *Stasi*. The examination made by the section responsible for keeping Allied vehicles under surveillance in East Berlin, however, revealed that the *Stasi* did not give credence to this "event." With an eye on the work he and Harrington were performing for the secret *OPS*, Mullis also made it known to the *Stasi* that American citizens doing propaganda work against the United States Army could incur the death penalty. And Harrington, on his part, let the *Stasi* know that he had lived in the United States under the threat of being eliminated, and that the Central Intelligence Agency (CIA) had repeatedly made attempts to hire him for spying.

As a foreigner living and working in the GDR, Harrington was kept under close surveillance by the *Stasi*. Thus his mail from, or to, citizens of the GDR and correspondents of "non-socialist foreign countries" was regularly controlled, and his departures from, and reentries into, the GDR through frontier posts controlled by GDR officials were duly noted.[15] In a summary report dated October 1968 Harrington was evaluated as follows: "Harrington has clear political views concerning the struggle of colored citizens of the USA for equality. He expresses this in his works."

In addition, Harrington was surrounded by several *Informelle Mitarbeiter* (*IM*) ("voluntary collaborators"), whose task it was to report to the *Stasi* on his activities and the statements made by him to others. For a while a woman close to Harrington at the *RBI* was used as an informant by the *Stasi*. However, the *Stasi* had discontinued using her long since "because of her apparent lack of cooperation." The same was true for Billy Mullis alias *"Bert Pierce."* He had, as was customary, signed a *Schweiger Verpflichtung* (enlistment and promise of secrecy) on November 2, 1961, concerning his collaboration with the *Stasi*. This was shortly before he could have possibly met Harrington for the first time. However, he was discharged soon afterward. In the following years, he repeatedly avoided another *Verpflichtung* (obligation) by pointing out that this would be an impediment to his regular work at *RBI*. However, in 1968 he became active for the *Stasi* again.

Harrington's association with Jewish leftists and foreign artists appears to be of interest to the informants and possibly to their *Stasi* superiors. It became apparent that Harrington's international views may not have been totally congruent with those of the GDR. *"Fatima,"* aka Christa Friedmann, née Roßberg, whose main field of observation was *RBI/OPS*, also reported on Harrington. She was an editor serving in the "Latin American Department" freelancing for *OPS* at the same time. However, the two most important *IMs* at *Radio Berlin International* who spied on Harrington and his later wife, Dr. Helma Richter,[16] were *"Stefan"* and *"Becker."* The name of the former was a pseudonym for *RBI* editor Irene Runge,[17] who was said to be "close to Jewish circles." On one occasion she states about Harrington: "Ollie frequently keeps company with foreign artists. He has contacts in Jewish circles. His political world view is not clear." Horst Böhme, aka *"Becker,"* had joined *RBI* in April 1959, working first in the *Deutsche Nahostredaktion* (the "editorial office of the Near East"), and from 1962 until 1966, as director of the *Dänische Redaktion* ("Denmark editorial office"), and from March 1, 1966, on as deputy editor-in-chief.

Harrington's Circle of Friends and Acquaintances

Due to his activities just mentioned and being a dedicated caricaturist before and after his arrival in the GDR, Harrington had a circle of friends and acquaintances with international dimensions. Some of them held important positions in the publishing business. In East Berlin, Harrington was on friendly terms with other African Americans, for example, Billy Moore or Aubrey Pankey, a singer and lecturer at the *Hochschule für Musik* (Academy of Music). He lost his life in a traffic accident in 1971. It seems probable that Harrington also kept in touch with Pankey's wife, Kathryn, née Weatherly, for professional reasons. She had worked as an "interpreter, editor and translator" at *Seven Seas Publishers* of the publishing house *Volk und Welt* from 1959 on, before becoming *Leitende Lektorin* (director) of the former, on July 1, 1967. Pankey, like Harrington, was especially interested in "wars of liberation and emancipation movements of people of color in Africa," the United States, and elsewhere, and had several titles published on these themes.

A wider circle of Harrington's documented acquaintances included German Americans, people from English-speaking nations, and Germans with personal, or special, ties to the United States. Some of these had already been communists of great renown in the thirties. Helga Lohr, for example, was born in Berlin but had emigrated and become a United States citizen. She had also joined the Communist Party of the United States in 1936. In the GDR, she still enjoyed the high respect of visiting American communist delegates. The *Stasi* knew of her that she belonged to writer Stefan Heym's acquaintances and that she regularly informed him of visiting Americans, whom she tried to put in touch with him. Lohr and her husband, George Lohr-Ohlwerther—he had once been a New York CPUS district organizer before his death in 1964—were categorized as *Rechte Liberale* (right liberals) because, according to the *Stasi*, "they openly spoke out against the GDR and did not conceal their hostility to 'the Party'" (i.e., the Socialist Unity Party) and the "leadership of the state." Lohr saw "a very good friend" in Harrington with whom she could discuss her personal problems. As Harrington had not mastered the German language, Lohr assisted him as his interpreter, particularly when he had discussions with (Party) functionaries. Apparently she also left the GDR, perhaps late in 1968, after her marriage with Arthur Boyd (McCullough) in order to return to the United States. When Harrington was asked by an informer (*IM*) about Boyd-Lohr's departure to West Berlin on February 19, 1969, Harrington pointed out that she was a United States citizen and that she had probably returned to that country. After the *Stasi* put Harrington under close observation, the following opinion was expressed about him: "His personal development is not yet clear. He thinks that a return to the United States is not yet possible for him. But he feels somewhat lonely in the GDR and not quite happy."

The names of Oliver Harrington, Walter Kaufmann, and Stefan Heym are given in a report to the *Stasi* dated July 22, 1976, as examples for the numerous personal contacts cultivated by the Englishman John Peet as director of the press department of the East German PEN center. Nothing else appears in the *Stasi* files accessible to the writer regarding his relationship with Harrington.

Peet had served as director of the Reuter agency in West Berlin before he went to East Berlin under spectacular circumstances on June 11, 1950. From there he soon edited the *Democratic German Report* for many years. He also served as a correspondent for the (British communist) *Labour Monthly* and regularly provided weekly commentaries for English-language programs broadcast by *RBI*. According to his file, Peet bundled his journalistic activities in 1976 concentrating on the publication of press releases and the editing of books for the PEN center.

Stasi surveillance of Harrington and the British expatriate Walter Kaufmann stemmed from their suspicions regarding the party and their view of the GDR's policies toward intellectuals and culture as too restrictive and narrow. Walter Kaufmann,[18] who was born in Berlin, appears in the *Stasi* files as a former British officer who had decided to live in the GDR. In World War II, Kaufmann had volunteered for military service in the Australian foreign legion. In the GDR, he worked as a journalist and writer. He joined the PEN Center in 1975 and rose to become its secretary general in 1983. An informer expressed the following opinion on Kaufmann and Harrington: "O. Harrington and Walter Kaufmann are persons who to some extent have misgivings regarding the culture policy of the Party and the Government." These misgivings were viewed as possible disloyalty and evidence of a potential threat to the GDR. An IM reported to the Stasi Harrington's openly expressed opinion that "the artists and intelligentsia are the experimenters of the world of tomorrow who are at present hemmed in and prevented from working (effectively) by the cultural functionaries and their policies."

Harrington's Public Political Activities

In all his public appearances in the GDR, Harrington seems to have made his moves with circumspection, but also spoke more directly on racial issues. In one situation, for example, he assumed the role of a loyal visitor to the GDR, when in an informal meeting between artists and the editor-in-chief of the *Monat*, Hilde Eisler. She became an *agent provocateur*. Thus she claimed that concerning a controversy about the publication of two of Stefan Heyms's novels, *König David Bericht* and *Lassalle*, the important point to be made was that it was not Heym but the functionaries who did have to change their views. According to the *IM*, Harrington's artist friends, Elizabeth Shaw and her husband René Graetz, enthusiastically agreed to this, but Harrington did not: "Oliver Harrington did not share this view. He stated that people being dissatisfied in the GDR did not know how well they were off here." On another occasion, an *IM* reports about Harrington, who had participated in a discussion with the latter's artist friends: "In the period in question the US citizen Harrington remained a quiet but interested listener." Another *IM* noted: "He seems to be hiding behind obstacles of language in order not having to express his views promptly."

However, when it comes to Harrington's participation in discourses with national or international dimensions that he has deep feelings about, he does not keep silent or reserved. Thus, he unhesitatingly expresses his personal views regarding racism in the United States and the wars of liberation in Africa, or the cultural policies toward *Kulturschaffende und Intellektuelle* (cultural workers and intellectuals) in the GDR. Harrington and his friends and acquaintances employ a somewhat unusual strategy in order to bring their constructive criticism regarding the themes mentioned above to the attention of high-ranking *SED* party functionaries and national government officials. They intentionally use the *Stasi* apparatus as a means of communicating with them on sensitive issues. One can hardly fail to note that due to their otherwise politically weak position, their views might have gone unnoticed.

Thus, one of Harrington's *IMs* reports to the *Stasi* dated May 22, 1968, a list of critical points that Harrington had explicitly listed for him: like some of his friends Harrington criticizes, for example, that "the problems of Negroes in the United States" are frequently played down by the *Kommunikationsmittel* (the media of communication) of the GDR. In addition, he is also dissatisfied about "how little is known" by "large parts of the GDR or the German population" about "the actual situation [existing] in the United States." Particularly "the race problem" is not "correctly evaluated in the GDR," and the people in "the working class," regrettably, have not yet understood that "the race problem is also a class problem" and the cruelty and explosiveness of life in the ghettos is not completely understood. In Harrington's eyes, "[the use of] violence can only be a response to white violence." He fears that the assassination of Dr. Martin Luther King was "an attempt to incite Negroes to violence in order to be able to destroy Negroes and their organizations."

With regard to Africa and its liberation movements, Harrington and his friends do not hide their deep dissatisfaction with the *Zickzackkurs* (zigzag course) followed by GDR diplomats and those of other "socialist countries":

> Harrington held [the view] that developments in the African states will gradually move in a direction being the result of the volatile and unclear diplomacy of the SU [Soviet Union] and other socialist countries. This will be detrimental to the cause of socialism, and socialism will be thrown back for many years.

In order to make this point, Helga Lohr once refers to General (Joseph Desire) Mobutu of the Democratic Republic of the Congo as a negative example.

Whereas Mobutu is in her eyes "one of the murderers of [Patrice Emery] Lumumba," Mobutu is cited "in GDR press releases" as a "legitimate head of state" and even made "a folk hero." She concludes that "such a policy is not understood in Africa, and the African liberation movements do feel betrayed by the GDR and sold to the enemies of Africa." Harrington agrees to these views. But the *IM* also emphasizes that Harrington "is quite familiar with these African problems," even more so, "since, among other things, he has been working for newspapers of African liberation movements." The whole conversation took place at Harrington's home between Lohr, the "informal collaborator," and himself on March 12, 1968.

The same *IM* dutifully mentions in a report about another meeting at Harrington's home, this time only between Harrington and himself on January 18, 1969, that Harrington, too, cites Mobutu as a negative example and that he has come to the following conclusion: "Above everything else, the [diplomatic] position concerning the Congo and General Mobutu has highly tragic consequences. One does not believe any longer in the honesty of the socialist states." In an IM's report dated May 22, 1968, dealing with Harrington's own ideology, he is accused of *Linksradikalismus* (left radicalism):

> His ideology tends towards left radicalism with a tendency of regarding revolution as an export product and armed uprisings as a means of problem solving. (In doing this he never employs Chinese slogans but rather positions being close to developments in Cuba.) [He has] contacts with Cuban citizens in the GDR.

Harrington's view of a positive GDR policy in Africa, which involved more support of African nationalistic movements, was clearly at odds with a less aggressive more conservative GDR foreign policy toward Africa.

The strategy of using the *Stasi* and its apparatus for political purposes of one's own can be extrapolated from the *Stasi* files even more distinctly, when the national cultural policy of the GDR is at issue. Thus it has become a common belief among *Stasi* officials that Harrington, due to his isolated position influence of some of his acquaintances, frequently voices his prejudice and opposition regarding the cultural policy of the GDR:

> In the GDR Harrington feels left alone by the social forces and organisations. Perhaps on the basis of this, H. has developed a certain prejudice and opposition over against the cultural policy of the GDR. All this is reinforced by his acquaintance with [Helga] Lohr, [Ingeborg] Hunzinger, and [Wolf] Biermann.

An informal collaborator reported that sculptor Ingeborg Hunzinger organized a meeting at Harrington's apartment on February 16, 1968, in the course of which the sculptor René Graetz complains about the "deficient specialized and expert knowledge" of "party functionaries" in his conversations with them. With an eye on Harrington the *IM* wrote:

Harrington is a case in point. He is an example for [i.e., the result of] deficient psychological and agitational knowledge. Harrington makes a living for better or worse in our socialist state of the German nation. Nobody has had the idea of availing himself of what is offered politically and artistically.

Those present at the meeting, probably unaware of the informal collaborator's presence, urged the *IM* to help organize an exhibition of Harrington's works.

At a private meeting, Harrington himself told the same *IM* that originally, after his immigration, he was received with enthusiasm but that "this enthusiasm soon became routine like a smile which dies on the lips and becomes a mania." Several informers duly report similar views expressed by Harrington and his friends to *Stasi* officials. But as one of these reports dated May 22, 1968, reveals, Harrington also uses his own situation on that occasion in order to draw attention to the problematic situation existing for foreign artists living in the GDR: "Harrington is deeply shaken that (official) organs or organizations do not care at all about foreigners living in the GDR or in Berlin. He feels abandoned and sometimes betrayed. There exists no department where he could go with his problems."

The strategy employed here was apparently used at an earlier date with some success, as an informer reports, who participated in a celebration held in the famous East Berlin artists' club *Möwe*. The party followed the opening of Harrington's exhibition *Dark Laughter*, which was part of the official celebration of Paul Robeson's seventieth birthday in April 1968. It was attended by the Heyms, the Pankeys, Elisabeth Shaw, and Ingeborg Hunzinger among others.

The latter tells her friends on this occasion that the *Sektion Bildhauer* (section sculptors) had a controversy with Paul Verner[19] under full control after having reported him to Hans Rodenberg.[20] The complaints by the artists about their poor working conditions and against the heavy-handed cultural policy of Verner, a member of the GDR's *Volkskammer* (People's Chamber) and first secretary to the SED Berlin District, to Rodenberg, also a member of the *Volkskammer*, probably contributed to the closer scrutiny of Ollie Harrington by the government. Rodenberg had also served as the deputy chairman of the *Ausschuß für Kultur* (cultural committee) of the *Volkskammer* since 1965. Charges that Verner made all the decisions himself, including what is art and what is not, illustrated the hierarchal and antidemocratic process in GDR cultural life. Rodenberg was shocked and after having a protocol made out, he has invited Paul Verner for a conversation. The informer continues: "Paul Verner has become rather nervous and meek. Hunzinger regards all this as a victory over these dogmatists of the Party and as a point of departure for further steps to be taken by the artist comrades."

It was perhaps due to all these activities, that Harrington was watched more carefully by GDR officialdom. Thus Carl (Winter) of the U.S. communist *Daily World* in his letter to Harrington dated August 2, 1977, refers to the project of an exhibition to be organized by the "GDR Artists' Union." However, after Harrington's exhibition "Dark Laughter," which opened on April 22, 1968, on the occasion of Paul Robeson's seventieth birthday, only a few of Harrington's exhibitions were documented in the files. The artists and intellectuals around Harrington therefore repeatedly complained with some justification that his exhibition "Dark Laughter" had hardly had an echo in the GDR press.

A few Harrington exhibitions are documented in the *Stasi* files such as the *Kulturhaus Potsdam Hans Marchwitza* exhibition, one of the *Kulturhäuser* (houses of culture) of the GDR. Another exhibition was held at the *Kleine Kulturbundgallerie* of the *Kulturbund der Deutschen Demokratischen Republik*[21] (i.e., the section *Berlin-Treptow*), which lasted from May 7 until June 30, 1978. And under the date of April 20, 1978, the director of the *Staatliches Museum Greiz* belatedly asks Harrington for two or three of his "works" to be added to the exhibition "Good Luck or Bad Luck to Be a Child?" The *Kulturhaus* of a factory, the *VEB Nadelwerk Ichtershausen* appeared to have organized an exhibition for Harrington sometime in May or June 1979.

Harrington received international recognition as well. This can be concluded from a letter sent to him by Seymour Joseph of the United States. The communist *Daily World* dated March 17, 1977, congratulated Harrington on having been awarded a gold medal for caricatures shown at the exhibition "Satire in the Struggle for Peace" in Moscow.[22] In addition to this recognition, the district administration of the *Stasi* responsible for the frontier crossing point *"Friedrichstraße* station" reported on May 3, 1981, that Harrington upon his "exit" told them that he had just returned from a trip to Cuba. In his letter to Harrington dated October 1981, Mark Rogovin, curator of the Peace Museum of Chicago, asked for his permission to have his cartoons and materials, which are still kept at the *Daily Worker's* office in New York, shown at the exhibition "Daumier to Doonsbury: Caricatures and Cartoons on War and Peace" to open on March 14, 1982. Gayle McKinney and Donald M. Griffith of the *Fountainhead Tanz Theatre* in West Berlin tried to get Harrington interested in the "Black Cultural Festival" planned for the period of March 3 until March 23, 1986. His works, ideas, and to a limited extent, Harrington, himself, traveled internationally despite the obstacles.

During his stay in the GDR Harrington's transatlantic discourses mainly consisted of close foreign contacts he kept with leading members of the communist parties of the United States, Great Britain, and most probably France, as well as so-called progressive people in these countries. Reciprocal visits and mutual support were given regarding private matters as well as public political activities. Thus one informer mentions in his report on Harrington's wife that "on the occasion of delegates of the CPUS visiting in the GDR there are always visits to Harrington's home." These visits would hardly have been possible had these delegates not considered the artist as being one of their own.[23]

As Harrington himself points out in one of his essays,[24] he counts among his friends of long standing the African American CPUS members Henry Winston and Jim (James E.) Jackson, as well as John Pittman, who was later to become editor-in-chief of the communist *Daily World* published in New York City. Harrington, who had joined its editorial staff from 1968 on, regularly sent two cartoons per week from West Berlin. John Pittman invited him to New York in 1972:

Harrington is received by the African American administrative director Dorothy Robinson at Kennedy Airport. Soon afterward, he is met by his friends Henry Winston, James E. Jackson, and John Pittman. Later on Harrington is sent to Chicago in order to give support to Ish Flory, the African American Communist Party candidate for governor in Illinois. In September 1986, Harrington received an invitation from the Pittman family for the celebration of John Pittman's eightieth birthday in an East Berlin restaurant.

The American communist connection to Harrington is further evidenced by another good friend, Charlene Mitchell of the National Alliance against Racist and Political Repression in New York City. In the United States presidential election of 1968, she was the first African American woman to run for president of the United States on a ticket of the CPUSA.[25] Mitchell asks Harrington for a poster to be used by her society in her personal letter dated August 31, 1977. Harrington continued his contacts with CPUS publishing organs into the 1980s, which continued to publish his works. John Pittman's wife, Margrit, also asked the artist, in her letter of February 1981, for a number of his graphics to be published in the *Daily World*. Harrington gave his okay in a cable sent by him on February 23, 1981, to Mary Moskowitz of the National Committee of the CPUS. On the same day, he cabled Brenda Steele of the periodical *Political Affairs*, in which he promises to submit his review of a Richard Wright biography before long.[26] On August 16, 1981, John Pittman wrote Harrington a letter in which he suggested that the latter ought to encourage Mike Zagarell, the national youth director of the CPUS and editor of the *Daily World*, and J. J. Johnson, editor of *Political Affairs*, to keep in touch with him permanently.

Harrington's contacts with *Daily World* communists were not always positive and sometimes involved the kind of stylistic and ideological micromanagement associated with GDR officials. His contributions to the *Daily World* were checked by cultural editor Adelaide Bean and one "Winnie," perhaps Carl Winter, as indicated in an October 17, 1977, letter. Harrington is subjected to tough criticism by Seymour Joseph in a March 17, 1977, letter:

> Frequently the victims in your cartoons are too helpless. And to accentuate that helplessness you often draw them as being emaciated. Some victims of colonialism and imperialism are, indeed emaciated from malnourishment. And there are times when such rendering is appropriate. But we [the editorial board] feel you ought to keep under tighter reign the metaphor of physical deformity, and come out more with the other aspect of victimization: resistance!

Joseph later continues this line of criticism suggesting the need for a more heroic depiction of the oppressed resisting repression: "You succeeded in your Chile poster, and you often succeed in your cartoons. But occasionally your cartoons convey defeat and depression." And with regard to Harrington's captions he added: "As for the captions, the main problem is wordiness and occasionally corniness." Harrington complained about this to James E. Jackson, when the latter visited him in (East) Berlin. Soon afterward, Joseph was pressured by Carl Winter to send a written apology to Harrington, which he did on June 29, 1977.

The recognition accorded Oliver Harrington by important officials of the Communist Party in America is evident in the invitation extended to him to by Margrit (Pittman) to meet the rising star of the Communist Party, Angela Davis. The African American Angela Davis paid an official visit to the GDR as a member of the Central Committee of the CPUS from September 10 until September 14, 1972. On orders from Erich Mielke, national minister for security of the state, a special *Stasi* staff is created to ensure her personal safety. In a file on Harrington containing papers dated between December 1978 and May 1979, there is the German text of a cable sent by Margrit (Pittman) to Harrington: "Can you come on Thursday in order to meet Angela? Please call, if possible—Margrit." It seems probable therefore that both women were in (East) Berlin at that time.

On several occasions, members of foreign communist parties, like the American and French parties, tried to give support to Harrington in his attempts to emancipate himself from, or gaining more leeway under, the *SED* regime of the GDR. Thus, as was already mentioned, an offer was extended to him by the Communist Party of France (CPF) to direct one of their publishing houses. James E. Jackson, an African American member of the National Committee of the CPUS in those days, contacted the Central Committee of the Socialist Unity Party in order to have Harrington accredited as a foreign correspondent of the *Daily World* in (East) Berlin, which would open up travel and artistic options for him.

The GDR government complied with this request, however, by imposing certain restrictions on Harrington at the same time. Thus he was again not allowed, as repeatedly requested by him, to "import written products from West Berlin into the capital of the GDR." In addition, as he had now become a foreign correspondent, he is put "under permanent observation at all border crossings." On the other hand, Harrington is given "an exit and entry visa being valid for multiple uses, which from now on is valid for half a year instead of three months as before." He is also given a so-called *Grenzempfehlung* (i.e., a special written recommendation to be used at border crossings). On his previous *Vierteljahresvisum* (quarterly visa), Harrington would go to West Berlin three times per week in order to ship his caricatures to the U.S. communist *Daily World* from there. For the GDR, Harrington's increased international recognition added to their propaganda campaign, but it also required continued monitoring, intelligence, and surveillance.

Conclusion

The research for this essay was based on materials gathered by informers who voluntarily spied on their friends, acquaintances, or colleagues, even if one bears in mind that a few of them held a protective hand over their *Zielobjekte* (subjects of observation). Next these materials were analyzed and interpreted by officers of the *Stasi*. For these reasons, Harrington and his friends and acquaintances are viewed through several distorted lenses.

Which image of Harrington comes across despite these drawbacks? That he was a dedicated African American Communist with an independent mind of his own throughout his lifetime. That he was a loyal foreign visitor to the GDR, but one who kept his eyes wide open on political conditions there and in other "socialist countries." That Harrington, together with his artist friends and acquaintances, tried to help improve the working and living conditions of "cultural workers and intellectuals" in the GDR. They did this by making their own constructive criticism on a number of issues important to them known to high-ranking government officials and *SED* party functionaries by availing themselves of the *Stasi* apparatus.

That from the relatively privileged position he had built for himself in East Berlin, he used his caricatures and writings to fight against racism and worldwide colonialism, in particular in the United States and South Africa.

But one ought to bear in mind as well that Harrington lived in the GDR in a period which a person close to him characterized to this writer as having been *schmuddelige Zeiten* (murky times). Despite that, Oliver Wendell Harrington, called Ollie Harrington, remains an important African American figure in the WW II and postwar periods: He had an impact well beyond white and African American communist circles in the United States, and several European and African countries. I hope that a book-length biography based on his career as a political activist, journalist, and caricaturist will be written one of these days.

Notes

1. Cf. Constance Webb, *Richard Wright* (New York: G. P. Putnam's Sons, 1968), 376 and note 4, 397–99; cf. also Ollie Harrington, "The Last Days of Richard Wright," *Ebony* (Chicago) (February 1961): 83–86, 88, 90, 92–94; "The Last Laugh," *Ebony* (Chicago) (February 1996): 122.

2. Ollie Harrington, "Why I Left America," in Oliver W. Harrington, *Why I Left America and Other Essays* (Jackson: University Press of Mississippi, 1993), 96f.

3. Ollie Harrington, "Look Homeward Baby," in *A Freedomways Reader*, ed. Ernest Kaiser (New York: International Publishers, 1977), 108.

4. "The Last Laugh," *Ebony* (Chicago) (February 1996): 122+.

5. Cf. Ernst Fischer, *Kunst und Koexistenz* (Hamburg: Rowohlt paperback, 1966), e.g. 70ff.

6. The government and the Socialist Unity Party of the GDR gradually enforced this dogma from the mid-1950s on in following the example of the Soviet Union. Cf. Hermann Weber, *DDR: Grundriss der Geschichte 1945–1990* (Hannover: Fackelträger-Verlag, 1976), 70.

7. Harrington, "Why I Left America," 108, 109.

8. This national committee supervised the radio personnel and the public and secret programs produced by them.

9. He did this for the first time during an authorized holiday from October 5 until 31, 1962, in Copenhagen in October 1962.

10. Ollie Harrington, "Look Homeward Baby," *Freedomways* 13 (1973): 138.

11. Cf. Walter White, *A Man Called White: The Autobiography of Walter White* (New York: Viking Press, 1948), 255ff.

12. M. Thomas Inge, ed., *Dark Laughter: The Satiric Art of Oliver W. Harrington* (Jackson: University Press of Mississippi, 1993), xvii, xxii, xxxii. For more general information on "Negro war correspondents," please cf. Ulysses Lee, *The Employment of Negro Troops*. United States Army in World War II, Special Studies (Washington, DC: Office of the Chief of Military History, 1966), 385.

13. Harrington, "Why I Left America," 101. Chester Himes, *The Quality of Hurt* (= *The Autobiography of Chester Himes*, vol. I) (Garden City, NY: Doubleday & Company, 1972), 178.

14. The letters *OPS* stood for "outpost station." (Thanks to Victor Grossman.) This program was kept so secret that even members of the *Stasi* wanted to learn more about it.

15. Harrington apparently did not use Checkpoint Charly as he could have done being an American citizen.

16. She first worked at the Department International Relations, moved on to the *Lateinamerikaabteilung/Portugiesisch* (around 1964/65) becoming the *Redaktionsleiter* ("director") of the *Südamerikanische Abteilung* ("South America Department") in 1970.

17. Barth et al., eds., 621.

18. Barth et al., eds., 358.

19. Barth et al., eds., 755.

20. Barth et al., eds., 608.

21. The *Kulturbund* was the central cultural organization of the GDR and was founded in July 1945. Cf. Bundesministerium für gesamtdeutsche Fragen, ed., *SBZ von A bis Z: Ein Taschen—und Nachschlagebuch über die sowjetische Besatzungs-Zone Deutschlands*, 6th rev. and enl. ed. (Bonn: Deutscher Bundes-Verlag, 1960), 225f.

22. Ollie Harrington, "Look Homeward Baby," in *A Freedomways Reader*, ed. Ernest Kaiser (New York: International Publishers, 1977), 103. Harrington writes in his essay that he once spent two and a half months in the USSR upon the invitation of the satirical magazine *Krokodil.*

23. In Harrington's files there are several entries indicating that he was a member of the Communist Party of the United States.

24. Ollie Harrington, "Look Homeward Baby," 104f., 108. International Publishers was owned by the CPUS.

25. Together with other African Americans, she was purged from the national committee of the party sometime before 1992 by Gus Hall.

26. Harrington reviewed Addison Gayle, *Ordeal of a Native Son* (Garden City, NY: Anchor Press, 1980), for *Political Affairs* June 1981, 18–22.

Works Cited

Die Bundesbeauftragte für die Unterlagen des Staatssicherheitsdienstes der ehemaligen DDR, Otto-Braun-Str. 70/72, Berlin-Mitte: MfS AIM 11143/ 62, MfS AP 779/64, MfS 6671/73, MfS AIM 15145/89, MfS HAXX 9520;MfS AP 56834/92, MfS HA II/13 843; MfS BdL/Dok 1497, MfS AP 55217/92, MfS A OPK 13243/91; ZAIG 9959, HAXX 10183; AS 104/86, AKK 2410/79, AP 624/92, AP 6668/73, AIM 7170/61 P/2, AIM 7170/61 P/3, AIM 7170/61 P/1; MfS AIM 15351/69 P 1, P 2, A I, A2, A 3, A IV, A V; HAXX/AKG VSH, MFS AP 1355/80, MfS AP 7973/68, MfS AIM 15787/89 665l/1; MfS AOP 17752/62, MfS AP 16817/78, MfS HA II/13 834, MfS HA II/13 1118, MfS AIM 8331/91, MfS Teilablage 126/80; MfS AIM 11422/85, MfS AP 4373/92, MfS AP 55229/92, MfS AP 14111/64, MfS AIM 2096/67, MfS HAV/3679, MfS HAII/13ZMA0318;MfS AIM 11422/85, MfS

AP 4373/92, MfS AP 55229/92, MfS AP 14111/64, MfS AIM 2096/67, MfS HAV/3679, MfS HA II/13ZMA0318;MfS AP 2771/84, MfS AIM 15382/85, MfS A 126/80.

Cole, Lester. *Hollywood Red.* Paolo Alto, CA: Ramparts Press, 1981.

Fischer, Ernst. *Kunst und Koexistenz.* paperback edition. Hamburg: Rowohlt 1966.

Grossman, Victor (Stephen Wechsler). *Crossing the River.* Amherst: University of Massachusetts Press, 2003.

Harrington, Oliver W. (Ollie). "The Last Days of Richard Wright." *Ebony* 16 (February 1961): 83+.

———. "Look Homeward Baby." *Freedomways*, 3rd quarter, 1973, 135–211. Repr. in *A Freedomways Reader*, ed. Ernest Kaiser, 94–112. New York: International Publishers, 1977.

———. "Rev. of *Ordeal of a Native Son by Addison Gayle.*" Garden City, NY: Anchor Press, 1980. *Political Affairs*, June 1981, 18–22.

———. "The Last Days of Richard Wright." *Ebony* (February 1961): 83–86, 88, 90, 92–94.

———. "Why I Left America." *Why I Left America and Other Essays.* Jackson: University Press of Mississippi, 1993.

Das Haus in der Französischen Straße. Vierzig Jahre Aufbau-Verlag. Ein Almanach. Berlin and Weimar: Aufbau-Verlag 1985.

Heym, Stefan. *Nachruf.* 3rd printing. München: C. Bertelsmann Verlag, 1988.

Hicks, Granville. *John Reed: The Making of a Revolutionary.* New York: Macmillan, 1936.

Himes, Chester. *The Quality of Hurt.* (= *The Autobiography of Chester Himes*, vol. I). Garden City, NY: Doubleday & Company, 1972.

Inge, M. Thomas, ed. *Dark Laughter: The Satiric Art of Oliver W. Harrington.* Jackson: University Press of Mississippi, 1993.

"The Last Laugh." *Ebony* 51, no. 4 (February 1996): 122+.

Lee, Ulysses. *The Employment of Negro Troops.* United States Army in World War II, Special Studies. Washington, DC: Office of the Chief of Military History, 1966.

Saunders, Frances S. *The Cultural Cold War.* New York: New York Press, 1999.

SBZ von A bis Z. Ein Taschen—und Nachschlagebuch über die sowjetische Besatzungs-Zone Deutschlands, ed. Bundesministerium für gesamtdeutsche Fragen, 6th revised and enlarged edition. Bonn: Deutscher Bundes-Verlag, 1960.

Webb, Constance. *Richard Wright.* New York: G. P. Putnam's Sons, 1968.

Weber, Hermann. *DDR.* Grundriss der Geschichte 1945–1990. Hannover: Fackelträger-Verlag, 1976.

Wer war Wer in der DDR, ed. Barth, Berndt-Rainer, Helmut Müller-Enbergs, and Jan Wielgohs, enl. ed. Frankfurt/M: Fischer Taschenbuchverlag, 1996.

White, Walter. *A Man Called White: The Autobiography of Walter White.* New York: Viking Press, 1948.

Exploding Hitler and Americanizing Germany

Occupying "Black" Bodies and Postwar Desire

DAMANI PARTRIDGE

Through an analysis of the figure of the "African American" GI in film, in popular culture, and in the daily life of post–World War II Germany this article explores the ways in which the presence of these occupying "black" bodies reconfigure social imaginations of "blackness," America, and processes of Americanization. It examines the shift from an era in which Billy Holiday identified black bodies as strange fruit swinging from southern trees to an era in which black bodies become a new way in which America can be accessed and Germany will be occupied. In the post–World War II era, one sees a critical movement from international outrage, as in the response to the French African occupation, toward much more open desire.

In her account, Tina Campt emphasizes the widespread reaction to the French African troops and their post–World War I occupation:

> As a Leipzig paper noted in a 26 May 1921 article titled, "Die farbigen Truppen im Rheinland" [The Colored Troops in the Rhineland]:
> What offends European sensibility in the use of Black troops is not their blackness but rather the fact that savages are being used to oversee a cultured people. Whether these savages are totally black or dark brown or yellow makes no difference. The prestige of the European culture is in danger. That is what is at stake. And precisely those peoples, those such as England and France that are dependent upon the dominance they exercise over colored peoples, should consider that with the degradation of Germany in the eyes of the colored, they degrade the white race and with this endanger their own prestige. (2004, 52–53)

In the post–World War II context, while there were also critiques of American consumerism versus German culture, through Hollywood and American music, Germans had, already in the Weimar era, been prepared for the entrance and even occupation by Americans. Along these lines, American blacks were not as "savage" or unfamiliar in the minds and representations available to everyday Germans. Germans openly desired and consumed "their culture." With the

American occupation, unlike the French one, the Americans also brought ideas (if not practices) of racial equality, candy, cigarettes, other consumer goods, and the Marshall Plan.

This historical context alongside my own contemporary observations has led me to examine the ramifications of having an "African American" occupier in post–World War II Germany, and further, how the figure of the black American soldier allows German access to America and American capital, particularly for white German women, but also for African and other Germans. What does the presence of the black body in postwar Germany do to conceptions of American-ness and to perceptions of "democracy?" If "Americanization" becomes learning to love or at least learning to perform black American masculinity, then how does this position complicate the subjectification of black Americans in Germany and in the United States? What does it mean for the African American soldier to be the image of accessibility and social mobility? What does he—the "foreign"/"black" subject in Germany—gain from this encounter? What does she—the German nation and the implicit normative subject—gain? (While this paper begins by assuming occupation as a gendered experience, its gendering will also be problematized below.)

As noted elsewhere (Partridge 2003):

After a screening of the film *Fremd Gehen. Gespräche mit meiner Freundin.*² at the February 2000 Berlin Film Festival, a pseudo documentary film about a German woman who is writing her dissertation while sleeping with a series of African-American men she meets at a US military base in West Germany, the audience breaks into a heated discussion:

GERMAN WOMAN: "There was nothing in the film that one couldn't say in ten minutes."

ANOTHER GERMAN WOMAN: "Black men are sex machines . . ."

YET ANOTHER GERMAN WOMAN: "[This is] racist and sexist. . . . [These are] discourses that should be over . . ."

(A man from Frankfurt speaks about the "Plantation Club," a former military club.) "My daughter told me, (switches to English) 'Black guys fuck better than whites.' (Back to German . . .) I was jealous."

FILM PRODUCER: "The woman was a Casanova. Normally when women sleep with lots of men, they're seen as being loose."

MODERATOR: "When I was 16, I was really intrigued by the army base . . . I also did it. I slept with a Black soldier. But I never talked about it. This film was emancipatory for me."

Of course this "emancipation" relies on occupying black bodies in a double sense—that is, as occupying foreign troupes, and simultaneously occupying the broader social imagination. The emancipation prefigures the ways in which the appropriation and use of African American bodily forms and performances will be necessary for recognition within Germany. Furthermore, the breadth of this sentiment is confirmed by an ethnographic investigation into citizenship and processes of racialization over the past nine years, in which I regularly visited dance clubs in which white German women go to meet black men and vice versa, while also conducting a range of semi-structured open-ended interviews with a broad cross-section of black men and white German women who have been involved in relationships with each other.

In 1996, after going to the group's meeting and conducting several interviews with members of *Eltern schwarze Kinder* (Mothers of Black Children)—a group in Berlin that consisted almost exclusively of white German mothers of black German children, I arranged for a follow-up group interview at one of the member's apartments. I began by asking them how they met their children's fathers, which led to an extended discussion about West German *Diskos* in the 1970s:

ANNA: I purposefully went to a *Disko* where they play Black music, where Black people come . . . At the time, it was a *Disko* where there were primarily Black Americans. There weren't so many Africans . . . only a few. It was fun. I liked the music. I liked their way of doing things . . . I liked the way they danced. And so, it was fun for me . . . First of all, it was someone very interesting. It was new for me. It was brilliant. I enjoyed it.

DAMANI (Interviewer): You enjoyed that fact that you were in love?

ANNA: No, that I . . . mmm . . . mmm . . . was in love with an African man. This was a completely new experience for me.

The conversation turned into one in which the four mothers completed one another's sentences, trying to articulate a broader moment and feeling, and ultimately suggesting the extensiveness of the types of feelings and experiences they described. The pervasiveness of this experience is further confirmed by my own observations and the historical shifts underway from the Weimar era through the post–World War II Americanized cultural explosion made possible by youth desire, Hollywood, jazz, and American occupation—with an extensive period of intervening Nazi repression. It contrasts sharply with what they described as the boringness and inactivity of German men.

MARIA (interrupting the discussion with Anna): . . . Can I add something to that? Do you know how it used to be? . . . I don't know when you met your husband [Anna]. I met mine . . . so, I'm talking about the time at the end of the 70s, 78/79 or 75. (Another woman speaks over her as she talks, interrupting with dates.) You know . . . yes . . . it was definitely sometime in the 70s.

ANNA: For me, it was in 73, exactly.

MARIA: And, and, ummm . . . When German *Diskotheken* in comparison were so that ummm . . . one was just left there sitting, you know, because no one came and asked you to dance. It was like that . . . either you know someone who you could eventually ask, or something, but Germans didn't just simply go and dance. And when you went to these *Diskotheken*, then you could be sure that you would just be waiting around the whole evening and then go home. That was it, you know? So, it was . . . it . . . I don't know . . . the way of living was different [in the Black *Diskotheken*].

The point here is not whether black men really produce a different feeling in the clubs they frequent, but the perception of the white German women who frequent these clubs, as well as the broader social imaginary beyond the clubs.

At the other side of Nazi-ism and "America as the enemy" are the willingness and the desire for America through black bodies. In the post–World War II moment, there seems to be a critical shift inasmuch as the occupying black soldier is now desired on a scale to which no one would have previously imagined, at least inasmuch as this desire is expressed openly and in public. The desire itself is part of a process of consumption and learning to consume, of rejecting the old nation, in search of something or someone new (i.e., the black GI as opposed to *Der Führer*).

In the life of filmmaker Leni Riefenstahl (see *The Wonderful Horrible Life of Leni Riefenstahl* 1995), one sees this shift as one that is emblematic of national desire through a nationally projected visual move from her emphasis on the Führer's body to her emphasis on Jessie Owens's, from *Triumph des Willens* (*Triumph of the Will* (a Riefenstahl film about Hitler and the Nazi Party)) to *Olympia* (a Riefenstahl documentary on the 1936 Berlin Olympics), from the idealized *Arian* body to Leni Riefenstahl's later fascination with the Nuba. Also in the World War II arena, Germans experience not only the defeat of their army, but the defeat of Max Schmeling by the African American boxer Joe Louis. Again, one should note the presence of the black GI and the subsequent social transformations experienced as a result of his occupation.

While other authors have pointed to the presence of African American GIs in terms of troubling race and gender norms (see Fehrenbach 2000; Höhn 2002; Poiger 2000), too little has been made of the critical nature of this occupation (both mentally and physically) to processes of Americanization. I understand Americanization here in terms of the particular modes of consumption, desire, and "democracy" that make capitalism viable in the form that one finds (and that is increasingly emerging) in contemporary Germany. Americanization is not simply abstract or ideological, but also includes the success and dominance of Hollywood (see Fehrenbach 1995), the emergence of jazz, rock and roll (see

Poiger 2000)—eventually called "black music"—and ultimately the movement toward "racial tolerance" and universal citizenship. While I am critical of the forms in which the latter two concepts get practiced (i.e., tolerance as opposed to respect, and the ways in which universal citizenship often actually still means only nationally acceptable belonging), the emergence of these shifts have been critical to contemporary life in postwar and post-wall Germany.

In a book entitled *Destined to Witness: Growing up Black in Nazi Germany* (a bestseller in Germany), the child of a German nurse and a Liberian diplomat, Hans Jürgen Massaquoi, describes his experience of American, British, and French occupation in post–World War II Germany as follows:

> It was gratifying for me to note that my skin color, which for so long I had regarded as my major liability, had almost overnight turned into an asset. During my previous, mostly clandestine, encounters with German girls, I rarely could escape the feeling of being used as forbidden fruit—quite willingly, I admit, but used nevertheless. Now I had the new, ego bolstering experience of being pursued openly and unabashedly because, as far as the fräuleins of the immediate post war period were concerned, black was definitely in. (Massaquoi 1999, 288)

In this account, one sees a shift from "strange fruit" to "forbidden fruit" to open desire—mobility that the American victory and the presence of the African American soldier as part of an occupying military force make possible.

Later in the work, Massaquoi relates experiences of American racism to the fact of German defeat. This suggests a transformation of the global position of African American GIs, as fighting for the American nation and occupying the German one eventually leads African Americans to change their social position even in America. A re-articulation of their bodies in the occupying context leads to this transformation. Furthermore, the presence of these troops suggests the possibility of a new embodiment for Massaquoi and other African Americans. As Massaquoi notes:

> Regardless of how poorly black GIs were treated compared with their white counterparts, I realized that physically, they were incomparably better off than the vanquished Germans. Having discovered that my resemblance to a black American had decided advantages in war-torn Germany, I resolved to continue my efforts to learn how to sound and act like one. Being able to study black GIs close-up, in their own habitat, struck me as serendipitous. (op. cit., 319)

The actual presence of black GIs is critical to the success of Massaquoi's performance, particularly because of the transformative links between official policy and the sociocultural politics of daily life—expressed in the post–World War II German context simultaneously through processes of Americanization and the increasing desire for African American bodies.

Linking social policy to everyday life, historian Heide Fehrenbach notes that, "Some of the most fervent clashes over postwar reconstruction occurred in the putatively 'apolitical' realm of culture—where politics could run rampant precisely because hard-nosed economists and political scientists considered it a tertiary sphere" (Fehrenbach 1995, 5). Along these lines, one should note the unintended impact of the African American GI's presence in shaping and reshaping the modes through which Americanization would take place, as well as access to processes of Americanization more broadly. Here, policy is lived not just through abstract ideologies or even immaterial desire, but through the direct experience linked to and informed by ideology and desire. As Fehrenbach (1995) and Uta Poiger's (2000) work suggest, not just the presence of GIs is critical, but this presence linked to a history of the German infatuation with Hollywood, and the consequential impact of jazz in its dance hall, "high cultural," and rock and roll forms.

However, while Fehrenbach notes the importance of "cultural" productions in shaping the politics of daily life, this is an arena that remains unexhausted. She writes: "Given the fact of military occupation, territorial division, and the radically altered political geography of the Cold War world, this quest to define an 'acceptable' post-fascist identity went hand-in-hand with the larger project of *native elites* to reestablish national integrity (both territorial and cultural) and political sovereignty" (Fehrenbach 1995, 6, my emphasis). Expanding on this work, my project seeks to understand the everyday lives of a broader public.

In an admittedly heterosexual and perhaps even heterosexist matrix, through her interviews and historical investigation, Tamara Domentat (1998) argues that American GIs fulfilled a void produced in the arena of a defeated postwar German masculinity. Amidst rape (which Germans widely reported in their contacts with Soviet Troops (see Fehrenbach 2005)) and occupation, "In the wake of defeat and occupation, German men lost their status as protectors, providers, and even (or so it seemed for a short time) as procreators" (Fehrenbach 2005, 49). As Fehrenbach, assuming heterosexual desire, also notes, "According to the first postwar census of 1946, the ration of German men to women was 100:126; numbers in urban areas were even more skewed. Adding to contemporary alarm was the official estimate that among the reproductively active 'marriageable' age groups, there was a mere 1,000 men for 2,242 women" (op. cit., 48). Within this context, according to Höhn (2002), "African American" GIs were more accessible to the postwar German subjects than their "white" male counterparts. While she at times functionalizes the relationships with American GIs as the result of "weak women" in search of a better life, Domentat captures the feeling of daily life in the *Nachkriegszeit* (see, for example, 1998, 164). She argues: "Doch die Trennung der Sphären konnte nicht verhindern, daß sich an ihren Schnittstellen im Laufe der Zeit ungezählte Affären, Beziehungen und Ehen zwischen GIs und deutschen Frauen entwickelten, die das poltische Bekenntnis zu deutsch-amerikanischen Freundschaft mit privater Substanz unterfütterten" (op. cit., 9). (The separation of spheres could not prevent the fact that at the intersections, over time, there would develop untold numbers of affairs, relationships, and marriages between

GIs and German women that would substantiate the political pronouncement of German-American friendship with private substance.) One should note that these affairs and relationships not only took place in a literal sense, but that they also took shape and played out in a virtual realm, that is, in the realm of desire, as one sees in the consumption habits of the German postwar generation. In this sense, Domentat's distinction between public and private seems dubious, particularly if "public life" excludes relationships that grew out of dance club encounters, movie theater visits, music listening habits, and consumption practices more broadly.

As Hans Jürgen Massaquoi's memoir makes clear, and as a number of feminist and Foucaultian works suggest, the private and the public, the political and the sexual, are necessarily linked. In a scene in which Massaquoi and his companion are forced to leave the army barracks of a new African American GI friend, Massaquoi describes the transformation that he and his white German friend, who was also in the process of becoming African American, undergo:

We quickly grabbed our overnight bags, said so long to Donald [an "African American" GI the two befriend], then jumped on the waiting weapons carrier whose driver, a black first lieutenant, was impatiently checking his watch. Exceedingly handsome and meticulously dressed in officer's twill, he was the first black U.S. Army officer I had seen. His friendly smile gave no indication how much, if anything, he knew about our plight. It filled me with an extraordinarily sense of pride when I watched the white MP at the gate come to attention and salute the black officer as we were leaving the post . . . Our unexpected eviction from the army post had made us gun shy and seriously diminished our enthusiasm for passing ourselves off as Americans. So instead of honoring the waiting hall reserved for Allied personnel with our presence, as had been our habit, we went to the German waiting hall instead. Dilapidated and bereft of any amenities that hall was packed with weary German travelers with battered suitcases and knapsacks. Many were munching on homemade sandwiches that they must have brought along since there were no food vendors anywhere within sight. We were almost hungry enough to swallow our pride and ask a German to let us have a couple of sandwiches in exchange for some cigarettes. But instead, we light up ourselves to appease our groaning stomachs. We immediately became the target of envious, if not hateful, stares from people who obviously felt that affluent Americans had no business in "their" waiting hall.

They weren't the only ones who felt that way. Two black MPs in white helmets and white belts had entered the waiting hall and headed straight for us. "Can you read English?" one of the MPs accosted me with an air of sarcasm. When I didn't quite get what he was driving at, he repeated his question, "Can you read English?"

"Of course I can read English," I finally replied, more annoyed than frightened by his interrogation. After all, I hadn't done anything wrong— for a change.

"Then read that," he ordered while pointing a mean-looking nightstick toward a large sign on the wall. The sign read, OFF LIMITS TO ALL AL-LIED PERSONNEL.

Before I could follow my inclination and respond with a flippant "So what?" the MP good-naturedly told us to stop giving him and his buddy a hard time and to take our you-know-whats to the Allied waiting room on the other side of the station where we belonged. He said he couldn't under-stand why we wanted to stay in this "dump" and hang out with the Krauts.

Werner and I couldn't either, for that matter, and within minutes we were enjoying—quite illegally—the generous hospitality of Uncle Sam in the waiting hall's comfortable USO canteen. (op. cit., 320)

This passage represents one of a number of moments in Massaquoi's life story in which his African American performance is substantiated. Of course his brown skin aids in his "authentication," but it could not be confirmed without also con-firming the success of his English, a language that Massaquoi never learned in school. Furthermore, the presence and successful performance of Massaquoi's white German friend who is also becoming an African American GI is crucial to Massaquoi's story of transformation and Americanization. In all of these mo-ments, the wealth and desirability of African Americans also have implications for the success and speed of processes of Americanization.

In a later passage, Massaquoi writes:

It was late afternoon by the time Werner and I felt we had seen enough of Nuremberg and decided to return to the *Hauptbahnhof.* On our way, we ran into three black GIs, who wanted to know what we were doing in ci-vilian clothes. "We're merchant marines sightseeing in Bavaria," explained Werner, without seeming to arouse suspicion.

"You guys are welcome to come to a dance at our barracks tonight," one of the GIs offered.

We were in no particular hurry to get back to Hamburg, and sensing new adventure, we accepted the invitation.

The GIs were stationed in Nuremberg's former *SS Kaserne*, a complex of massive three-story brick barracks that not too long ago had housed a divi-sion of Hitler's military elite. Except for the missing swastika, which had been chiseled from the wreath in the claws of the giant stone eagle emblem above the entrance gate, the barracks seemed untouched by war.

Expecting to be asked to leave at any moment, Werner and I were on a constant alert for inquisitive MPs or other military officials who might object to our presence. But everyone treated us like long-lost brothers. The only hitch came when we were about to enter the auditorium for the dance and an officious soldier seated behind a table at the door stopped Werner to ask, "You sure you're colored?"

Without hesitating for even a split second, the blond and blue-eyed Werner indignantly replied, "What do you think?"

The soldier shrugged apologetically and let Werner pass.

The huge hall was jam-packed with hundreds of black GIs and their German dates. (op. cit., 323)

The reference to "black GIs and their German dates" suggests the relevance and importance of African American soldiers to processes of Americanization even if the same type of encounter is not possible (at least not at this point) in much (if not most) of the United States. This centrality of African American bodies as sites of access to America and processes of Americanization is also emphasized by Massaquoi's performance and the performance of his white German friend.

Finally, describing the general scene of Americanization, and postwar transformation through desire for the black soldier's American body, Massaquoi notes:

It was quite apparent from the choreographed-looking jitterbug acrobatics put on display by the fräuleins and their black GI partners that they had plenty of practice. Watching the rapturous expressions on the young women's perspiring faces as they "jived" to what the Nazis had always derided as *Negermusik*, I was sure that if the Fuehrer hadn't blown out his brains the mere sight of his cherished *Deutsche Mädchen* with the "apelike creatures" would have killed him. (op. cit., 323–24)

Here, as in other places, one sees the importance of pleasure as a vehicle for motivating consumption. One sees how American modes of pleasure and consumption were so central to postwar German culture. In many ways, the centrality of these media forms predicts Germany's future and even what became the untenability of "actually existing socialism" inasmuch as it (like Americanized capitalism) relied on the "right" to consume (see Verdery 1996) but could never quite meet the productive expectations of consumptive desire.

Uta Poiger puts Americanized consumption in a historical context and links its success to the willing participation of German youth. She notes: "While many U.S. government programs in the 1940s and 1950s sought to prove to Germans that the United States was a land of high culture, East and West German officials, like authorities in the Weimar Republic and the Third Reich, grew increasingly worried about the impact that American movies, jazz, and boogie-woogie had on German youth" (2000, 32). Here, a youthful desire for pleasure exceeds the possibilities of formal regulation. Moreover, pleasure and desire as forms of occupation mean that at some point, Americanization could proceed without the threat of the military presence; and yet, the military presence has been crucial to the accessibility of American, and particularly African American, bodies.

While Poiger, like others, gives a somewhat functionalist account of American GI/German relations—emphasizing official rhetoric as opposed to everyday encounters—it is clear from the scenes that Massaquoi describes and that persist in contemporary Germany (see above, and Partridge 2003) that pleasure and desire exceed function.[3] Poiger writes:

During the 1940s, many of the relationships between German women and
U.S. soldiers were based on a need for food, consumer goods, and protection. That is not to say that mutual affection could not play a role; certainly numerous relationships ended in marriage. But in the minds of many
Germans, the food or nylon stockings that German women received from
their American lovers, or the dances they danced with them, confirmed a
link that had a long history in German anti-Americanism: the link between
consumption and the oversexualization of women. And even more so than
in the interwar years, Germans now related these phenomena to the weak-
ness of German men. (2000, 36)

However, the success of jazz, rock and roll, and American cinema in their official
and unofficial articulations (including officially sanctioned jazz projects in postwar East and West Germany) that she observes at a number of other junctures
in her book, belie this observation, particularly when one takes into account the
types of social taboos one had to break in order to enter into these relationships,
particularly with African American soldiers. While American policy makers attempted to orchestrate the success and influence of American popular culture
in contemporary Germany (see Poiger 2000), it is clear that the success of the
German embrace is deeper and more genuine than policy alone can account
for, particularly given American policy makers' official distaste for relationships
between African American GIs and German women, and their refusal in most
cases, to sanction their attempts to marry (see Höhn 2002; Poiger 2000).

Exploring the types of dance scenes that Massaquoi describes above, in fiction film through the movement from the desire for Hitler to the desire for black
America, Rainer Werner Fassbinder makes *The Marriage of Maria Braun*, a film
that examines the life of a West German woman in the World War II and postwar periods.[4] In the very first shot of *Maria Braun*, the image of Adolf Hitler
that fills the screen explodes. It later becomes apparent that this explosion is
necessary to make room for the later entrance/imagination/body of the African
American soldier. While Maria, the main character, marries Hermann Braun (a
German soldier) in this first scene, the marriage—the union between the white
German woman and white German masculinity—is also troubled. In the ceremony, the objection to this union comes in the form of the American bomb that
forces the couple to dive for cover and eventually to be separated (because of the
war). Then, one sees how the administration of the state-sanctioned marriage
itself explodes as a close-up reveals the *Standesamt* (civil registry office) sign
being propelled to the ground and papers flying everywhere. Maria, determined
to complete the official state-sponsored ceremony (a determination that mirrors
the West German determination for national solidarity) asks as she finds one
paper on the ground: "Where should I sign?" In an off-tone, cries of a scream-
ing baby foreshadow the birth of a new and troubled nation, inalterably (as we
will learn) penetrated by various forms of Americanization. Within this context,
Maria learns not only to desire, but also to perform, moving from desire to "self-
sufficiency" and future explosions. In *The Marriage of Maria Braun*, Maria learns

new forms of consumption, new forms of desire, and the English language. She learns to become cosmopolitan through lessons administered by the African American soldier Bill.

Through the visual and aural language of this film, one begins to understand African American occupation in multiple senses. This includes the senses in which the black body becomes an occupying force, but also the sense in which the black body occupies the social imagination, and furthermore, the sense in which occupying the black body becomes a possible if not necessary mode through which Germans become Americanized and, by extension, modern (i.e., "rational" consumers in a "democratic" nation).

In one scene, the "African American" soldier Bill teaches Maria English. She repeats after him in a bout of seeming confusion before he eventually corrects her: "I am black and you are white." "No," he counters, "I am black and *you* are white." "I am white and you are black," she concludes. Here, it takes going through the "black" body to become "white" again. It takes occupying "black" bodies— that is, proceeding through a phase of national "inferiority," in order to find the new German nation.

In her book *GIs and Fräuleins: The German-American Encounter in 1950s West Germany*, Maria Höhn gives a historical context for how the relationship between Bill and Maria Braun might have been seen in the 1950s. She notes:

> Even more troubling [to conservative German commentators and officials] than the prostitutes were the many German women from respectable backgrounds who nonetheless associated with American GIs. Their Americanized demeanor and behavior evoked much consternation, and their willingness to live in common-law marriages with white and black American GIs marked them as sexual as well as racial transgressors. Conservatives reserved their greatest outrage, however, for their own charges. Instead of expressing outrage over the goings-on in their communities, the local population was busily figuring out how to participate in the American-induced boom. (2002, 10)

In her book, much of Höhn's focus centers on the presence of African American and white American GIs in the immediate postwar period and the outraged response of conservative commentators. She is also interested in the ways in which these relationships challenged American Jim Crow norms. However, her analysis often stays close to official debates, with less emphasis on the transformative power of unofficial desire.

Nevertheless, pointing toward the accessibility of black GIs, in comparison to white soldiers, Höhn suggests:

> Germans were stunned at how well the black soldiers treated them, but black soldiers were equally amazed that most Germans approached them with much more tolerance than did white American soldiers. In the aftermath of Germany's bitter defeat, many Germans preferred the black GIs

to the white soldiers, because black GIs were more generous with their food rations. Black GIs also did not approach the defeated Germans with the sort of arrogance that many of the white soldiers displayed. Because of the humiliation of their defeat, Germans also experienced a certain kinship with the black GIs, convinced that black GIs, just like themselves were treated as second-class citizens by white Americans.

The encounters of black GIs with Germans were so positive that the African American press in the United States repeatedly described the experience of the GIs in Germany to indict American racism at home. *Ebony*, for example, reported in 1946 with much surprise on how cordially most Germans treated blacks: "Strangely enough, here where Aryanism ruled supreme Negroes are finding more friendship, more respect and more equality than they would back home—either in Dixie or on Broadway." While providing wide selections of photos of interracial fraternization, *Ebony* concluded, "Many of the Negro GIs . . . find that democracy has more meaning on Wilhelmstrasse than on Beale Street in Memphis." (op. cit., 90–91)

Part of what Germans liked more must have also related to their desire for "palatable" black bodies as opposed to pure "African" ones, particularly when one considers the then recent success of Jesse Owens and Joe Louis in their very public defeats of Adolf Hitler and Max Schmeling (see also the historian Fatima El-Tayeb's work on the European-wide outrage over the presence of French troops of African descent in the *Rhineland* [El-Tayeb 2001] and Tina Campt's investigation in *Other Germans* [Campt 2004, also quoted above]).

What Höhn (2002) describes as a preference for black GIs is substantiated by the image and accessibility of Mr. Bill in *The Marriage of Maria Braun* compared to the official American all-white military establishment pictured in the form of the military tribunal that sentences Maria Braun's husband to prison after he takes the blame for her killing Mr. Bill when the husband finally returns from a Soviet war prison and finds his wife in a sexually explicit encounter. The introduction of a new kind of establishment also promoted scenes of accessibility, not just to African American music, but also to black bodies. In spite of the presence of underground jazz clubs in the Nazi era, "Another new kind of enterprise that suddenly appeared in the villages of both Kaiserslautern and Birkenfeld counties was the nightclub" (Höhn 2002, 111; see also Poiger 2000). The presence of nightclubs even in German villages next to American army bases represents a movement of clubs from the underground to the main stream, from the city to the rural enclave. Here, one finds a genealogy for what have become the clubs where African men now go to dance with German women and vice versa in the contemporary era. The stakes, however, have been transformed. In the 1950s, processes of Americanization get articulated through the need to fulfill American and be fulfilled by Americanized desire as part of the process of gaining access to economic capital and American bodies. The other side of this process relies on the ways in which Germans learn not only how to produce the products, but also how to consume. Furthermore, they begin to understand consumption not as a privilege, but as a right unequivocally associated with what they then, learning from Americans, call "freedom." A transformation of German gender norms and the significant desire of German youth are critical to this process (see Poiger 2000).

Along these lines, Höhn observes: "Young women also flocked to the garrison communities because they had read colorful descriptions in the national press of the never-ending dollar supply of the American GI. The descriptions of Baumholder as the 'El Dorado of West Germany' or as the 'Alaska on the Westwall' in the national press always stressed that this was 'the land where milk and honey flow, that is, where the $ and the DM roll'" (2002, 128). One should note the confluence of disdain and desire mobilized by the national press attention to relationships between GIs and German women, with a particular emphasis (according to Höhn) on relationships between black GIs and white German women. She goes on to note, "At a time of high unemployment, especially for women, many desperate souls responded to these enticing tales" (op. cit., 128). It seems both interesting and problematic, however, that Höhn refers to these women as "desperate," in the sense that she assumes the rhetoric of the conservative critics. Furthermore, as noted above, the emphasis on dollars and desperation could potentially lose sight of the critical importance of pleasure and desire in these encounters.

Höhn suggests later in her work: "Church-affiliated welfare workers worried incessantly that parents were not up to the task of protecting their young from the seductions of the dollar" (op. cit., 163). "In order to protect young German women from the GIs and their dollars, church-affiliated welfare workers also spun a tight web of surveillance around all those families considered at risk." In fact, it was "the nation" as a whole that was "at risk," and the nation as a whole (if one takes German unification into account) that succumbed. Again, one needs to move beyond the dollar as the only, or even primary, motivation for the ensuing "adventure." The imagination of a black threat becomes, in the post–World War II context, the articulation of a national desire. This is the story underlying Höhn's narrative of moral resistance from conservative Germans.

Policing the sexuality and desire of young white German women is not merely an afterthought or side effect of German conservatives guarding against a larger process of "Americanization"; to the contrary, protecting and determining sexual practices is central to national self-definition. In this sense, the success of processes of Americanization do not depend solely upon the desire for Coca-Cola or the desire to consume in toto, but more importantly upon how access is obtained—that is, through the bodies of black American GIs who are more accessible, more resisted, and thus more intriguing and more desired (due to the broader social belief in their increased sexual danger). In a number of places, Höhn notes the disproportionate attention the national media paid to relationships between African American GIs and white German women. In some sense, this attention both backfires and comes too late. The tabooization and attempts at social policing are restricted by the fact of occupation. The ensuing relationships are made possible by the types of "freedoms" that African American GIs would not be able to enjoy in the United States, but that become tenable in Germany as a result of their having fought in the war, the transportation of African American images to popular German media, and, according to Höhn, the American military's response to communist critiques of American racism. In Germany, America was more accountable to its claims of freedom than laws, social rules, and authorities allowed in the United States, who, in the 1950s, still enforced antimiscegenation and Jim Crow laws in a significant number of states.

Finally and critically, "Due to the occupation statute, German police officers could not conduct vice raids without the assistance of American military police (MPs). Unless accompanied by the MP, German law-enforcement officers could not check the identification of a German woman if she was in the company of an American GI" (op. cit., 183). Höhn adds, "The limits put on their authority was particularly abhorrent to German police officers if the woman was in the company of a black soldier" (ibid.). While this law was later changed to allow German authorities to at least police German women, it is significant in terms of the history of German authorities' inability to police the desire for the occupation of black bodies. Furthermore, one should note that the black-only bars next to post–World War II army barracks did not mirror their American equivalents in the sense that they weren't black only, but in fact bars with black men and white German women.

In many ways, this process is prefigured in the Weimar era success of jazz, a type of music, as Poiger (2000) notes, that is simultaneously associated with modernity, American *Negern* (Negroes/Niggers), and that exceeds the formal dimensions of what one understands today as a narrower art form. It included spirituals, instrumental music, and even rock and roll. As occupiers and victors, the presence of African American GIs in postwar Germany suggests a new legitimacy for a previously suppressed and repressed desire (particularly in the Nazi era, where jazz had to be Germanized in order to be legal [see Poiger 2000]). The presence of "real" African Americans in the German landscape suggests the possibility of "authentic" access, the fulfillment of a historically repressed/suppressed desire.

In writing about the relationship between American GIs and presumably white German women, the film historian Annette Brauerhoch writes about "'Fräuleins' [the German women who desire American GIs] as a representation of 'nation'" (2003, 1). If this is true, then, as I have argued, the nation is desiring black men.

In the film *Fremd Gehen* (Heldmann 1999—see above), Brauerhoch plays the contemporary white German woman who sleeps with a series of African American GIs on a U.S. Army base near Frankfurt in almost daily encounters with the black soldiers. She also wrote the script for this pseudo-autobiographical-documentary film. In the related academic piece, she notes: "Most of the accounts of this phenomenon of the 'Fräuleinswunder' have concentrated on a view from the outside, relegating the women under consideration to the status of objects of history" (2003, 1). Here, one should note the linguistic relationship between "Fräuleinswunder" and Wirtschaftswunder.[5] In other words, inasmuch as the occupation by African American soldiers is desired, Germany/she can have un-limited access to wealth and "liberation."

Along these lines, one should note the ways in which black GIs become objects in Brauerhoch's analysis, her film, and the broader national social imaginary. She argues in the related talk: "This paper will try to take their perspective as subjects who can be considered as foreigners in many aspects of the 'Americanization' of Germany" (ibid.). Brauerhoch refers to these as "foreign affairs," implicitly mak-ing a link between actions taken in bedrooms and the transformation of foreign policy. Noting links between conflicting forms of Americanization, she writes: "The Hollywood production code with its rule against representations of 'mis-cegenation' was in its main outlines copied by the guidelines for the German Voluntary Board of Censors (Freiwillige Selbstkontrolle was established in 1948)" (op. cit., 3). And yet, ironically, it is not antimiscegenation laws, but the act of desiring black bodies that becomes one of the only avenues through which many German women (and men) experience Americanization, and thus the possibil-ity of personal and social transformation. Brauerhoch continues: "In departing from norms of proper female behavior by actively pursuing sexuality, and lead-ing promiscuous lives without marriage, the Fräuleins established a form of fe-male subjectivity which was threatening to an emerging concept of a developing new national identity, in which gender roles served to re-stabilize the system" (op. cit., 4). To some extent, this claim is overstated, inasmuch as the entire na-tion embraces processes of Americanization. Here, German women who desire American GIs begin a public negotiation not only of their gender roles, but also of the nation and its Americanization. Brauerhoch refers to the "Fräuleins" as "protofeminist rebels against normative gender-restrictions and Nazi induced racial propaganda" (op. cit., 1). In many ways, this is the type of resistance that could be predicted inasmuch as that which is most forbidden is often that which is also most acutely desired. Curiosity is aroused by the power of repeated denial. However, black American male occupation changes the significance and mean-ing of this desire.

Conclusion

In this paper, I have pointed to some of the multiple ways in which the figure of the black American soldier and the fact of his occupation, both his militarized presence in Germany and his appropriation through performance and desire, have become critical to postwar German transformation and processes of Amer-icanization. The success and the desire to occupy and be occupied, to love one's occupation, are predicated on his presence, as they are also predicated on the presence/absence of German women, German men, African American women, and those Tina Campt refers to as "Other Germans" (see Campt 2004), among others.

And yet, after the fall of the Wall, as African American GI numbers diminish, there is again an increased tension between national self-determination and the desire for Americanization. The desire, however, is no longer facilitated by the actual presence of African American bodies in large numbers, but by the persistence of an imagination linked to the ever-increasing consumptive possibilities.

Notes

1. This work was inspired by the Berkeley-Tübingen-Wien-Harvard working group call for an interdisciplinary conference on Americanization in 2003 in Tübingen, Germany. In it, I link what are perceived as strictly political economic trends (i.e., Fordism, Taylorism, rationalization, and industrialization) to everyday practices, the fact of desire, and the critical importance of the presence of black bodies as the transporters of this process. In addition to the members of this group, I would like to thank members of the Turkish-German Studies Group at the University of Michigan, as well as participants and organizers of the conference "Crossovers: African Americans and Germany," at the Westfälische Wilhelms-Universität in Münster, Germany.

2. In German, *Fremd Gehen* is usually used to refer to having an affair when someone is already in a committed relationship (i.e., going astray). In this case, it is also used to refer to the literal meaning of "going foreign."

3. As Heide Fehrenbach finds: "In a survey conducted in the early 1950s, German social workers queried German women to determine why they become involved with black troops. (Tellingly, this question was not posed to women who fraternized with white troops.) On the basis of interviews with 552 women, social workers concluded that for 56 percent "material benefits were decisive": "For the women themselves, it was naturally a great inducement to satisfy their hunger with American canned foods, and, in addition, obtain tasty treats, cigarettes, silk stockings and money from their colored boyfriends." However, such incentives were not the only motivation, as social workers found. Of the remaining 44 percent of women polled, 27 percent responded that they had chosen African American lovers on the basis of affection or love, and 17 percent said they were motivated by sexual curiosity, carnal desire, or 'simply the wish not to be outdone by their friends who already had Negro boyfriends'"(65).

4. Even in the arena of consumer goods "canned food" is enhanced by desire that exceeds the function of eating to avoid hunger.

In my analysis, it is clear to me that fiction film is just as critical to daily life as other forms of sociocultural production and critique.

5. This is a term that refers to Germany's economic miracle after the Second World War. While a somewhat antiquated term, "Fräulein" refers an unmarried woman.

Works Cited

Brauerhoch, Annette. "Foreign Affairs"—"Fräuleins as Agents," Panel VI. Germanness and Gender. http://www.unc.edu/depts/europe/conferences/Germany_celeb9900/abstracts/brauerhoch_ annette.html (accessed April 4, 2003).

Campt, Tina. *Other Germans: Black Germans and the Politics of Race, Gender, and Memory in the Third Reich.* Ann Arbor: University of Michigan Press, 2004.

Domentat, Tamara. *"Hallo Fräulein": deutsche Frauen und amerikanische Soldaten.* Berlin: Aufbau-Verlag, 1998.

El-Tayeb, Fatima. *Schwarze Deutsche: der Diskurs um "Rasse" und nationale Identität 1890–1933.* Frankfurt: Campus, 2001.

Fassbinder, Rainer Werner. *The Marriage of Maria Braun.* (A co-production of Albatros Film-Michael Fengler/Trio Film-WDR.) Burbank, CA: RCA/Columbia Pictures Home Video, 1986.

Fehrenbach, Heide. *Race after Hitler: Black Occupation Children in Postwar Germany and America.* Princeton, NJ: Princeton University Press, 2005.

———. "Of German Mothers and '*Negermischlingskinder*': Race, Sex, and the Postwar Nation." In *The Miracle Years: A Cultural History of West Germany, 1949–1968,* ed. Hanna Schissler. Princeton, NJ: Princeton University Press, 2000.

———. *Cinema in Democratizing Germany: Reconstructing National Identity after Hitler.* Chapel Hill: University of North Carolina Press, 1995.

Heldmann, Eva. *Fremd Gehen. Gespräche mit meiner Freundin.* Deutschland, 1999.

Höhn, Maria. *GIs and Fräuleins: The German-American Encounter in 1950s West Germany.* Chapel Hill: University of North Carolina Press, 2002.

Massaquoi, Hans Jürgen. *Destined to Witness: Growing Up Black in Nazi Germany.* New York: William Morrow and Company, 1999.

Müller, Ray (director). *The Wonderful horrible life of Leni Riefenstahl* [video recording]. New York: Kino International Corp., 1995.

Partridge, Damani James. "Becoming Non-Citizens: Technologies of Exclusion and Exclusionary Incorporation after the Berlin Wall." Dissertation, University of California, Berkeley, Department of Anthropology, 2003.

Poiger, Ute. *Jazz, Rock, and Rebels: Cold War Politics and American Culture in a Divided Germany.* Berkeley and Los Angeles: University of California Press, 2000.

Verdery, Katherine. *What Was Socialism, and What Comes Next?* Princeton, NJ: Princeton University Press, 1996.

Reconstructing "America"

The Development of African American Studies in the Federal Republic of Germany

EVA BOESENBERG

In this article, I discuss the development of African American Studies in the Federal Republic of Germany since the 1950s. My contribution thus reflects a West German perspective; it is based primarily on the annals of the *German Association for American Studies* (*Deutsche Gesellschaft für Amerikastudien, DGfA*).[1] Although I will occasionally refer to parallel developments in the German Democratic Republic, this is not a history of African American Studies in East Germany. Other contributors to this volume such as Astrid Haas cover various aspects of East German scholars' inquiries into African American literature and culture. A comprehensive picture of African American Studies in Germany would require a synthesizing of their data with my own findings, which is beyond the scope of this chapter.

I will further concentrate on literary and cultural studies. Focusing primarily on research, I will identify several "generations" of scholars in African American Studies and their respective research agendas. In order to contextualize the developments in academia, my investigation requires at least a brief consideration of the political and cultural situation in which the respective scholarship was undertaken, the impact of U.S.-American financial support and international exchange programs, as well as the role of academic organizations such as the *DGfA* and the Collegium on African American Research or CAAR.

My chapter is divided into five sections. In the first section, "With a Little Help from Our Friends," I examine the emergence of African American Studies in connection with postwar cultural politics. Next, I discuss the maturation of African American Studies in the Federal Republic of Germany. It is followed by a consideration of the intersections between African American Studies and gender studies in German academic discourse since the 1980s. I subsequently analyze the increasing internationalization of African American Studies before offering some comments on current developments in the field.

"With a Little Help from Our Friends": The Foundational Phase of African American Studies in West Germany

American Studies in Germany are very much a product of the cold war, and African American Studies are no exception. Like American Studies generally, they have been informed by a continuing, if not always explicit engagement with German fascism. Although U.S.-American literature and history have been taught at German universities since the nineteenth century,[2] it was only after World War II that American Studies emerged as a distinct academic field in West Germany. The establishment of American Studies Centers in Frankfurt, Berlin, and Munich formed part of a larger movement, generously supported financially as well as logistically by the U.S. Government and its cultural institutions that resulted in the creation of American Studies institutes and chairs throughout much of Western Europe. Relatedly, national and international networks of scholars such as the *Deutsche Gesellschaft für Amerikastudien* and the European Association for American Studies (EAAS) were founded in 1953 and 1954, respectively.

As Jules Chametzky has convincingly argued, the postwar expansion of American Studies held a particular appeal for German scholars eager to reconnect with "the world's mainstream," to "negotiate the abyss" resulting from the years of fascism. In this respect, American Studies possessed a political, even "quasi-activist" character, a fact recognized by leading figures such as Arnold Bergsträsser. The field appeared particularly promising for effecting an "intellectual 'normalizing' of the situation," as Chametzky terms it.[3] The circumstance that a number of the older American Studies scholars in Germany had condoned and some had even actively supported the Nazi regime would have intensified the longing for such an "escape."[4]

If American Studies in Germany were self-consciously international in the 1950s, they were resolutely interdisciplinary as well. In the absence of an independent institutional basis for American Studies, however, most of the practitioners held positions in U.S.-American literature (generally within English departments) or, less frequently, in U.S.-American history. Other disciplines, such as political science, economics, geography, or sociology produced at best individual scholars specializing in the United States, a pattern reflected in the membership of the *DGfA* to this day. This was the institutional framework within which African American Studies developed.

African American Studies began in earnest, I would argue, when Charles H. Nichols, who had formerly taught at Hampton Institute, became director of the John F. Kennedy Institute in Berlin in the fall of 1959. Until his return to the United States ten years later, Nichols published and lectured extensively on African American literature and culture, even appearing in educational radio broadcasts (*Schulfunk*) in 1963. In 1962, his book *Many Thousand Gone: The Ex-Slaves' Account of Their Bondage and Freedom* appeared as the first volume of the Kennedy

Institute's new monograph series. Except for some unusual cases such as Heinz Rogge, who published two articles on Langston Hughes and the language of jazz fans in 1956, it was U.S. guest professors, many of whom came under the auspices of the Fulbright Program, who undertook research, taught, and gave lectures on African American culture throughout the 1950s. Kenneth Stampp spent the summer semester of 1957 in Munich; Edward Clark taught the first course on a black subject, "The Image of the Negro in American Fiction," at the University of Kiel in 1958.

As the title of one of Nichols's lectures, "Die Bereicherung der amerikanischen Kultur durch die Neger" ("The Contribution of African Americans to American Culture") attests, these scholars sought to communicate to a German audience the vital role black cultural productions played in the context of the most "advanced" and modern nation. Interestingly, Nichols's description of blacks as "phantoms" in white U.S.-American literature prefigures Toni Morrison's later revisionary move in her 1993 Nobel Prize acceptance speech, which contributed significantly to the emergence of Whiteness Studies.[5]

Academic interest in African American subjects grew in the early 1960s, in many cases clearly due to the increasing visibility of the civil rights movement in the United States. The eighth annual conference of the *DGfA*, held in Heidelberg in 1961, for instance, considered "Die Entwicklung der rassischen Integration im amerikanischen Erziehungswesen" ("The Development of Racial Integration in the American Educational System").[6] The first dissertations on African American writers and racial segregation in schools and universities were completed in 1960 and 1961 (in Freiburg and Köln).

Scholarly investigations of African American culture were energized by performances of renowned black writers and artists who visited Germany, often with financial support from U.S. Government agencies. In Berlin, for example, James Baldwin's play *The Amen Corner* was presented by a U.S.-American cast; the Alvin Ailey Dancers appeared in the *Akademie der Künste;* the *Berliner Festspiele* focused on Africa and authors of the African diaspora in 1964. Demands for the establishment of Black Studies programs at U.S.-American universities stimulated further debate in German academic circles.[7] The first German scholars began to teach African American literature in Göttingen and Mainz in 1961. Slowly but surely, the number of such courses climbed in the 1960s: they were offered in Hamburg, Kiel, Frankfurt, Munich, Köln, and other places. By the late 1960s, an average of five courses in African American Studies were annually taught at West German universities.

Yet it is clear that in this early phase, the fate of African American Studies in Germany depended heavily on the efforts of committed individual scholars. Both Nichols and Chametzky recalled the marginal role of African American Studies and African American literature during their time in Germany.[8] When Nichols left Berlin in 1969, research in African American culture abruptly ceased at the Kennedy Institute. Throughout the 1960s, the input of U.S.-American academics remained crucial for the field. Although some younger German scholars, many of them trained by African American professors, were beginning to specialize in

African American Studies, the German contribution to what was then a barely recognized specialization within American Studies remained tenuous indeed.

African American Studies Come of Age: 1968 and After

The fertile political climate of the late 1960s and the expansion of the West German universities in the 1970s represented a productive context for the emergence of African American Studies as a distinct subfield of American Studies in Germany. This time, it was younger German academics, many of whom had spent longer periods of time in the United States, who took the lead. As the German university system began to respond to the far-ranging methodological and organizational challenges mounted by the student movement, they showed a marked interest in cultural and literary theory in keeping with the times' revisionary spirit, questioning many of the assumptions that had traditionally shaped American Studies in their home country.

The early 1970s mark the beginnings of sustained academic interest in African American culture in German academia. In 1970, Peter Freese and Volkhard Brandes published on James Baldwin and on the role of Africa for the freedom fight of black Americans respectively; in 1971, Werner Sollors's "Bibliographic Guide to Afro-American Studies" appeared in the *Jahrbuch für Amerikastudien*, to be supplemented in the next edition. In 1972, Günter Lenz, Werner Sollors, Martin Christadler, Arno Heller, and Uwe Bruhns contributed scholarly articles on James Baldwin, Amiri Baraka, Ralph Ellison, and civil rights. The next year, Eckhard Breitinger's influential collection *Black Literature* came out, and Werner Sollors completed his dissertation, as did Marion Berghahn and Udo Jung. Berndt Ostendorf explored "Black Poetry, Blues, and Folklore," Kurt Otten offered an interpretation of Richard Wright's work. Altogether, there were an unprecedented eleven publications in African American Studies.

Scholarly monographs, essay collections, and articles quickly followed during the 1970s and early 1980s, many of them milestones of the discipline in a German context: Peter Freese (ed.), *Growing up Black in America* (1978); Heinz Christian Lüffe, *Zur Textkonstitution afro-amerikanischer Initiationsliteratur* (1980); Klaus Ensslen, *Einführung in die schwarzamerikanische Literatur* (1982); Angelika Krüger-Kahloula, *Motivgeschichte und Anthropologie der afroamerikanischen Erzähltradition* (1984); and others. Scholars such as Wolfgang Binder and Fritz Martini specifically explored the literature and culture of the Caribbean. Other topics frequently discussed include the civil rights and black power movements, with particular attention devoted to the person of Martin Luther King Jr., African American music, slavery, and black English.[9]

Perhaps not coincidentally, East German Americanists began to examine African American literature and culture around the same time. For them, the civil rights movement also played a pivotal role, supporting an interpretation of contemporary African American writers as "unmittelbare [. . .] Fortsetzer des proletarisch-revolutionären Erbes der 30er Jahre," as Eberhard Brüning, who later wrote about the Black Liberation Movement and American Drama, phrased it.[10] Horst Ihde's research resulted in articles on John Oliver Killens (1968) and the contributions of black slaves to U.S.-American culture ("Der Beitrag der Negersklaven zur Kultur der USA," 1971). Friederike Hajek, who compared Richard Wright's *Native Son* to Theodore Dreiser's *An American Tragedy* in a 1974 article, later published a monograph on *Black Liberation Movement und Autobiographie* in 1984. African American authors received considerable attention from GDR scholars. Many of these publications, which were often produced under difficult circumstances (with limited access to secondary literature, for instance), made important contributions to the development of the field.

Without slighting the achievements of the many individuals who participated in and promoted the growth of German African American Studies during this phase, I think it is fair to say that three scholars were particularly influential in the 1970s and 1980s: Berndt Ostendorf, Günter Lenz, and Maria Diedrich. Ostendorf, who began as a literary scholar, later counted African American history among his specialties as well. After researching and teaching in Freiburg and Frankfurt, he shaped the American Studies program in Munich with such congenial partners as Klaus Ensslen and Hartmut Keil.

Ostendorf's research was generally marked by a cultural studies approach. In his classic *Black Literature in White America* (1982), he emphasized the interactions of African American folklore and black literature. His collection *Gettoliteratur*, which came out in 1983, took what one might call a comparative approach to cultural marginalization and literary production. *Creolization and Creoles* (1997) later focused on processes of hybridization central to African American language and culture. Generally, Ostendorf's critical turn from multiculturalism (*Multikulturelle Gesellschaft*, 1994) to transnationalism (*Transnational America*, 2002) can be said to mirror a gradual paradigm shift in German African American Studies also noticeable in the writings of other scholars such as Günter Lenz. Ostendorf's most recent publications include *Iconographies of Power: The Politics and Poetics of Visual Representation* (2003) and *Cultural Interactions: Fifty Years of American Studies in Germany* (2005), both coedited with Ulla Haselstein.

Maria Diedrich can perhaps best be described as a one-woman powerhouse in African American Studies. Her dissertation, *"Kommunismus im afro-amerikanischen Roman"* (1979), already discussed a crucial and controversial issue in African American literature. The year she completed her *Habilitation* on the slave narrative, in 1986, she also published five articles on black subjects, singlehandedly contributing more than a third of the seventeen publications in that area listed in *Amerikastudien/American Studies*. She has continued to write and edit unflaggingly throughout her career, producing among other works *Love across Color Lines: Ottilie Assing and Frederick Douglass* (1999). The volumes she coedited— *The Black Columbiad* (1994), *Black Imagination and the Middle Passage* (1999), *Mapping African America: History, Narrative Formation, and the Production of Knowledge* (1999), and *Monuments of the Black Atlantic* (2004)—documented some of the most original work in African American Studies undertaken by European scholars, and stimulated further inquiry into the subjects discussed in the texts. In her most recent publication, *Crossing Boundaries: African American Inner City and European Migrant Youth* (2004), she addresses an issue of pressing concern for contemporary social and cultural policy on both sides of the Atlantic.

Maria Diedrich's work has clearly been informed by her intensive studies with Nathan Irvin Huggins of Harvard University. Teaching in Hannover before she came to Münster, she in turn inspired and encouraged many younger (especially female) scholars to specialize in black literature and/or culture. I will discuss her pivotal role as the cofounder and first president of CAAR below. But she has also been a powerful voice outside of academia, seeking to foster black-white dialogue in a number of political arenas.

Günter Lenz finally was a formative presence at the *Zentrum für Nordamerika-Forschung* (*ZENAF*) in Frankfurt, and subsequently at Humboldt University in Berlin. Due to their geographic and at times also ideological proximity to the Frankfurt School and its Critical Theory, one might call Lenz and his colleagues the "Frankfurt School of African American Studies." They produced an impressive array of "Critical Race Theory" in the 1980s, perhaps best exemplified by such volumes as *History and Tradition in Afro-American Culture* (1984) and *Reconstructing American Literary and Historical Studies* (with Bröck-Sallah and Keil, 1989).

In addition to an interest in literary and cultural theory he shared with Ostendorf, the writings of Günter Lenz explored the intersections between music and literature in black culture and investigated the role of African American authors such as Ishmael Reed for an understanding of postmodernity. He also edited a volume on representations of African Americans in documentary films (*Afro-Amerika im amerikanischen Dokumentarfilm*). His work consistently reflected his theoretical engagement with "European contexts and intercultural relations," as the subtitle of a 1995 publication attests. In later years, Lenz concentrated specifically on urban spaces as sites of transculturation and black identity formation (*Postmodern New York City*, 2003). With his assistant Klaus Milich, he established the Du Bois lecture series, and later the Distinguished Du Bois lecture series at Humboldt University.

At least in the 1970s and the early 1980s, the research of German scholars in African American Studies such as Diedrich, Ostendorf, and Lenz was clearly animated by a countercultural spirit. As Ostendorf once put it, they understood themselves as representatives of "the other America." At different points in time, the "big three" held important positions in the *DGfA*. Beyond that, they were key players in establishing cultural studies as a central, perhaps even dominant mode of academic inquiry within German American Studies, a development whose beginnings can be located in the *DGfA*'s 1983 annual convention, which was titled *"Amerikastudien als Kulturwissenschaft: Modell- und Paradigmenwechsel"* ("American Studies as Cultural Studies: Changing Models and Paradigms"). In this, they were indebted to scholarly debates at U.S. universities, whose impulses they absorbed during extended research periods spent in the United States, and productively transformed in their own writing. It was Günter Lenz who managed to introduce "culture" as a distinct field in *DGfA* membership profiles. Today, two thirds of all members claim cultural studies as their area of expertise by checking the appropriate box.

But Frankfurt was especially influential for another reason as well. For Lenz mentored two younger scholars, Anne Koenen and Sabine Bröck, whose work had a profound impact on German African American Studies in its next phase, to which I now turn.

Engendering African American Studies

Although Maria Diedrich had already analyzed issues of gender in her earlier work, the publication of Anne Koenen's dissertation *"Zeitgenössische afroamerikanische Frauenliteratur: Selbstbild und Identität bei Toni Morrison, Alice Walker, Toni Cade Bambara und Gayl Jones"* in 1985, and Sabine Bröck's Ph.D. thesis *"Der entkolonisierte Körper: Die Protagonistin in der afroamerikanischen weiblichen Erzähltradition der 30er bis 80er Jahre"* three years later represented the point of departure for an extensive consideration of gender issues in African American literature and culture by German scholars that continues to this day.[11]

In this, too, German researchers benefited from work undertaken in the United States, where the emergence of Black Feminist Criticism was signaled by seminal studies such as Barbara Christian's *Black Women Novelists* (1980), Cherríe Moraga's and Gloria Anzaldúa's *This Bridge Called My Back* (1981), and Gloria Hull and colleagues' *But Some of Us Are Brave* (1982), which included Barbara Smith's influential essay "Towards a Black Feminist Criticism." The substantial body of innovative and challenging scholarship produced by black female critics like Mary Helen Washington, Nellie McKay, Claudia Tate, Hazel Carby, Hortense Spillers, and Joanne Braxton, as well as scholars such as Susan Willis, Barbara Johnson, Michael Awkward, Houston A. Baker, and Henry Louis Gates Jr., informed the research undertaken at German universities throughout the 1980s and early 1990s. Issues of sexuality and heteronormativity were also raised by German critics, particularly in conjunction with a critical engagement of Audre Lorde's and Barbara Smith's writings. However, neither within nor outside of African American Studies did queer theory ever gain the prominence it attained in U.S.-American critical discourses.

Analyses of race and gender by German critics were facilitated by the increasing adoption of cultural studies with their attention to social stratification. The *DGfA* conference on *"Frauen in Gesellschaft und Kultur der USA: Neue Ansätze in den Amerikastudien"* (1984) ("Women in U.S.-American Society and Culture: New Perspectives in American Studies") thus followed almost logically upon the already mentioned 1983 convention devoted to *"Amerikastudien als Kulturwissenschaft."*

This line of inquiry was also sustained by the phenomenal success of African American women writers, which climaxed in Toni Morrison's Nobel Prize for Literature (1993) and, more controversially, Steven Spielberg's movie version of Alice Walker's *The Color Purple*. By then, names like Maya Angelou, Paule Marshall, June Jordan, Gloria Naylor, and Gayl Jones were well known not only to literary critics, but also to a wider German readership. Yet, the reception of their writing in Germany was not necessarily unproblematic, as Anne Koenen pointed out.[12] Still, energized by all of these developments, scholars such as the indefatigable Tobe Levin, also of Frankfurt, Dorothea Fischer-Hornung, Susanne Opfermann, Bettina Friedl, Renate von Bardeleben, Stephanie Sievers, Sylvia Mayer, Heike Rafael-Hernandez, Carmen Birkle, Therese Steffen, Sabine Sielke, Sieglinde Lemke, Heike Paul, and many, many others, including myself, undertook research on a wide range of African American female authors and black women's cultural productions.

The frequently feminist work produced in this context accelerated the reconstruction of the U.S.-American literary canon taught at German universities, and challenged the more mainstream versions of American Studies to review their research agendas. Although I would not claim that a gender-sensitive African American Studies put gender on the map in German American Studies—distinguished theorists of gender come to mind whose research focused on other issues, most notably perhaps Renate Hof and Gisela Ecker—they had a significant impact on the process. This productive relationship between black cultural studies and gender studies remains an important factor in American Studies as they are currently practiced in Germany.

Internationalizing African American Studies after the End of the Cold War

The fall of the wall, or rather the consequences of German reunification effectively terminated the career of the majority of East German scholars in American Studies, African American Studies included. GDR Black Studies ceased to exist, even if individual academics continued their research in new institutional frameworks.[13]

At the same time, the growing importance of inner-European academic exchanges, to some extent encouraged by the closer economic and political ties within the European Union, was reflected, in African American Studies, by the foundation of CAAR in 1992. International cooperation in African American Studies was not exactly new, and its transatlantic variety had been of major importance for Black Studies in Germany throughout. Virtually all younger scholars in the field have spent extended periods in the United States for research purposes, benefiting enormously from the expertise of their mostly African American colleagues as well as the resources of U.S. universities, above all the W. E. B. Du Bois Institute at Harvard under Henry Louis Gates Jr. Tendencies toward internationalizing African American Studies became more conspicuous in three great conferences on "African Americans and Europe" held in Paris during the 1990s, which were co-sponsored by U.S.-American institutions like Harvard, Columbia, the University of Mississippi, and the Sorbonne.

But this process attained a different quality with CAAR. The organization provided an *institutional* basis for sustained academic debate both among European scholars and between European and U.S.-American scholars in African American Cultural Studies.[14] Taking the transnational character of black culture Paul Gilroy had outlined so forcefully in *The Black Atlantic* as its point of departure, the founding statement of CAAR envisioned the practice of African American Studies as "international, interdisciplinary, inter-racial, comparative, and collegial." In particular, CAAR was designed to transcend "the artificial distinctions between disciplines like African American studies, Caribbean studies and African studies, to name only a few." In recognition of the field's history, the articles also underlined the political quality of research in African American Studies.[15]

Cofounded, among others, by Maria Diedrich and Berndt Ostendorf, CAAR became the focal point of African American Studies in Germany, counting many Germans among its most consistent supporters. Beginning in 1995, its biannual conferences offered both continuity and a forum for a large spectrum of diverse research interests pertaining to black literature and culture. The CAAR newsletter facilitated communication among the members, supplying them with information about upcoming events, new publications, and so forth. The monograph series, published in Münster, enhanced the visibility of scholarship produced by—mostly European—specialists in black culture and showcased new approaches to some of the field's vital issues.

As the organization's first president, Maria Diedrich was essential for the success of this organizational venture. During her tenure from 1992 to 2001, CAAR broadened its membership base as well as the scope of its activities. Vibrant, inspiring conferences were held in Puerto de la Cruz, Tenerife, in Liverpool, and in Cagliari. The only CAAR conference held in Germany so far took place in Münster. It is hardly surprising that Diedrich has remained a formative presence in CAAR even after she stepped down as its chair.

The trend toward internationalization that resulted in the flourishing of CAAR was not unique to African American Studies. In the early 1990s, there was a resurgence of interest in the EAAS throughout Western Europe as scholarly organizations from formerly communist countries began to join the association. In the United States, both the American Studies Association and the Modern Language Association declared their commitment to internationalizing American Studies. In what is perhaps the closest parallel to the establishment of CAAR, MESEA, the Society for Multi-Ethnic Studies: Europe and the Americas was founded in Heidelberg in the year 2000. Like CAAR, MESEA has since contributed significantly to the visibility of African American Studies in Germany.

Current Developments

While German African American Studies scholars thus tend to participate in both transatlantic and European research networks, they are also beginning to turn their scholarly gazes back to Germany, exploring interactions among

African Americans, Africans, and black and white Germans in the context of *both* German and black diasporic cultures. A number of conferences devoted to these "crossovers," to cite one of the titles, have been held at the University of Massachusetts, Münster, Berlin, and Mainz, which has established itself as a very productive locus of inquiry in African American Studies over time. Projects such as the "Black Atlantic" exhibition, designed by Paul Gilroy, Tina Campt, and Fatima El-Tayeb and shown in Berlin in 2004, which highlighted the fact that parts of the African diaspora are German, also testified to a great interest on the side of nonacademic German audiences.

In their current studies of African/American/German encounters, German academics are profiting from the groundbreaking work of Afro-German scholar-activists such as May Ayim, Ika Hügel-Marshall, and Katharina Oguntoye,[16] as well as the publications of African American specialists on German history and culture like Tina Campt and Michelle M. Wright. Issues such as the repercussions of colonialism and constructions of "blackness" in German culture, which have been hotly debated by feminist and/or internationalist activists since the 1980s, are now being addressed in academic contexts as well.

Sabine Broeck, with her research on the influence of the civil rights movement on German culture, Maria Diedrich (again), Jürgen Heinrichs and Peggy Piesche are among the scholars most visible in these projects, contributing both West and East German perspectives on black/German intersections. There is a significant overlap between their research interests and contemporary Whiteness Studies, advanced in Germany by Susan Arndt, Eske Wollradt, Maischa Eggers, Martina Tißberger, Daniela Hrzan, and Gabriele Dietze, to name only a few. The fact that there is a growing number of academic networks that connect scholars investigating these issues, including the Black European Studies (BEST) and Crossovers: African American and German Interactions, suggests a serious interest and a promising future for this emergent field.

But perhaps the picture I have drawn here appears too rosy. There is as yet no chair in African American Studies or even African American Literature at any German university, nor is there an African American Studies program, at least to my knowledge. At any rate, much remains to be done. This short history of African American Studies in the Federal Republic of Germany has been sketchy as well as preliminary. Much further work is needed to adequately represent the complex trajectory of German academic engagement with African American culture.

Yet, what I have traced here amounts to the transformation of African American Studies from a minor field into an esteemed, even prominent segment of U.S.-American Studies in contemporary Germany. In addition to the scholars already mentioned, academics as diverse as Udo Hebel, Alfred Hornung, Ulf Reichardt, Ruth Mayer, Elisabeth Schaefer-Wünsche, Klaus Benesch, Willie Raussert, Dorothea Löbbermann, Bärbel Tischleder, and a host of others are actively engaged in expanding the horizons of African American Studies in German academic contexts. African American guest professors like Hortense Spillers, Joanne Braxton, Melba Joyce Boyd, Robert Reid-Pharr, and others continue to provide much-appreciated intellectual impulses. But for younger generations of German Americanists, I would venture to say, the study of African American literature and culture is no longer something exotic but an unquestioned, in many cases particularly cherished, part of doing American Studies. From the vantage point of the recent past, this may be a small, but by no means insignificant achievement.

Notes

1. The *Mitteilungsblatt* of the *DGfA*, published annually since 1955, contains information, among other things, on courses taught in American Studies, guest professorships, and guest lectures in the previous academic year, as well as the topics of the society's annual conferences. The bibliography of works published in American Studies during the last year generally appears in the society's journal *Amerikastudien/American Studies*, a quarterly. Most of the information on African American Studies in the GDR was derived from the *Zeitschrift für Anglistik und Amerikanistik, ZAA*.

2. Brumm, 10.

3. Chametzky in JFK, 89. He continues: "I speak hesitantly about the need to leap out of *their* skins, their identities, as it were, in the aftermath of so much horror. Not to be German—to be European, say [. . .], or better yet, for some, to be identified with things American—far away and new, fresh and without guilt, this must have been an operative, though not always acknowledged, motive and drive for many Germans who turned positively towards American Studies" (90).

4. For the composition of the early *DGfA* membership, cf. Grabbe. Ursula Brumm has pointed out the decisive role of scholars returning from U.S.-American exile after the end of fascism for establishing American Studies in the Federal Republic of Germany.

5. Nichols, 19; Toni Morrison, *Playing in the Dark: Whiteness and the Literary Imagination* (New York: Vintage, 1993).

6. The treatment of the "race question" in the context of teaching English in high schools had already been the subject of a teacher training seminar held in Hamburg in 1956. The phrasing of the 1961 *DGfA* conference title implies that there was as yet no widespread discomfort with terms such as "rassisch."

7. Nichols, 20.

8. This also held true for women's literature and the writing of nonwhite authors generally. Thus Jules Chametzky's 1964 article, "Notes on the Assimilation of the Jewish American Writer: Abraham Cahan to Saul Bellow," based on a lecture he had given in Berlin in 1963, represented "the first study published in a German periodical investigating American Jewish writers as a literary ethnic group." Chametzky, 92, 94–95; Nichols, 19.

9. Aribert Schroeder has informed me that a number of articles on African American Studies were published in journals expressly concerned with the teaching of American Studies in this period. Unfortunately, time constraints prevented me from investigating the matter more fully for this version of my article.

10. Brüning, *Weimarer Beiträge* 16 (1970): 182. One of the earliest pieces of GDR scholarship in African American Studies was Heinz Wüstenhagen's essay on James Baldwin (published in 1965), which he described as "Versuch einer ersten Einschätzung."

11. Hajek also published an article on *"Ethnizität und Frauenemanzipation: Der afro-amerikanische Roman nach den 6oer Jahren"* in 1984, but considerations of gender did not influence GDR African American Studies to the extent they did in the West.

12. Anne Koenen in Milich, *Multiculturalism in Transit*.

13. Most of those still active eventually joined the *DGfA*.

14. The original plan to establish an "International African American Research Association" with chapters on different continents proved not to be feasible. CAAR was initially designated as the European section of this umbrella organization.

15. *CAAR Newsletter* 1 (spring 1993): 3.

16. *Farbe bekennen,* perhaps their most well known publication, constituted a milestone in Afro-German Studies.

Works Cited

Breitinger, Eckhard, ed. *Black Literature: Zur afrikanischen und afroamerikanischen Literatur.* München: Fink, 1979.

Diedrich, Maria, Henry Louis Gates Jr., and Carl Pedersen, ed. *Black Imagination and the Middle Passage.* New York: Oxford University Press, 1999.

Diedrich, Maria. *Crossing Boundaries: African American Inner City and European Migrant Youth.* Münster: Lit, 2004.

Diedrich, Maria. *Kommunismus im afro-amerikanischen Roman: das Verhältnis afroamerikanischer Schriftsteller zur Kommunistischen Partei der USA zwischen den Weltkriegen.* Stuttgart: Metzler, 1979.

Diedrich, Maria. *Love across Color Lines: Ottilie Assing and Frederick Douglass.* New York: Hill and Wang, 1999.

Diedrich, Maria, Carl Pedersen, and Justine Tally, ed. *Mapping African America: History, Narrative Formation, and the Production of Knowledge.* Hamburg: Lit, 1999.

Diedrich, Maria, and Joanne Braxton, ed. *Monuments of the Black Atlantic: Slavery and Memory.* Münster: Lit, 2004.

Ensslen, Klaus. *Einführung in die schwarzamerikanische Literatur.* Stuttgart: Kohlhammer, 1982.

Freese, Peter, ed. *Growing up Black in America.* 1978.

Freitag, Christian H. *Die Entwicklung der Amerikastudien in Berlin bis 1945.* Berlin: Freie Universität, 1977.

Georgi-Findlay, Brigitte, and Heinz Ickstadt, eds. *America Seen from the Outside: Tpocis, Models and Achievements of American Studies in the Federal Republic of Germany.* Berlin: Freie Universität, 1990.

Grabbe, Hans-Jürgen. "50 Jahre Deutsche Gesellschaft für Amerikastudien." *Amerikastudien/ American Studies* 48, no. 2 (2003): 159–84.

Hajek, Friederike. *Selbstzeugnisse der Afroamerikaner: Black Liberation Movement und Autobiographie.* Berlin: Akademie-Verlag, 1984.

Hoenisch, Michael. "Zum Begriff der Tradition in der Amerikanistik der DDR." *Amerikastudien— Theorie, Geschichte, interpretatorische Praxis,* ed. Martin Christadler and Günter H. Lenz, 104–27. Stuttgart: Metzler, 1977.

Krüger-Kahloula, Angelika. *Die List des Schwächeren: Motivgeschichte und Anthropologie der afroamerikanischen Erzähltradition.* Frankfurt: Campus, 1984.

Lenz, Günter, ed. *Afro-Amerika im amerikanischen Dokumentarfilm.* Trier: Wissenschaftlicher Verlag Trier, 1993.

Lenz, Günter, and Klaus J. Milich, eds. *American Studies in Germany: European Contexts and Intercultural Relations.* Frankfurt: Campus, 1995.

Lenz, Günter, ed. *History and Tradition in Afro-American Culture.* Frankfurt: 1984.

Lenz, Günter, and Utz Riese, eds. *Postmodern New York City. Transfiguring Spaces—Raum-Transformationen.* Heidelberg: Winter, 2003.

Lenz, Günter, Hartmut Keil, and Sabine Broeck-Sallah, eds. *Reconstructing American Literary and Historical Studies*. Frankfurt: Campus, 1990.

Lenz, Günter, and Peter J. Ling, eds. *TransAtlantic Encounters: Multiculturalism, National Identity, and the Uses of the Past*. Amsterdam: VU University Press, 2000.

Lüffe, Heinz Christian. *Zur Textkonstitution afro-amerikanischer Initiationsliteratur*. Frankfurt: Peter Lang, 1980.

Milich, Klaus J., and Jeffrey M. Peck, eds. *Multiculturalism in Transit: A German-American Exchange*. New York: Berghahn Books, 1998.

Morrison, Toni. *Playing in the Dark: Whiteness and the Literary Imagination*. New York: Vintage, 1993.

Nichols, Charles H. *Many Thousand Gone: The Ex-Slaves' Account of Their Bondage and Freedom*. Leyden, 1963.

Oguntoye, Katharina, May Opitz, and Dagmar Schultz, eds. *Farbe bekennen: Afro-deutsche Frauen auf den Spuren ihrer Geschichte*. Berlin: Orlanda Frauenverlag, 1986.

Ostendorf, Berndt. *Black Literature in White America*. Brighton: Harvester u.a., 1982.

Ostendorf, Berndt. *Amerikanische Gettoliteratur: Zur Literatur ethnischer, marginaler und unterdrückter Gruppen in Amerika*. Darmstadt: Wissenschaftliche Buchgesellschaft, 1983.

Ostendorf, Berndt. *Creolization and Creoles: The Concepts and Their History with Special Attention to Louisiana*. Odense: University Odense, 1997.

Ostendorf, Berndt. *Multikulturelle Gesellschaft: Modell Amerika?* München: Fink, 1994.

Ostendorf, Berndt. *Transnational America: The Fading of Borders in the Western Hemisphere*. Heidelberg: Winter, 2002.

Ostendorf, Berndt, and Ulla Haselstein. *Iconographies of Power: The Politics and Poetics of Visual Representation*. Heidelberg: Winter, 2003.

Ostendorf, Berndt, and Ulla Haselstein, eds. *Cultural Interactions: Fifty Years of American Studies in Germany*. Heidelberg: Winter, 2005.

Sollors, Werner. "Bibliographic Guide to Afro-American Studies." *Jahrbuch für Amerikastudien* 16 (1971): 213–22.

Sollors, Werner, and Maria Diedrich, eds. *The Black Columbiad: Defining Moments in African American Literature and Culture*. Cambridge, MA: Harvard University Press, 1994.

Wüstenhagen, Heinz. "James Baldwin's Essays und Romane: Versuch einer ersten Einschâtzung." *Zeitschrift für Anglistik und Amerikanistik* 13 (1965): 117–57.

Contributors

EVA BOESENBERG is professor of North American literary and cultural studies at Humboldt University Berlin. Her publications include *Gender _ Voice _ Vernacular: The Formation of Female Subjectivity in Hurston, Morrison, and Walker, Chancen und Grenzen des Dialogs zwischen den Geschlechtern*, and *Money and Gender in the American Novel, 1850–2000*. Among her research interests are African American literature and culture, critical whiteness studies, gender studies, representations of intercultural couples in U.S.-American literature, and the cultural significance of sports.

SABINE BROECK is professor of American studies at the University of Bremen. Her teaching and research focus on the intersections of race, class, gender, and sexualities, with a historical emphasis on modernity, slavery, and the black diaspora; her work also has a strong postcolonial bent. Her most recent publication in the field is "Blackness and Sexualities in the Interracial Diaspora," in Wright and Schuhmann, eds., *Blackness and Sexualities* (2007). She is president of the Collegium for African American Research (CAAR).

LARRY A. GREENE is professor of history in the Department of History at Seton Hall University. His research interests are in the fields of African American, Civil War, and World War II history. He is the co-author with Lenworth Gunther of *The New Jersey African American History Guide* (1996) and co-editor with John B. Duff, of *Slavery: Its Origins and Legacy* (1975). He is the author of numerous articles on Harlem and African Americans in New Jersey. He is the co-author with Diana Linden of "Charles Alston's Harlem Hospital Murals: Cultural Politics in Depression Era Harlem," *Prospects* (vol. 26, 2002).

VICTOR GROSSMAN, is a freelance translator, journalist, English teacher, lecturer, and book author. He is the author of two books on U.S. history and his autobiography, *Crossing the River: A Memoir of the American Left, the Cold War, and Life in East Germany* (2003).

ASTRID HAAS received her Ph.D. in English and American studies from the University of Münster, Germany, where she wrote a thesis entitled *Stages of Agency: The Contributions of American Drama to the AIDS Discourse*. She holds a master's degree in art history from the same university and has written on American and European theater, African American literature, and modern and contemporary art from Europe and the Americas. She is one of the editors of *Von schönen und anderen Geschlechtern: Schönheit in den Gender Studies* (Frankfurt/Main: Lang, 2004).

MARIA HÖHN is professor of history at Vassar College. Höhn teaches German history and in much of her work has explored how American forms of racism, brought to post–World War II Germany through the U.S. military, impacted German debates on race. She is the author of *GIs and Fräuleins: The German American Encounter in 1950s West Germany (*Chapel Hill: University of North Carolina Press, 2002). She is also the co-editor of *Over There: Living with the U.S. Military Empire from 1945 to the Present* (Duke 2010), and the co-author of *A Breath of Freedom: The Civil Rights Struggle, African American GIs, and Germany* (Plagrave 2010) and *Der Kampf um die Bürgerrechte: Afroamerikanische Soldaten und Deutschland* (VBB 2010).

MISCHA HONECK teaches history at the University of Heidelberg and recently finished his dissertation which explores cultural contacts and coalitions between German Forty-Eighter revolutionaries and American abolitionists in the Civil War period. His areas of specialization are theories of the Enlightenment, antebellum America, transnational cultural and intellectual history, and the contemporary American novel.

LEROY HOPKINS is professor of German at Millersville University. His research interests include African-American history in Pennsylvania (especially Lancaster County) and cross-cultural contact (African and German). His publications include "Writing Diasporic Identity: Afro-German Literature since 1985," in *Not So Plain as Black and White: Afro-German Culture and History, 1890–2000,* ed. Patricia Mazòn and Reinhild Steingröver (2005) and "Afro-German Diasporic Studies: A Proposal," *Preserving Heritage: A Festschrift for C. Richard Beam*, ed. Joshua R. Brown and Leroy T. Hopkins (2006).

FRANK MEHRING is assistant professor at the department of cultural studies of the John F. Kennedy Institute for North American Studies at the Free University of Berlin. His current project is dedicated to transcultural confrontations of German immigrants and the promise of American democracy. His publications include *Karl/Charles Follen: Deutsch-amerikanischer Freiheitskämpfer* (2004), *Sphere Melodies: Die Manifestation transzendentalistischen Gedankenguts in der Musik der Avantgardisten Charles Ives und John Cage* (2003), and *Sight & Sound: Naturbilder in der englischen und amerikanischen Romantik* (2001).

ANKE ORTLEPP is professor of American history at the University of Munich, Germany. Her research interests include the history of travel and tourism, gender history, urbanism, the history of space, design, and architecture. She recently completed a cultural history of air travel in postwar America. Her publications include *Auf denn, Ihr Schwestern! Deutschamerikanische Frauenvereine in Milwaukee, Wisconsin* (2004) and *Mit den Dingen leben: Zur Geschichte der Alltagsgegenstände,* co-edited with Christoph Ribbat (2009).

BERNDT OSTENDORF is professor emeritus of North American cultural history at the Amerika Institut of the University of Munich, Germany. His publications include *Black Literature in White America* (1982), *Die multikulturelle Gesellschaft: Modell Amerika?* (1995), and *Transnational America: The Fading of Borders in the Western Hemisphere* (2002). Areas of interest include the cultural history of immigration, the politics of difference, American religions, multiculturalism, popular culture and the culture industry, New Orleans, and American music.

DAMANI PARTRIDGE is an assistant professor in the Department of Anthropology and at the Center for Afro-American and African Studies at the University of Michigan. In addition to teaching the undergraduate and graduate courses "Race and Displacement," "Citizenship and Non-Citizens," "Urban Anthropology," "The Races of Sexuality and the Sexualities of Race," "Diasporic Aesthetics," and "The Anthropology of Europe," he is currently completing the revisions for his book manuscript *Becoming Non-Citizens: Technologies of Exclusion and Exclusionary Incorporation into European "Human Rights."*

ARIBERT SCHROEDER for many years taught at the Department of English at Heinrich-Heine-Universität Düsseldorf. He is now Akademischer Oberrat im Ruhestand. His research interests include American racial minorities and American studies. His publications and reviews have focused on these fields.

JEFFERY STRICKLAND is assistant professor of history at Montclair State University. In 2003, he earned his Ph.D. in history at Florida State University with a specialization in United States urban history. His dissertation focused on the social, economic, and political interaction between German immigrants and African- Americans in Charleston, South Carolina, during Reconstruction and is forthcoming. His publications include "The Whole State Is on Fire_: Criminal Justice and the End of Reconstruction in Upcountry South Carolina," *Crime, History & Societies* (December 2009) and "How the Germans Became White Southerners: German Immigrants and Their Social, Economic, and Political Relations with African-Americans in Charleston, South Carolina, 1860–1880" *Journal of American Ethnic History* (Fall 2008).

Index